A Purgatorial Flame

A Purgatorial Flame

Seven British Writers in the
Second World War

Sebastian D. G. Knowles

University of Pennsylvania Press
Philadelphia

The author gratefully acknowledges permission to quote from published works. These are listed at the end of this volume, after the Index.

Copyright © 1990 by the University of Pennsylvania Press
Printed in the United States of America

Library of Congress Cataloging-in-Publication Data

Knowles, Sebastian David Guy.
  A purgatorial flame : seven British writers in the Second World War / Sebastian D.G. Knowles.
     p.   cm.
  Includes bibliographical references.
  ISBN 0-8122-8213-2
  1. English literature—20th century—History and criticism. 2. World War, 1939-1945—Literature and the war. 3. War in literature. I. Title.
PR478.W67K56   1990
820.9′358′09044—dc20   –89-25114
                                                                                      CIP

For
K.G. J.C.K

Contents

viii   Contents

Acknowledgments

Never has so little owed so much to so many. This book would have been impossible without the assistance of the following people. Thanks to John Campbell, for a good word at the right time, to Mike Davis, for information on certain theological matters, to Maria DiBattista, for all her help, especially on Woolf, to Margaret Doody, for all the detective fiction, to Lady Eccles-Hyde, for a summer's research in Italy, to Paul Fussell, for comments on the first chapter, to John Gross, for pointers on a train, to Samuel Hynes, for reading the manuscript in partial form and for a conversation in a pub near the British Museum, to Ned Jackson, for analogies to everything, to Bart Kahr, for *The War Artists*, and to Walt Litz, who has done so much for me and for this book that I shall bring this sentence to a close. To Leigh Barrows, for not running out of gas, to Scott Leonard, for proofreading the final text, to Mary and Anne Manson, for help with chapters II and VII respectively, to Margarita, for the daily crossword, to Neil, because I said I would, to Floyd Romesberg, for train spotting, to Dave Weber, computer guru, and to my parents, *sine quibus non* as always.

Though none of what follows has been published before, various parts of this manuscript have been aired at the European Seminars at Syracuse, the Siena College Conferences on World War II, the T. S. Eliot Centennial Conference at Orono, Princeton's Dunwalke, and conferences in Boone, Denver, East Lansing, Oneonta, and Philadelphia. Thanks to all those met along these ways, especially to Gordon Beadle, Vincent Sherry, Carroll Terrell, and Walter Ullmann, whose advice and encouragement have made this a much better book than I could have written myself.

I would also like to acknowledge the financial assistance of the College of Humanities and the Office of Research and Graduate Studies at the Ohio State University, and the professional assistance of the staff of the University of Pennsylvania Press, especially Alison Anderson and Amanda Boyask.

For millions now life is steeped in flame--often indeed a literal flame. Most of the peoples of Europe have passed, or are passing, through a very furnace of adversity. We pray that the flames kindled by the fury of the oppressor may be transmuted into a fire like that which guarded the secret of happiness on Dante's mountain.

Lucy Redpath, *Dante and the Present War*

Preface: Where the War Poets Were

> I wished the effect of the whole to be Purgatorial which is much
> more appropriate.
>
> Eliot.

In 1941, Tom Harrisson, one of the founders of Mass Observation, made
an early assessment of British Second World War literature. He dismissed
it all as completely unreadable:

> For two years, urged on by the editor of *Horizon*, I have read literally every
> book which has anything to do with the war, reportage, fiction or fantasy.
> Every month I have tried to sum up my curious learning into a report for
> *Horizon*. Month after month I have let the editor down. For I have become
> totally, immeasurably bogged, engrossed in bad reading.[1]

To reach this conclusion, Harrisson ploughed through Basil Woon's *Hell
Came to London* (1941),* with its text "liberally bespattered with bomb
noises: 'Whee-ee-eesh . . . bloo-oomp!' "[2] He learned to distinguish Lieu-
tenant-Colonel Hutchison's enormously popular *The W Plan* (1939) from
its sequel, *The V Plan* (1941), in which the Germans are defeated through
the construction of a Channel tunnel. He suffered *The Death of Lord Haw-
Haw* (1940) and *Poindexter Crashes the Fifth Column* (1941). Harrisson
divided his reading into seven categories: evacuation novels, diaries, Dun-
kirk books, R.A.F. books, Blitz books, espionage books, and peace books.
Taken together, the library of the literature of World War Two amounted
to "a cataract of tripe."[3] Harrisson found only one book to recommend
highly: Rex Warner's *The Aerodrome* (1941).

Not one of the works studied here could be said to rest on any of
Harrisson's seven shelves. *Put Out More Flags* (1941) is no more an evacuation novel than *All Hallows' Eve* (1945) is a Blitz book. *Little Gidding*

---

*The first reference to every primary text cited is followed by the work's year
of publication in parentheses. When the initial date of publication is misleading,
the year of writing is substituted.

(1942) will be found to treat the air raids very differently from John Strachey's *Digging for Mrs Miller* (1941) or John Carstairs' *Whatho She Bumps!* (1941). Harrisson read novels, generally first efforts, that were prompted by the war. The modernists were writers before 1939; their writing responds to the war more by necessity than by design. In his introduction to *In Parenthesis* (1937), David Jones writes of the difference: "I did not intend this as a 'War Book'—it happens to be concerned with war."[4] Elizabeth Bowen makes the same distinction in her preface to *Ivy Gripped the Steps* (1946): "These are all wartime, none of them *war*, stories. There are no accounts of war action even as I knew it—for instance, air raids."[5] All wartime writing is "concerned with war." But for Waugh and Williams, for Woolf and Eliot, the subject is more than war: the second war is incorporated into the modernist field of vision as was the first.

Modernism did not end conveniently in 1939, to resume as Contemporary Literature in 1945. The editors of the otherwise very useful *Spatial Form in Narrative* betray this common perception:

> "Modernist" refers to works written between the end of the nineteenth century and World War II—works that are experimental and often involve spatial form. "Contemporary" designates a similar class of works written since World War II.[6]

The Second World War did not mark a hiatus in British literature; the progress of literary thought continued through into the forties. This study will center on the war work of seven British modernists: Woolf, MacNeice, Eliot, Tolkien, Lewis, Williams, and Waugh. None of the seven is generally considered a war writer, but all wrote their finest or most mature work under the shadow of the Second World War.*

Virginia Woolf was acutely aware of the coming war when she began *Between the Acts* in 1938, and the book was rewritten in wartime. MacNeice's *Autumn Journal*, written in the last months of 1938, is a warning of a future war as well as a valedictory to a dying present. In

---

*Only a handful of them are generally considered modernists. The argument that the modernist label is earned, and should not be so easily affixed to less celebrated writers like Louis MacNeice and Charles Williams, dies hard, and this book is trying to put it to rest. "Modernist" need not be a medal pinned to the chests of a changing pantheon of canonical illuminaries; the term may be allowed to embrace any author who falls into step with the march of twentieth-century literary ideas. If this book fails to bring modernism into the Second World War, it will not be because it restricts itself to the officers' mess.

Little Gidding, Eliot tries to make sense of the nonsense of the Blitz; the fantasies of the Inklings also transform the direct experience of war. Evelyn Waugh traces the progress of the war from the Munich conference to war's end in *Work Suspended* (1939), *Put Out More Flags* (1941), *Brideshead Revisited* (1945), and *Sword of Honour* (1952–1961). The following examination of these representative writers attempts to extend the compass of British modernism into World War Two.

Cyril Connolly, with Harrisson, would have found such a project patently absurd: for him the forties were "five years of total war and five more of recrimination and exhaustion during which the Modern Movement unobtrusively expired." W. W. Robson judged that "The 1940s were one of the worst periods of English literature." Randall Stevenson, in his very comprehensive study *The British Novel Since the Thirties*, quotes these disparagements as straw targets, in order to establish the presence of a literature of the Second World War.[7] Orwell consciously sets himself up as such a target in a 1941 letter to the *Partisan Review*:

> So far as I know, nothing of consequence is being written, except in fragmentary form, diaries and short sketches for instance. The best novels I have read during the past year were either American or translations of foreign books written several years earlier. There is much production of anti-war literature, but of a one-eyed irresponsible kind. There is nothing corresponding to the characteristic war books of 1914-18.[8]

Orwell exaggerates on three counts. First, his judgment in April 1941 is premature, cast before the publication of either Henry Green's *Caught* (1943) or Eliot's *Little Gidding*. Second, by April 1916 very little of consequence had been written either. And third, though Green and Eliot respond very differently to the war, they both respond as civilians. Orwell is quite deliberately looking in the wrong direction.

So, less deliberately but no less provocatively, was Fleet Street. Not long after the start of the war, the popular press began to drum up the notorious cry, "Where are the war poets?" Rarely has such a tiresome question encouraged such an illuminating response. Nothing was better calculated to goad the literary world into a spirited defense of its war work. As a *Horizon* manifesto put it: "*The Times* and other papers asked why this war produced no poets. The poets wrote essays on why they couldn't write poetry."[9] The hectoring reached a climax with an editorial in the *Times Literary Supplement* of 30 December 1939. "To the Poets of 1940" was a summons to literary arms: "It is for the poets to sound the trumpet call."[10] The pages of London literary journals were soon covered with attempts to unfixe this *idée*. Spender and Graves discussed the subject in *The Listener*, Connolly and Waugh in *Horizon*, and Eliot in *Common Sense*. Keith Douglas wrote on the subject while stationed in Tunisia in 1943.* All provided separate explanations for the perceived decline in poetry during the war.

It is difficult to see why these arguments were necessary: the charge is easily denied. The Second World War was no less a literary war than its predecessor. The conventional depreciation of its poetry has never been justified; Linda Shires' *British Poetry of the Second World War* has laid that commonplace to rest. Not all of the poetry is as bad as A. A. Milne's war verse:

> I march along and march along and ask myself each day:
> If I should go and lose the war, then what will Mother say?
> The Sergeant will be cross and red, the Captain cross and pink,
> But all I ever ask myself is, What will Mother think?[11]

Catherine Reilly's indispensable "biobibliography," *English Poetry of the Second World War*, lists 2,679 poets, 831 from the armed forces.[12] Reilly concludes her introduction with a persuasive compromise:

> The poetry of the Second World War has not yet attracted as much literary and critical attention as that of the First World War but it is a popular misconception that the poetry of the second war is inferior to that of the first. A more accurate assessment would be that the First World War produced some outstanding poetry by a relatively small number of poets, while the Second World War produced a great deal more good poetry.[13]

Orwell's sweeping dismissal and Reilly's reappraisal of the literary output of the fighting forces share a common yardstick: both compare the present war to the past one. Throughout the Second World War, Douglas, Alun

---

*These six responses are as follows: Stephen Spender, "War Poetry in this War," *The Listener*, 26, 16 October 1941, 539; Robert Graves, "War Poetry in this War," *The Listener*, 26, 23 October 1941, 566; Cyril Connolly, "Comment," *Horizon*, III, #13 (January 1941), 5–7; [Evelyn Waugh], "Letter - Why Not War Writers?," *Horizon*, IV, #24 (December 1941), 437–38; T. S. Eliot, "Poetry in Wartime," *Common Sense*, XI, #10 (October 1942), 351; Keith Douglas, "Poets in This War," [May 1943], rpr. in *A Prose Miscellany*, comp. and ed., Desmond Graham, 117–20.

Lewis, Keyes, and others cannot escape the poetry of the First War. At the front, the poet struggles under the burden of World War One.

The Greater War shadowed an entire nation. Malcolm Muggeridge writes of the preparation for war at the end of *The Thirties*:

> Now old uniforms were brought out, put away long ago; old songs were remembered, thought to have been forgotten; old ways were resumed, old emotions experienced, old hopes revived. No new war was possible, so an old one would have to suffice. Out of the past, a ghost was summoned up, intervening years cancelled; out of the past, a corpse was disinterred.[14]

The diaries of 1938–39 are riddled with comparisons to August 1914. On the first of September 1938, Harold Nicolson fears that "we may get into the same mess as in 1914—namely, give the Czechs the impression that we shall fight for them, and the Germans the impression that we shall not."[15] A year later, his sense of *déjà vu* is more oppressive:

> It looks as if war will burst upon us tomorrow. Again that curious contrast with 3rd August 1914! Then we were excited by all these events and there was a sense of exhilaration. Today we are merely glum.[16]

Virginia Woolf's haunting entry for 28 August 1938 reads: "A single step—in Cheko Slovakia—like the Austrian Archduke in 1914 & again its 1914. Ding dong ding dong."[17] She reminds herself a month later to "Give the pre-war atmosphere" in her biography of Roger Fry: an atmosphere she experiences as well as recreates.[18]

Faced with a second war, the war poets do not dry up, they simply draw from old and half-empty wells. There were two separate wells of First World War poetry. Stephen Spender writes, in response to the admonition from the *Times Literary Supplement*, of the shallower well:

> At the beginning of the last war Rupert Brooke and others were 'trumpets singing to battle'. Why did not Rupert Brooke step forward 'young and golden-haired' this time? No doubt, in part, precisely because one had done so last time.[19]

Rupert Brooke is dead; there is little room for him in the Second World War. Neither is there much water in the deeper well. For many World War Two poets, the horror and the pity of war had already been expressed at its highest intensity, distilled to its most refined pitch. The First World War became an entirely original literary response to war. From the Bible

and Homer to Tennyson and Kipling, the poet had been on the side of
the victors: war poetry was patriotic until the moment a literary country,
such as Napoleonic France or Edwardian England, began to lose. On or
about 1 July 1916, war poetry changed. Douglas writes of the change in
"Poets in This War":

> Rupert Brooke, who might have seemed our ready made herald and bard,
> appeared superannuated in a moment and wandered away fittingly, from a
> literary point of view, to die in a region of dead heroes. Instead, arose Owen,
> to the sound of wheels crunching the bones of a man scarcely dead; Sassoon's
> tank lumbered into the music hall.[20]

"Poets in This War" continues to address the silencing influence of Owen
and Sassoon on the Second World War poet:

> The poets who wrote so much and so well before the war, all over the world,
> found themselves silenced, or able to write on almost any subject but war. Why
> did all this happen? Why are there no poets like Owen and Sassoon who lived
> with the fighting troops and wrote of their experiences while they were enduring
> them?
>   The reasons are psychological, literary, military and strategic, diverse. There
> are such poets, but they do not write. They do not write because there is
> nothing new, from a soldier's point of view, about this war except its mobile
> character. There are two reasons: hell cannot be let loose twice: it was let loose
> in the Great War and it is the same old hell now. The hardships, pain and
> boredom; the behaviour of the living and the appearance of the dead, were so
> accurately described by the poets of the Great War that everyday in the bat-
> tlefields of the western desert—and no doubt on the Russian battlefields as
> well—their poems are illustrated. Almost all that a modern poet on active service
> would be inspired to write, would be tautological.[21]

Douglas' own debt is clearest in "Desert Flowers": "Living in a wide
landscape are the flowers - / Rosenberg I only repeat what you were saying."[22] Roy Fuller speaks of the First World War poets as begetters of the
poets of the Second in "Another War": "Our fathers felt these things
before / In another half-forgotten war."[23] Alun Lewis remembers Edward
Thomas in an elegy to him, and in the closing lines of "All Day it has
Rained . . .": "Edward Thomas brooded long / On death and beauty—till
a bullet stopped his song."[24] "Hell cannot be let loose twice": the poets
actually fighting the war are keenly aware of this tautology.
    The Auden circle draws from wells dug in a more recent war. For the
poets of the Left, the old war is not World War One, but the war with

Spain. C. Day Lewis suggests this in the "Dedicatory Stanzas" to his 1940 translation of Virgil's *Georgics*. Day Lewis is especially irritated by Fleet Street's *ubi sunt*. He defends himself against the stale and weary cry in two separate poems, "Where are the War Poets?" and "Dedicatory Stanzas." "Where are the War Poets?" explains that his silence is a result of his distaste for propaganda:

> They who in folly or mere greed
> Enslaved religion, markets, laws,
> Borrow our language now and bid
> Us to speak up in freedom's cause.[25]

His earlier justification, in the stanzas dedicated to Spender, is more compelling:

> Where are the war poets? the fools inquire.
> We were the prophets of a changeable morning
> Who hoped for much but saw the clouds forewarning:
> We were at war, while they still played with fire
> And rigged the market for the ruin of man:
> Spain was a death to us, Munich a mourning.
> No wonder then if, like the pelican,
> We have turned inward for our iron ration,
> Tapping the vein and sole reserve of passion,
> Drawing from poetry's capital what we can.[26]

Here, the literary drought of the poets of the Left becomes attributable to the Spanish Civil War. Once again, the Second World War is too much like an earlier war.

Spender's response to the *Times Literary Supplement* presents this argument: "the poetry of the war of democracy versus fascism had already been written by English, French, Spanish, German and Italian émigré poets during the past five years, and particularly during the Spanish war."[27] Samuel Hynes comments:

> For the 'thirties generation, the battle had already been fought and lost; the final curtain had fallen on the tragedy of the decade, and what followed was not essentially a part of the drama. For the writers *as writers*, the appropriate response to the end of the 'thirties was silence, or a retrospective brooding over what had happened.[28]

The Spanish Civil War was the Auden circle's World War One; it was also their World War Two. The Spanish Civil War led to some of the group's best work, to "Spain, 1937" and to *Autumn Journal*. The poems of the Spanish war often eerily anticipate the coming world war. And after 1939, with the flight of Auden and the beginning of war, the circle broke.

As Douglas suggests, there were practical as well as psychological reasons for the apparent shortfall: "The reasons are psychological, literary, military and strategic, diverse." Trench warfare had been ideally suited for war poetry, with its long bouts of waiting, waiting to go over the top. With the collapse of the Maginot Line in 1940 came the collapse of trench warfare in the Western European theatre. France fell, as Churchill said, before a few thousand motor vehicles. Even if either side had ever wanted to see trenches again, tanks rendered them obsolete. Keith Douglas, himself a tank commander, underscores this new mobility as the chief difference between the wars: "there is nothing new, from a soldier's point of view, except its mobile character." The Second World War, with its quickly shifting regiments, its twenty-four-hour surveillance, and its virtually global scope, made quick heroes and destroyed poetry. The long transfixed stretches of time that the Great War had offered its poets all but disappeared.

Censorship also played a significant part. The second war was much more of a propaganda war: M.I.5 took to distinguishing between black, gray, and white propaganda according to the shades of truth in any public statement. One reason may have been that the Axis Powers weren't as good at propaganda. Another more searching reason lay in Chamberlain's sincere belief that pieces of paper could convince the Germans not to fight. He is reported to have said on one occasion during the Twilight War that "as soon as the Germans realize they cannot win, they will fold."[29] The Twilight War was Chamberlain's kind of war, fought with leaflets instead of bombs. Propaganda led to paranoia: the maintaining of a diary during military service was forbidden lest it should fall into enemy hands. The hundreds of letters Owen wrote to his mother before his death in 1918 simply would not have passed through the censors. The Imperial War Museum is full of small diaries written in microscopic hands by soldiers at the front and found upon them. To write anything at all was subversive; to write poetry in the sardonic, lacerative spirit of the first war was next to impossible.

There may be a sociological explanation for the relative absence of poetry from the lines. From Sir Walter Raleigh to Lord Tennyson, nine out of every ten writers of poetry in Britain had been from the upper classes.* Fully a third of the poets writing from the front in the Second World War were from Oxbridge. But it is a comparatively small third.† In the second war poets simply did not sign up in such numbers. In 1914 the elite went eagerly to war, expecting a big show and a quick Waterloo. The aristocracy flocked in, full of dreams of Empire, under the spell of Rupert Brooke. A generation died. The Second World War found them more wary. Parents who had seen their families fall before the myth procured soft jobs in the Intelligence for their sons rather than sending them off into the Infantry. Many joined "the few," the R.A.F., where opportunities for individual heroism soon became much greater. Evelyn Waugh is, not unexpectedly, the most elegant expounder of this elitist argument. Ian Kilbannock rehearses it before Crouchback in *Officers and Gentlemen* (1955):

> 'Delightful fellows, heroes too, I dare say, but the Wrong Period. Last-war stuff, Guy. Went out with Rupert Brooke.'
> 'You find us poetic?'
> 'No,' said Ian, stopping in his path and turning to face Guy in the darkness. 'Perhaps not poetic, exactly, but Upper Class. Hopelessly upper class. You're the "Fine Flower of the Nation". You can't deny it and *it won't do*.'
> In the various stages of inebriation, facetiously itemized for centuries, the category, 'prophetically drunk', deserves a place.
> 'This is a People's War,' said Ian prophetically, 'and the People won't have poetry and they won't have flowers. Flowers stink. The upper classes are on the secret list. We want heroes of the people, to or for the people, by, with and from the people.'[30]

If British non-contemporary literature is written by an upper middle-class—and most of the writers studied here fall into this category, whether from Bloomsbury or Mayfair—then British literature stayed at home.

Eliot's response to the media's search for war poets raises a further practical point. His "Poetry in Wartime" is perhaps the most considered of all the poets' apologetics. Eliot separates war poetry into two familiar

---

*See Sir Arthur Quiller-Couch's argument in *The Art of Writing*, quoted in the final chapter of *A Room of One's Own*: "It may seem a brutal thing to say, and it is a sad thing to say: but, as a matter of hard fact, the theory that poetical genius bloweth where it listeth, and equally in poor and rich, holds little truth" (Virginia Woolf, *A Room of One's Own*, 111).

†Of the 831 poets writing from the lines, 513 were university educated, 355 at Oxbridge. Cf. Catherine Reilly, *English Poetry of the Second World War*, vii–ix.

wells: "We may mean patriotic poetry, that is to say poetry which expresses and stimulates pride in the military virtues of a people. Or we may be asking for poets to write poetry arising out of their experience of war."[31] Eliot contends that patriotic poetry is never especially good, that "There is no first-rate poem about the victory over the Armada, or the Battle of Trafalgar."[32] Regarding the poetry of experience, Eliot argues that the experience of modern war is primarily on a trivial level: "When these poets write about the war, it is mostly about some limited experience, even trivial experience."[33] Patric Dickinson, in his introduction to the quixotic anthology *Soldiers' Verse* (1945), agrees: "The Total War of 1939–45 has naturally produced very little war-poetry. For as the scope of war has enlarged the scope of poetry has diminished. The small incident engrosses the poet."[34] For Eliot, these trivial incidents include "cold, discomfort, or the boredom of waiting at an isolated post."[35] Waiting will be seen to occupy a central place in war literature on all fronts of the Second World War.

Eliot concludes, in a typically perverse application of Wordsworth's "recollected in tranquillity," that soldiers will be unable to assess the impact of the war until the war is over:

> [. . .] the bigger experiences need time, perhaps a long time, before we can make poetry of them. You cannot understand war—with the kind of understanding needed for writing poetry—or any other great experience while you are in the midst of it; you can only record small immediate observations. And when, after the war, the experience has become a part of a man's whole past, it is likely to bear fruit in something very different from what, during time of war, people call "war poetry."[36]

Keith Douglas argues almost precisely the same thing in Tunisia six months later. For Douglas, boredom and waiting are also the two great subjects of war poetry:

> The long inaction on all fronts was not inspiring; everyone was too used to inaction. Dunkirk was over almost before most people had rubbed the sleep out of their eyes; inaction, as far as most soldiers were concerned, began again. This produced, as it was bound to, an amount of loitering, fed-up poetry, vaguely relatable to some of Turner's poems 1914-1918.[37]

Again, the comparison with the poetry of the Great War. Douglas closes his argument, as Eliot does, with the same stress on reimagined experience: "Meanwhile the soldiers have not found anything new to say. Their experiences they will not forget easily, and it seems to me that the whole body of English war poetry of this war, civil and military, will be created after war is over."[38]

This delayed solution was unacceptable to the writers of *Horizon*'s manifesto: "At the beginning of the war, it was assumed that the function of the creative writer was to write a good book about the war ... after the war. Experience of two years of war has shown to writers that their function is to write a good book about the war *now*."[39] *Horizon*'s call to immediate action was sounded by a host of luminous figures, including George Orwell, Stephen Spender, Alun Lewis, and Cyril Connolly. The group's solution was to establish an Official Group of War Writers. In the next issue of *Horizon*, an anonymous "Combatant" replied to the suggestion with strangely familiar derision:

> But what do your chums propose doing? They will like to form an Official Group; they would go on jaunts to the Americas and Dominions; they would have 'the facilities of journalists' which, as far as I have seen, merely means the privileges of commissioned rank without its obligations—cheap railway tickets, entrance to ward-rooms and officers' messes and investitures; they would 'co-ordinate war-effort emotionally'. Cor, chase my Aunt Nancy round the prickly pear! The General Staff love initials; they would, I am sure, rejoice to put an armlet, D.A.E.C.W.E. on someone's arm and call him Deputy Assistant Emotional Co-ordinator of War Effort.[40]

The diction is unmistakable, especially when compared with *Put Out More Flags*. Ambrose Silk reacts to Fitzrovia's preparations for war in the same way: "Cor chase my Aunt Fanny round a mulberry bush, thought Ambrose, what a herd."[41] The two relatives circumambulate in the same orchard: the "Combatant" is clearly Evelyn Waugh.*

Cyril Connolly had a second solution of his own to the fools' inquiry, which he published as the leader of the January 1941 issue of *Horizon*. Of all the responses, it is the most epigrammatic, and the most convincing:

> About this time of year articles appear called 'Where are our war poets?' The answer (not usually given) is 'under your nose'. For war poets are not a new kind of being, they are only peace poets who have assimilated the material of war. As the war lasts, the poetry which is written becomes war poetry, just as inevitably as the lungs of Londoners grow black with soot.[42]

*The appearance of this letter in the Waugh Collection at the University of Texas supplies external evidence for this claim.

This simplest answer provides the definition of war literature assumed here. The Second World War was, in literary as in military terms, a civilian's war. Its literature comes from those fighting at home. The literature of the home front is directly engaged in war in a way it could never be in the First World War. The search for an original literary response to the Second World War must turn to the works of its civilians. The German conscript in Owen's "Strange Meeting" knows of wells sunk too deep for war:

> Then, when much blood had clogged their chariot-wheels,
> I would go up and wash them from sweet wells,
> Even with truths that lie too deep for taint.[43]

These are the wells, healing wells brimming with pure water, from which the seven writers draw. The literature of the Second World War can be found, as Connolly put it, "under your nose."

I. The Literature of the Second World War: Anticipation, Experience, Reimagination

While England Slept: The Literature of Anticipation

> 'Poor Ricky', he said, 'If this army is anything like the last he must be in purgatory.'
>
> Allingham.

The literature of the Second World War can be divided, like Gaul, into three parts. Eyes front, eyes side, eyes back. The years of Chamberlain's Ministry (May 1937–May 1940) were, in literary as in geopolitical terms, years of anticipation, looking ahead to a war future. The literature written between the fall of France and VE-Day (May 1940–May 1945) directly records a war present, realizing a war-torn London in vivid and immediate detail. At the other end of the scale, those writing after the war provide an uneasy coda in their reimaginings of a war past. The Literature of Reimagination is by far the largest of the three groups, wide enough to encompass works as distantly related as Bowen's *The Heat of the Day* (1948) and Le Carré's *A Perfect Spy* (1986). The full range of the literary effect of the Second World War in Britain can be drawn only from this three-fold perspective.

A comprehensive account would be divided into the three taxonomic categories of Anticipation, Experience, and Reimagination—but such a broad sketch is beyond the particular focus here. This study does not pretend to a general overview of a decade of British literature. The literature of the American and Continental wars has also been set aside. The task is not to provide a dizzying kaleidoscope of loosely connected texts, but to allow, somewhat myopically perhaps, seven very good writers to speak for the British literary experience of World War Two. Waugh's *Sword of Honour* will represent the Literature of Reimagination in chapter VI;

Little Gidding and the works of the Inklings will serve for the Literature of Experience in chapters IV and V; chapters II and III will center on the anticipatory works of Woolf and MacNeice.

The Literature of Anticipation is a phenomenon peculiar to the Second World War, and restricted enough in its definition to permit close attention on a wide scale. No war before or since has produced so considerable a body of prophetic texts. For some, especially for Orwell and the Auden circle, the approach of war is so shatteringly obvious that their writings can hardly be called anticipations. H. G. Wells, in the 1926 edition of *The Outline of History*, calmly presents 'A Forecast of the "Next War." ' [1] S. Fowler Wright's novel of 1935 has the preternaturally prophetic title *A Prelude in Prague: A Story of the War of 1938*. Anthony Beavis, in *Eyeless in Gaza* (1936), predicts "another war quite soon—about 1940, he thought."[2] Orwell writes in his wartime diary that "Since 1934 I have known war between England and Germany was coming, and since 1936 I have known it with complete certainty."[3] Above this in the entry for 8 June 1940 is an even more far-reaching prediction: "At any rate, I have known since about 1931 (Spender says he has known since 1929) that the future must be catastrophic."[4] Orwell appears to be in competition with Spender on this one: anything you can have foreseen I can have foreseen earlier. But that Orwell writes all this in 1940 does not detract from his extraordinary foresight. By September 1938 and the travesty in Munich, no such foresight was needed.

The main dates of the rapidly moving Munich crisis may be quickly outlined here. Hitler, feigning outrage at the condition of the Sudeten Germans on the borders of Czechoslovakia, had been threatening to attack throughout the summer. On August 3 Lord Runciman was sent to Prague by Chamberlain to pressure Czechoslovakian acquiescence to Hitler's demands. These talks broke down, and by August 27 Mussolini's Ambassador asked Ribbentrop to inform him when the attack would take place. On September 7 the French, prepared to fight for Czechoslovakia, inquired of England whether they were ready to do the same. On September 12 the Cabinet sent to M. Bonnet the verbal equivalent of an unsigned blank check: "while His Majesty's Government would never allow the security of France to be threatened, they are unable to make precise statements of the character of their future action, or the time at which it would be taken, in circumstances that they cannot at present foresee."[5]

Such equivocation encouraged Hitler to stall negotiations with the Czech President Beneš, and on September 15 the Sudeten Nazi leader,

Henlein, fled to Germany. On the same day, Chamberlain flew to Berchtes-gaden, and agreed to the secession of the Sudetenland. Beneš was forced to accept these terms, and a week later Chamberlain flew to Godesberg, only to find Hitler demanding a complete military takeover of the Sude-tenland by the first of October. The French army mobilized, as did the British fleet; by September 28 Chamberlain was ready to announce war to the House of Commons. As he reached the close of his speech a message from Hitler summoned him, with Daladier and Mussolini, to Munich. The effect on the House, as Nicolson records in his diary, was electric:

> That, I think, was one of the most dramatic events which I have ever witnessed. For a second, the House was hushed in absolute silence. Then the whole House burst into a roar of cheering, since they knew that this might mean peace.[6]

Beneš was not invited. On September 30, Chamberlain returned from Germany for a third time, having capitulated on Beneš' behalf to Hitler's terms, and pronouncing "peace with honour."

In the political sphere the reactions to Chamberlain's piece of paper were swift and direct. Mosley's hatchet-job on Chamberlain, *On Borrowed Time: How World War II Began*, records the following dialogue between two French delegates to Berchtesgaden, MM. Stehlin and Léger: *"Mais enfin, l'agrément, c'est un soulagement." "Ah oui, un soulagement! Comme quand on a merdé dans sa culotte!"** Duff Cooper, the First Lord of the Admiralty, resigned on the spot. Churchill rose against considerable op-position to speak of "a total and unmitigated defeat."[7] Churchill had been a parliamentary Cassandra throughout the thirties. He had spoken against Hitler's reoccupation of the Rhineland in 1936, fearing that *"The creation of a line of forts opposite to the French frontier will enable the German troops to be economized on that line, and will enable the main forces to swing round through Belgium and Holland."*[8] As soon as his predictions had been proved partially right, and Chamberlain proved utterly powerless to prevent them from coming true, Churchill's political prestige snowballed. Opposition groups within the government formed around Churchill and Anthony Eden almost immediately.

The public reception was no less negative. The reaction of Balfour's niece to the first Munich agreement, ten days earlier, may be taken to be representative in all but its violence:

*"But anyway, the agreement is a relief." "Yes, a relief! As if one had crapped in one's trousers!"

The morning begins by Baffy Dugdale ringing me up. She said she had been sick twice in the night over England's shame, and that at breakfast she read *The Times* leader. She came upon the words, 'The general character of the terms submitted to the Czechoslovak Government could not, in the nature of things, be expected to make a strong *prima facie* appeal to them.' Having read these words she dashed to the lavatory and was sick for a third time.[9]

The Unity Theatre performed the pantomime *Babes in the Wood*, with Chamberlain as the Big Bad Wolf. Louis MacNeice, in his poetic record of the period, *Autumn Journal*, had no illusions about the meaning of the Munich conference:

> But once again
>   The crisis is put off and things look better
> And we feel negotiation is not vain—
>   Save my skin and damn my conscience.
> And negotiation wins,
>   If you can call it winning,
> And here we are—just as before—safe in our skins;
>   Glory to God for Munich.[10]

MacNeice's sickened sarcasm at Chamberlain's "peace with honour" is typical of all those who anticipate the war. The cartoonist David Low had been prophesying war in the pages of the *Evening Standard* for years. His "Stepping Stones to Glory," printed on 8 July 1935, depicted Hitler goose-stepping over the backs of political leaders from "Rearmament" to "Rhine-land Fortification" to "Danzig" to "??" to "!!" to "Boss of the Universe." After Munich, Lord Beaverbrook no longer pulled the cartoons off his newspaper's pages. Like Churchill, Low's credibility increased with every previsioned catastrophe: "As someone who had been proved resoundingly correct about Hitler, moreover, Low found himself with a reputation not simply as a cartoonist but, on the international scene at least, as a prophet."[11]

George Orwell played the soothsayer's role to the hilt. *Keep the Aspidistra Flying* (1936) displays a Tiresean certainty of the coming war:

> Our civilisation is dying. It *must* be dying. But it isn't going to die in its bed. Presently the aeroplanes are coming. Zoom - whizz - crash! The whole western world going up in a roar of high explosives.[12]

Homage to Catalonia (1938) is an account of the Spanish Civil War until the last paragraph, when, without warning, Orwell jars the book into the future:

> Down here it was still the England I had known in my childhood: [...] all sleeping the deep, deep sleep of England, from which I sometimes fear that we shall never wake till we are jerked out of it by the roar of bombs.[13]

Coming Up for Air (1939) continues this Tiresean note. *"It's all going to happen,"* George Bowling assures us:

> All the things you've got at the back of your mind, the things you're terrified of, the things that you tell yourself are just a nightmare or only happen in foreign countries. The bombs, the food-queues, the rubber truncheons, the barbed wire, the coloured shirts, the slogans, the enormous faces, the machine-guns squirting out of bedroom windows.[14]

Orwell has foresuffered all: here he anticipates the post-war world of his *Nineteen Eighty-Four* (1949).

The pre-war artist, whether politician, poet, or painter, was more than prophet. In preparing for a war the literature of Munich did not merely look forward. The literature of the Second World War looks at the war in the future, in the present, and finally in the past; similarly, writers preparing for the war either look forward, to its outbreak, laterally, to wars fought elsewhere, or backward, to the First World War and visions of a lost past. In her introduction to the period, "Endings and Beginnings," Linda Shires writes of 1939 as "a year when the past broke off from the present, when the present itself became fragmentary, and when the future was uncertain."[15] The time is out of joint; to come to terms with this disjointed time the writers in the years before war attempt to weave it into a seamless whole. The war is anticipated in time future, time present, and time past.

W. H. Auden is a central figure in the future group. The pre-war poems of Auden's *Another Time* (1940) face almost exclusively forward. "In Memory of W. B. Yeats" casts forward to "the dogs of Europe" (95)* and "the guts of the living" (93):

---

*W. H. Auden, *Another Time* (New York: Random House, 1940), 95. References to this edition of *Another Time* in this section will appear within the text.

In the nightmare of the dark
All the dogs of Europe bark.
And the living nations wait,
Each sequestered in its hate. (95)

"It's Farewell to the Drawing-room's Civilized Cry" is a preparation piece as well as an elegy. Its first title, for *The Listener* in February 1937, was "Song for the New Year"; the New Year comes "with gas and with bomb" (13). In *Another Time*, the future is immediate and inescapable: in "Spain, 1937" it arrives "To-morrow" (91). The present is prepared for "a future of marriage" with "the hairy and clumsy bridegroom" (39) in "Poem XXIV," titled "Crisis," for the *Atlantic Monthly* in September 1939. The original title of "Poem IX," for *The Spectator* of 25 August 1939, was "The Prophets." "Gare du Midi" announces that a "terrible future may have just arrived" (41). By "Dover" the soldiers are killing "Their pauper civilian future" (46). The "terrified / Imaginative child" (36) of "Not as That Dream Napoleon" knows that "he has to be the future" (37) and walks about in the present world. In each case the future is directly implicated, if not actually contained, in the present. *Another Time* is the present time; the title poem describes no other time but our own: "It is to-day in which we live" (49).

At times Auden's prophetic fervor can result in too liberal a use of the benefits of hindsight. False prolepsis is an especial problem when discussing the Literature of Anticipation.* In Evelyn Waugh's *Work Suspended*, the painter Mr. Plant dies some months before the war, leaving on his easel the picture of "a one-armed veteran of the First World War meditating over a German helmet."[6] The painting has the highly prophetic title "Again?"—or did in 1949. When part of the story was first published in *Horizon* in 1939, all the easel held was a picture of the Queen Mary, with the innocuous title, "Too Big?" Auden's revisionary compulsion often opens him up to the charge of false prolepsis. "Voltaire at Ferney," written in February 1939, begins: "Perfectly happy now, he looked at his estate"

---

*Shaw was guilty of this in the first war: his preface to *Heartbreak House* implies that the bulk of the play was written before 1914, allowing Irvine and Henderson, among others, to admire the work's clairvoyance. But the research of Stanley Weintraub has taken the edge off that prophecy, revealing that the play was written largely during the war.

(28). Auden changes this after the war to "Almost happy now." "Spain, 1937" is buried after the fall of Barcelona.*

Sometimes, though, the foreshadowing is the result not of contrivance but of the coincidence of history. For the present group, the war is not anticipated, but fought in front of them. With the poets of the wars before the war, in Spain and China, it is frequently difficult to determine whether the war is prophesied or actually experienced. Auden is also a member of this lateral group:

> If war was the experience to be prepared for, then one way of preparing was obviously to seek war out, to journey beyond that frightening border and to return with the truth. Auden and Isherwood's *Journey to a War* is Literature of Preparation in this sense: it is *the* war-book of the period just before war became the Second World War.[17]

Journey to a War (1939) begins with the Second World War in the far distance: "Here, though the bombs are real and dangerous, / And Italy and King's are far away."[18] But this initial gulf between the present and future theatres of war is crossed by "The Ship," the third poem of *Journey to a War*:

> Somewhere a strange and shrewd To-morrow goes to bed
> Planning a test for men from Europe; no one guesses
> Who will be most ashamed, who richer, and who dead.[19]

The poem was written while sailing to the Sino-Japanese war; soon all of Europe will be on the liner. The two lateral worlds are compressed together with electric economy at the close of "Sonnet XVI":

> And maps can really point to places
> Where life is evil now:
> Nanking; Dachau.[20]

Dachau, the first Nazi concentration camp, was established in 1933. But Auden could not have possibly known, in 1939, the force of that last word: sometimes his foresight is real.

---

*Auden addresses a related charge in the *Collected Shorter Poems*, suppressing any poem dishonest in its expression of "feelings or beliefs which its author never felt or entertained" (*Collected Shorter Poems*, 15). But the omission of "Spain, 1937" for its teleological view of history is insincerity of a graver kind.

Stephen Spender's *The Still Centre*, published in May 1939, compresses the future with the present of the Spanish rather than the Sino-Japanese war. Spender's "Thoughts During an Air Raid," though it first appeared in the *New Republic* on 18 May 1938, reads like a poem of the Blitz:

> [...] A hundred are killed
> In the outer suburbs. Well, well, I carry on.
> So long as the great 'I' is propped upon
> This girdered bed which seems more like a hearse,
> In the hotel bedroom with flowering paper
> Which rings in wreaths above, I can ignore
> The pressure of those names under my fingers
> Heavy and blank as I rustle the paper,
> The wireless wail in the lounge margin.
> Yet supposing that a bomb should dive
> Its nose right through this bed, with me upon it?[21]

Were it not for the phrase "hotel bedroom," and the poem's publication, if considerably revised, in Spender's *Collected Poems* under the heading "Poems about the Spanish Civil War," there is nothing to suggest here that "Thoughts During an Air Raid" was written two years before the first bomb was dropped on London. "A Stopwatch and an Ordnance Map," "The Bombed Happiness," and "War Photograph" retain the same unsettling ambiguity; the suppression of detail allows Spender to write of both a future England and a present Spain.

C. Day Lewis blurs this line between prophecy and present experience even further in *Overtures to Death*. In "Bombers," the planes fly over both worlds: "Black as vermin, crawling in echelon / Beneath the cloud-floor, the bombers come."[22] "Newsreel" maintains the same tension between journalism and prophecy as *Homage to Catalonia*. The English watch the Spanish Civil War in the cinema's "dream-house," soon to be jerked out of their "womb-deep sleep":

> Oh, look at the warplanes! Screaming hysteric treble
> In the long power-dive, like gannets they fall steep.
> But what are they to trouble -
> These silver shadows to trouble your watery, womb-deep
>   sleep?

See the big guns, rising, groping, erected
To plant death in your world's soft womb.
Fire-bud, smoke-blossom, iron seed projected -
Are these exotics? They will grow nearer home.

Grow nearer home - and out of the dream-house stumbling
One night into a strangling air and the flung
Rags of children and thunder of stone niagaras tumbling,
You'll know you slept too long.[23]

For the Auden group, the best means of anticipation is to keep one's eyes squarely upon a war in the present.

The third way to prepare for a future war is to look back at a past one. The proleptic return to the past, the forward look backward, is the way of the one charter member of the Auden group not yet mentioned. Louis MacNeice meets his *déjà vu* on Primrose Hill, "Whose summit once was used for a gun emplacement / And very likely will / Be used that way again."[24] The Londoners in *Autumn Journal* say to one another "This must be wrong, it has happened before, / Just like this before, we must be dreaming." Orwell's George Bowling remembers the pre-war atmosphere of July 1914 in *Coming Up for Air*:

> GERMAN ULTIMATUM; FRANCE
> MOBILISING
>
> For several days (four days, wasn't it? I forget the exact dates) there was a strange stifled feeling, a kind of waiting hush, like the moment before a thunderstorm breaks, as though the whole of England was silent and listening.[25]

Orwell is writing in September 1938: his writing is both a recollection of pre-war 1914 and a reaction to the Munich conference.

Coming Up for Air looks back at a past war, and at a past world. "To get my nerve back before the bad times begin," Bowling returns to his childhood fishpond in Lower Binfield.[26] (Gordon Beadle has identified Lower Binfield as Henley: the names of Bowling's fishing companions, Lovegrove and Barnes, are inscribed upon the Henley war memorial.) As Hynes has written of the Literature of Anticipation, "if you examined the past honestly, as a displaced person might examine his belongings before he fled his home, you might find what was worth saving: and if you imagined the future fully and without flinching, you might be able to survive it."[27]

Bowling reaches back into his past to protect himself against the future: all he finds there is an urban swamp full of broken bedsteads and lorry-loads of tarblocks.

Virginia Woolf also tries to bring the past into the present through the pageant at Pointz Hall. In this expression of the valedictory impulse, this attempt to place history under glass, Woolf had good company. For pre-war England, the pageant acted as a combination time-capsule and placebo, in both cases a quick pill to reassure oneself of tradition and to block out its imminent discontinuity. On 8 July 1939, Kenilworth Castle mounted an enormous pageant, with a cast of over two thousand. It rained; but *The Times* could still rhapsodize over its evocation of a dying age:

> And, incredible as it must seem to us, it was an England unawakened by railway whistles and the roar of aeroplanes, an England with an ear for lesser sounds, so that the jingle of harness that was heard this afternoon within and without this fortress, where trees grow in the base-court and in crevices of the masonry, more than anything else aroused its former life.[28]

The production at Kenilworth Castle was one of an almost continuous parade of pageants before the war. The first week of August 1938 saw pageants at Blenheim Palace, and at Kempford in Gloucestershire. The Church of St. Magnus the Martyr put on a pageant of nursing in July; a week later the women's league of health and beauty held an Empire pageant at Wembley.

By 1938, pageants were well established as a literary sub-genre. Anthony Powell's *From a View to a Death* (1933), takes place during a village pageant, as does Charles Williams' *Descent into Hell* (1937). The playwright of Williams' pageant, John Struther, is modelled on Eliot, who wrote *The Rock* in 1934. *The Rock* is also a source for Christopher Fry's pageant, *The Boy with a Cart* (1938), first performed in Steyning, Sussex, 20 miles from Monks House.* *The Boy with a Cart* begins with "The People of South England" chanting in the same incantatory rhythm as Woolf's villagers:

> In our fields, fallow and burdened, in grass and furrow,
> In barn and stable, with scythe, flail, or harrow, [...]
> God providing, we dividing, sowing, and pruning;
> Not knowing yet and yet sometimes discerning.[29]

---

*The play has since been forgotten, though it had a notable revival under John Gielgud at the Lyric in 1950, with Richard Burton in the title role.

Forster wrote two pageants before the war, *The Abinger Pageant* (1934) and *England's Pleasant Land* (1938). *England's Pleasant Land* provides a large part of Miss La Trobe's material in *Between the Acts*, as will be seen in chapter II. Virginia Woolf began *Between the Acts* as a defence against the future, unifying the present by recapturing the past. She too is unable to stall the powerhouse of history; in 1938, there is only the trying.

For many writers, Charles Dickens offered a way out. A total of 299,000 complete sets of Dickens were ordered through three London dailies in 1934.[30] By 1939, Dickens seems to have been upon every literary bedside table: Evelyn Waugh, Virginia Woolf, Harold Nicolson, George Orwell, and Graham Greene were all reading Dickens in the war. Woolf was reading *Nicholas Nickelby* "by way of a refresher" in April 1939.[31] In Greene's *The Ministry of Fear* (1943), Arthur Rowe reads Dickens "as people used to read the Bible, over and over again till he could have quoted chapter and verse."[32] Some were to find him impossibly remote. Nicolson, who was also reading *Nicholas Nickelby*, exclaimed "How unreal Dickens is!" in his diary four days before war was declared.[33] Waugh wrote to his wife at the end of the war: "I have just read *Dombey and Son*. The worst book in the world."[34] There were many ways of returning to the past. All were anticipatory in their attempt to stave off the future; all were certain to fail.

The Literature of Anticipation was sure of its failure. The prophets of the late thirties were right that England, old England, couldn't last, but they were right for the wrong reasons. All these writers, from Auden to Orwell, from MacNeice to Woolf, saw the end as an Armaggedon from the air. The spectre of General Guilio Douhet haunts their works. Douhet's *Command of the Air*, with its stress on civilian bombing, its acceptance of chemical warfare, and its resignation to total war, had spawned a widespread hysteria. The Literature of Anticipation was waiting for Douhet; like his Beckettian counterpart, Douhet never came. He did not need to.

Orwell's skies are black with bombers—this is the way the world ends, not with a whimper but a bang. The members of the Auden circle present the war in terms of air attack, in "Song for the New Year," "Journey to a War," "Thoughts During an Air Raid," "Bombers," and "Newsreel." These are not just enemy planes; the planes above the spinster are England's. Their presence is an equally unsettling reminder of the war to come. The R.A.F. drops the bomb that falls on Lower Binfield in *Coming Up for Air*. British planes disrupt Forster's pageant at Dorking and Miss La Trobe's pageant at Pointz Hall. The growing threat of British planes is pressed further in Auden's "Ballads," as the lunatic James Honeyman is taken for a German:

> Suddenly from the east
> Some aeroplanes appeared,
> Somebody screamed: "They're bombers!
> War must have been declared!"

> The first bomb hit the Dairy,
> The second the cinema,
> The third fell in the garden
> Just like a falling star. (68)

Honeyman blows up the three places of his past: "On their left a United Dairy, / A cinema on their right. / At the bottom of his garden / He built a little shed" (65). In Woolf, in Forster, in Auden, and especially in Orwell, the planes bomb the past. And they are all R.A.F. planes. Douhetism has crossed the Channel; British planes are equally a threat to a past which backward-looking authors of the time are finding impossible to preserve.

The literature of the Chamberlain years anticipates a war future; the literature of 1940–1945 directly records a war present; the literature of the post-war period recreates a war past. Those writing while England slept were wide awake, with their eyes front, eyes side, and eyes back. Orwell's major work of the thirties falls into this three-part pattern. *Keep the Aspidistra Flying* looks fearfully ahead to a catastrophic future; *Homage to Catalonia* looks to the Spanish Civil War; *Coming Up for Air* looks backward to a lost past. All three are anticipations of the Second World War. In looking in these three directions, Orwell and other writers of the late thirties mirror the larger spectrum of the literature of the Second World War. Each third is itself a triad: what develops is a nine-fold requiem in the time of war.

Purgatory: Waiting in the War

> Let us now consider the future in the light of the last cantos
> of the *Purgatorio*.
>
> Redpath.

For all the voices in this requiem, the war was primarily a time of waiting. Whether anticipated, experienced, or remembered, the war entered a suspended world. Waiting is the central theme of the Literature of Experience. For Eliot, the central subject of the soldier-poet is "the boredom of waiting"; for Douglas, long inaction leads to "loitering, fed-up poetry." *East Coker* (1940) instructs the soul to "wait without hope";[1] Steffi still waits for the soldier of Douglas' *"Vergissmeinnicht."* In *The Secret Vanguard* (1941), Michael Innes' detective, Inspector Appelby, describes wartime as "normal and waiting: the contradiction alone could express it. Waiting."[2] "Waiting" was a popular Service song during the war, with verses of varying respectability:

> 'I'll be *wai*-tin' for you, *At* Oflag Seventy-three-ah!
> I'll be *wai*-tin' for you, don't look out for me-ah!
> Lift up your froat you'll bleed like a goat,
> *whoops* your adam's apple!'[3]

Charlie Luke sings this verse to Margery Allingham's detective Albert Campion in *The Tiger in the Smoke* (1952). Luke proceeds to remember the 1944 raids in chilling terms:

> 'Remember V 2's? The whole city waiting. Silent. People on edge. More waiting. Waiting for hours. Nothing. Nothing to show. Then, strike a light! Suddenly, no warning, no whistle, wallop! End of the ruddy world! Just a damned great hole and afterwards half the street coming down very slowly, like a woman fainting.'[4]

Luke's harrowing reimagination returns Campion, and the novel, to the transfixed world of the Second World War.

Waiting is above all the stress of the Literature of Anticipation. Graham Greene's recent republication of his 1937–1939 journal in *Granta* is called "While Waiting for a War."[5] Malcolm Muggeridge captures Parliament's abeyance in 1937, just prior to Chamberlain's accession of Baldwin as Prime Minister:

Parliament, reflecting the mood of those it represented, gave an impression of waiting - like the elderly inmates of a private hotel waiting for the post, though they have no particular reason for expecting a letter; or waiting for evening to come and the blinds to be drawn, though they have no particular reason for preferring evening to day. A strange apathy was apparent, occasionally broken when some event, exceptionally violent, impelled attention [...] Soon this clamour died away, and the old apathy returned; the waiting, no one knew for what.[6]

By 1938 the waiting had become obsessive. Virginia Woolf describes the days before Munich in her diary: "we are beginning to feel the herd impulse: everyone asks everyone, Any news? What d'you think? The only answer is, wait & see."[7] Mr. Jeavons says much the same thing in *At Lady Molly's* (1957), Anthony Powell's recreation of two pre-war worlds: " 'Wait and see,' said Jeavons. 'That was what Mr. Asquith used to say. Didn't do us much good in 1914.' "[8]

With the outbreak of war, everyone expected this waiting to stop. But nothing happened: "war was coming, coming, coming; then came, and lo! there was no war."[9] During the eight-month period between the British declaration of war on 3 September 1939 and Churchill's succession of Chamberlain as wartime Prime Minister on 10 May 1940, the waiting simply intensified. Cyril Connolly's leader for the first issue of *Horizon* proclaimed that "At the moment civilization is on the operating table and we sit in the waiting room."[10] Churchill referred to the period as "Twilight War," appropriating the expression from Chamberlain himself, who wrote three weeks into the war:

One can see already how this war twilight is trying people's nerves. Without the strong centripetal force of mortal danger, all the injustices, inconveniences, hardships and uncertainties of war-time are resented more and more.*

This gestation period before the fall of France earned a variety of epithets. Malcolm Muggeridge dubbed these months the "contraceptive" war.[11] Evelyn Waugh offered a more ebullient sobriquet in the dedicatory letter

---

*Neville Chamberlain, Letter, 23 September 1939, quoted in Keith Feiling, *The Life of Neville Chamberlain*, 424. Churchill quotes this source in "The Twilight War," the second book of *The Second World War*: 'Mr. Chamberlain in a private letter published by his biographer described this phase as "twilight war"; and I find the expression so just and expressive that I have adopted it as the title for this Book' (422).

to *Put Out More Flags*: "that odd, dead period before the Churchillian renaissance, which people called at the time the Great Bore War."[12] Even the Germans had a phrase for it, calling it *Sitzkrieg*. American detective slang provided the most familiar epithet with "the phoney war."*

Preparations at home for the war that refused to come ranged from the comic to the chilling. Chorus girls in London prior to their evacuation to the country were forced to practice milking cows on canvas udders, while swimming pools were made ready for the burial of the anticipated dead. A man was accused of signalling to the Germans with his cigar: "he was puffing hard to make a big light and pointing it at the sky." An Army officer commandeered the nation's supply of permanganate of potash with the intention of staining the trenches from the Wash to the Severn to render them invisible from the air. 280,000 mongrel cats and dogs were killed in September, for fear of epidemic. A number of suicides were reported to have resulted from listening to BBC news bulletins. Fellow civilians presented a far more compelling danger than the enemy: the number of automobile accidents nearly doubled with the national ban on the use of headlights. Of the nearly 1800 casualties recorded in the first two months of hostilities, the black-out was responsible for over 1100, the German Army for none. Not until 20 April 1940 was the first British civilian killed by the Germans on British soil. James Isbister, an Orkney labourer, thus became perhaps the least likely hero of the war.†

This early pantomine hysteria soon waned, turning to a dispirited disease. Private W. C. Brodie recorded in his wartime diary that "By the

---

*The word "phoney" is of uncertain origin. The first O.E.D. supplement gave the following spurious etymology: "This..word..implies that..a thing so qualified has no more substance than a telephone talk with a suppositious friend." More recent editions of the supplement no longer cite this source. Eric Partridge's essay on "Slanguage" for the R.A.F. anthology *Slipstream* (1946) gives an even more fanciful derivation: '*phoney* has been borrowed from the American underworld, which itself borrowed (and then corrupted) it from the English underworld *fawney*, a finger-ring, the transition being through "Brum" jewellery' (*Slipstream*, 63).

†Neither is James Isbister very likely to be related to Powell's artist, Horace Isbister. Sources for the information in this paragraph are as follows. "Chorus girls": Page, Leitch, and Knightley, *Philby*, 121; "A man was accused": E. S. Turner, *The Phoney War on the Home Front*, 65; "An Army officer": Interview with K.G.J.C. Knowles; "280,000 mongrel cats": Turner, 113–14; "A number of suicides": Muggeridge, 66n; "Fellow civilians": Turner, 68; "Of the nearly 1800 casualties": Muggeridge, 335; "James Isbister": *The Illustrated*, 20 April 1940, 1–6.

middle of January 1940 although the M.O. had an adequate supply of shell dressings, he did not possess one aspirin."[13] Mollie Panter-Downes wrote for the *New Yorker* in early 1940 that "Anti-aircraft people have been on the job guarding London since August, and most of them would probably sob with delight at the sight of a few Heinkels." She remarked upon the "strange, somnambulistic quality" of "this curious, trancelike period."[14] The phoney war simply prolonged the waiting, continuing the war of nerves.

Britain was first waiting for the war, then waiting for it to start in earnest, and finally waiting for the bombs to fall. Leonard Woolf, in *The Journey not the Arrival Matters*, characterized the civilian experience of war as

> negative emptiness and desolation of personal and cosmic boredom, the feeling that one is endlessly waiting in a dirty grey railway station waiting-room, a cosmic railway station waiting-room, with nothing to do but wait endlessly for the next catastrophe.[15]

The literature of the Second World War distills not the pity of war, as the poetry of Wilfred Owen did, but its paralysis. The paralyzed waiting suffered throughout Britain during the war pervades its literature. The sense of passive suffering that the war induced found its most common literary expression in the metaphor of purgatory. Purgatory was only one such expression, but the figure provides the deepest literary connection between the writers studied here. It also brings a decade of British literature into sharper focus, since the recourse to the figure of purgatory was fairly widespread from the late thirties to the early fifties.

Dante's vision of purgatory, especially, besets the British literary world during the war. In Auden's "New Year Letter," written for New Year's Day, 1940,

> [. . .] wakened from a dream of glory,
> We find ourselves in Purgatory,
> Back on the same old mountain side
> With only guessing for a guide.[16]

Auden's epigraph to "Crisis," published in the *Atlantic Monthly* on 3 September 1939, is from the *Purgatorio*.* Laurence Binyon and John

---

*W. H. Auden, "Crisis," *Atlantic Monthly*, 164, 3 September 1939, 358–59.

Sinclair publish their renditions of the *Purgatorio* in 1939; Dorothy Sayers works on her translation throughout the war. Edmund Wilson ends his thirties journal with two references to the *Purgatorio*. Thomas Merton begins his journal in 1939 with a discussion of Dante; his *Seven Storey Mountain* (1948) was started during the war. Ezra Pound helped Binyon with his translation of the *Commedia*, and especially the *Purgatorio*, before the war; his 83rd Canto, written in Pisa at the end of the war, raises the shade of Arnaut Daniel. According to Conrad Knickerbocker, Malcolm Lowry's *Lunar Caustic* was conceived in 1940–1941 as a purgatorial sequel to *Under the Volcano*, the second part of a modern *Divine Comedy*: "*Lunar Caustic*, he once said, was only Purgatory."* Thomas Mann's *Doctor Faustus* (1947), written in America during the war, begins with an epigraph from *Inferno II*; in that work, Leverkühn, who dies in 1940, sets verses of the *Purgatorio* to music.†

One group of writers, in particular, makes a concerted and apparently deliberate return to the metaphor: the Inklings—Charles Williams, C. S. Lewis, and J. R. R. Tolkien. Tolkien writes of a Middle Earth throughout the war, but leaving *The Lord of the Rings* (1948) aside, his most unambiguous recreation of purgatory is the lovely allegorical fable, "Leaf By Niggle." Tolkien admits this in a letter to Peter Hastings, the manager of the Newman bookshop, in 1954:

To conclude: having mentioned Free Will, I might say that in my myth I have used 'subcreation' in a special way (not the same as 'subcreation' as a term in criticism of art, though I tried to show allegorically how that might come to be taken up into Creation in some plane in my 'purgatorial' story *Leaf by Niggle* (Dublin Review 1945)) to make visible and physical the effects of Sin or misused Free Will by men.[17]

The epigraph reads: "*Of my sowing such straw I reap. O human folk, why set the heart there where exclusion of partnership is necessary?*" (*Purgatorio* 14, 85–87). Auden, like Eliot and many others, used the *Temple Classics* translation by Thomas Okey.

*Conrad Knickerbocker, introd., Malcolm Lowry, *Lunar Caustic*, 7. Lunar caustic, or silver nitrate, is itself a purgative.

†Thomas Mann, *Doctor Faustus* (Harmondsworth: Penguin with Secker & Warburg, 1968), 158. On the subject of musical settings, Benjamin Britten wrote his "Serenade for Tenor, Horn, and Strings" during the Second World War; the Blitz is captured unforgettably in the Dirge, in which the tenor sings of a purgatorial flame: "The fire will burn thee to the bare bane, / And Christe receive thy saule."

Tucked in parentheses, and dropped into quotation marks, the word 'purgatorial' quietly brings "Leaf by Niggle" into line with the greater part of the literature of the war. And the quotation marks suggest more than this: the 'purgatorial' is deliberately attempted, in response to a particular conversation or a particular review. That conversation was probably with the Inklings; all three rework the *Purgatorio* during the war.

Lucy Redpath places the world of 1940 squarely in the context of Dante's vision of purgatory in *Dante and the Present War* (1941): "Let us now consider the future in the light of the last cantos of the *Purgatorio*."[18] Her essay envisions, in somewhat tremulous rhetoric, the world passing through Dante's flame:

> For millions now life is steeped in flame—often indeed a literal flame. Most of the peoples of Europe have passed, or are passing, through a very furnace of adversity. We pray that the flames kindled by the fury of the oppressor may be transmuted into a fire like that which guarded the secret of happiness on Dante's mountain.[19]

It is hoped that the more familiar infernal flame will be transmuted into the refining flame of *Purgatorio* 27, through which Dante must pass to reach Beatrice and Paradise: Redpath moves from the *Inferno* to the *Purgatorio*.

Eliot, Spender, and Isherwood do likewise. In "What Dante Means to Me," Eliot states that the second movement of *Little Gidding* was "intended to be the nearest equivalent to a canto of the Inferno or the Purgatorio [...] that I could achieve."[20] Elsewhere, Eliot is more precise about these intentions: "I wished the effect of the whole to be Purgatorial which is much more appropriate."[21] Stephen Spender, reviewing Laurence Binyon's translation of the *Purgatorio* in January 1939, also comments on the appropriateness of the work for the time: "Modern man lives in an Inferno, or, at best, a Purgatory which is fairly easy to relate to Dante's view of the *Divine Comedy*."[22] Like Eliot, Spender does not initially distinguish between Inferno and Purgatory, but as the war approaches, he restricts himself to the *Purgatorio*. In a letter to Christopher Isherwood dated 3 August 1939, Spender writes: "One has to look on everything in life as experience, and imagine one is in a kind of purgatory."[23] Making a similar transition, Isherwood describes the return to post-Munich London in *Down There on a Visit* (1959) as "a conducted tour, similar to Dante's tour of the Inferno. But this Inferno is more of a Purgatorio."[24] Dante, and especially the *Purgatorio*, is found to be a particularly appropriate subtext for the Second World War.

Dante's *Purgatorio* is one part of the larger metaphor, one cornice on the mountain. Yeats' last play, *Purgatory*, was published in early 1939. Eliot professed to dislike the title because "I cannot accept a purgatory in which there is no hint, or at least no emphasis upon Purgation."[25] Eliot's difficulty points to the possibility of different purgatories. What is purgation for one modernist is not necessarily purgation for another. Modernists generally assumed Dante to be a poet of the affirmative way; against the affirmation of images witnessed throughout the *Purgatorio* there runs the negative way of St. John of the Cross. Both Eliot and Williams invoke the works and philosophy of St. John of the Cross as well as Dante throughout their war work. The fire to which Eliot's ghost returns in *Little Gidding* is both Dante's *"foco che li affina"* (26, 148)* and St. John's *The Living Flame of Love*.

Between the way up and the way down, between Dante and St. John, there lies a middle, more secular way. As Eliot writes in *Little Gidding*:

There are three conditions which often look alike
Yet differ completely, flourish in the same hedgerow:
Attachment to self and to things and to persons, detachment
From self and from things and from persons; and, growing
  between them, indifference.[26]

Those who do not choose to write of purgation, who are in Eliot's sense indifferent to its theological force, nevertheless provide acutely experienced visions of a secular purgatory. Both Waugh's *Put Out More Flags* and Woolf's *Between the Acts* present the guiding metaphor of the time in a third form, in the image of limbo.† Between the final acts of Miss La

---

*Dante Alighieri, *Purgatorio*, vol. II of *The Divine Comedy* (1939; rpt. New York: Oxford University Press, 1961), 26, 148. "The fire that refines." References to this edition of the *Purgatorio* will appear within the text. Minor discrepancies in the various editions of Dante's text have been silently brought into line with the Oxford edition. Where the meaning of the Italian is not either obvious or paraphrased in the main text, I shall provide a pedestrian translation of my own in a footnote.

†Though Waugh formally entered the Catholic church a decade earlier, he is still, in 1940, a long way from the religious conviction expressed after *Brideshead Revisited* in 1946: "So in my future books there will be two things to make them unpopular: a preoccupation with style and the attempt to represent man more fully, which, to me, means only one thing, man in his relation to God" ("Fanfare," 56). This is not to say that Waugh is anti-clerical in the 1930s, just keenly aware of those who are.

Trobe's pageant, the audience is captured sitting in limbo: "All their nerves were on edge. They sat exposed."[27] The limbo imagined by Ambrose Silk in *Put Out More Flags* is much more congenial: "But Limbo is the place. [...] Limbo for the unbaptized, for the pious heathen, the sincere sceptic."[28]

Ambrose Silk's afterworld is clearly inspired by Dante's limbo, the first circle in Hell. Limbo cannot be mistaken for purgatory, for limbo is not a waiting world. Unless one has the good fortune to be a friend of Beatrice, there is nothing to look forward to. But limbo and purgatory can be conflated in certain respects. The presence of Virgil in the *Purgatorio* brings limbo into purgatory; Statius, encountered by Virgil on the mountain, asks for news of Hell's first circle. The Second World War is always both hell and purgatory. It is a question of perspective, as C. S. Lewis makes beautifully clear in *The Great Divorce* (1945). A ghost, arriving in heaven, asks where he has come from. A Spirit replies that "You have been in Hell: though if you don't go back you may call it Purgatory."[29]

The two places must be distinguished theologically, but can be considered together metaphorically, as images evinced and conditioned by a particular historical situation. Limbo may be understood, in Dante, as the heathen equivalent of a terrace in purgatory; one might similarly perceive limbo, in the literature of the Second World War, as the secular equivalent of an image of the *Purgatorio*. One could argue that limbo is found in the less theologically committed works of Waugh, Woolf, and Isherwood, rather than in those of Eliot, Williams, and Tolkien, because the tranquil, directionless worlds of Mayfair and Bloomsbury do not require the sense of active journeying in the *Purgatorio*. Beckett's perception of Joyce's purgatory, in *Our Exagmination [...] of* Work in Progress, applies equally to the waiting worlds in Waugh and Woolf:

> A last word about the Purgatories. Dante's is conical and consequently implies culmination. Mr. Joyce's is spherical and excludes culmination [...] In the one movement is unidirectional, and a step forward represents a net advance: in the other movement is non-directional - or multi-directional, and a step forward is, by definition, a step back.[30]

Miss La Trobe's audience is unable to step either forwards or backwards; Ambrose Silk does not care to do so. They rest "between / The live and the dead nettle" in Eliot's hedgerow, in the pathless way of indifference.[31] The energy in the secular vision is more static than kinetic.

Why should purgatory be such a particularly appropriate myth during wartime? One pragmatic answer may be the new availability of Dante in translation. Dante came late to English: English literature began to show a widespread awareness of the *Commedia* only with the translations of Henry Francis Cary, who started, quite properly, with the *Purgatorio* in 1797. Thomas Okey's facing-page translation, published by Temple Classics at the turn of the century, opened to the modernists a comparatively unexplored territory. The work of Sinclair and Binyon provided wartime writers with the most literal and the most poetic of modern translations: their appearance in 1939 is no historical accident. The recourse to purgatory is a response to the historical situation, a response for which there are as many reasons as writers returning to the myth.

For most writers, purgatory was the best expression of a world in waiting. Purgatory is primarily, as Ezra Pound described "Araby," "a vivid waiting."[32] The waiting-rooms of Cyril Connolly and Leonard Woolf open onto the massive waiting-room of purgatory. In *Out of the Picture* (1938), MacNeice's epitaph to a dying present, the artist and his model exchange the following dialogue:

> MOLL. What did he want to paint it for anyway?
>   Crucifying himself, living in a fool's purgatory.
>   Though I must admit there is something about the eyes.
>   [PORTRIGHT *bursts in from the landing door, running.*]
> PORTRIGHT. Hullo!
> MOLL. Hullo! Where's your lady?
> PORTRIGHT. Waiting for me. Waiting.[33]

"Fool's purgatory" is more than a play on "fool's paradise," more, even, than an expression of the state of Portright the artist. The word captures the suspension of a time, the suspended world of London in 1938, as Portright's subsequent repetition of "waiting" implies.*

---

*The world may be waiting for a war, but Portright is waiting for a woman. In "Heavy Date," Auden imagines the world waiting as a lover would for the war:

All mankind, I fancy,
When anticipating
Anything exciting
  Like a rendez-vous,
Occupy the time in
Purely random thinking,
For when love is waiting
  Logic will not do. (*Another Time*, 55)

As Barthes has it in *A Lover's Discourse*, love is always a profound waiting. All the

Purgatory is not just a place of suspended animation, it is also a place of very gradual ascent. Christian writers turned to the *Purgatorio* as a source of hope. Dr. Elliott-Binns preached from Westminster Abbey in 1938 on *Dante and the World To-day*, holding the example and the values of the *Commedia* as a remedy for a world approaching war.[34] Writers in time of war commonly turn to Dante, but in the Second World War the emphasis shifts. The flames of the First World War were seen as inescapable; in the Second, they offered the hope of relief and redemption. The First War drew upon the *Inferno*, the Second turned to the *Purgatorio*. What literature remains to be written after the Third World War will probably draw upon the *Paradiso*.

For some, then, the return to the myth of purgatory was spurred by faith. The doctrine of Purgatory was first formulated by Gregory the Great, and was subsequently affirmed by the Catholic Church at Lyons (1274), Florence (1439), and the final *sessio* at Trent (December 3, 1563).* As Zoé Oldenbourg puts it in *Massacre at Montségur*, Purgatory evolved for economic as well as spiritual reasons.[35] Since the church's monies in the Middle Ages came principally from Masses for the Dead, to give souls a way-station before they entered heaven immeasurably increased the number of hours a soul had to be prayed for. In time of war, the presence of this way-station was a godsend to believers. Purgatory was the place for the unshriven soldier dying beside you, for the relative missing presumed dead. For Anglicans like Eliot and Williams, purgatory was more Dante than doctrine. But for Evelyn Waugh, the only practicing Roman Catholic studied in depth here, purgatory assumed a religious force by the end of the war. Lord Marchmain's act of grace at the close of *Brideshead Revisited* sends him directly to a Catholic purgatory.

For many writers, purgatory reappeared with such persistence because of its position between two sets of worlds. Mount Purgatory lies between heaven and hell, and between heaven and earth. War, as hell on earth, also occupied a halfway-world. For David Jones, "the war itself was a

members of the Auden circle experience *l'attente* at its most painful directly before the war. MacNeice has lost his wife; Spender, Auden, and Isherwood have all undergone emotional crises of their own. This gives the waiting they present a personal cutting-edge: history is only one of the factors brought into and conditioning the myth of purgatory.

*According to Jacques Le Goff in *The Birth of Purgatory*, the word *purgatorium* was coined at some point between 1170 and 1180. The importance of Purgatory in Catholic doctrine has been downplayed since Vatican II.

parenthesis."[36] On the 29th of April 1938, Woolf is "in a dazed state, hovering between 2 worlds."* MacNeice is "isolated in a temporary limbo between two worlds" in 1940.[37] The suspensions are Dantesque: between these two worlds, past and future, heaven and hell, lies the middle-ground of purgatory. Agatha Monchensey, in the *The Family Reunion* (1939), looks to this middle-ground:

> You and I,
> My dear, may very likely meet again
> In our wanderings in the neutral territory
> Between two worlds.[38]

Eliot's compound ghost in *Little Gidding* inhabits that neutral territory, walking peregrine "Between two worlds become much like each other."[39] In Williams' *Descent into Hell*, a single door opens "in two worlds at once."[40] The passageway opens upon *Little Gidding*'s world, upon the world of London during the Blitz, above all, upon a purgatorial world.

The Family Reunion, written under the shadow of war, is also a play of purgation. Agatha says to Harry:

> You are the consciousness of your unhappy family,
> Its bird sent flying through the purgatorial flame.
> Indeed it is possible. You may learn hereafter,
> Moving alone through flames of ice, chosen
> To resolve the enchantment under which we suffer.[41]

The Family Reunion even suggests why purgation is necessary. Before purgatory must come a fall; expiation requires a sin. A literature which turns to purgatory as a driving myth is driven by guilt. According to Agatha:

> It is possible that you have not known what sin
> You shall expiate, or whose, or why. It is certain
> That the knowledge of it must precede the expiation.[42]

*Virginia Woolf, 29 April 1938, *Diary*, V, 138. Woolf may be referring to Matthew Arnold's "Stanzas from the Grande Chartreuse," where Arnold imagines himself "Wandering between two worlds, one dead, / The other powerless to be born" (ll. 85–86).

Harry must fight in expiation of the sins of his family, resolving the enchantment of a generation sleeping into war. His mother dies as the clock stops in the dark: her birthday candles are blown out, the play ends, and the war begins.

Ghosts walk between the worlds: in *The Family Reunion*, the Eumenides walk free. The compound ghost peregrinates in *Little Gidding*; in Williams' war work the passageway between the worlds is packed with wandering ghosts. The *Purgatorio* gave the literature of the Second World War the complete realization of a supernatural world. The nightmare of the war was often felt to be a hallucination, as the diaries of Waugh and Woolf attest. While defending the Irish coast of Cornwall in July 1940, Waugh admits to "a sense of unreality"; Virginia Woolf confesses in 1938 that "I dont feel that the crisis is real."[43] In this mind-twilight, fantasy could become a parachute. Dante's hallucinatory vision is at some reach a fantasy; the fantasy worlds of Tolkien, Lewis, and Williams all defer to the patron saint of the literature of the fantastic.

It should be mentioned that the *Purgatorio* was a significant influence upon six centuries of European literature before Chamberlain took office in 1937. The modernists, especially, were no strangers to Dante; Charles Williams and Eliot repeatedly attempted to rework Dante in modern terms. Pound's sixteenth canto opens in such a reworking of purgatory. The entire structure of the *Cantos* is loosely based upon the *Commedia*:

> For forty years I have schooled myself [...] to write an epic poem which begins 'In the Dark Forest' crosses the Purgatory of human error, and ends in the light, and 'fra i maestri di color che sanno.'[44]

But it is worth remembering that these lines were written in 1944. And Pound wrote the Pisan cantos in the nearest actual representation of a part of Dante's purgatory that the Second World War provides: imprisoned, in a cage, in Tuscany. Joyce's *Finnegans Wake*, like the *Cantos*, is in large part the recreation of a purgatorial world. Beckett underscores this in *Our Exagmination*: "In what sense, then, is Mr. Joyce's work purgatorial? In the absolute absence of the Absolute."[45]

"On this earth that is Purgatory," as Beckett has it later in his essay, the image of purgatory is never very far away. Waiting is an essential part of all worlds. It is the essence of love, of baseball, of anything that develops slowly. If all modernist literature is to be reread, as Joseph Frank and the proponents of spatial form insist, then the act of reading is itself a waiting.

Purgatory did not appear in 1939 out of thin air, fabricated from the whole cloth of the historical situation. The question, in the Second World War, is one of degree. For the home front, the war was a paralyzed time of perpetual waiting, punctuated by unpredictable staccato bursts of incredible violence. Purgatory, whether perceived as a waiting world, a place of ascent, a middle-ground, or a place of expiation, is for the writers in the Second World War both a response and an escape.

Myth: The Tesseract of Literature and History

> In the greatest moments of Dante and Shakespeare, in, say *The Tempest* or the climax of the *Purgatorio*, we have a feeling of converging significance [. . .].
>
> Frye.

The myth of purgatory is both the expression of a waiting world, and a release from it. It may seem impossibly naive to hold literature accountable to history in this way, to impose the same naturalist perspective on, say, Virginia Woolf, that one might presume for Joyce. But literature is always conditioned by history, and especially in time of war. So Samuel Hynes has argued in his preface to *The Auden Generation*: "I assume that a close relation exists between literature and history, and I think that this relation is particularly close in times of crisis, when public and private lives, the world of action and the world of imagination, interpenetrate."[1] The barrier between the two collapses; at moments of catastrophe all writing becomes chronic.

Literature cannot be considered in an ahistorical vacuum, nor is it simply a field for the force of history. Auden rightly insists that the place of literary criticism lies between these twin poles:

> The important and complicated relation between an artist and the age in which he lives has been the downfall of many an excellent critic. Some, denying its importance, have regarded works of art as if artists—and critics too—lived exclusively in the timeless and spaceless world of the spirit; others, denying its complexity, have assumed that a work of art is a purely natural product, like a pebble on a beach, totally explicable in terms of its physical causes.[2]

As Bernard Bergonzi writes in *Reading the Thirties*, the polarities must be reconciled:

> Literary texts remain unique entities, but they inevitably enter into relations with other texts, either by the same author, in a context of personal development; or by other, contemporary authors, in a group context of shared attitudes and influences. So, too, in astronomy do single stars form constellations, and constellations form galaxies, even though, in the end, everything consists of single stars.[3]

For Bergonzi, the thirties form "a collective text, the trans-individual product of a generation, possessing, like the *oeuvre* of an individual author, a number of regular and recurring features."[4] The spatial relation of contemporaneous texts is the fundamental assumption of literary history, an assumption both valuable and dangerous. Its value lies in the discovery of the coherence that the myth of purgatory appears to provide the literature of the Second World War. Its danger lies in the trivializing of individual experience.

Throughout the thirties, writers in Britain were reaching towards a myth. C. S. Lewis pointed to the general need for one in a letter to Owen Barfield in 1939:

> By the bye, we now need a new word for the "science of the nature of myths", since "mythology" has been appropriated for the myths themselves. Would "mythonomy" do? I am quite serious. If your views are not a complete error, this subject will become more important; and it's worth while trying to get a good word before they invent a beastly one. "Mythológic" (noun) wouldn't be bad, but people would read it as an adjective. I have also thought of "mythopoeics" (cf. "metaphysics"), but that leads to "a mythopoeician", which is frightful; whereas "a mythonomer" (better still "The Mythonomer Royal") is nice.*

Lewis agrees with Barfield, who was trying to publish a volume of poetry based on the Orpheus myth, that the need for myth will be greater during the coming war.

Candidates for the position of Mythonomer Royal would have certainly included Auden, though his mythical framework did not fully develop

---

*C. S. Lewis, Letter to Owen Barfield, undated (between 8 February 1939 and 5 April 1939), *Letters*, 163. The letter continues: 'Or shall we just invent a new word—like "gas". (Nay, sir, I meant nothing.)' "Gas" is a suggestive analogy, derived, as Beckett's Murphy realizes, from χάος: myth will bring order to the impending chaos.

until the late thirties.* Hynes' contention that "the Myth of the Thirties begins with Auden" holds true for the Myth of the Thirties both as objective and subjective genitive.[5] The Apocalypse Poets were also mythonomers, reintroducing myth in 1939 as an integrating and humanizing force in poetry. Critics followed the turn towards myth: Maud Bodkin's *Archetypal Patterns in Poetry* (1934) spawned a host of mythonomies in the thirties. As crisis turned to catastrophe, the separate searches for myth convened in a general attempt to breathe meaning into the experience of war. A dominant myth of the forties, objective genitive, was purgatory.

Reviewing *Ulysses* in 1923, Eliot anticipates this need to aestheticize and organize the war experience:

> [Myth] is simply a way of controlling, of ordering, of giving a shape and a significance to the immense panorama of futility and anarchy which is contemporary history.[6]

" 'Ulysses', Order, and Myth" is not just a review, it is a statement of purpose. The paragraph containing this celebrated definition begins: "In using the myth, in manipulating a continuous parallel between contemporaneity and antiquity, Mr Joyce is pursuing a method which others must pursue after him" (483). In 1964, Eliot was to reject part of this remark— "To say that other writers must follow the procedure of *Ulysses* is [...] absurd"—but he does not recant completely.[7] The Joycean way may be passed by, but the mythic way must still be pursued. Eliot, in 1942, is one of these pursuers; like Joyce twenty years earlier, Eliot needs a myth to come to terms with contemporary history. The myth of purgatory lies behind *Little Gidding*, as Eliot responds to the futility and anarchy of a world at war.

Eliot's argument offers a penetrating reason for the recourse to the myth of purgatory. Mircea Eliade locates the modernist return to myth in

> an attempt to restore this historical time, freighted as it is with human experience, to a place in the time that is cosmic, cyclical, and infinite. In any case, it is worth noting that the work of two of the most significant writers of our day—T. S. Eliot and James Joyce—is saturated with nostalgia for the myth of eternal repetition and, in the last analysis, for the abolition of time.[8]

*For a penetrating discussion of the development of myth in Auden's poetry, see Lillian Feder, *Ancient Myth in Modern Poetry* (Princeton: Princeton University Press, 1971), 136–80.

Joseph Frank quotes these lines at the close of "Spatial Form in Modern Literature."* Frank then concludes that the modernist compression of past and present is a flight from historicity:

> By this juxtaposition of past and present, as Allen Tate realized, history becomes ahistorical. Time is no longer felt as an objective, causal progression with clearly marked-out differences between periods; now it has become a continuum in which distinctions between past and present are wiped out.⁹

But modernism, as Eliot realized, is more than an escape from history, it is an attempt to bring it significance. Modernist literature must be considered both spatially and temporally. No one suggests that *Ulysses* should first be read backwards; spatial form simply places a new value on the experience of rereading. The same is true on the larger narrative level of history. For Eliade, myth is a *regressus ad uterum*; its purpose is to recover the past, to erase the work of time. The countless valedictories to a dying world, the open-air pageants that country seats all over England staged before the war, bear witness to this regression. But the escape to the past is an escape from and within the present. *Chronos* becomes *kairos* when a present moment is charged with past and future significance—but that moment can only attain atemporal significance within the context of its present. The escape to myth is still of necessity a response to history; myth does not appear in Eliot at the expense of time.

The superposition of antiquity and contemporaneity, seen in *Ulysses*, Barnes' *Nightwood*, and "Stetson! / You who were with me in the ships at Mylae," creates myth. Myth results from the tesseracting of temporal forms: the idea is Eliot's, whose practical example is *Ulysses*.† If modernism "has been engaged in transmuting the time world of history into the timeless world of myth,"¹⁰ as Frank has said, then the literature studied here provides a further practical example of Frank's formulation. If "The mythic is the polar opposite of what we mean by the historical," as Philip Rahv writes in *The Myth and the Powerhouse*," then in modernism these opposites are resolved.

Rahv accuses those who resort to what Larkin derisively called a "myth-kitty" of ignoring the powerhouse of time: "what the craze for myth

---

*Frank's theory of spatial form originated in G. Wilson Knight's spatial reading of Shakespeare; the broader consequences of his theory can be traced back to Eliot through their mutual friend, Allen Tate.

†The image of the tesseract is Madeleine L'Engle's: cf. *A Wrinkle in Time*.

represents most of all is the fear of history."¹² Rahv clinches his argument with Blake's celebration of *chronos*: "Eternity is in love with the productions of time."¹³ That the line is one of the *Proverbs of Hell* does not help Rahv's argument. *Autumn Journal* gives the argument the lie; in Louis MacNeice's long poem, myth and history are joined together. It is such a production of its time that though Barcelona fell between its writing and its publication, MacNeice let his now hopelessly dated call to arms stand. Events are narrated in strictly chronological order, while underneath lies a waiting myth, the myth of Persephone. Euhemerism, the search for a historical source for myth, has long been out of critical fashion. A historical explanation is rarely tendered for the origin or reappearance of a particular myth. But in the Second World War, each of the separate tropes that comprise the myth of purgatory is chained to the force of history.*

To take an example: the literature of the war makes continual reference to the supernatural, specifically to the image of the returning spectre. In Yeats' *Purgatory*, the ghosts of the Old Man's parents return to haunt him into a false expiation: his father is "A dead, living, murdered man!"¹⁴ The ghost of the war stalks Nick Jenkins in Powell's *The Kindly Ones* (1962):

> Like one of the Stonehurst 'ghosts', war towered by the bed when you awoke in the morning; unlike those more transient, more accommodating spectres, its tall form, so far from dissolving immediately, remained, on the contrary, a looming, menacing shape of ever greater height, ever thickening density.¹⁵

Keith Douglas somewhat playfully introduces a returning ghost on 4 May 1940:

> By a happy accident, one of THE CHERWELL staff was passing the locked door of Merton library at dead of night, when the medieval essence of Duns Scotus passed easily through its woodwork, and accosted him in friendly Latin. Although the spirit at first declined, he was at length persuaded to write an article for THE CHERWELL, which is now in the hands of the translators.¹⁶

Ghosts walk through Forster's pageant of 1938, *England's Pleasant Land*, and through Louis MacNeice's *Autumn Journal* of the same year. In C. Day Lewis' "Passage from Childhood," "one more ghost" walks "in a

---

*The verb is Larkin's: "A 'war' poet is not one who chooses to commemorate or celebrate a war but one who reacts against having a war thrust upon him: he is chained, that is, to a historical event, and an abnormal one at that" (Philip Larkin, "The War Poet," 159).

glacial sleep."[17] Osbert Sitwell's *Poltergeists* was published in 1940. "More ghosts!" thinks George Bowling on his return to Lower Binfield in *Coming Up for Air*.[18] *All Hallows' Eve* opens with the ghosts of Lester and Evelyn walking through the streets of London, halfway between the living and the dead; *Descent into Hell*'s John Struther is only a shade different from the ghost in *Little Gidding*.

The Second World War is so preoccupied with the returning shade for several reasons. For Forster, and the countless others who turn from the future to recapture the past, these are the ghosts of a dead heritage, re-minders of a lost world. For writers during the war itself, the ghosts result from the appalling proximity of the other world. In the close presence of death, the barrier between the here and the hereafter is smashed. The peopling of their poetry with ghosts becomes both a reassurance and a resurrection. Writers could at least ensure a creative after-life: the ghost of Wilfred Owen's murdered victim in "Strange Meeting" sustains the German soldier's memory long after his death. The most immediate his-torical source for all the ghosts is Adolf Hitler:

> Hitler provided an age with its image—'I proceed like a somnambulist.' Eyes glazed and unseeing, mind blank and unthinking, arms reaching forward to touch but never touching, step confident but directed nowhere—such was his and Time's march, observed by all with helpless absorption.[19]

The ghost in the literature of the war is frequently a *doppelgänger*. Pauline, in *Descent into Hell*, feels it "coming up at her pace—*doppelgänger, doppelgänger*."[20] Just prior to her encounter with the ghost of herself, Pauline recalls lines from Shelley's *Prometheus Unbound*:

> *Doppelgänger*, the learned called it, which was no comfort. Another poet had thought of it; [...]
> *The Magus Zoroaster, my dead child,*
> *Met his own image walking in the garden.*[21]

Harry Monchensey meets his double in *The Family Reunion*, as Agatha's allusion to Henry James' "The Jolly Corner" implies:

> Yes. I mean that at Wishwood he will find another Harry.
> The man who returns will have to meet

The boy who left [. . .] he will have to face him—
And it will not be a very *jolly* corner.*

Each figure compounded in *Little Gidding*'s ghost is in some way a *doppelgänger*, as the appendix illustrates. Auden's American title for *New Year Letter* was *The Double Man* (1940). Eliot changed the title for publication in England, perhaps because the trope had, by 1940, already become a cliché.

The *doppelgänger* assumed a prominent place in Second World War fiction. In H. G. Wells' novel of ideas, *Babes in the Darkling Wood* (1940), a behaviorist presents schizophrenia as part of "a new psychology."²² His name is, appropriately, Gemini. Gemini walks around pre-war London limping, "the almost disembodied ghost of a highly improbable future. . . ."† The title character of Patrick Hamilton's *Hangover Square: Or the Man with Two Minds* (1941) is George Bone, a schizophrenic whose mind periodically "clicks" from Mayfair dropout to sexual murderer. George Bowling, returning to Lower Binfield, feels like Wells' original double, the invisible man: "Did you ever read the story of H. G. Wells's about a chap who was in two places at once [. . .] Well, it was just like that."²³ Nancy Whitmore, in Henry Green's *Back* (1946), is the spitting image of her step-sister: "there she stood alive, so close that he could touch, and breathing, the dead spit, the living image, herself, Rose in person."²⁴ Crouchback and Apthorpe are both forced to use walking-sticks in *Men At Arms* (1952): Guy feels "haunted by Apthorpe in the role of *doppelgänger*."²⁵

Detective fiction was particularly fond of the image of the double man. Albert Campion begins Margery Allingham's *Traitor's Purse* (1941) much as Christopher Tietjens begins *No More Parades*, suffering from amnesia acquired in the war. Allingham's *The Tiger in the Smoke* begins with a chase through the fog after a double for Major Elginbrodde. The work of Michael Innes is full of doubles during the war. In *The Secret Vanguard*,

*T. S. Eliot, *The Family Reunion*, 18. For a further discussion of this passage, see chapter IV.

†H. G. Wells, *Babes in the Darkling Wood*, 129. Incidentally, the "darkling wood" of the title is Dante's: Stella, Gemini's friend, dreams that "she and Gemini were wandering in a dark wood at twilight; it was a very dark wood and it was growing darker" (237). Her dream is especially Dantesque in its conclusion: "The ebony darkness about her became positive. It became an intensity of vision that transcended sight" (238).

Appelby provides an infallible shibboleth by which a double can be identified:

> "Give a man two copies of a photograph of himself, one positive and the other negative, with a story such as I put up. He will pick out the negative one— the *wrong* one—as himself, because that's how he knows himself in the mirror. But give the copies to an impostor—an impersonator—and he will choose the positive one—the *right* one—because that's how he knows the person he's impersonating."[26]

In Day Lewis' *Minute for Murder* (1947), one of the very few detective novels actually set in the war, Strangeways must talk a schizophrenic off a ledge.[27] Shell-shocked by the war, Merrion Squires is prepared, like Septimus Smith after the first war, to jump.*

The *doppelgänger* has been floating about since Narcissus. But the literature of war does not use the trope in the same way as the Romantics did. In the nineteenth century the idea was a romantic self-annihilation, as in Schubert's "*Doppelgänger*" and Shelley's Magus Zoroaster. The crowning nineteenth-century appearance of the myth comes at the close of *The Mayor of Casterbridge*, as Henchard sees the Skimmington-ride effigy of himself floating in the pond in which he drowns. In the Second World War, the significance of the *doppelgänger* is historical rather than psychoanalytic. The image expresses not an uneasiness of self but an imbalance of history, not a fractured identity as much as a fractured world. The shell-shocked amnesiacs of World War One return in force in the Second World War; the mental disability of Campion, Squires, Tietjens, and Septimus Smith is not personal but induced by war. The return of the *doppelgänger* is the production of its time, as all literary tropes are in time of catastrophe.

---

*After the war, the image continued to play an important part in detective fiction. In Innes' *The Case of the Journeying Boy* (1949), Mr. Thewless catches sight of a second Humphrey Paxton and recalls that "in folklore there is no more certain presage of disaster than to meet oneself face to face—to meet what the Germans call one's *Doppelgänger*" (125). Christie's *There is a Tide* (1948) and Tey's *Brat Farrar* (1949) end with the unmasking of pretenders to the Cloade and Latchett estates respectively. *Brat Farrar*, though the war is in no way its subject, takes the psychological possibilities of the *doppelgänger* to a level unmatched in popular fiction: "In Tey, however, the device seems more a splitting and dividing of personalities into opposite and controllable parts. Simon is irresponsible and dangerous; Pat, it appears, was good and kind [. . .]. The traits of both Simon and Patrick are then recombined in Brat, Patrick's double, who is both criminal and angel" (Sandra Roy, *Josephine Tey*, 97).

The danger in assuming the spatial relation of texts within a common historical context is that the resulting coherence is flat and frequently trivial. It reduces the modern refashioning of purgatory to a series of mythemes, climbing the mountain terrace by terrace. Such a structuralist approach would complement an analysis based on Frank's spatial form splendidly. As James Curtis has remarked, there are 'striking similarities between "Spatial Form in Modern Literature" and another remarkably influential essay, "The Structural Study of Myth." '[28] But it has been said of Lévi-Strauss that though he "has perhaps found the harmony, [...] he has certainly lost the melody."[29] Similarly, the search for spatial form in a group of texts, rather than in one alone, ends up as a sounding of Forster's "great chords." What follows is structured not by terraces but by travellers, by melodies rather than common chords.

The study of MacNeice expands to the poets commonly associated with him, the study of Williams embraces the Inklings, the study of Waugh branches out to the re-visions of the war. T. S. Eliot and Charles Williams often walk together, as, to some extent, do Evelyn Waugh and Virginia Woolf. The same tropes are sounded over and over again in the period, with such clarity that one artist occasionally appears to be consciously echoing another. Auden's "Autumn 1940" can sound breathtakingly familiar:

Time remembered bear witness to time required,
The positive and negative ways through time
    Embrace and encourage each other
    In a brief moment of intersection.[30]

"Autumn 1940" is also the epilogue for *The Double Man*, which Eliot published and edited as director of Faber & Faber. Both *Little Gidding* II.ii and "Autumn 1940" open at dawn after an interminable or timeless night; both bring the positive and negative ways emphatically together. The war is truly an "intersection time";[31] poets write so consistently in the same key that accidental harmonies sounding through their works become inevitable. The "still point of the turning world," for instance, first appears in Eliot's "Coriolan" in 1931. It is borrowed by Williams for *The Greater Trumps* (1932), borrowed back by Eliot in *Burnt Norton* (1936), and then passed from Williams' *Descent into Hell* (1937) to Eliot's *East Coker* (1940) to Williams' *All Hallows' Eve* (1945). A discussion of the Second World War in terms of theories of influence is clearly wrong from the start.

Equally misplaced, though very beguiling, would be a discussion using the terms of the theories of Jung and Frye. Jung's term for such an echo-chamber effect was "synchronicity." This connecting principle explains the concatenation of meaningful coincidences within time, just as the archetype explains such coincidences within the subconscious. Archetypes, for Jung, "manifest themselves mainly through their ability to *organize* images and ideas";[32] for Frye, the archetype is "a symbol which connects one poem with another and thereby helps to unify and integrate our literary experience."[33] The myth of purgatory does serve as an organizing force for a decade of modern British literature; an associative cluster of recurrent images draws the period together in much the same way that the archetypes of Jung create our collective unconscious, and those of Frye focus our literary experience.

But the touchstone of purgatory differs irreconcilably from the archetype as defined by Jung and Frye. First, Frye never mentions purgatory as an archetype: *The Anatomy of Criticism* betrays an Anglican consciousness throughout. Frye maintains a dual view of the cosmological world, allowing only two undisplaced myths, two possible anagogic levels. He writes in *Fables of Identity* that

> Again, for poets, the physical world has usually been not only a cyclical world but a "middle earth," situated between an upper and a lower world. These two worlds reflect in their form the heavens and hells of the religions contemporary with the poet, and are normally thought of as abodes of unchanging being, not as cyclical. The upper world is reached by some form of ascent, and is a world of gods or happy souls. [...] The definitive literary example of the journey of ascent is in the last half-dozen cantos of Dante's *Purgatorio*.[34]

But there is a middle ground on the theological level as well. Dante's *Purgatorio* is not merely an ascent but also a suspended world. Frye is wrong to restrict the possibility of cosmological reference to the two opposed camps of apocalyptic and demonic metaphor.

A second, and more fundamental, difficulty with both Jung and Frye is that neither system allows for a historical basis for its archetypes. Jung's synchronicity is acausal: a connected event is not historically but psychically induced. Frye's view that literature generates its own recurrent images permits him to work in an ahistorical vacuum: a historical explanation is never considered for the origin or the reappearance of any particular myth.

With Walter Burkert, Frye believes that mythic structures are anthropo-morphic; his archetypes and recurrent images are rooted in human nature rather than in history. The belief that archetypes can be historically con-ditioned constitutes this study's chief divergence from the theories of these two great paleontologists.

The chorus of responses to the paralysis of war is univocal enough to suggest that the return to the myth of purgatory may be directly condi-tioned by history. Purgatory has reappeared throughout Western literature ever since its birth in the twelfth century. But at no other time in literary history is its presence as concentrated as in the years of the Second World War. Frye writes in *The Anatomy*:

> In the greatest moments of Dante and Shakespeare, in, say *The Tempest* or the climax of the *Purgatorio*, we have a feeling of converging significance, the feeling that here we are close to seeing what our whole literary experience has been about, the feeling that we have moved into the still center of the order of words.[35]

British literary experience moves toward that still center during the war. For T. S. Eliot, the Inklings, and Evelyn Waugh, purgatory is a real presence in the war work. For Virginia Woolf and Louis MacNeice, it is only the waiting that matters, but the faith and the love and the hope are all in the waiting. The purgatorial flame kindles slowly in the literature of the Second World War. In *Between the Acts* and *Autumn Journal* it will seem barely alight; with *Four Quartets* it will blossom into fire; by *Sword of Honour* and *A Dance to the Music of Time* it will die down. The impor-tant thing, for these seven writers and for their wartime readers, is to keep it lit.

II. The Looking-Glass War: Warping the Contemporary Record in *Between the Acts*

> All their nerves were on edge. They sat exposed. [...] They were neither one thing nor the other; neither Victorians nor themselves. They were suspended, without being, in limbo.
>
> Woolf.

The nature of Woolf's response to the real world in her last novel has been widely debated. The work has long been considered an anticipation of the coming war. But Mitchell Leaska's tremendous edition of the earlier and later typescripts has shown *Between the Acts* to be essentially a product of the war rather than its prophet. Only a third of the book was even drafted before the appeasement talks in Munich. *Between the Acts* went through a series of drafts before it reached the unfinished state it was left in at Woolf's death. Through these drafts can be traced a definite and very unexpected progression. As Leaska has said, "The Earlier Typescript of *Pointz Hall* and the published text of *Between the Acts* are, by virtue of their differences of semantic direction, fundamentally different novels" (PH, 29).* The presence of the real world is the index of that difference; by tracking the contemporary, one can trace the passage from *Pointz Hall* to *Between the Acts*. The study of the various stages of writing and rewriting reveals Woolf's vision, and revision, of the real.

The four stages of writing can be conveniently dated by Hitler's successive invasions of Eastern European countries. Woolf's writing is so strongly tied to political events that each invasion marks a new stage in her typescript. The first covers the period from Austria to Czechoslovakia, the second from Czechoslovakia to Poland, the third from Poland to the Lowlands, and the fourth from the fall of Holland and Belgium to her

---

*Mitchell Leaska, ed., *Pointz Hall: The Earlier and Later Typescripts of* Between the Acts, by Virginia Woolf (New York: University Publications, 1983), 29. References to any part of *Pointz Hall* in this chapter, whether typescript, holograph, or commentary, will appear within the text, prefaced by the letters PH.

death in 1941. Each phase has a particular, distinct response to the Second World War. In the first, Woolf prepares for a war that she, along with most literary and political figures of the pre-war, has seen coming for years. The first stage looks forward, marked by the prevision of a war future. The second stage, written between 30 September 1938 and 3 September 1939, looks the other way. It is dominated by the pageant, Woolf's attempt, again with many others, to put history under glass. The third stage, the eight months of the Twilight War, finds Woolf unable to write. Not until the fall of France in June 1940 does she write the final act of Miss La Trobe's pageant, and of her last novel. In this fourth stage she also rewrites the book, transforming *Pointz Hall* into the unfinished, and very unsettled, text of *Between the Acts*.

The published version is uncertain not only as an unpolished and incomplete text but as a response, in its bizarre relation to the real world. Woolf's early typescript is tied to the record of current events in an extraordinary way. Woolf dates the typescript only fourteen times in its 238 pages, and each point in the novel beside a date touches a point in contemporary history. Each time, the borders between the novel and reality are crossed; the real world reaches into the novel through direct reference to a real event. Alex Zwerdling, in *Virginia Woolf and the Real World*, has shown Woolf to be increasingly possessed by the real world in her novels and essays, and sees that *Between the Acts* "reflects the impact on her of the extraordinary circumstances of the time."[1] The dates point to these reflections, signalling moments in the novel affected by contemporary history.

But these reflections shine through the looking-glass. As Woolf becomes more and more possessed by the appalling reality of the modern world, her grasp on that reality grows weaker and weaker. When Woolf rewrites her text in 1940, the historical glosses are either transformed or written out completely. On 30 July 1939, Woolf dates her first typescript for the last time. Flavinda then enters, to confront "a great clock face, the hands pointing two minutes to the hour" (PH, 135). Two minutes later, at nine o'clock, the clock brings the act to a close: "The clock strikes nine. They embrace. Curtain" (PH, 137). The great clock face has an obvious symbolic value, representing the modern world ticking towards its own destruction. Rewriting this episode in 1940, Woolf makes one small hair-raising change. Flavinda enters at three minutes to seven—*and it still strikes nine*. The time is thrown out of joint. Woolf transforms the stock symbol of her original timepiece to convey a far darker message about the fantastic machinery of war.

The dates, in the form they appear in the early typescript, together with the contemporary references in the typescript to which they correspond, are as follows:

2nd April 1938
  "Summer Night. 1...The Lamp" (PH, 33)

[April 22-26, 1938]
  "M. Daladier [...] has been successful in pegging down the franc"
  (PH, 46)

May 11th [19]38 stopped.
  "the forthcoming <play> <entertainment>" (PH, 52)

Begun May 20th [1938]
  "A girl who lives down our way [...] used to go out with the Guards"
  (PH, 54)

July 3rd [1938]
  "Who noted the silence, the emptiness?" (PH, 61)

1st Aug. [19]38
  "one thirty-five on a June morning in the hall" (PH, 62)

Aug. 6th [1938]
  "sixteen men, perfectly innocent men, had been shot" (PH, 70)

22nd Aug. [1938] / 29th Aug. [1938]
  "At any moment, guns would rake that land into furrows" (PH, 75)

Sept. 16th [1938] / Sept. 19th [1938]
  "by the conflict between the news in the paper" (PH, 80)

Oct. 7th 1938
  "even now in 1938, on this day of light variable winds" (PH, 92)

5th Feb. 1939 / Feb. 27th [1939]
  "The doom of sudden death hanging over us" (PH, 121)

July 30th [19]39
  "the hands pointing two minutes to the hour" (PH, 135)*

*A note on parentheses: the editorial markings in Leaska's edition of *Pointz Hall* have been greatly simplified for the purposes of this study. < > indicates a later emendation to Woolf's typescript by the author, either an insertion or a deletion. [ ] signifies an ellipsis, or an editorial statement, by Leaska, Bell, or myself. ( ) is either an honest parenthesis, or gives a page reference.

The chronological study of these corridors into the real world reveals Woolf's warping of the contemporary record in *Between the Acts*.

2nd April 1938: "Summer Night. 1 . . . The Lamp" (PH, 33). On the second of April, 1938, Woolf began what was to become *Between the Acts*. Two weeks earlier, Hitler had marched into Austria: "The public world very notably invaded the private at MH. last week end. Almost war: almost expected to hear it announced" (V, 131).* From the start, *Between the Acts* is a personal reaction to a world waiting for a war. The public invasion of her private world triggers *Between the Acts* in two ways; it is an invasion of privacy, and an invasion of her past. Two years later, when Paris fell, the Woolfs were at Penshurst. Leonard Woolf remembers, in *The Journey not the Arrival Matters*, the peculiar juxtaposition of past and future that resulted:

> Friday, June 14, the Germans took Paris, and we spent the day incongruously— or from another point of view appropriately—with history being made so catastrophically across the Channel—for we took a journey from the present into the past. Virginia had never been to Penshurst.[2]

Penshurst, for the Woolfs, was "an epitome of English history."[3] Her new book, not yet titled *Pointz Hall*, will invoke the values of Penshurst. With "Almost war" pressing in, she imagines her book as an escape from the fragmented modern world into a complete whole: "Summers night: a complete whole: that's my idea" (V, 133).

The first pages of the early typescripts spin directly from Woolf's first injunction. The first paragraph is a perfect circle, beginning and ending with an oil lamp:

> Summer Night.
> 1 . . . The Lamp.
>   Oh beautiful and bounteous light on the table; oil lamp; ancient and out-of-date oil lamp; upholding as on a tawny tent the falling grey draperies of the dusk; seen across the valley; not a wandering light like the car's; but steady; assurance to the next house over there in the darkness that the <fleet> <ships> have reached harbour after the day's toil; circled by gaitered legs; slippered feet; and dogs couchant; <lamp that> presides over truth; when the active

---

*Virginia Woolf, 22 March 1938, *The Diary of Virginia Woolf*, ed. Anne Olivier Bell, V (London: Harcourt Brace Jovanovich, 1984), 131. References to the diaries in this chapter will appear within the text, prefaced by the appropriate Roman numeral.

and the urgent slip their vestments and become disapparelled; rid of the five fingers; five toes; money in the pocket; and brooches and watches; when the whole emerges <at top like a many-scaled fish,> all its parts now visible, not evanescent and vanishing and immortality broods; and death disappears; and the moment is for ever; yet sleep has not leathered the eye; nor doped the mind; on the contrary, the mind released from shepherding the body to knock at this door, to observe that fur, that rag, that window, that grating, this, that and the other, surveys the whole unembarrassed by the part; unimpeded; oil lamp, that calls out the colour in the faded, <matches> <unifies> the discordant <in unity; God or Goddess;> accept the praise of those dazzled by daylight; drowned by uproar; oil lamp. (PH, 33)

In 1938, this call to unity has a hypnotic force; the oil lamp, ancient and out-of-date, unifies the discordant as the past unifies the present. Two years later, Woolf has snapped out of the trance. After Munich, the declaration of war, and the fall of France, the opening sentence is radically different: "It was a summer's night and they were talking, in the big room with the windows open to the garden, about the cesspool" (7).* The incantation reappears as part of "The Moment: Summer's Night" in 1940. By the time "The Moment" is written, the lotus-eater prose has become narcotic: "Let us do something then, something to end this horrible moment, this plausible glistening moment."⁴ In the world of 1940, the shimmering moment is a dangerous fake.

In her first paragraph, Woolf embraces the past, an overture she finds herself increasingly unable to make. In the longest addition to the opening scenes in the early draft, Isa's passage through the library shows Woolf attempting to recapture the past, and then shrugging it off to reach the present. Isa starts with *The Faerie Queene*, and Keats. She turns from poetry to biography: "Or a life—not a poem?" She discards biography for history: "Or not a person's life—a country's life." And finally, she turns from history to science, ending with "Darwin's Descent of Man" (PH, 54). She passes from a commitment to the values and meaning of literary tradition to a dispassionate and evolutionary understanding of mankind. In the early typescript, this process compasses ten pages: Isa's library is described in as much detail as that of Jacob Flanders. Three pages on Chaucer turn to a discussion of the Crusades, and Marlowe. These pages, in revised form, return in "Anon" and "The Reader"; they are excised from *Between The*

---

*Virginia Woolf, *Between the Acts* (Harmondsworth: Penguin, 1953), 124. References to this edition of *Between the Acts* in this chapter will appear within the text.

Acts.[5] In the last version, Isa simply enters the library, exclaims "The library's always the nicest room in the house" (18), and recites a quick catalogue of books within it. Her catalogue hurtles from Spenser to Darwin; the past is brushed aside to make room for the present. While *Pointz Hall* begins as a record of Britain's past, the war presses on Woolf the necessity of a contemporary document. The library scene cannot stay.

[*April 22-26, 1938*]: "*M. Daladier [...] has been successful in pegging down the franc*" (PH, 46). Together with the injunction of "a complete whole," Woolf projected, on 26 April 1938, an ending affirming the values of community: " 'I' rejected: 'We' substituted: to whom at the end there shall be an invocation?" (V, 135). Throughout the book these values are betrayed. With blood on his shoes, Giles denies the possibility of an invocation to them: " '*We?*' said Giles. '*We?*' " (80). Miss La Trobe does end her pageant as Woolf intended to end her novel, with a solemn invocation to the values of community. Miss La Trobe separates her audience into "*scraps, orts, and fragments*" (131), but in a *coup de grâce* the gramophone brings them, if only for a moment, together again. Music has been already presented as a force of unity—"Music makes us see the hidden, join the broken" (86)—and here its counterpoint underscores the possibility of connection and coherence:

> Like quicksilver sliding, filings magnetized, the distracted united. The tune began; the first note meant a second; the second a third. Then down beneath a force was born in opposition; then another. On different levels they diverged. On different levels ourselves went forward; flower gathering some on the surface; others descending to wrestle with the meaning; but all comprehending; all enlisted. (131)

The pageant concludes, with this paragraph, in a call for unity: "To part? No. Compelled from the ends of the horizon; recalled from the edge of appalling crevasses; they crashed; solved; united" (132).

But the invocation goes unheard. The message simply does not get across: throughout the pageant the audience fails to translate its message into present-day terms. Wind carries away the words of the villagers; no one pays attention to Phyllis: "Her voice petered out. No one was listening" (70). Even Isa, so receptive to the meeting of Carinthia and the Prince, cannot reproduce that love. She misquotes their lines, and mocks, in front of William Dodge, what she once found "enough":

> 'Hail, sweet Carinthia. My love. My life,' he quoted.
> 'My lord, my liege,' she bowed ironically. (76)

For a time, Miss La Trobe's audience seems to have grasped her meaning. Streatfield asks "Surely, we should unite?" (134). The affirmation of the gramophone—*"let us retain whatever made that harmony"* (137)—leads to an explosion of conversation. The spectators disperse into groups of "cronies" (138); even the parking arrangements bring the audience together: "cars, push bikes, and cycles were crowded together" (137). Many go straight from Pointz Hall to church, but those who do remain end the book as bitterly isolated as they began. When the music dies away the pageant's message is unheeded.*

The catalyst for this reaction, as for Woolf's reaction against the past, is the war. The invocation is immediately questioned by the query mark in Woolf's initial diary entry: "to whom there shall be at the end an invocation?" The war has already begun, for Woolf, with the invasion of Austria. Her original decision to end *Pointz Hall* with a celebration of the ideals of community cannot stand up as Austria leads to Czechoslovakia leads to Poland and war. The conversation following the well-wrought lamp makes this new direction clear. Desultory in the published version, the talk in the early text is more wide-ranging, more literate, and more prophetic. Reference is made to the Napoleonic wars, to the Greek war for liberation, and to World War One. Napoleon appears three times in the early version: "In the Napoleonic wars [...] in the Napoleonic wars [...] No, he did not remember the Napoleonic wars" (PH, 37). Byron, mentioned briefly in *Between the Acts*, receives a parenthetical obituary in *Pointz Hall*: "Byron; who died at Missolonghi well over a century ago" (PH, 35). This gratuitous allusion to the Greek war sets the stage for a completely lost sequence which brings up the First World War.

Byron is compared to Edward Thomas, in whom Rupert Haines reveals an unexpected interest:

> "Did you ever hear, Sir" (so he called the old man) "of a chap" (here he hesitated as if from awkwardness at trespassing clumsily into some higher sphere) "of a poet" (he made the correction as if he stood in the presence of a superior) "called" (he brought the name out pursing his lips) "Thomas?"
>
> Oliver touched the mottled cover of Byron with the tips of his fingers; yellow one was with tobacco juice. He also raised his eyebrows.

*For a further discussion of isolation and intimacy in *Between the Acts*, see the second section of chapter VI. The historical slant of this chapter precludes a study of theme and narrative here; purgatorial elements in *Between the Acts* are explored later, in conjunction with *Put Out More Flags*.

"Thomas?" he repeated. "A surname," said Haines.

Whereupon, there was a collision between the ladies. For Mrs. Perry, whose goose eyes always seemed like a bill about to gobble some pea, said, "Thomas," and Mrs. Giles very slowly raised her head, swanwise, and, as if certain weights had moved into position behind her eye, making the shallow heavy; the surface dark, said, "Old Man's Beard!"

[...]

" 'I like the Cuckoo' is it? and the deaf man who hears a voice. . . . " They quoted; remembered; forgot; stumbled.

"I wish," she said, shifting in her chair as they came to an end of what they remembered, "I'd known him - Did you, Mr. Haines?" He shook his head.

"I doubt," said old Oliver, "I doubt . . . ." He lengthened his lips a little and smiled. "I doubt that we should altogether have approved." <He was thinking of Lord Byron.> (PH, 38–39)

In its painstaking presentation of the collisions and tensions of everyday speech, this passage approaches the mandarin style of late Henry James. The colliding conversations converge upon the central conflict of World War One. "The Cuckoo" is Edward Thomas' poem; the conversation centers on his death. "Old Man's Beard" is superimposed upon "Thomas," and the plant is a botanic symbol of death. The excised connection between Lord Byron and Edward Thomas is both literary and military. Not only did they both die in wartime, they both, as Mitchell Leaska points out, wrote poems with "go no more a-roving" in the refrain.* These references to the earlier war, and Thomas' link to Byron as a tragic literary hero, are all written out in the published version.

Woolf anticipates the war in her early draft of *Between the Acts* by raising the ghosts of poets of the First World War. Edward Thomas is discussed in the opening conversation, and Rupert Brooke makes a brief appearance at the close of the first draft. Miss La Trobe, feeling "the horror and the terror of being alone" (146) descend upon her, decides to go to the Inn. The terror is added in the late typescript, and probably stems from "The Moment: Summer's Night": "Then comes the terror, the exultation; the power to rush out unnoticed, alone."† But for every gain in the late

---

*" 'So we'll go no more a-roving' is among the well-known lines of Byron. A less familiar poem, however, again by Edward Thomas, is called "An Old Song" the chorus of which runs: 'I'll go no more a-roving / With you, fair maid' " (PH, 193).

†Virginia Woolf, *Collected Essays*, II, 296. Together with this existential terror, Miss La Trobe's tribadism is first expressed at this point in the late typescript. The actress, Peter, who shared her rooms in the early version (PH, 175), now shares

typescript something is lost. In the early version, the Inn has a name: "Every night she drank at the Green Man with the farmhands" (PH, 175–76). Grantchester's pub and its most celebrated customer disappears. Rupert Brooke goes the way of Edward Thomas; the glances to the earlier war are dropped.

The pre-Munich section of *Between the Acts* responds directly as well as allusively to the events that lead up to September 1938. Bartholomew reads that "M. Daladier [. . .] has been successful in pegging down the franc" on page 21 of the early typescript: that is, between April 2 and May 11, 1938. Throughout the month of April, lead articles in *The Times* were devoted to the rising franc. On 22 April, the franc had become so over-valued that "M. Reynaud wanted [. . .] the franc exchange on London pegged at about 175f." By 26 April, *The Times* could report that "The declaration made by M. Daladier [. . .] disposes of all the rumours about the franc."[6] Woolf appears to have drawn from an actual *Times* article: but in the final draft, Bartholomew is reading the same article, though the scene is now set in June 1939. The newspaper is a full year out of date. That Daladier is permitted to peg down the franc from April 1938 to June 1939 reveals Woolf's attitude to contemporary history. Woolf's manipulation of the newspaper shows her to be at once aware of the modern world and unafraid to twist its documents to her own fictional ends. Woolf's oversight is deliberate, warping the threads of fact in her fiction. The record is twisted to permit Bartholomew's overriding concern with Daladier's franc. But the record is still there.

May 11th [19]38 stopped.: "the forthcoming <play> <entertainment>" (PH, 52). On the ninth of May, 1938, E. M. Forster rang up Virginia Woolf for "some literary help about a quotation in a pageant" (V, 139). Immediately *Pointz Hall* is given its dramatic centre. Five lines later in the same diary entry Woolf writes that "Pointz Hall is to become in the end a play." Two days later, the typescript bears its second date. With that date appears the first reference to the coming pageant: Lucy holds "a notice of the forthcoming <play> <entertainment>" (PH, 52). As the parentheses indicate, Virginia Woolf is unsure of the drama's precise nature. Not until 29 August is the entertainment determined to be a pageant, following a string of pageants in the summer of 1938. But the seed of

---

her bed (PH, 432). But the left hand takes away what is given with the right: with the addition of this detail, the name of the actress, with its suggestive rhyme, is excised.

the pageant originates in Forster's two works written for the village of Abinger.

The presence of E. M. Forster in *Between the Acts* is established upon the title page. Woolf's provisional title, *Pointz Hall*, was derived from "Sir Poyntz Claverly" in Thackeray's *Pendennis*. Her second title comes from Forster's *Passage to India*. After the Chandrapore Club's performance of *Cousin Kate*, Mrs. Moore rediscovers the mosque where she first encountered Dr. Aziz:

> 'Oh, yes - that's where I got to - that's where I've been.'
> 'Been there when?' asked her son.
> 'Between the acts.'[7]

Whether this is a deliberate gloss is arguable; though Miss La Trobe's pageant is hardly as slight as Forster's *Cousin Kate*, Lucy Swithin certainly owes something to Mrs. Moore. In any event, the title is an afterthought, decided upon only a month before Woolf's suicide: "Finished Pointz Hall, the Pageant: the Play—finally Between the Acts this morning" (V, 356). This homage to Forster, if it is such, acknowledges a profound debt. For Forster provides the inspiration, and much of the material, for the driving force in *Between the Acts*, the pageant itself.

Forster does not provide the central conceit of Woolf's novel with a single phone call. The pageant he calls about, and a similar pageant written four years earlier, bear similarities to Miss La Trobe's pageant so striking that they can scarcely be attributed to coincidence. Renée Watkins has remarked on the parallels between Forster's first pageant and the one in *Between the Acts*: "In its basic scheme, Virginia Woolf's pageant imitates one written by E. M. Forster and put on in 1934 at the village of Abinger."[8] *The Abinger Pageant* of 1934 presents the history of a rural community from the Domesday Survey to the modern desolation, charting "*the history of a village lost in the woods.*"[9] Forster's villagers have spent "*Centuries of life amongst obscure trees and unnoticed fields*";[10] Woolf is also concerned with the anonymous voice of history. Act IV begins with "the other voice speaking, the voice that was no one's voice [. . .] the voice that wept for human pain unending" (126).

This voice, laboring and anonymous, has been heard before in Woolf's work. On 20 July 1925 Woolf wrote, "I want to read voraciously & gather material for the Lives of the Obscure—which is to tell the whole history of England in one obscure life after another" (III, 37). As Werner Deiman has said, Woolf compresses the pageant of history into a single obscure voice in *Jacob's Room* ("That old man has been crossing the Bridge these six hundred years")[11] and in *Mrs. Dalloway*: "Through all ages—when the pavement was grass, when it was swamp, through the age of tusk and mammoth, through the age of silent sunrise, the battered woman [. . .] stood singing of love." When she stops singing, "the pageant of the universe would be over."[12] For Deiman, "Both the elderly man of *Jacob's Room* and this woman become in a very real way the embodiment of history."[13] Woolf reflects in June 1940 that the wartime writer is forced to be anonymous: "It struck me that one curious feeling is, that the writing 'I', has vanished. No audience. No echo" (V, 293). Miss La Trobe does not acknowledge her applause: her pageant, "Anon," and "The Reader" are all histories in the anonymous voice.

Forster's pageant closes, as Miss La Trobe's does, with a diatribe against the modern world addressed directly to the audience:

Houses, houses, houses! You came from them and you must go back to them. Houses and bungalows, hotels, restaurants and flats, arterial roads, by-passes, petrol pumps and pylons—are these going to be England? Are these man's final triumph?[14]

Woolf's loudspeaker, "megaphontic, anonymous," attacks the same targets: *"Take for example [. . .] Mr M's bungalow. A view spoilt for ever"* (130). The loudspeaker also announces the coming of war: *"Consider the gun-slayers, bomb droppers here or there. They do openly what we do slyly"* (130). In 1934, the Woodman's lines, a checklist for any budding Pylon Poet, do not ask to be read as a prevision of war. But for *The Times*, at least, the lines projected beyond the dark satanic mills of Birmingham and Leeds to those of the Ruhr. The *Times* review of *The Abinger Pageant* highlights many details, not present in the text, which reappear in *Between the Acts*. The rural setting necessitated the "driving of a flock of sheep off the arena"; one of the programme advertisements read "Get your milk from the cows that are taking part in the pageant." *The Times* reported that "motorists had to abandon their cars and walk a long way upon leaf-mould paths between trees to reach the old rectory hollow where the pageant was presented." The final words of the review make it clear that such a nostalgic setting merely served to fix the audience's eyes upon the future: "Could the sunny trees, within whose circle we sat, withstand for long these influences of the time which are alien to these gentle players?"[15] Time is hurrying near, and no amount of looking backward can stop its advance.

By 1938, the time of Forster's second Abinger pageant, the advance of Time has become an onslaught. Forster's pageant play, *England's Pleasant Land*, was first performed on 9 July 1938, at Dorking, a village approximately forty miles north of Monks House. Though Virginia Woolf wanted to go, she was unable to attend any of its three performances: "We tried to get to Morgan's pageant—I heard it was lovely; but another engagement prevented, most tiresomely."[16] Though the play was not published by the Hogarth Press until 1940, after the first draft of *Between the Acts* had been completed, a program was published for the pageant, complete with full text, the day of its first performance. That text frequently anticipates *Between the Acts*. The play opens with a conversation about a cesspool: "Consider that dreadful pond behind us from which pestilent vapours arise each night."[17] Act Two opens upon "The Domesday Garden Party," a late Victorian picnic complete with parasols, bad music, and a cockney policeman called Bumble. Woolf's "Picnic Party" is set in "About 1860" (115), and the cockney policeman's name is Budge. A winding sheet is woven in both plays: "And weave your winding sheet till fair / England be your sepulchre!" in Forster, and *"Where the worm weaves its winding sheet"* (129) in Woolf.* Forster's pageant closes, as does Woolf's, with the revelation of the modern world, or "The Pageant of Horrors": "(*They dance and beckon to a procession of little bungalows which gradually fill the stage. Motor cars, motor bikes, motor buses, paper and empty tins. In the distance,*

---

*E. M. Forster, *England's Pleasant Land*, 50. Frieder Stadtfeld has unearthed two more originals for Woolf's winding sheet, in Webster's *The White Devil* and Blake's "Auguries of Innocence." In this double reference he sees a conflation of Isa's adulterous love for Rupert Haines and Mrs. Manresa's "lust" (72):

> In den Alliterationen von *"Where the worm weaves its winding sheet"* verbindet sich Giles' Todsgewissheit unmittelbar mit der Verurteilung von Isas "infidelity" und einer Kritik an Mrs. Manresas "lust." Denn in demselben Augenblick, in dem er Isas Leidenschaft für den *gentleman farmer* Haines durch die Anspielung auf die anklagenden Worte Flamineos verdammt,

>   − ô Men
> That lye upon your death-beds, and are haunted
> With howling wives, neere trust them, they'le remarry
> Ere the worme peirce your winding sheete

> erkennt er in Mrs. Manresas allzu freien Gunstbeweisen die apokalyptischen Vorzeichen des Untergangs:

> The Harlot's cry from Street to Street
> Shall weave Old England's winding Sheet.

(Frieder Stadtfeld, "Virginia Woolfs Letzter Roman," 67–68)

more motor vehicles and masses of adverts.)"[18] "The Horrors of the Present" crush "The Ghosts of the Past": Forster's pageant warns against a future chaos.

These ghosts exit, in Forster's pageant, to music by Vaughan Williams, a Lento passage that became part of the Prelude in the Fifth Symphony. Vaughan Williams also wrote a "Funeral March for the old order" for the pageant, reworked into the first movement of the Fifth Symphony. The old order marches out to a chorus singing Vaughan Williams' own translation of Horace's ode, *"Eheu fugaces"*: "Swiftly they pass, the flying years, / No prayers can stay their course."[19] Woolf's three pageants, the old man's, the battered woman's, and Miss La Trobe's, are all set to music. For the old man, "It seems as if we marched to the sound of music; perhaps the wind and the river; perhaps these same drums and trumpets - the ecstasy and hubbub of the soul."[20] The woman in *Mrs. Dalloway* sings of love, and of the same ecstasy of the soul. Miss La Trobe's gramophone plays an unidentified work of majestic counterpoint that sounds vaguely High Baroque. The composition that closes Forster's first Abinger pageant, a setting by Vaughan Williams of Psalms 84 and 90, became the festival anthem "O How Amiable." The closing pieces for both Abinger pageants are like the music on the gramophone: homophonic, majestic, and easily taken, by a villager, for High Baroque. In lamenting the passing of an old order unable to continue before a present disorder, the three pageants share common themes; some of these themes may be musical as well as literary.

In his preface to the 1940 edition of *England's Pleasant Land*, Forster recounts some of the unexpected occurrences which took place during the performance: "And of course aeroplanes messed about overhead and anticipated the final desolation. But there was also a lovely flock of white pigeons, which descended on one occasion among the ghosts."[21] It is hard to believe that Woolf, who "heard it was lovely," did not also hear of these unrehearsed moments in the pageant. In Woolf, the swallows perch on the wall, foretelling a future liberation: "The swallows - or martins were they? - The temple-haunting martins who come, have always come ... Yes, perched on the wall, they seemed to foretell what after all *The Times* was saying yesterday" (127). In Woolf, the aeroplanes scream overhead, foretelling a future desolation: "The word was cut in two. A zoom severed it. Twelve aeroplanes in perfect formation like a flight of wild duck came overhead" (134).

For both writers, a grandfather clock represents the inevitable march of time towards the future. In *England's Pleasant Land*, a clock is presented to Squire George, the developer-aristocrat, by his disgruntled village: "we'd like to mark the occasion by presenting you with this clock. (*A hideous clock is unveiled—well-drilled applause.*)"[22] In *Between the Acts*, the clock strikes nine in the last scene Woolf drafted before the war. Just prior to the appearance of the great clock face, Lady Harranden asks Sir Spaniel Lilyliver to marry her. He takes her meaning: "*Had it been written in letters of gold, fifty feet high, visible from Paul's Churchyard to the Goat and Compasses at Peckham, it could have been no plainer*" (94). So the published version has it, but the early typescript places the pub in Hammersmith. The change is probably made for the alliteration of "Paul's," "Peckham," and "plainer." But with the change a glance to Forster is lost. According to Leaska, Hammersmith may recall Joe Ackerley's flat there: "Possibly she thought Hammersmith might, to those who knew them, be connected to E. M. Forster and Joe Ackerley" (PH, 443). Leaska is probably correct that this is a suppressed reference to Forster, and to Forster's affair with a friend of Ackerley's, a Hammersmith policeman called Harry Daley.[23] Hammersmith, after all, also suggests Abinger Hammer.

Begun May 20th [1938]: "A girl who lives down our way [. . .] used to go out with the Guards" (PH, 54). Hammersmith also suggests Lucy's hammer, taken from Bart's cupboard to nail the placard on the Barn. This hammer changes hands many times: it is now Lucy's, now the assaulted girl's in Isa's fictional *Times* article, originally a miner's in the real London *Times*. The hammer's trail begins with the rape Isa reads about in the newspaper her father-in-law has dropped:

'A horse with a green tail . . .' which was fantastic. Next, 'The guard at Whitehall . . .' which was romantic and then, building word upon word she read: 'The troopers told her the horse had a green tail; but she found it was just an ordinary horse. And they dragged her up to the barrack room where she was thrown upon a bed. Then one of the troopers removed part of her clothing, and she screamed and hit him about the face. . . .' (18)

Isa treats the article as a work of fiction, a work she writes, "building word upon word," herself. She even rewrites the article; when Lucy enters the room carrying a hammer, Isa incorporates it into her text: "The girl screamed and hit him about the face with a hammer" (20). The lines between fact and fiction are blurred; the newspaper article reaches out and grabs a hammer from its proper place on Bartholomew's shelf. The lines are blurred even further with the discovery that the hammer in Isa's revised article actually has a basis in fact.

Though such an article would seem incongruous in the modern London *Times*, or at least the pre-Murdoch *Times*, lurid columns of this kind often appeared at the foot of its middle pages during the thirties.* The first version of the newspaper account appears on the thirty-fifth page of the early typescript. Three pages earlier in the same scene the text is dated "Begun May 20th." And on 20 May 1938, *The Times* carried an article in which a hammer is a murder weapon. William Parker, a miner, discovers his wife strangling their two children. His report of the incident sounds rather like Jude Fawley at Christminster:

> 'I saw my wife standing beside the cot with her hands round the two-months-old boy's neck. I said "What are you doing" and she said "You are too late" and threw the little boy into the cot. She grabbed at a poker and struck at me. I ran into the scullery. [. . .] She struck at me again. I hit her with a hammer. She fell down.'[24]

This melodrama lends *Between the Acts* its hammer. Isa recasts her *Times* article after Lucy's entrance; Woolf borrows from an actual account to provide Isa with the implement that reveals the recasting.

The presence of William Parker's hammer in *Between the Acts* is an unmistakable augury of a world at war. Woolf's diary entry for 6 September 1939 describes the modern destruction in terms of a hammer smashing a jar:

> It seems entirely meaningless—a perfunctory slaughter, like taking a jar in one hand, a hammer in the other. Why must this be smashed? Nobody knows. This feeling is different from any before. And all the blood has been let out of common life. [. . .] Of course all creative power is cut off. (V, 235)

This passage touches *Between the Acts* at several points. The bloodletting recalls both the blood pouring from Miss La Trobe's shoes as she feels

---

*The Torso case, still unsolved, broke in March 1938 and was widely covered throughout the spring. On April 13, the day Daladier became Prime Minister of France, an assault on an artist was reported: "She walked back into her room and this man, along with another man, entered and closed the door. She told them to get out, and as they came towards her in a threatening attitude, Mrs. Holland picked up a pair of blunt scissors and threatened to kill them. Then they left" (*The Times*, 13 April 1938, 9, col. 1).

her creative power failing her at the close of the pageant (125), and the blood on the white canvas of Giles' shoes after he crushes the toad-snake (72). Giles' violent action sullies his canvas shoes; Miss La Trobe's canvas is blank. Blood circulates through both metaphors; the war is the impetus for Giles' action, and the cause of Miss La Trobe's aporia. Further, the hammer is not placed into the victim's hand until after Woolf's hammer/jar metaphor of Autumn 1939. The victim's assailants and her choice of weapon both suggest that her rape fictionalizes the rape of Austria. (This phrase was in general circulation before the war: Sir Winston Churchill titles his chapter on Hitler's takeover of Austria in *The Gathering Storm* "The Rape of Austria.")

Lucy's provision of a hammer for the victim in Isa's *Times* article crosses the boundaries of reality into a looking-glass world. Two other moments blur the lines between reality and fantasy: Bart rises from his chair at the summons of Lucy's reading, Miss La Trobe writes the words that Giles and Isa will speak. In each of these three moments, Woolf weaves fact and fiction into a Möbius strip. J. Hillis Miller has taken issue with the image of the Möbius strip as a critical analogy here, arguing against the use of a spatial metaphor for a non-visual paradox.[25] But this is precisely why the image is so appropriate. And each crossover is made only in the final text: the Möbius strip is woven late.

Miss La Trobe does not write the words that Giles and Isa will speak until the latest holograph version of the book. Nothing comes to her in the pub in the early typescript. In the late typescript she hears "the first words of the play" (PH, 432), but there is no hint that the Olivers are to speak them. Only in the penultimate draft does she see where the lines are to be spoken: "It wd. be midnight; the figures hardly perceptible. A great rock perhaps?" (PH, 549). The setting reveals Giles and Isa, imagined in "some high place among rocks" (152), to be the play's speakers. The published version makes this identification clearer: "there would be two figures, half concealed by a rock" (146).

Similarly, only in the last version does Bart rise to leave the room and the novel at the dictates of Lucy Swithin's *Outline of History*. Lucy reads the following:

'England,' she was reading, 'was then a swamp. Thick forests covered the land. On the top of their matted branches birds sang...' [...]
'Prehistoric man,' she read, 'half-human, half-ape, roused himself from his semi-crouching position and raised great stones.' (151–52)

In between these two readings, Bart rises from a semi-crouching position, half-man, half-hound: "As a dog shudders its skin, his skin shuddered. He rose, shook himself, glared at nothing, and stalked from the room. They heard the dog's paws padding on the carpet behind him" (151). Bartholomew's metamorphosis into a figure from Lucy's text, anticipated in Grace's five-second entrance as a monster at the beginning of the book, does not appear in the early typescript. The *Outline of History* reaches into Pointz Hall after the outbreak of war.

The third crossover, Isa's appropriation of Lucy's hammer, appears in the final version as "The same chime followed the same chime, only this year beneath the chime she heard: 'The girl screamed and hit him about the face with a hammer' " (20). The first version is very different, twice: 'Every year the same chime followed the same chime; [...] But she changed, *it* changed—the thing that was behind <the wall>: today <"it" was> "the girl screamed; and hit him about the face" ' (PH, 56). First, Lucy Swithin's hammer appears in the victim's hand only in the final version. And second, the wall, the pageant's symbol of civilization, disappears. The early version places the girl behind the wall, anticipating the pageant's metaphor, and further identifying her rape as the rape of civilization by a modern world. Isa does not know there will be a wall in the pageant: the wall, like the hammer, tangles the threads of fact in her fiction. But the skein is knotted between the two drafts. In adding one symbolic reference to the war—the hammer—and deleting the other—the wall— Woolf takes back with one hand what she gives with another. In the last version of *Between the Acts*, Woolf creates a looking-glass reality that mirrors her contorted response to the war. Sometimes the war is written out; at other times the real world is refracted in a distorting glass.

July 3rd [1938]: "Who noted the silence, the emptiness?" (PH, 61). There follow three dated entries which make no reference to contemporary history. "July 3rd [1938]" introduces "The Dining Room," a short and introspective scene before the entrance of the diners:

> But who observed the dining-room? Who noted the silence, the emptiness? What name is to be given to that which notes that a room is empty? This presence certainly requires a name, for without a name what can exist? And how can silence or emptiness be noted by that which has no existence? [...] Certainly it is difficult to find a name for that which is in a room, yet the room is empty; for that which perceives pictures, knife and fork, also men and women; and describes them; and not only perceives but partakes of them, and has access to the mind in its darkness. And further goes from mind to mind and surface

to surface, and from body to body creating what is not mind or body, not surface or depths, but a common element in which the perishable is preserved, and the separate become one. Does it not by this means create immortality? (PH, 61)

This ruminative section on the presence of a narrator, lost in the published version, is critical for students of Woolf's narrative technique, but unimportant for students of literary history. The dining room scene was written just after a trip to Scotland and the Lake District, a week's holiday that seems to have blotted out the war. The date simply indicates a return to the manuscript after a short hiatus, and a return home.

1st Aug. [19]38: "one thirty-five on a June morning in the hall" (PH, 62). The second and third of these ahistorical entries avoid history in a progressively more complex way. The dates August 1 and August 6, 1938 serve not to relocate the manuscript but to dislocate it further. The sections written beside these dates both pretend to a contemporary account, and in both the account is wrong. The narrator, whose existence has been debated in the preceding scene, finally gives the novel a date: "At this moment, one thirty-five on a June morning in the hall at Pointz Hall" (PH, 62). Here, it is June 1938; Woolf later places her audience in limbo on a "June day of 1939" (PH, 160). The month is mentioned three times in the typescript. The third reference comes with the pageant: "half-past three on a June day in 1939" (57). In the first version, it is "1938, on this day of light variable winds" (PH, 92). The year seems to be immaterial: Bart is allowed to read a year-old newspaper. *Between the Acts* does not attempt to record contemporary events accurately; Woolf is unafraid to distort the real.

Aug. 6th [1938]: "sixteen men, perfectly innocent men, had been shot" (PH, 70). Giles reads in the morning paper, already the source of a great deal of misinformation, that "sixteen men, perfectly innocent men had been shot, others exiled, just over there across the flat land—there were only seventy miles of it—between them and the sea" (PH, 70). This article was written between August 1 and August 6, 1938; the approaching war was as obvious to Woolf before Munich as after. The details imply that Giles' article is taken from an actual event, yet careful search of *The Times* for the first week of August has yielded no report of sixteen men, exiled or shot, innocent or otherwise. The Battle of the Ebro is being fought in Spain, the Germans are stiffening their defences at the Maginot Line, but Giles' article does not appear in *The Times*. With each date, Woolf reaches out from the fictional world of Pointz Hall to fix her novel upon facts. And sometimes, as in this case, it is a false reach. The sixteen men have no counterpart in the real world, unless Virginia Woolf came across them in the press cuttings she was sifting through for her biography of Roger Fry. The lines may refer to the Easter Rising of 1916. Many were exiled as a result; Yeats' "Sixteen Dead Men" commemorates those who died: "O But we talked at large before / The sixteen men were shot" (ll. 1–2). In this case, the reach to the contemporary world would be contorted further by reference to an earlier war.

Woolf does return to the first war—she has been seen to return to its poetry—in preparing for the second. As Munich approaches, Woolf returns directly to the pre-war world of 1914. Her work on Roger Fry has already brought her deeply into that world: on 20 September 1938 she writes "Give the pre-war atmosphere" (V, 173), referring to the atmosphere before World War One and the pre-war atmosphere of the present. Her diary entry for September 5 reads: "Its odd to be sitting here, looking up little facts about Roger & the M[etropolitan] M[useum]. in New York, with a sparrow tapping on my roof this fine September morning, when it may be the 3rd Aug 1914 ... " (V, 166). Virginia Woolf feels that it's the day before war two days before the Nazis stopped pretending to negotiate with Czechoslovakia. While Churchill is reassuring his constituents on 27 August 1938 that "War is certainly not inevitable,"[26] Woolf, on the 28th, is resigned to war. In one of the most lyrical moments in her diary, she places her August world squarely in the context of 1914: "A single step—in Cheko Slovakia—like the Austrian Archduke in 1914 & again its 1914. Ding dong ding dong" (V, 164). As she writes these words the Rodmell church bell is ringing: "Ding dong bell. ... ding dong—why did we settle in a village?" (V, 164). Isa hears these chimes in *Between the Acts*, and for her they signal the coming of war.

The bells are an incomplete text, as Isa realizes, listening to the bells from the lawn: "Isa, half-way across the lawn, listened. ... Ding, dong, ding, ... There was not going to be another note" (144). As the gathering disperses at the close of the pageant, the church bell rings only three times: "Ding dong. Ding ... Rather a cracked old bell" (139). The missing note can be heard in two ways. Like the gramophone's truncated "*Un..dis. ...* " (140), the bells may sound the breakdown of communication, ringing the changes on an amputated world. The pageant has been full of fragmented texts, from the words of the villagers lost in the wind to the shards of mirror reflecting the "*scraps, orts, and fragments*" (131) of the modern world. Constable Budge concludes the third act of the pageant with a paean to the values of *"Ome"* (120), the dropped aitch perhaps suggesting that such a home is beyond the modern grasp. The bells stop because the service is beginning, the congregation is seated. "Ding dong ding dong" describes the domino effect of war: perhaps the absence of the final note suggests that the war has been forestalled. Woolf allows the bells to contain this contradiction. The ambiguity of the bells, like the give-and-take of the wall and the hammer, illustrates a text violently at odds with itself, ambivalent in its response to war.

22nd Aug. [1938] / 29th Aug. [1938]: "At any moment, guns would rake that land into furrows" (PH, 75). Woolf hears Rodmell's bells on Sunday the 28th of August; a day later she dates her typescript for the eighth time in the first five months of writing. The preceding page has "22nd Aug." at its foot, indicating that *Pointz Hall* is continued after a week's respite. Three paragraphs into the scene, Giles buckles under the pressure of the political situation:

> Giles nicked his deck chair into position, with a jerk, thus expressing his irritation with the kind of nonsense Aunt Lucy talked. Thus he showed his impatience with a set of old fogies who sat and looked at views, over coffee and cream, when the whole of Europe—over there beyond the flat was bristling like a—to express the idea of guns pointed, planes about to take flight, each with a bomb in its tail—he had only the ineffective word "hedgehog." At any moment, guns would rake that land into furrows; splinter the spire of Bolney Minster into smithereens. (PH, 75)

This is the first real mention of war. With it, Woolf signals a new direction in her novel. The book is suddenly charged with a contemporary validity. With the assault on Czechoslovakia in September 1938 whatever rosy appeal to unity Woolf may have originally intended dies out completely. From here on the book becomes a direct response to a war world, and all pleas for unity turn self-destructive or parodic. With Munich, anticipation is exchanged for experience. *Between the Acts* enters a second stage in Autumn 1938; the "pre-war atmosphere" is discarded for an acute consciousness of the present.

Giles, irritated at Lucy's blissful ignorance of the war, tries to lay the blame on her: "And the blame for the guns rested somehow upon Aunt Lucy [. . .] She could have done something last century, before he was born" (PH, 75). This is Giles', and Woolf's, first attempt to ascribe responsibility for the coming war. Giles exonerates Lucy eventually, remembering her husband, "dead in the prime of life, when a lamp exploded" (PH, 75). Giles' accusation disappears in the published version, together with any mention of the death of Lucy's husband. But though Woolf writes out the war by the end, with Munich she is writing it in. The exploding lamp shatters the values that began *Pointz Hall*, the values of Penshurst, of the oil lamp, of a "Summer Night." By the end of August the war is real: "War seemed round the corner again" (V, 165).

On 15 September 1938, Chamberlain flew to Berchtesgaden for the first time. By this point, Woolf had drafted the first third of the book, up to the opening procession of the pageant. In that third the coming war is vividly clear. In fact, there is more mention of the war in the first draft of this section than in the second: Woolf suppresses her prophecies of the war during the Blitz. The scenes written before Munich bring up the war, only to have Woolf excise these once-proleptic references in the published text. Mrs. Manresa is a spokesperson for the war effort in the early version, giving speeches on "Our brave boys" (PH, 65) to packed houses. This is in 1938: by 1940, when everyone is doing this, Mrs. Manresa leaves the meeting hall. Writing in the war, Woolf writes the war out. References to old wars are cleared away to make room for the new. Time and reality, in the late versions of *Between the Acts*, disintegrate under the pressure of the war.

After Munich, the lines between reality and fantasy come down. As Hitler mobilized towards the Sudetenland, Woolf wrote in her diary: "What would war mean? Darkness, strain: I suppose conceivably death. And all the horror of friends: & Quentin . . . All that lies over the water in the brain of that ridiculous little man. Why ridiculous? Because none of it fits. Encloses no reality" (V, 166). Here rests the explanation of Woolf's distortion of reality in the modern world: Hitler himself encloses no reality. Her next diary entry begins: "I dont feel that the crisis is real" (V, 167). By this she does not deny its existence, she perceives the crisis rather as a monstrous fantasy: "All these grim men appear to me like grown up's staring incredulously at a child's sandcastle which for some inexplicable reason has become a real vast castle, needing gunpowder & dynamite to destroy it" (V, 167). Only her biography of Roger Fry staves off the tide: "what a help he remains—in this welter of unreality" (V, 167). *Pointz Hall* is written in the midst of that welter, and the real becomes unreal.

Sept. 16th [1938] / *Sept. 19th [1938]: "by the conflict between the news in the paper"* (PH, 80). On September 16th, with Chamberlain in Germany and all England waiting, Woolf has Giles remember the irritation she made him feel on the 29th of August, "bred in him that morning, by the conflict between the news in the paper and the talk over the fish" (PH, 80). He recalls nicking his deck chair into position, a nervous tic he will repeat before stamping the snake to death. The conflicts between idle conversation and current events, between the Allied and the Axis Powers, between the real and the unreal, are all caught in the monstrous unity of snake and toad:

> There, couched in the grass, curled in an olive green ring, was a snake. Dead? No, choked with a toad in its mouth. The snake was unable to swallow; the toad was unable to die. A spasm made the ribs contract; blood oozed. It was birth the wrong way round - a monstrous inversion. So, raising his foot, he stamped on them. The mass crushed and slithered. The white canvas on his tennis shoes was bloodstained and sticky. But it was action. Action relieved him. He strode to the Barn, with blood on his shoes. (72–73)

Giles' crushing of the toad-snake is described in such vivid detail as to render the scene wholly fantastic. The hyperrealism of its description prevents it from becoming real. The figure of the snake unable to swallow, the toad unable to die, is clearly allegorical, so much so that it does not need to be real. And yet the allegory is just as clearly that of the modern world, choking itself to death.

Alex Zwerdling has read the snake as an image of Munich, citing an entry in Woolf's diary: 'During the Munich Crisis, when air raids seemed imminent, Woolf heard an announcement on the radio that "all poisonous snakes at the Zoo would be killed, & dangerous animals shot" and recorded her phantasmagoric "Vision of London ravaged by cobras & tigers." '[27] Other points in the early typescript suggest that Giles' action is inspired by the travesty at Munich. The scene was written after Chamberlain's third visit to Germany, at some point after October 7, 1938. Forster's essay, "Post-Munich," describes this period as "The state of being half-frightened [. . .] These mixed states are terrible for the nerves."[28] Before Giles discovers the mixed state of snake and toad he speaks of "disillusionment," while the gramophone reiterates its closing refrain, "Dispersed are we" (PH, 108). These expressions of the general spirit of shame and despair after Munich were written out in the late typescript. But Giles' "nicking his chair into its notch" (72) just prior to the snake-scene is written in, recalling his earlier action. The recollection indicates that his anger and disillusionment are directed at current events rather than at Mrs. Manresa or the "snake in the grass" William Dodge (55).

Though the snake-scene is unreal, it is intended to reflect the real event of the appeasement talks. Virginia Woolf blurs the lines of reality and fantasy because the real world has become monstrous. The distorted reality of toad and snake is an exact mirroring of the distorted reality of Munich. Horrific fantasy mirrors horrific fantasy. Miss La Trobe speaks for Woolf at the end of the play: " 'Reality too strong,' she muttered. 'Curse 'em!' She felt everything they felt" (125). Reality is too strong: the newspaper turns into a monster in Bartholomew's hands, scaring the wits out of his grandchild. The monstrous shame of Berchtesgaden finds its way into Giles' garden. The modern world, a "welter of unreality," returns to Lucy Swithin's swamp.

Oct. 7th 1938: "even now in 1938, on this day of light variable winds" (PH, 92). Unable to write during the peak of the Munich crisis, Woolf begins Pointz Hall again a week after the reprieve, dating the typescript "Oct. 7th 1938" (PH, 90). This is the first time since the beginning of the typescript that she has written the year in full. Munich has tilted Woolf's forward glance to a solid stare at the present, forcing the novel to confront the contemporary. But the date is wrong. Woolf writes "I'm taking a frisk at P.H." (V, 179) on October the sixth. The line "even now in 1938, on this day of light variable winds" (PH, 92) is revised, in October 1940, to "about three-thirty on a June day 1939" (PH, 311). By the end of her life dates have ceased to mean anything. There may be a second, more disturbing reason for Woolf's warping of the contemporary record in the late typescript of *Between the Acts*. Leaska has remarked upon several "curiosities of logic" in the book, noting especially that though the chauffeur cannot say who lives at Pointz Hall, Mrs. Manresa can read the family name clearly on the sign-post. He concludes that *"Pointz Hall* is not a novel but a play in which such irregularities are considered dramatic license" (PH, 205). But perhaps the inconsistency, the blurring of fantasy and reality, is not deliberate. Daladier's year-long concern for the franc may actually be an oversight; the clock may strike nine instead of seven by accident. In this case it is Woolf's own grasp of time and reality that is failing her; the collapse is internal as well as external.

5th Feb. 1939 / Feb. 27th [1939]: "The doom of sudden death hanging over us" (PH, 121). The early typescript is dated at only two further points in the rest of its 238 pages, once marking a hiatus from the 5th to the 27th of February, 1939, during an exceptionally social month in London, and once with the appearance of the clock on 30 July 1939. The late typescript is not dated at all until its 187th and final page, when she writes, triumphantly, "22nd Nov. 1940" (PH, 440). Again, the date is wrong; Woolf begins her diary of November 23rd: "Having this moment finished The Pageant—or Poyntz Hall?" (V, 340). The confusion in the dating of her three suicide notes, finally resolved by Nigel Nicolson in his appendix to the last volume of the letters, demonstrates how unimportant actual time has become to Woolf at the end of her life. In the introduction to this volume, Nicolson writes that Virginia Woolf suffered at the end from "a combination of fantasy and fear."[29] Woolf loses touch with reality and actual time by the end, entering the twilight world of mind time. It takes Lucy Swithin "five seconds in actual time, in mind time ever so much longer" (11), to distinguish Grace from her ancestors. The book is re-written in this mind time. It owes something to Bergson, as it always has in Woolf, but in Woolf's last novel the effect is richer and more strange: mind time warps reality.

July 30th [19]39: "the hands pointing two minutes to the hour" (PH, 135). The grandfather clock appears twice in Woolf. More obviously, it gives the pageant its wittiest line in providing a hiding place for Valentine: "[Flavinda] has eloped, to put it plainly, with the entrails of a timepiece, the mere pendulum of a grandfather's clock" (102). Like Forster's clock, it is enormous: "Some screens painted with walls represented the Palace, upon which was hung a great clock face, the hands pointing two minutes to the hour" (PH, 135). In the published version, the hands stand at three minutes to seven rather than two minutes to nine, a bizarre rescription that flies in the face of reality. Like Forster's clock, it has an obvious symbolic value, a time-bomb hanging on the wall that Mr. Page later understands as civilization: "Civilization (the wall) in ruins" (126). It marks the close of the last scene Woolf was to write before the declaration of war: "The clock strikes nine. They embrace. Curtain" (PH, 137). With these lines, Woolf brings down the curtain on her last novel, not to raise it again until January 1940. The curtain draws the novel temporarily to a close, as the parallel curtain and projected embrace closes Between the Acts itself.

The second appearance of the grandfather clock is excised from the published version of Between the Acts. As the inhabitants of Pointz Hall gather in the living room, the sound of Bartholomew's paper provokes a flurry of images in Isa's mind: "The paper crackled. The second hand jerked on. M. Daladier had pegged down the franc. The girl had gone skylarking with the troopers. She had screamed. She had hit him. . . . What then?"

(150). In an undated holograph version of this scene, the clock ticks far more ominously: "The second hand of the foreign news had jerked on again" (PH, 553). The foreign news has a second hand; the modern world is a time-bomb, as it was in the pageant. "Tick, tick, tick" (124) goes the gramophone; the clock's hands are set two or three minutes before the zero hour. It is impossible to be certain when this reference to the foreign news was put in, though the state of the text suggests a late date, possibly 1940. But Woolf decided to take the reference out, again writing out the war.

The curtain which the clock brings down finally rises on Giles and Isa, in a scene set in the prehistoric past of Lucy's *Outline of History*. In the published text, the scene is both a present heart of darkness and a future embrace. That Giles and Isa are speaking at all seems to be a positive step, and when Miss La Trobe hears their first words her tree is "pelted with starlings" (147). But if the title is taken to refer to the acts of war, the beginning of a new act can only mean the start of a new war.* In earlier versions, the affirmative reading is all but lost. The last lines were these: "Then, the rage which they had suppressed all day burst out. It was their part—<to tear each other asunder,> to fight" (PH, 188). These lines cast a long shadow over the whole of the preceding day, and project forward into a far bleaker future than Woolf's last version affords. The previous conversations between Isa and the father of her children are suddenly infused with hate. As Leaska has said, "The first ending is in fact so different from that of the published text that everything leading up to it must be read with different emphases and focuses of attention" (PH, 29).

If Miss La Trobe is the playwright of this final act, Lucy Swithin designs the set. Her reading from the *Outline of History* provides the backdrop for the scene: " 'Prehistoric man,' she read, 'half-human, half-ape, roused himself from his semi-crouching position and raised great stones' " (152). In the two earlier versions of this line, Swithin's set is far more foreboding. ' "Prehistoric man," she read, "half-human, half-monster, rose from his semi-crouching position and fashioned a weapon." <That was the end>' (PH, 439). Man is now not half-ape but half-monster, as Bart, behind *The Times*, was half-monstrous to his grandson (13). He fashions weapons rather than raising stones; his work is not creative but destructive. In an

---

*Leaska has argued, on the analogy of fire-proof safety curtains in theatres, that "the raised curtain, in a time of war, meant imminent annihilation" (PH, 450).

undated but probably later version of the scene, this weapon is specific and dangerous, and Woolf sets the line apart on the page:

> Prehistoric man raised himself from his crouching position & fashioned an axe. (PH, 555)

The parenthetical statement "<That was the end>" becomes, in the holograph, "the <last> words of the story of the dawn of the world" (PH, 555). For Lucy, the last trump is sounded, the resolution is apocalyptic. All this finality is lost in Woolf's last version. The apocalypse is delayed.

The future war will be played out on a private and public stage, on both a personal and a political level. Zwerdling has written that ' "War" for Woolf meant the conflict between individuals as well as between nations."[30] Throughout the book the coming conflict is internal and external, and both conflicts are made more vivid in earlier versions of the text. The earlier conclusion, especially, is a far bleaker vision in both registers. Returning to the novel in 1940, Woolf mutes that negative vision. She is deeply uncertain of her response to war, and her second ending reflects that uncertainty. *Between the Acts* is both a valedictory to a dying England, and a contemporary response to war. Half the book places an old world under glass, the other half presses its face to the glass in front. Woolf looks forward and backward, and the book is caught between the two worlds.

Woolf originally conceived of a "fantastic Pointz Hall" (V, 137), a fable to relieve herself from the arduous task of Fry's biography. With the war this resolution does not fade but is confronted with an equally firm resolve to present the modern world. The fantasy turns to nightmare. Throughout the typescripts Woolf writes the war in and then out, uncertain as to the final thrust of the work. Rescription in *Between the Acts*, whether the excision of a pre-Munich anticipation of war, the warping of a contemporary reference, or the weaving of fact and fantasy, ties the novel into knots. On the 29th of April, 1938, a month after beginning *Between the Acts*, Woolf is "in a dazed state, hovering between 2 worlds" (V, 138). These are the worlds of past and future, of heaven and hell, between which lies a purgatorial present. *Pointz Hall* is begun with a commitment to the past and an awareness of the future; *Between the Acts* is rewritten in the purgatorial world of a predicted twilight, a half-way world between reality and fantasy, a war captured through the looking-glass.

III. "And with a great future behind him": Louis MacNeice Prepares for War

They introduce Louis at a pause in his life, isolated in a temporary limbo between two worlds, looking back over his past and forward to a future which for him as for all British subjects was in 1940 dark and uncertain.

Dodds.

In 1937, MacNeice had an extraordinary dream. The nightmare is recorded in his 1940 memoir, published posthumously as *The Strings are False*:

Shortly after seeing the film of Dr. Mabuse I had the following dream. I had been invited to a houseparty. The party was given on a little peninsula in a marshy lagoon at the end of nowhere; the other side of the lagoon was invisible. The peninsula consisted of a long neglected garden in the centre of which was a knoll on top of which was a house. This house was a skeleton; the boards of the walls and floors had gone, there remained only the structural beams and the staircase. There were many people—everyone I knew—being social in the garden, but I, having arrived late, went straight through them up to the house where I unpacked my suitcase and laid out my spongebag and brush and comb and—I think—some books upon the floor, i.e. upon the ground. Then instead of joining the other guests, I went up the staircase and picked my way over the joists which had supported the upper floor (I have always liked climbing over ruined houses). While I was perched up there it happened. The alarm. Like sirens or bells but you could not hear it, it was more like the shiver on a pond when a breeze comes on it out of nothing. At once the people in the garden began flooding down towards the entrance in the narrow neck of the peninsula, like beasts fleeing from a forest fire [Text uncertain]. For They were coming. I hurriedly climbed down, ran after my friends who were by now nearly all at the entrance. The sky was getting darker and the air itself denser and breathing like an animal asleep. But as I caught them up I remembered my suitcase. I knew it was unimportant, what was of vital, of final importance was escape. All the same I went back up the knoll to the house, collected my belongings, put them in my suitcase, and carried it down the garden which by now was empty of people. I found myself walking along an overgrown path and in the flower borders on either side there was growing, instead of flowers, a regular row of swords planted with the point up as regularly as tulips, curving shining swords. I hurried on to the neck of the peninsula and there was a wall of rough stones, in it a little Gothic gateway such as you find in Victorian rockeries. In this gateway there stood a soldier in khaki with a fixed bayonet. I stopped in front of him. He remained fixed with a fixed bayonet. A terrifying imbecile cackle made me look behind and there at my left shoulder stood Dr. Mabuse from the film, cackling and leering; he had a great bush of orange-red hair. On sight of him I awoke.[1]

Fritz Lang directed two films with Dr. Mabuse as the title role, *Dr. Mabuse the Gambler* (1922) and *The Last Will of Dr. Mabuse* (1932). Though MacNeice does not specify which film he saw, it is more likely to have been the latter. Banned by Goebbels and smuggled to France, *The Last Will of Dr. Mabuse* was intended, as MacNeice took it, to be a warning of Hitler's rise to power. As Lang wrote in 1943, "This film was made as an allegory to show Hitler's processes of terrorism."[2] Kracauer suggests that "this self-interpretation smacks of hindsight," and perhaps he is right.[3] But whether or not Lang's foretelling is fortuitous, the film was perceived by viewers as widely different as Joseph Goebbels and Louis MacNeice as a premonition of Nazi Germany. MacNeice's reaction to Dr. Mabuse in 1937, and his memory of this reaction in 1940, are both triggered by the tyrant gambler Adolf Hitler.

MacNeice's nightmare of swords and bayonets, sirens and bells, is a confrontation with Fascism.* MacNeice returns instinctively to the ruined house, collects his belongings, and puts them in his suitcase. Faced with the coming war, MacNeice turns back to recapture the past. As Hynes has said of *Coming Up for Air*, coincidentally sharing MacNeice's imagery, "if you examined the past honestly, as a displaced person might examine his belongings before he fled his home, you might find what was worth saving."[4] Henry Green uses the same image in his 1939 autobiography, written at, and written about, the same time as *The Strings are False*: the memoir is titled *Pack My Bag*. And after the R.A.F. accidentally drops a

---

*Orwell also experiences the pre-war world as a nightmare: "For several years the coming war was a nightmare to me" ("My Country Right or Left," in *Collected Essays*, 538–39). Auden's "In Memory of W. B. Yeats" is written "In the nightmare of the dark" (*Another Time*, 95). These global nightmares are to be expected with a world asleep. Orwell's 1937 bombers interrupt "the deep, deep sleep of England"; Day Lewis' 1938 warplanes break "your watery, womb-deep sleep"; Mollie Panter-Downes describes England in 1939 as "somnambulistic," "trancelike." *Autumn Journal* ends with a lullaby to a waiting world: "Sleep, my body, sleep, my ghost" (XXIV).

bomb on Lower Binfield, Orwell's Bowling sees the blood mingle with the marmalade, and returns "to the George to pack my bag."[5]

MacNeice, Green, and Orwell are packing up. MacNeice's preface to *The Strings are False* ends with "Anyway I will look back. And return later to pick up the present, or rather to pick up the future."[6] E. R. Dodds, MacNeice's friend and editor of *The Strings are False*, writes of these lines: "They introduce Louis at a pause in his life, isolated in a temporary limbo between two worlds, looking back over his past and forward to a future which for him as for all British subjects was in 1940 dark and uncertain."[7] For Auden in *Another Time*, past and future are "the poles between which our desire unceasingly is discharged."[8] The Literature of Anticipation that prepares for the future by returning to the past oscillates between these poles. Henry Green's *Pack My Bag* is not wholly an escape; Green is very aware of the war breathing down his neck. He constantly draws bitter comparison between past and future: "'For what?' was the cry in 1913. It will be the same this time."[9] The Second World War suddenly surfaces from reflections on childhood lepidoptery: "It was thought less cruel to use gas than to stick them on pins. Our difference is, now we are older, we may die both ways at one time."[10] The butterfly net leads to the bayonet: Green casts back to a past life and ahead to a future which "our deaths have bought."[11] *Coming Up for Air*'s position in this argument is fairly clear. All three writers look not to the future or to the present but to the past, and in the entrails of that dead past haruspicate the future.

This third method of anticipating the war is more subtle than prophecy or direct experience. R. L. Cook has said that "No other modern poet has depicted the dying throes of the life that was swept away by the war as directly or as vividly as MacNeice."[12] One can go further than this: it is a forward-looking farewell, the grim farewell of a Roman gladiator. *"Morituri te salutamus"* is translated twice in *Autumn Journal*. "Les Neiges d'Antan," from MacNeice's play *Out of the Picture*, is written, as the title suggests, in the *ubi sunt* tradition. But the poem misses the snows of tomorrow as well as those of yesteryear:

> What's become of them? What's becoming of us?
> Look ahead, Long-Sighted Jim,
> What do you see in the future dim? (80)*

*Louis MacNeice, *Collected Poems of Louis MacNeice* (London: Faber & Faber, 1966), 80. References to poems in this edition of the *Collected Poems* in this chapter

In August 1939, MacNeice wrote a group of poems quietly reflecting on a lost Ireland, which he called "The Coming of War." After the war, in a rare act of revisionism, MacNeice retitled them "The Closing Album." In these two titles rests the essence of this third kind of Literature of Anticipation. The present is both a coming on and a closing in. The blood is beginning to get mixed up with the marmalade; MacNeice, with Green and Orwell, must take stock "before the bad times begin."[13]

Louis MacNeice takes stock in a more comprehensive and a more personal way than any other poet of the pre-war period. His poetry expresses a profoundly individual reaction to a general malaise, and deserves particular consideration in its anticipation of the war. Louis MacNeice has always been the square peg in the Auden circle, resisting an easy amalgamation with Spender and Day Lewis, and suffering from the association. At his best MacNeice resembles Eliot more than he does Auden; at his worst he rarely falls as far short as the other members of the group. *Autumn Journal*, a verse record of the fall of 1938, is MacNeice's finest poem, and arguably the finest long poem of the twentieth century. The work is divided into twenty-four cantos, each approximately a hundred lines long, and written in a highly complex form that only a classicist or a campanologist could love. Its settings range from Brighton to Barra, from Birmingham to Barcelona. *Autumn Journal* will receive here, as it has nowhere else, the close attention that such a strangely difficult and beautiful work demands.

In the foreword to *Poems 1925–1940*, MacNeice bids his most elegiac farewell to the past world: "I am collecting mine not because I am dead, but because my past life is. Like most other people in the British Isles I have little idea what will happen next."[14] The centerpiece of this collection is *Autumn Journal*:

> "Autumn Journal," the long topical poem I wrote in the Fall of 1938, is in a sense a failure; it fails in depth. I had foreseen that failure. We shall not be capable of depth—of tragedy or *great* poetry—until we have made sense of our world.[15]

It cannot be overemphasized that MacNeice's work of this time is not an ending but a beginning: "I have little idea what will happen next." But where others anticipate the war with constant reference to a forbidding future, MacNeice's emphasis is on the past. Auden looks forward, occa-

will appear within the text. References to *Autumn Journal* will be cited by canto rather than page number.

sionally glancing back; *Autumn Journal* looks backward, occasionally glancing forward. The net result, the anticipation of war, is the same. This uneasy balance between anticipation and farewell, the shifting emphasis from future to past, creates in *Autumn Journal* an extraordinary pulse.

This pulse is also generated in the poem's form. MacNeice first uses the form in "Carrickfergus," written in the year of his nightmare, 1937. As in the dream, the poem looks backward in its anticipation of war. "Carrickfergus" prepares for a future war by returning to a past one; the poem, especially in the last three stanzas, is vague enough to refer to both world wars and precise enough to refer to only both:

> The steamer was camouflaged that took me to England—
>   Sweat and khaki in the Carlisle train;
> I thought that the war would last for ever and sugar
>   Be always rationed and that never again
>
> Would the weekly papers not have photos of sandbags
>   And my governess not make bandages from moss
> And people not have maps above the fireplace
>   With flags and pins moving across and across—
>
> Across the hawthorn hedge the noise of bugles,
>   Flares across the night,
> Somewhere on the lough was a prison ship for Germans,
>   A cage across their sight. (69–70)

Each quatrain in "Carrickfergus" consists of a strong and a weak pair. The weak endings are unrhymed, though their metrical connection draws them silently together. "England" is paired with "sugar," "Bugles" with "Germans," and both pairs imply a semantic connection. Alternating with these uneasy couplings, the strong rhymes ("train / again," "night / sight") punctuate each quatrain, closing each stanza off with a certain degree of finality. *Autumn Journal* draws its form from "Carrickfergus," and sustains the quatrain form through 2400 lines. What is begun in "Carrickfergus" reaches its height in *Autumn Journal*.

While working on *Autumn Journal*, MacNeice wrote to T. S. Eliot, then director of Faber & Faber, of the strength of this form: "It [*Autumn Journal*] is written throughout in an elastic kind of quatrain. This form a) gives the whole poem a formal unity but b) saves it from monotony by allowing it a great range of formal variations."[16] MacNeice rings all the possible changes on this flexible form in *Autumn Journal*. The form of "Carrickfergus" is *pfpf*, where "p" marks an unrhymed weak ending, and "*f*" a rhymed strong ending. *Autumn Journal* sometimes rhymes the first and third rather than the second and fourth (*fpfp*), occasionally the first and fourth (*fppf*), rarely the second and third (*pffp*). Once even the weak endings are rhymed (*pfpf*), to very unsettling effect. In *Modern Poetry* (1938), MacNeice talks of his years spent in Oxford studying "Significant Form." He concludes that the term, if only self-reflexive, is next to meaningless:

> It had not occurred to me that the theory of Significant Form, which I took from Clive Bell, is a contradiction in terms. In any object, poem or picture, which shows 'significant form', according to this theory, the shape is valuable *for the shape's own sake*. But 'significant', on any analysis, ought to mean significant of something outside itself.[17]

In his "elastic kind of quatrain," MacNeice develops a truly significant form. The tension between the weak and strong pairs is a perfect mirror of the tension between future and past, around which *Autumn Journal* revolves.

The first eight cantos of *Autumn Journal* alternate between the present and the past, an alternation underscored by the rhyme. The quatrains in the odd cantos have the strong rhymed couplet in the 2nd and 4th position (*pfpf*). The even cantos bid farewell to Platonic ideals, to an anonymous woman, to Spain, and to the world of 1931 respectively, and they are all in *fpfp* form. Compare the end of Canto V—

(p) And a train begins to chug and I wonder what the morning
(*f*)   Paper will say,
(p) And decide to go quickly to sleep for the morning already
(*f*)   Is with us, the day is to-day. (V)

—with the end of Canto VI:

(*f*) Not knowing that our blunt
(p)   Ideals would find their whetstone, that our spirit
(*f*) Would find its frontier on the Spanish front,
(p)   Its body in a rag-tag army. (VI)

Instead of an end-stopped present, the reader is left hanging in an unresolved past. The form of *Autumn Journal* is cunningly adapted to its context; the structure engages in an unsettled dialectic which mirrors the pre-war world of Autumn 1938.

The effect of the rhyme-shift from odd to even cantos is to unsettle the past; the effect of the *time*-shift is to blur the distinction between past and present, allowing recollection and experience to spill into one another. Though Canto I is set in the present, it mourns the passage of that present world. MacNeice's farewell to the past is also a farewell to the dying present. This peculiar state of nostalgia for a lost present is rehearsed a year earlier in *Out of the Picture*. The play closes with an auctioneer taking bids on a civilization up for sale:

> It is your last chance which is here and now—
> The naked legs of children laced with foam,
> Waving their spades around a tower of sand—
> It is going, going, among the flux of words,
> Three thousand years of a wordy civilisation,
> Tags and slogans, nursery rhymes and prayers
> Resolved at last to a drowning gasp for breath.
> Our world is going, going—going for a song, [. . .]
>   GOING   GOING   GOING   GONE[18]

The auctioneer's images reappear in *Autumn Journal*: children build sand-castles in the first two cantos: "The building of castles in sand" (I), "I must go out to-morrow as the others do / And build the falling castle" (II). The image of "naked legs of children laced with foam" perhaps makes a second appearance as "the brown lace sinking / In the empty glass of stout" of Canto III. Not until after Munich does MacNeice confess the futility of castles in the sand against the oncoming tide of war: "Castles are out of date, / The tide flows round the children's sandy fancy" (XVI).

In *Out of the Picture*, as in Canto I, MacNeice is acutely aware of the future pressing upon this dying present. In the play the coming war is announced on an off-stage radio. Though the initial stages of the war seem to parody Chamberlain's feeble efforts at appeasement, these lines were written a year before Munich:

> The peace Conference is still in session at Geneva but the governments of the different countries are expected to withdraw their representatives at any minute.

At the adjournment for afternoon tea this afternoon, little hope was expressed of a satisfactory solution being arrived at. In the opinion of experts the declaration of war by at least five if not more of the leading nations is imminent within the next twenty-four hours. Details of today's discussion are not yet available for publication but half a dozen white papers and blue papers will, it is hoped, be issued within a month or two. Armies are reported to be massing on the Volga, the Rhine, the Rhone, the Danube, the White and Blue Niles, and the Yangtze Kiang.[19]

By the play's close the parody turns apocalyptic, macabre, almost Circean:

> PORTRIGHT. Then for God's sake let's have some music.
> *[Turns on* RADIO.*]*
> RADIO. . . . and that is all that now remains of Paris. The destruction was completed under schedule time [*sic*]. The remaining population is calculated at not more than—
> *[*PORTRIGHT *turns it off to jazz.* MOLL *appears carrying two candles and dressed in a most sumptuous négligé belonging to* CLARA.*]*[20]

The present and the future worlds have collided: the same thing happens in *Autumn Journal*. MacNeice travels "to London and down the ever-moving / Stairs" (I), stairs which lead inexorably towards the future. "Meeting-Point" reinforces this reading in its stopped stairs, which create a still point out of time:

> Time was away and somewhere else,
> There were two glasses and two chairs
> And two people with the one pulse
> (Somebody stopped the moving stairs):
> Time was away and somewhere else. (167)

In Canto I, the conveyor belt keeps moving; time is here and omnipresent. Future time, the coming of war, is inescapable; even the rhyme raises its presence:

> But the home is still a sanctum under the pelmets,
>   All quiet on the Family Front,
> Farmyard noises across the fields at evening
>   While the trucks of the Southern Railway dawdle . . . shunt. (I)

"Pelmets," the strips of cloth placed over windows to conceal curtain fittings, begs to be rhymed with "helmets." But it is a weak ending, and thus unrhymed: the suggestion of "helmets" is left hanging, strengthened by the reference to Remarque.

In capturing the past, then, MacNeice is also preparing for the future. Time present and time past are both perhaps present in time future and time future contained in time past. All the farewells, when examined closely, are compromised by an awareness of the coming war. MacNeice's departure from Southern England in Canto I, his renunciation of Plato in Canto II, his recollection of an unnamed woman in Canto IV, his elegy for Spain in Canto VI, and his memory of Birmingham in Canto VIII, all insist upon the approaching war. All these past shadows, and all these foreshadowings, are held within the present, within a contemporary record of the last five months of 1938. As Dedalus says to himself in "Scylla and Charybdis," "Hold to the now, the here, through which all future plunges to the past."[21]

Canto I begins with an unreadable adjective:

Close and slow, summer is ending in Hampshire,
    Ebbing away down ramps of shaven lawn where close-clipped yew
Insulates the lives of retired generals and admirals
    And the spyglasses hung in the hall and the prayer-books
        ready in the pew
And August going out to the tin trumpets of nasturtiums
    And the sunflowers' Salvation Army blare of brass
And the spinster sitting in a deck-chair picking up stitches
    Not raising her eyes to the noise of the 'planes that pass. (I)

How is the summer "close"? Not in the sense of proximate, for MacNeice is distanced from the world he describes: "I am in the train too now and summer is going / South as I go north" (I). Not in the sense of oppressive, or stale, for it is the city to which he journeys that will have a "packed and stale and pregnant air" (I). "Close-clipped yew," in the second line, emphasizes the word's singular importance in repeating it so soon, and raises further possibilities for its interpretation. The word is not an adjective; it must be taken separately, as both a noun and an imperative. This is the close of summer; close the old world down. The close-clipped tree is a yew not solely for the sake of an unimaginative rhyme: this is a dying world. The countryside is passed and past; summer is going, and going south. Right from the first word of *Autumn Journal*, MacNeice makes it clear that his eyes are fixed upon the past.

The slow death of the closing world is established not only in the first word of the first line, but in the first of the second. "Ebbing": MacNeice sees the approach of war as a flood-tide.* The six "Novelettes" from *Plant and Phantom* (1941), four of which were written before the war, present an ebbing world facing the tidal wave of the future. "The Old Story" ends with an old man who "watched the water / Massing for action on the cold horizon" (171). "Provence" ends with another old man on a beach: "Down on the beach, / His wife and three of his three children dead, / An old man lay in the sun, perfectly happy" (175). The total devastation of the old man's world—"three of his three children"—cripples the perfect happiness of the last line. In "The Gardener," the third of the novelettes, a third old man leaves the world of Summer 1939:

And memory ebbed
Leaving upon the shore
Odd shells and heads of wrack
And his soul went out in the ebbing
Tide in a trim boat
To find the Walls of Derry
Or the land of the Ever Young. (174)

These lines expand upon the "ebbing" of *Autumn Journal*'s second line. Like "close," the word appears twice in quick succession, a rarity that in MacNeice always calls attention to the metaphorical force of the word itself. "Ebbing" is allowed to hang fire at the end of the line until resolved by "Tide," as "going" waits to be resolved by "South." In *Autumn Journal*, the world of Southern England, like the gardener's soul, is leaving on the ebbing tide. The yew is "close-clipped," the lawn "shaven," horticultural details that bring the soul of the gardener and the soul of England even closer together.

Seated by his compartment window, MacNeice watches the images of his past pass by him at about twenty-five miles an hour. The rush of images is unbroken by any punctuation whatsoever. The first sentence comes to an end after twenty lines and twenty-one "Ands," most of them beginning a line. MacNeice's memory is anacoluthonic, a waterfall of irrepressible

*He is not, of course, the only one to do so: Stephen Spender writes in "The Uncreated Chaos" of "The bursting tide of an unharnessed power / Drowning the contours of the present" (*The Still Centre*, 25).

free-association strongly reminiscent of the close of *Homage to Catalonia*. The similarities are so striking that it is worth quoting Orwell in full:

> And then England—southern England, probably the sleekest landscape in the world. It is difficult when you pass that way, especially when you are peacefully recovering from sea-sickness with the plush cushions of a boat-train under your bum, to believe that anything is really happening anywhere. Earthquakes in Japan, famines in China, revolutions in Mexico? Don't worry, the milk will be on the doorstep tomorrow morning, the *New Statesman* will come out on Friday. The industrial towns were far away, a smudge of smoke and misery hidden by the curve of the earth's surface. Down here it was still the England I had known in my childhood: the railway-cuttings smothered in wild flowers, the deep meadows where the great shining horses browse and meditate, the slow-moving streams bordered by willows, the green bosoms of the elms, the larkspurs in the cottage gardens; and then the huge peaceful wilderness of outer London, the barges on the miry river, the familiar streets, the posters telling of cricket matches and Royal weddings, the men in bowler hats, the pigeons in Trafalgar Square, the red buses, the blue policemen—all sleeping the deep, deep sleep of England, from which I sometimes fear that we shall never wake till we are jerked out of it by the roar of bombs.[22]

Both reveries are in grudging and deeply qualified praise of Southern England. Both watch the world passing before them on a train going north to London. Orwell's England reads the *New Statesman*; MacNeice's mourns "the passing of the Morning Post." Orwell's "railway-cuttings are smothered in wild flowers"; MacNeice's "trucks of the Southern Railway dawdle . . . shunt / Into poppy sidings for the night" (I). Both are dying worlds: MacNeice's "close-clipped yew" is Orwell's "willow."* MacNeice's spinster cannot hear "the noise of the 'planes that pass"; Orwell's England will be woken by a "roar of bombs."

MacNeice's farewell to Plato in Canto II, like his farewell to Southern England in Canto I, sustains a muffled threat. In renouncing Plato's ideal world, MacNeice is forced to greet an actuality become horribly real. MacNeice broke with Plato well before *Autumn Journal*, renouncing "Pure Form" two years earlier in *Modern Poetry* for its "escape from the actual to some transcendent reality on the pattern of Plato's Forms."[23] *Autumn Journal* continues this movement away from Plato towards a celebration of the actual. In his book on Yeats' poetry in 1940, MacNeice reaffirms Auden's creed that poetry must be "*about* something," must be concrete,

---

*The passing of England's railway stations, with their richly evocative names, is mourned in Flanders and Swann's elegy, "Slow Train."

political, and functional.²⁴ If Plato has no room for the poets in his kingdom, the poets have no room for him in theirs: "Good-bye the Platonic
sieve of the Carnal Man / But good-bye also Plato's philosophising; / I
have a better plan" (II).

At the center of Canto II's better plan, an Aristotelian spider weaves
an entelechy of forms:

> Only the spider spinning out his reams
>   Of colourless thread says Only there are always
> Interlopers, dreams,
>   Who let no dead dog lie nor death be final;
> Suggesting, while he spins, that to-morrow will outweigh
>   To-night, that Becoming is a match for Being. (II)

Aristotle is later discovered watching "the insect breed" (XII), giving this
reading of an Aristotelian arachnid further credibility. In the closing quatrain of his valedictory to Oxford, MacNeice bids the ordering principles
of Platonic thought a second farewell:

> Good-bye now, Plato and Hegel,
>   The shop is closing down;
> They don't want any philosopher-kings in England,
>   There ain't no universals in this man's town. (XIII)

"Ain't" refers directly back to *Out of the Picture*, written two years before.
Portright, an artist whose oxymoronic name already suggests an irrecon-
cilability, speaks for Plato:

> PORTRIGHT. The true artist has his eye not on a particular person but on a
> transcendent model which exists in the world not of Becoming but of Being.
> Miss O'Hara and all the other models of your ordinary hand-to-mouth
> painters belong in the world of Becoming. This picture was painted from
> the immortal pattern, the Platonic Idea.
> 2ND MAN. Platonic Idea! I told you so. Those ain't Miss O'Hara's legs.²⁵

The second man speaks for the MacNeice of *Autumn Journal*, and for a
modern world whose trust in immutable values has been badly shaken.
"There ain't no universals in this man's town" casts an unnerving shadow
forward to a world without ideals, Platonic, Hegelian, or otherwise.

Generally speaking, the departure from Plato's cave is a rude awakening:

"I must leave my bed and face the music" (II). Aristotle's spider suggests that "to-morrow will outweigh / To-night." He spins in a twilight world:

> Spider, spider, twisting tight—
>   But the watch is wary beneath the pillow—
> I am afraid in the web of night
>   When the window is fingered by the shadows of branches. (II)

The spider, here compounded with the sheer terror of Blake's tiger, spins a chaotic actuality in the absence of Platonic ideals. Cantos XII and XIII continue the running denunciation of Plato, and here that actuality is more specifically military. Plato's incommensurability with the present world preparing for war is made explicit:

> Remember the sergeant barking at bayonet practice
>   When you were small;
> To kill a dummy you must act a dummy
>   Or you cut no ice at all.
> Now it is morning again, the 25th of October,
>   In a white fog the cars have yellow lights;
> The chill creeps up the wrists, the sun is sallow,
>   The silent hours grow down like stalactites
> And reading Plato talking about his Forms
>   To damn the artist touting round his mirror,
> I am glad that I have been left the third best bed
>   And live in a world of error. (XII)

Again, the rhyme reveals its significant form, emphasizing the breakdown of "Forms" in leaving the strong quatrain ("yellow lights / stalactites") for a variation on the weak quatrain unique to Canto XII. For the first and only time, the weak endings are rhymed. Canto XII breaks from the alternating pattern pfpf / fpfp, rhyming "mirror" with "error," "pedal" with "meddle," "crisis" with "thesis." The hesitancy of the crisis world is captured in these quavering rhymes; its incompatability with Plato is suggested in the overturning of the expected form.

In the second and third quatrains above, the mood and meter shifts; MacNeice's present is drastically different from his childhood world. And yet the presence of the war is unmistakable in the sergeant's schoolground bayonet practices. The past world contains the future war. Learning the

classics is described as marching "to the field-marshal's blue-pencil baton";
the classical student may be "called to the bar or the barracks" (XIII).
Finally, in the wittiest abnegation of Platonic ideals, the war trumpets its
presence over everything:

> So blow the bugles over the metaphysicians,
>   Let the pure mind return to the Pure Mind;
> I must be content to remain in the world of Appearance
>   And sit on the mere appearance of a behind. (XIII)

Taking leave of Platonic forms, MacNeice is forced to recognize the reality
of bugles.

The farewell in Canto IV is a very different kind of leave-taking:

> September has come, it is *hers*
>   Whose vitality leaps in the autumn,
> Whose nature prefers
>   Trees without leaves and a fire in the fire-place;
> So I give her this month and the next
>   Though the whole of my year should be hers who has
>   rendered already
> So many of its days intolerable or perplexed
>   But so many more so happy;
> Who has left a scent on my life and left my walls
>   Dancing over and over with her shadow,
> Whose hair is twined in all my waterfalls
>   And all of London littered with remembered kisses. (IV)

In a bracket with few contenders for the crown, the fourth canto of *Autumn
Journal* stands unacknowledged as the most beautiful love-lyric in British
modernism. The elastic quatrain is again perfectly suited to his subject,
the innate tension of the form mirroring both her paradoxes and his
ambivalence towards her:

> And though I have suffered from your special strength
>   Who never flatter for points nor fake responses
> I should be proud if I could evolve at length
>   An equal thrust and pattern. (IV)

The weak form, *fpfp*, gives each stanza a final, sometimes heartbreaking, lilt. MacNeice cradles his memory as he would a glass: "Only let it form within his hands once more— / The moment cradled like a brandy glass" (84). Much of the poem's immediacy lies in MacNeice's integrity towards his subject. The speaker does not idealize his love:

> Off-hand, at times hysterical, abrupt,
>   *You* are one I always shall remember,
> Whom cant can never corrupt
>   Nor argument disinherit. (IV)

He does not need to:

> Whose words would tumble over each other and pelt
>   From pure excitement,
> Whose fingers curl and melt
>   When you were friendly. (IV)

MacNeice never explicitly reveals, in the poem or anywhere else, whom he celebrates here. He leaves his love anonymous for three reasons. The least compelling one is that, for all the concrete details which give her description so much authenticity, MacNeice insists that his love is abstract, chosen almost at random. Much later in *Autumn Journal* he writes:

> Sweet my love, my dear, whoever you are or were,
>   I need your company on this excursion [. . .]
> Here, where we think all this, I need you badly,
>   Whatever your name or age or the colour of your hair. (XXII)

This self-indulgent vision of a nameless love culminates in a mechanical desire for "The age-old woman apt for all misuse / Whose soul is out of the picture" (XXII). The phrase "out of the picture" sends the reader back to the play, specifically to Moll's speech at the end of Act I: "Whom you love is comparatively unimportant / Any tree or shrub will give you a line on the landscape."[26] MacNeice does not identify her because the individual makes no difference: as with most romantics, the object of desire is not a matter of much significance.

The second reason for the suppression of the name is quite the reverse. The individual makes all the difference in the world, so much difference that MacNeice refuses to divulge her identity. An anonymous woman walks through MacNeice's writing from 1937 to 1940. "Trilogy for X," written in Summer 1938, introduces her in the title. The work is in many ways a preparation piece for *Autumn Journal*, with the same imagery as the longer work for a similarly proleptic effect. The woman is never mentioned by name, but the love is the same:

> But now when winds are curling
>   The trees do you come closer,
> Close as an eyelid fasten
>   My body in darkness, darling;
> Switch the light off and let me
>   Gather you up and gather
> The power of trains advancing
>   Further, advancing further. (89)

Winds curl in "Trilogy for X" as her fingers do; like the winds above, her mind in Canto IV is "like the wind on a sea of wheat." The train's parting thrust recalls the "equal thrust and pattern" of Canto IV's last line.* "Leaving Barra," another anonymous love-lyric, ends with the same exposed endearment as the fourth line quoted above: "Like the dazzle on the sea, my darling" (88). "Leaving Barra" is clearly in honor of Nancy Sharp, the artist with whom MacNeice travelled to Barra and the rest of the Hebrides in 1937, who illustrated *Zoo* and *I Crossed the Minch* in 1938, and to whom *The Earth Compels* (1938) is dedicated. This has led Robyn Marsack to conclude that the dark lady of *Autumn Journal* is Nancy Sharp, for "Leaving Barra" has, as Marsack suggests, many images in common with Canto IV.[27]

This conclusion may seem unlikely, even absurd, in the light of MacNeice's painful divorce just two years before. Surely the most obvious candidate is MacNeice's ex-wife, Mariette. And if not, Nancy Sharp was by no means the only woman in his life since his wife left for America with a graduate student. In *The Strings are False*, MacNeice withholds his customary frankness to introduce yet another anonymous woman:

---

*Trains have been a sexual image already in *Autumn Journal*: "And the train's rhythm becomes the *ad nauseam* repetition / Of every tired aubade and maudlin madrigal" (I). Spender's "Midlands Express," from *The Still Centre*, puts this conceit more bluntly: "All England lies beneath you like a woman / With limbs ravished" (38).

After that I went about with—
    of whom I cannot write, but who was for me what is called
      an education—
or rather illumination;
    so feminine that I sometimes felt like leaving the country at once
    [Text uncertain];
and so easily hurt that to be with her could be agony.
    She could be so gloomy as to black-out London
and again she could be so gay
    that I would ask myself where I had been before I knew her
and was I not colour-blind then.
    Of all the people I have known she could be the most radiant.
Which is why I do not regret
    the hours and hours of argument and melancholy,
the unanswerable lamentations of someone who wanted to be happy
    in a way that was just not practical.[28]

This passage was actually written in prose, but prose with the same cadence as the poetry of *Autumn Journal*. Arranged in that cadence, the anonymous figure clearly becomes the woman of Canto IV. She has the same radiance, the same ambivalence. MacNeice's lack of regret almost soars into poetry, the poetry of

So I am glad
    That life contains her with her moods and moments
More shifting and more transient than I had
    Yet thought of as being integral to beauty. (IV)

Even the woman's London-ness ties the two memories together. The figure in *Autumn Journal* is deeply rooted in London: all of London is "littered" with her kisses (IV), her return is imagined "across the London roofs" (XI), "The pigeons riddle the London air" before her (XIX). The absence of any reference to Nancy Sharp elsewhere in *The Strings are False* makes this cryptic figure's identity certain. Every significant woman in the poet's life is mentioned, except the woman with whom he spent three years, Nancy Sharp.*

---

*Eleanor Clark, with whom MacNeice fell in love in America, is also mentioned anonymously in *The Strings are False*: "At this time I met someone whom according

The anonymous woman is all women, one woman, and not a woman at all. That she has the ability, in *The Strings are False*, to black-out London ties her closely to the approaching war. As relations with the woman in Canto IV worsen, she gradually acquires a symbolic force. The dark lady is a symbol, as she was in "Trilogy for X," of the war. Nancy Sharp reappears in Cantos XI and XIX, and with each reappearance MacNeice's love for her is progressively more bitter. The "white / Smoking stub" she leaves on a plate in Canto IV becomes a grate "full of ash" in Canto XI. In MacNeice, ash signifies a decaying love, and a decaying world. When MacNeice, in *Modern Poetry*, called Eliot the "poet of cigarette stubs"[29] he was surely thinking of the cigarette ends in the river's tent, symbols of a dead love in a dead land. In "Trilogy for X," "some sit smoking, flicking / The ash away and feeling / For love gone up like vapour" (88). In "Eclogue Between the Motherless," the second speaker "can drop the ash on the carpet since my divorce" (48). But the ash implies more than a lost love in "The Heated Minutes": "the world piles with ash / From fingers killing time" (86). His falling out of love with Nancy Sharp, witnessed in the smoking stub at the cafe, prefigures the coming of war: "No one can stop the cycle; / The grate is full of ash but fire will always burn" (XI).

The later two cantos praising her with faint damns also describe a gradual decay in communications. Her words tumble and pelt in Canto IV, but in Canto XI she is "At times intractable, virulent, hypercritical, / With a bitter tongue." By Canto XIX the breakdown is complete:

Now I could see her come
Around the corner without the pulse responding,
    The flowery orator in the heart is dumb,
His bag of tricks is empty. (XIX)

This progressive inability to communicate heralds the coming of war in MacNeice's pre-war poetry. Without the ability to understand one another war is inevitable. The soldier at the close of "Trilogy for X" has a purely destructive, purely selfish mind: "Mind in the trigger-finger, / And a flight

to fairy story logic I was bound to meet but according to common sense never. A woman who was not a destroyer" (204). But she cannot be the woman in Canto IV, since MacNeice did not meet Eleanor Clark until his trip to America in 1939. Eleanor Clark subsequently married Robert Penn Warren, who was, in 1942, in the opposite camp of the Pure Poetry debate.

of lead connecting / Self and horizon" (91). The closing image of "Christmas Shopping" is of a lighthouse which "Moves its arms like a giant at Swedish drill whose / Mind is a vacuum" (96). In both these images of the empty mind, it is the absence of communication which terrifies MacNeice.

Autumn Journal is an attempt to establish communication with the past, with his selves, with his loves, with his sacred places. Without these links the mind lives in severed silence. MacNeice foresees this silence as far back as 1936, in his "Postscript to Iceland":

> With the fear of loneliness
> And uncommunicableness;
> All the wires are cut, my friends
> Live beyond the severed ends. (74)

The ambiguity of "my friends" in its position at the close of the line allows "live" to be both indicative and imperative, a syntactic ingenuity worthy of Auden, the poem's dedicatee. The poem ends with a premonition of war:

> Our prerogatives as men
> Will be cancelled who knows when;
> Still I drink your health before
> The gun-butt raps upon the door. (75)

By 1939 the wires have been cut, and the gun-butt is part of the landscape. In the presentation of his gradually alienated love for Nancy Sharp, MacNeice quits part of his past world and draws closer to the coming war. The private past becomes a metaphor for the public future: the X in "Trilogy for X," and in Canto IV, stands for the memory of Nancy Sharp and for the coming of the Second World War.

The essential bond between the two lovers, and the essential bond between MacNeice and his past, is honesty. MacNeice does not mince his words in appreciating Nancy Sharp, and neither did she:

> And I shall remember how your words could hurt
>   Because they were so honest
> And even your lies were able to assert
>   Integrity of purpose. (IV)

"Integrity of purpose" is, above all, the key-note of MacNeice's relation to past history in *Autumn Journal*. Writing of the poem's failure in the foreword to *Poems 1925–1940*, MacNeice insists that it succeeds in this: '"Autumn Journal" remains a journal—topical, personal, rambling, but failing other things, honest.'[30] By honesty, MacNeice meant a respect for the truth of a moment, however qualified that past impression may become in light of later events or later beliefs. This allows the assumption throughout that MacNeice is the speaker of his poem, for the honesty of *Autumn Journal* does not permit the cultivation of a persona.

This honesty can be contrasted with the obverse honesty of Auden, whose loyalty was to scientific truth, the objective rather than subjective integrity of a poem. Auden revised, tinkered with, and even cut poems he later disagreed with; MacNeice rarely changed a word. In leaving "Spain, 1937" and "September 1, 1939" out of his *Collected Poems*, Auden afforded two of his most accessible serious poems the status of non-poems. Auden's major difficulty with "Spain, 1937" was its view of History: "History to the defeated / May say Alas but cannot help or pardon" (ll. 91–92). Auden felt, perhaps, that this could be construed, in Edward Mendelson's phrase, as "meliorative" history, a justification of the victor. If so, no one could confuse Auden's past with his present beliefs; the coda to "Archaeology," one of Auden's last poems, shows that he ultimately held the opposite view:

What they call History
is nothing to vaunt of,

being made, as it is,
by the criminal in us:
goodness is timeless.[31]

MacNeice's attitude to his poetry is something like that of Auden's History. He prefaces *Autumn Journal* with a note that says Alas—*"I am aware that there are over-statements in this poem [. . .] There are also inconsistencies"*— but sees no need to pardon: *"But I was writing what I have called a Journal"* (101). This allows for a vivid and unmediated poetry, free from the hindsight and false prolepsis which can bedevil authors with less commitment to the actual.

Everything is recorded in scrupulous and immediate detail, down to the most apparently trivial observation. As MacNeice lies in bed, "a car having crossed the hill accelerates, changes / Up, having just changed down" (V).* The poem keeps time with a chronometric rigidity, beginning on August 1, 1938, Bank Holiday Monday. The autumn is divided into twenty-four sections, each with a recognizable date: "This is Tuesday / The 25th of October, 1938" (XII), "A week to Christmas" (XX), "December the nineteenth" (XXII). "Cobb has bust the record" (V): John Cobb did break the land-speed record on 15 September 1938, doing 350.25 m.p.h. on the Bonneville Salt Flats. "The Australians have lost their last by ten / Wickets" (V): the Australians did indeed lose the last Test by an innings. Hogg defeats Lindsay on 27 October 1938, and MacNeice duly records the bye-election in Canto XIV. Philip Larkin, in his obituary for Louis MacNeice, praised the "brilliantly quotidian reportage"[32] of *Autumn Journal*: the immediately verifiable events lend it an immediate veracity.

MacNeice's presentation of the Spanish Civil War holds especially strictly to this "Integrity of purpose." The Spanish Civil War, with its shifting fortunes and sympathies, seems to have inspired a new faith in the subjective impression, the unmediated vision as against the didactic accuracy of a scientific truth. Spender writes in his preface to *The Still Centre*, the third part of which is entirely concerned with the Spanish War, that "Poetry does not state truth, it states the conditions within which something felt is true."[33] The poetry of the Spanish Civil War is the poetry of the present; and *Autumn Journal* retains that actuality. Auden excises "Spain, 1937"; MacNeice leaves in his rallying cry for Barcelona even though that city fell before the poem was published: *Thus the section about Barcelona having been written before the fall of Barcelona, I should consider it dishonest to have qualified it retrospectively by my reactions to the later event* (101). Unqualified, the closing lines of Canto XXIII stand bitterly ironic, eternally sounding a false note of already crumbled hope: "Listen: a whirr, a challenge, an aubade— / It is the cock crowing in Barcelona."

Canto VI is the first of the Spanish cantos, remembering Spain as MacNeice saw it on a trip with Anthony Blunt at Easter in 1936. Again, that memory is shot through with anticipations of a future war. MacNeice

---

*Two cantos later, MacNeice invests a second automobile with symbolic significance: "And as I go out I see a windscreen-wiper / In an empty car / Wiping away like mad and I feel astounded / That things have gone so far" (VII). Canto V begins the change into a more optimistic gear.

returns to the world of Spain, to a world just before the civil war, happily oblivious to the coming cataclysm: "And we thought the papers a lark / With their party politics and blank invective" (VI). The one Cassandra is blithely ignored: "And we met a Cambridge don who said with an air / 'There's going to be trouble shortly in this country' " (VI).* In this un-preparing world MacNeice shows the present day in miniature, hinting at Britain's crisis in looking backward at a world before an outbreak. Barcelona's sirens wail for England, and the city has fallen by the time the words are read. The two worlds are woven together by shared images. The "peeling posters" (VI) of Spain are carbon copies of the "posters flapping" (V) in Britain. "A vulture hung in air / Below the cliffs of Ronda" (VI), as the vultures "are gathered together" in "Les Neiges d'Antan" (81), "back the eagles" (VIII), and "pick the corpses clean" (XVIII). *Autumn Journal*'s structure also emphasizes the conjoining of the Spanish and British pre-war worlds. Canto VI is sandwiched between two cantos set in the British present. And that present has the presence of Hitler firmly imbedded within it: "Hitler speaks / And we cannot take it in" (V), "Hitler yells on the wireless" (VII).

The visitors to Spain in Canto VI are day-trippers, who do little but "drink and think and loiter." They reveal their ignorance of the coming Civil War in every lazy action: the ranks of dominoes are "deployed." In the surrounding cantos, this bourgeois blinkered perspective becomes a general failing. "Tarts and negroes / Loiter" (V) as well as the bourgeoisie. The taxi-driver in St. John's Wood reveals the same nonchalance as those deploying dominoes in coffee-houses: " 'It turns me up / When I see these soldiers in lorries' [...] It turns me up; a coffee, please" (VII). But as in Spain, the upper-middle classes are the most oblivious to current events:

> But did you see
> The latest? You mean whether Cobb has bust the record
>   Or do you mean the Australians have lost their last by ten
> Wickets or do you mean that the autumn fashions—
>   *No, we don't mean anything like that again.*
> No, what we mean is Hodza, Henlein, Hitler,
>   The Maginot Line. (V)

---

*This harmlessly previous don recalls Myles Crawford in "Aeolus": reminded of Austria-Hungary by the horses in Deasy's letter, he thinks "Going to be trouble there one day" (*Ulysses*, 132).

For some, cricket is more important than Czechoslovakia. In Hitchcock's *The Lady Vanishes*, the British gentleman trapped by a blizzard in a Czechoslovakian village in 1938 barks across the telephone, "What's happening to England?," referring to the cricket team rather than the country. As Isherwood puts it in *Down There on a Visit*, there are those "to whom Hutton's record test-match score of 364 is still the most important event of the month."*

MacNeice's attack on the bourgeois mentality is badly needed: even a person as actively concerned as Harold Nicolson is prisoner to this perspective. Nicolson closes his diary of 1938 with "It has been a bad year. Chamberlain has destroyed the Balance of Power, and Niggs got a third. A foul year."³⁴ These lines are probably ironic; there is nothing ironic about Spender's description of the sound of distant guns in Valencia: "the guns making a rather hollow pleasant popping noise like the drawing of corks."³⁵ Neither does a tinge of irony save Auden's bourgeois perspective in "Spain, 1937":

> Tomorrow for the young the poets exploding like bombs,
> The walks by the lake, the weeks of perfect communion;
>   Tomorrow the bicycle races
> Through the suburbs on summer evenings. But today the struggle.
>
> Today the deliberate increase in the chances of death,
> The conscious acceptance of guilt in the necessary murder;
>   Today the expending of powers
> On the flat ephemeral pamphlet and the boring meeting.†

Orwell's indictment of the complacency of these lines in "Inside the Whale" is well known:

---

*Christopher Isherwood, *Down There on a Visit*, 160. Though England won the fourth Test, by the whopping margin of an innings and 579 runs, Australia retained the Ashes. This is perhaps not an insignificant detail, considering that ashes are, for MacNeice, a sign of a decaying world. The cup of "Take away this cup" (V) is double-handed; the Ashes and the cup of Christ's suffering are both symbolic vessels that Britain would gladly do without. The appearance of the word "Trophy" two lines above also suggests this second reading.

†W. H. Auden, "Spain, 1937," ll. 81–88, as quoted in "Inside the Whale." By *Another Time*, "the necessary murder" had been changed to "the fact of murder." There is some debate whether the change was made before or after Orwell's essay.

The second stanza is intended as a sort of thumb-nail sketch of a day in the life of a "good party man." In the morning a couple of political murders, a ten-minutes' interlude to stifle "bourgeois" remorse, and then a hurried luncheon and a busy afternoon and evening chalking walls and distributing leaflets. All very edifying. But notice the phrase "necessary murder." It could only be written by a person to whom murder is at most a *word*.[36]

Orwell and MacNeice are attacking similar attitudes. The blissful and usually deliberate ignorance they deride is best exemplifed by Mr. Norris: ' "Well, well," observed Mr. Norris, taking his cup, "we live in stirring times; tea-stirring times." '[37]

This mincing voice comes under savage attack at the end of Canto VII: "The hill grows bald and bleak / No longer one of the sights of London but maybe / We shall have fireworks here by this day week." The anti-aircraft battery upon Primrose Hill is nothing more than a display of Roman candles and Catherine wheels; "this day week" is the voice of a well-bred nanny's boy. The tourists who discover Spain before the storm become a whole society of Britons perceiving the present with the same tripper's perspective. Spain, especially Barcelona, is "a whirr, a challenge" in Canto XXIII. In Canto VI, the reflection is in calmer waters, and consequently more precise. In leaving Spain, the trippers forget their present, and ignore their future:

And next day took the boat
  For home, forgetting Spain, not realising
That Spain would soon denote
  Our grief, our aspirations. (VI)

For MacNeice the past and present worlds are mirror images of one another; gradually in *Autumn Journal* the two worlds co-inhere, become one and the same. This schizochronic perception of time comes to a head in Canto VIII, with MacNeice's memories of his years in Birmingham in the early thirties:

Eight years back about this time
  I came to live in this hazy city
To work in a building caked with grime
  Teaching the classics to Midland students. (VIII)

Birmingham is, like London, a "hazy city." Writing of this return to Birmingham in *The Strings are False*, MacNeice makes the parallel with London clear:

> The next morning Primrose Hill looked so forlorn that I took the train to Birmingham, stayed with John Waterhouse. We spent the day listening to the radio. The faces in the street were just as lost as in London.[38]

Birmingham revisited is interspersed with images of the present day.

The juxtaposition points up the differences as well as the similarities between past and present:

> That was then and now is now,
> Here again on a passing visit,
> Passing through but how
> Memory blocks the passage.
> Just as in Nineteen-Thirty-One
> Sun shines easy but I no longer
> Docket a place in the sun—
> No wife, no ivory tower, no funk-hole. (VIII)

Mariette has left him by 1938; he has left his ivory tower for a brazen one. The Brazen Tower is MacNeice's term for a poetry that is forced by the pressure of contemporary events to abandon the personal for the political, to exchange a private face for a public place. In "The Poet in England Today," an article of 25 March 1940, he writes of these twin towers: "Some of the poets who renounced the Ivory Tower were ready to enter a Brazen Tower of political dogma; [...] Bad logic demanded a choice between the Towers, but salutary self-deceit allowed many of the Brazen school to leave the door open."[39] MacNeice leaves the door open in *Autumn Journal*, allowing his personal past to filter into the political present. Thus the distance between Birmingham and London is not as wide as "That was then and now is now" initially suggests. Birmingham's spiritual unreadiness before the depression mirrors London's before the war. In the Birmingham canto, "The soul was deaf to the mounting debit, / The soul was unprepared" (VIII). Modern London is also a soulless world: the soul is "forfeit" (II), and "out of the picture" (XXII). The denial of Plato's universals in 1938 amounts to a renunciation of the soul; "it is too late / To save your soul with bunting" (XVI).

The strongest connection between the old world and the present one is the Birmingham train, which "ran down the line / Into the sun against the signal" (VIII). The train that runs against the signal going to Birmingham is coupled to the train MacNeice takes in Canto I, hurtling past fields to London, rushing past signals towards war. The train has been a universal symbol for the modern industrial world well before *Women In Love*; in the thirties, the train pulls away from the present and plunges headlong into future history. In March 1937, having presented the facts of Germany's covert rearmament to an unreceptive Parliament, Churchill recalled to himself these lines from a turn-of-the-century volume of *Punch*:

"Who is in charge of the clattering train?
The axles creak and the couplings strain;
And the pace is hot, and the points are near,
And Sleep has deadened the driver's ear;
And the signals flash through the night in vain,
For Death is in charge of the clattering train."[40]

The image of the train out of control is most hauntingly expressed at the end of Powell's *Casanova's Chinese Restaurant* (1960):

Once, at least, we had been on a Ghost Railway together at some fun fair or on a seaside pier; slowly climbing sheer gradients, sweeping with frenzied speed into murky depths, turning blind corners from which black, gibbering bogeys leapt to attack, rushing headlong towards iron-studded doors, threatened by imminent collision, fingered by spectral hands, moving at last with dreadful, ever increasing momentum towards a shape that lay across the line.[41]

Moreland's Ghost Railway, like Churchill's clattering train, is an image of the coming war: two pages later, the Furies bring "in their train war."[42]

Mr. Norris' train and Orwell's train at the end of *Homage to Catalonia* are similar only in their destination. Their terminus, the terminus of Gascoyne's long black pullman in "Farewell Chorus," is war:

Let us fill
Our final fiery glass and quickly drink to 'the Pre-War'
Before we greet 'the Forties', [...]

> Even while underneath the floor are whirling on
> The wheels which carry us towards some Time-to-Come.[43]

Trains have played an important part in MacNeice's pre-war vocabulary; in "Departure Platform" the train leaves at the zero hour:

> It leaves at three-fifteen—with lifting pistons—
> > The zero hour;
> Opposite in corner seats we hope for nearness
> > And dearness in what is wrongly called the distance.[44]

The departure time is the same in Gascoyne's "Zero," written in September, 1939: "For this is Zero-hour."[45] The zero hour appears twice in *Autumn Journal*, once in Canto V as "the zero / Hour of the day," and once at the close of the Birmingham canto: "Arguing for peace / While the zero hour approaches" (VIII). At the zero hour in Canto V, "a train begins to chug and I wonder what the morning / Paper will say"; the second zero hour brings Birmingham into the modern world.

The hour is, in 1938, postponed. By the end of Canto VIII MacNeice's diary has reached the 29th of September, and the Munich conference:

> But once again
> > The crisis is put off and things look better
> And we feel negotiation is not vain—
> > Save my skin and damn my conscience.
> And negotiation wins,
> > If you can call it winning,
> And here we are—just as before—safe in our skins;
> > Glory to God for Munich. (VIII)

MacNeice's disgust at Chamberlain's successful efforts at appeasement, so typical of those who anticipate the war, signals a change in tone. Cyril Connolly, speaking of *Autumn Journal* in a radio broadcast of 1966, called the poem "almost journalism - the total effect is that of a complete phase of the thirties, post-Munich depression one might call it, absolutely realized and felt in every line of the poem, even when it's about something else."[46] This otherwise accurate remark is in one sense seriously inaccurate, for MacNeice's integrity to the principle of contemporaneity prohibits the failure of Munich from affecting the events of August and September. The first eight cantos are not products of "post-Munich depression." With Canto IX, however, the mood shifts. MacNeice's farewells become more conclusive: "It was all so unimaginably different / And all so long ago" (IX). His voice is more often bitter, and the threat of future war in his memories of the past rises more readily to the surface.

The middle cantos take place almost entirely in the past. MacNeice returns to Classical Greece in Cantos IX to XIII, Oxford in XIV, Ireland in XVI, a Yeatsian past in XVIII, and the Old Masters in XX. Each vision is both unimaginably long ago and a sometimes brutal reminder of the imminent future. The Classicists spend their time "working the dying fall" (IX). "These dead are dead" (IX), and will be. The women pour "Libations over graves," and one must try to "imagine oneself among them" (IX). "Call no man happy / This side death" (IX) says the teacher, lecturing on the past in the present, and *vice versa*. Twice in Canto XII the gladiators salute the Emperor, and both times the scene shifts from a classical to a modern context: "Those who are about to die try out their paces. / Now it is night," "(The Emperor takes his seat beneath the awning, / Those who are about to die . . .) Come, pull the curtains closer" (XII). The field-marshal's baton and the bugles blown over the metaphysicians in Canto XIII have been mentioned as prefigurations of war. The journey back to Oxford is "damp and dark and evil," a "Plunge to Henley or Hades" (XIV).

Canto XVI, MacNeice's memory of Ireland, is *Autumn Journal*'s longest section, and one of the most despairing:

> And she gives her children neither sense nor money
> Who slouch around the world with a gesture and a brogue
> And a faggot of useless memories. (XVI)

The memories are not completely useless, since they presage the future. MacNeice's Ireland is "a world of bursting mortar," of "bombs in the turnip sack, the snipers from the roof" (XVI). Through the land there beats the pounding of drums: "Drums on the haycock, drums on the harvest, black / Drums in the night shaking the windows" (XVI). Since *Out of the Picture*, drums have been associated with the coming war.* The play introduces Time, the limping God:

*MacNeice is not the only one to make this fairly primitive association. Auden muffles the drums in *Another Time*'s "Funeral Blues"; Gascoyne hears them coming

> Swinging between
>   Crutches he comes
> To an overture
>   Of buried drums.[47]

Throughout *Autumn Journal* the drums sound louder and louder, from the carpet-sweepers advancing "like a tank battalion / In answer to the drums" (V) to "Drums in the trees" (VII). Ireland, as MacNeice remembers it, was "ready to fight" (XVI); the crescendo of drums expresses that readiness, and allows the past to blur into the future.

The vision of Time slouching into the future also raises Yeats' rough beast. In 1938 MacNeice was researching his book on Yeats' poetry, which he was to publish after Yeats' death. Some of the book may actually have been written during this time: in his introduction to the book MacNeice writes: "I had only written a little of this book when Germany invaded Poland."[48] Canto XVI begins with MacNeice "reading the memoirs of Maud Gonne," and contains an ironic invocation to "Kathaleen ni Houlihan!" His discussion of the relative merits of Plato and Aristotle while in a schoolroom in Canto XII is a startlingly familiar situation. And Canto XVIII, a farewell to the pastoral world, sounds rather like Yeats' Happy Shepherd fifty years on:

> Sing us no more idylls, no more pastorals,
>   No more epics of the English earth;
> The country is a dwindling annexe to the factory,
>   Squalid as an after-birth. (XVIII)

> The woods of Arcady are dead
> And over is their antique joy
> Of old the world on dreaming fed;
> Grey Truth is now her painted toy.[49]

Canto XVIII also recalls Yeats in its diction: "yesterday's magic coat of ragged words" is unmistakable. Two members from Yeats' trio of Saint, Hunchback, and Fool are summoned to protect the modern world from the onslaught of the future:

in "Snow in Europe": "But when the great thaw comes, / How red shall be the melting snow, how loud the drums!" (*Collected Poems*, 80).

> [. . .] call the hunchback,
> The gentleman farmer, the village idiot, the Shropshire Lad,
> To insulate us if they can with coma
> Before we all go mad. (XVIII)

The hunchback and the idiot are called, but the saint is not chosen—his omission brings into question the restorative power of the Yeatsian landscape. "Et in Arcadia Ego": in the pastoral world one finds "sheep that breed and break their legs and die" (XVIII).

The Old Masters of Canto XX are revered, in a rapidly changing present, for their ability to encapsulate the changeless past:

> Where in their frames
> Other worlds persist, the passions of the artist
> Caught like frozen flames. (XX)

The Old Masters, and the values they freeze-frame, are celebrated in Auden's "Musée des Beaux Arts." But the ship passes Icarus by; in *The Dog Beneath the Skin* (1935) these values are savagely attacked by Destructive Desmond. In Spender's "The Past Values," published in *The Still Centre*, the painters are equally at odds with the present time:

> Alas for the sad standards
> In the eyes of the old masters
> Sprouting through glaze of their pictures!
>
> For what we stare at through glass
> Opens on to our running time.[50]

In MacNeice the present is also "out of the picture"—and further, the past artists foreshadow the coming war. "These arrogant Old Masters / Swoop and loop and lance us"; Sebastian is "calmly waiting the next arrow" (XX). All the past visions, from Greece to Ireland, from Yeats to Rembrandt, are qualified by the future world. MacNeice compromises his pastoral reflections, scattering death throughout the pages of his past.

In the centre of all these past worlds, Canto XV presents an eerie reverse. The rakes revelling in "Shelley and jazz and lieder and love and hymntunes," in "Strip-tease, fireworks, all-in wrestling, gin" (XV), are confronted with ghosts from all the past. The rakes live in the tomorrowless present that Isherwood remembers in *Down There on a Visit*: "For example, I'm on my way back today from a weekend in Paris, where I got tomor-rowlessly drunk, had tomorrowless sex, and made several people a lot of tomorrowless promises."[51] Rather than revisiting past ghosts, the ghosts come to visit the present. Like Eliot's "familiar compound ghost," they are one and many, and half-recognizable:

> But something about their faces is familiar;
>   Where have we seen them before?
> Was it the murderer on the nursery ceiling
>   Or Judas Iscariot in the Field of Blood
> Or someone at Gallipoli or in Flanders
>   Caught in the end-all mud? (XV)

These spectres come from childhood and church, from hell and two fronts of World War I. In these last respects they are also spectres of a future hell, a future war. The past and future world face a *carpe diem* present:

> Sufficient to the moment is the moment;
>   Past and future merely don't make sense
> And yet I thought I had seen them . . .
>   But *how*, if there is only a present tense? (XV)

Here MacNeice presents, in antithesis, the conception of time that binds the whole journal together. "Past and future merely don't make sense": past and future not only make sense but are one and the same. In looking backward the rake looks forward; he cajoles his companion not to look back at the spectres: "don't / Look just yet, just give them time to vanish" (XV). In living in the present the rake is blind; MacNeice sees spectres in both directions:

> This little pig went to market—
>   Now I think you may look, I think the coast is clear.
> Well, why don't you answer?
>   I can't answer because they are still there. (XV)

The half-rhyme "clear / there" is one of the very few in *Autumn Journal*. It serves to distinguish the two voices, literally and spiritually faced in different directions. The false note is deliberate, creating an uncertain, unbalanced atmosphere, and bringing Canto XX to a harrowing close.

The spectres come from hell, and in that origin they are a reminder of the future as well as the past of this thirties world. *Autumn Journal* begins with a descent into hell: "And so to London and down the ever-moving / Stairs" (I). MacNeice's underground is as infernal as Eliot's in *Burnt Norton*. In this hell MacNeice will see strangely familiar compound ghosts. Eliot and MacNeice have more than a descent into the London Underground in common. The two classicists share a healthy obsession with form: Eliot experiments with strong and weak endings in *Little Gidding*'s dawn encounter. And MacNeice frequently lifts from Eliot wholesale. The Radio Announcer in *Out of the Picture* cries "Hypocrite auditeur, mon semblable, mon frère";[52] "The Sunlight on the Garden" offers the lines "We are dying, Egypt, dying" (84). Both of these are allusions to allusions; MacNeice also borrows Eliot's voices:

Fire in Troy, fire in Babylon, fire in Nineveh, fire in London
FIRE FIRE FIRE FIRE
The buckets are empty of water, the hoses are punctured,
The city main is cut off, the holy well is dry,
There is no succour in the dusty ground, the metallic sky,
No rock will spout with water at the prophet's rod. (81)

"Les Neiges d'Antan," from which these lines are taken, sees a second Waste Land in the coming war. Four of Eliot's cities have fallen, there is no water but only rock, and even the promise of an Eastern reassurance has been broken. Once the present world has entered hell, it stays there. The drive to Oxford takes his car via "Henley or Hades" (XIV), the departing steamer on the way to Paris "cries to hell" (XXII). MacNeice reverses the Gloria in Canto II: "Glory to God in the Lowest, peace beneath the earth, / Dumb and deaf at the nadir." The pre-war world is an Inferno: earth has fallen into hell.

The image of war as hell is nothing new: what is new and different is the introduction into this hell of a usually welcome face:

And I think of Persephone gone down to dark,
    No more a virgin, gone the garish meadow,
But why must she come back, why must the snowdrop mark
    That life goes on for ever? (II)

April is the cruellest month: Persephone brings war as well as spring. Persephone becomes a powerful and perverted metaphor for MacNeice's horror of the future. She is both married—"The future is the bride of what has been" (XXIV)—and virgin: "the future remains a virgin / Who must be tried again" (XVII). Virgin and bride, her return is fresh in the eternally recurring cycle of the seasons. But MacNeice's Persephone is more the wife of Hades, "what has been," than the daughter of Demeter, "Who must be tried again." MacNeice looks back again and again, desperately trying to keep Persephone in hell. But no amount of backward glances can keep her in her place.

In these backward glances the Persephone myth undergoes a further perversion: MacNeice conflates Persephone with Eurydice. The myth of Orpheus was a popular one as the war began: Spender's "No Orpheus No Eurydice" appeared in *The Still Centre*, and Auden's "Orpheus" was published in *Another Time*. David Gascoyne wrote "Orpheus in the Underworld" in 1937. Owen Barfield wrote to C. S. Lewis in 1939 of his unsuccessful attempts at a volume of poetry tentatively titled *Orpheus*.[53] As Orpheus, MacNeice is perpetually looking back, at the ghosts of Canto XV, at the "burning city" of Canto VIII, attempting to freeze the future by capturing the past. In a glorious inversion of the myth, MacNeice turns to look Eurydice full in the face, trying to stall her advance. But she keeps on coming.

As *Autumn Journal* progresses, Orpheus resigns himself to her advance:

Sleep serene, avoid the backward
    Glance; go forward, dreams, and do not halt
(Behind you in the desert stands a token
    Of doubt—a pillar of salt).
Sleep, the past, and wake, the future. (XXIV)

Lot's wife is the primary gloss here, as it was in Canto VIII: "And no look back to the burning city. / That was then and now is now." But the burning city, at which it skills not to look back, is Dis as well as Sodom. The burning city takes the third form of Barcelona in Canto XXIII:

I admit that for myself I cannot straiten
    My broken rambling track
Which reaches so irregularly back
    To burning cities. (XXIII)

In all these representations the city is clearly modern London as well. Hell has risen to earth: Orpheus is forced to allow Eurydice to return.

MacNeice's use of the Persephone / Eurydice myth is not simply ironic. True, she is immediately a war future, but by the time of her appearance in the final canto, MacNeice has come to accept this:

> The New Year comes with bombs, it is too late
>   To dose the dead with honorable intentions:
> If you have honour to spare, employ it on the living;
>   The dead are dead as Nineteen-Thirty-Eight. (XXIV)

The quatrain is glossed by Auden's "Song for the New Year," which comes "with gas and with bomb,"⁵⁴ and by MacNeice's "Plain Speaking": "I am I although the dead are dead" (188). MacNeice faced the wall in Canto III; he must learn to "face the music" (II). The distant future is a positive force which Orpheus embraces as well as accepts. There have been intimations of future rejoicing in the early cantos: "And in the end—with time and luck—to dance" (III). At the end of Canto XIV, "the sun caresses Camden Town, / The barrows of oranges and apples." This suggestion of spring blossoms in the final cantos of *Autumn Journal* into an affirmation of the future, culminating in the closing lines: "there will be sunlight later / And the equation will come out at last" (XXIV). MacNeice's later poem, "Return," written in February 1940, rejoices in the return of Demeter, in a similar sunlight:

> The acclamation of earth's returning daughter,
> Jonquils out of hell, and after
> Hell the imperative of joy, the dancing
> Fusillade of sunlight on the water. (190)

With the approach of Christmas MacNeice invests Persephone's rebirth, and Eurydice's return, with religious significance, and allows the poem to draw to an optimistic close.

The soul, out of the picture for so much of *Autumn Journal*, begins to find its voice:

> Still there are still the seeds of energy and choice
>   Still alive even if forbidden, hidden,

> And while a man has voice
> He may recover music. (XVIII)

Up until this point, the cantos have alternated between the p*f*p*f* and *f*p*f*p forms, excepting the denial of Platonic forms of Canto XII. One would thus expect Canto XVIII to have the weaker of the two forms, *f*p*f*p. But the last quatrain, quoted above, is the only one in the canto to rhyme the first and third lines. And in that switch back to the expected pattern MacNeice marks the "choice / voice" quatrain as a complete change of mood, in which the poem rights itself both in form and content. The rhyme-pair is also notable in that it is used three times in *Autumn Journal*. As it is extremely rare to find MacNeice using the same rhyme-pair twice, this repetition is certainly deliberate, giving the rhyme an added force and finality, and tying together the three quatrains in which the rhyme-pair is used. The first instance, "moral choice / mad voice," appears just ten lines before; the third is in Barcelona: "Here at least the soul has found its voice / Though not indeed by choice" (XXIII). The absence of a mediating weak unrhymed line between "voice" and "choice" brings home the rhyme with even greater force. MacNeice believes that the free soul can find its voice, that "the equation will come out at last." Having tried to keep the future at bay in a series of backward glances he allows himself to look forward to its advance.

This resounding affirmation, in the short term, rings very false. The advance is more of an onslaught. The backward glances have anticipated a future of snipers and field-marshals and hanged men. The three choice/voice pairs are all slightly compromised. "Choice" is first rhymed with "mad voice"; the soul finds its voice in Barcelona "not indeed by choice." In the quatrain that closes Canto XXIII the word "still" appears three times, suggesting a fundamental inertia; man only "may" recover music. And to find and liberate the soul is necessary but not sufficient: "we cannot ever / Live by soul alone" (XXI).

The unsettled future predicted in the last cantos is paralleled in the disintegration of the poem's form. Canto XX is broken in two. In the last four cantos the ordered rhyme scheme goes completely hay-wire. Canto XXI alternates irregularly between *f*p*p*f* and p*f*p. Canto XXII alternates equally irregularly between *f*p*f*p and p*f*p*f*. Canto XXIII continues the inner-outer rhyme of XXI, and in the last canto every possible permutation of MacNeice's elastic quatrain is used. In turning from the past MacNeice faces a more terrifying prospect than he pretends to suggest. The immediate future must be suffered first: as MacNeice writes before Munich, the world is "now preparing to essay good through evil / For the sake of Prague" (VII). Evil first: as in *Between the Acts*, the fight precedes the embrace. There will be sunlight "later," the equation will come out "at last." All that is extremely remote: the more recent future is another, more terrifying, time.

MacNeice has "a great future behind him," as Lenehan says of Moses in "Aeolus."[55] The past and future worlds in *Autumn Journal* have been the primary concern so far: the suspended present, London in the autumn of 1938, may be seen as purgatorial. Canto XII begins in the twilight present:

> These days are misty, insulated, mute
>> Like a faded tapestry and the soft pedal
> Is down and the yellow leaves are falling down
>> And we hardly have the heart to meddle. (XII)

This is the only canto in the poem where the weak endings are rhymed, to very unsettling effect. A sense of uneasiness is also captured metrically: "The night grows purple, the crisis hangs / Over the roof like a Persian army" (VIII). The position of "hangs," suspended at the end of the line, suddenly vivifies the suspense of the pre-Munich world.*

But it is unnecessary to suggest that MacNeice's expression of the uneasiness of a waiting world is purgatorial. As MacNeice is the square peg in the Auden circle, so is he the square peg in the theory. To circumscribe his work with purgatorial themes and Dantean parallels would be to open a watch with a crowbar. Reference to Dante is made throughout *Autumn Journal*: the schoolboys hope to obtain "A season ticket to the Vita Nuova" (X). And *Autumn Sequel* (1953), a companion piece that continues the themes and reflections of *Autumn Journal* in twenty-six cantos, is actually written in terza rima. MacNeice's debt to Dante is unmistakable; it would nevertheless be a mistake to reduce *Autumn Journal* to a reworking of the *Purgatorio*. In Canto XXI, MacNeice presents a purgatorial flame:

> O fire, my spendthrift,
>> May I spend like you, as reckless but

---

*Compare Britten's 5/8 setting of Owen's "At a Calvary near the Ancre" in the *War Requiem*: "One ever hangs | where shelled roads part."

> Giving as good return—burn the silent
> Into running sound, deride the dark
> And jump to glory from a single spark
> And purge the world and warm it. (XXI)

But this is more the flame of his poetry—"burn the silent / Into running sound"—than the flames of Barcelona and the coming war.

All that may be said, and it is enough, is that *Autumn Journal* is closer to the *Commedia* than any other English poem of this century. Dante's progression up the mountain allegorizes the discovery of the soul; flesh and blood at the beginning, casting shadows everywhere, his soul becomes lighter, the journey easier, as he climbs upwards. MacNeice also charts the gradual awareness of the soul's importance, finally grappling, as Dante must, with the roots of conscience: "I have thrown away the roots of will and conscience, / Now I must look for both" (XXIII). Both MacNeice and Dante are Aristotelians; MacNeice's second canto renounces the Platonic soul in favor of Aristotle's. Dante's fourth does the same:

> *e questo è contra quello error che crede*
> *ch' un'anima sovr'altra in noi s'accenda.* (4, 5–6)*

Both love and hate their native land: MacNeice's denunciation of Ireland—"*Odi atque amo*" (XVI)—echoes Dante's bitterly ironic diatribes against Florence.† Finally, both are masters of their form, unconstrained by the complexities of their rhyme-schemes.

It may seem presumptuous to compare MacNeice with Dante in this last regard, but the extraordinary variegation afforded in MacNeice's elastic quatrain, and the reflection of content in that variance, does allow the sustained comparison with Dante's terza rima. *Autumn Journal* suffers from what may be described as a phrenic schizochronia. MacNeice's unresolving, perpetually unbalanced form skillfully expresses the uneasiness of time present, the blurring of time present with time past, and the tensions between time past and time future. The elastic quatrain mirrors the two levels of the personal and public worlds, seen in continual conflict

---

*"And this is against the error which holds that each soul illuminates a higher soul in us."

†MacNeice's mixed feelings towards his homeland, though they are taken from Catullus, sound very much like Quentin Compson's. The cry "*Odi atque amo*" rings with the same searing ambivalence as "I don't hate it!"

throughout *Autumn Journal*. It reflects the unreliability of Platonic ideals. And it illuminates MacNeice's ambivalence to Nancy Sharp, to Ireland, and to the rest of his past. Such a form can surely be compared with the form of the *Commedia*.

MacNeice prepares for the future by keeping his eyes firmly fixed on the past. While waiting for a war he becomes several different characters, touching upon all the sacred places of his past. In these backward glances MacNeice most nearly follows Dante. All of Dante's characters on the Mountain of Purgatory are waiting, and all of them return to their past. In MacNeice, the recapturing is an escape, in Dante, an atonement. The one is an anticipation of war, the other an anticipation of grace.

IV. The Co-inherence of the Ways: *Little Gidding* in the Blitz

The Co-inherence of the Ways: The Way Up

> *Those who have known purgatory here know it hereafter—so shall you learn when enveloped by the coils of the fiery wind, in which you must learn to swim.*

Eliot.

In *Little Gidding*, the central text of the Literature of Experience, the channel between history and literature is direct: "the passage now presents no hindrance" (LG, 120).* Why autumn, John Hayward asks, querying "autumn weather" in an early draft of *Little Gidding*, and Eliot replies "because it *was* autumn weather—it is supposed to be an *early* air raid—and to throw back to Figlia che piange" (HG, 184).† Eliot confronts the air raid directly and retreats from it; *Little Gidding* is both a response to and an escape from war. Why purgatory, Hayward could have asked, and he would have received the same answer: "Because it *was* purgatory, and to throw back to the *Commedia*." Eliot, like his public, needs a metaphor for the Blitz. For Eliot, as for many others, the most appropriate metaphor is Dante's *Purgatorio*.

Eliot stressed in two post-war interviews that his writing in the war

---

*T. S. Eliot, *Four Quartets* (London: Harcourt Brace Jovanovich, 1971), LG, 120. References to this edition of *Four Quartets* in this chapter, the following chapter, and the appendix will appear within the text, prefaced by the appropriate initials.

†T. S. Eliot, Letter to John Hayward, 5 August 1941, quoted in Dame Helen Gardner, *The Composition of* Four Quartets, rev. ed. (London: Faber & Faber, 1980), 184. References to any part of this edition of Gardner's work in this chapter, the following chapter, and the appendix will appear within the text, prefaced by the initials HG.

was a direct response to history. To Donald Hall in 1959, he said: "The form of the *Quartets* fitted in very nicely to the conditions under which I was writing, or could write at all."¹ To John Lehmann in a 1953 interview for the *New York Times Book Review*, he went further:

> "Even 'Burnt Norton' might have remained by itself if it hadn't been for the war, because I had become very much absorbed in the problems of writing for the stage and might have gone straight on from 'The Family Reunion' to another play. The war destroyed that interest for a time: you remember how the conditions of our lives changed, how much we were thrown in on ourselves in the early days? 'East Coker' was the result—and it was only in writing 'East Coker' that I began to see the Quartets as a set of four."²

The last three quartets are the direct result of Eliot's being "thrown in" on himself during the war. According to Dame Helen Gardner in *The Composition of* Four Quartets, the war sense evolved during the process of writing: "There is nothing in the original notes to suggest that Eliot's experiences in the air raids were to play a part in his poem; they thrust themselves in as he wrote" (HG, 169).

It is difficult to conceive of the *Four Quartets* as war poetry, but this is how they were first perceived. For a starving literary world the quartets came as a sacred relief; as Gardner has written, the poems "spoke so powerfully to our condition in the dark years when they first appeared" (HG, viii). The publication of each successive quartet—*East Coker* in 1940, *The Dry Salvages* in 1941, and *Little Gidding* in 1942—was gratefully received as the poetic expression of a shared war experience. The war is present in all four: *Burnt Norton*, first published in 1936, was revised in 1944 to glance at the war. The fifth line of the second movement originally read "And reconciles forgotten wars" (HG, 84). In 1944, when all four quartets were published together, the line was changed to "Appeasing long forgotten wars" (BN, 51). Gardner writes that the change was made to avoid the repetition of "reconcile," which reappears among the stars some lines later.* This is certainly so,

---

*See revised edition of HG. In the first edition, Gardner believed that the 1936 text also read "Appeasing," necessitating a laborious argument for its change from "reconciling" in the draft version to "Appeasing" in 1936, back to "reconciling" in 1941 and finally to "Appeasing" in 1944. "I used to think that the change from 'Appeasing long forgotten wars', the reading in CP, to 'And reconciles forgotten wars', the reading of BN, published in 1941, showed a sensitiveness to the political overtones of the word 'appeasement' in the period just after the Munich Agreement,

but there is another reason. "Appeasing," especially in the war context, unmistakably raises the policy of appeasement of Neville Chamberlain. The reference to a pre-war Munich is written in to draw *Burnt Norton* into the whole of *Four Quartets*, allowing the complete work to be considered as a poetic response to war.

The best evidence for the *Four Quartets* as war literature is the perception of the work by its war readers. Melville Chaning-Pearce, in the *Nineteenth Century*, saw the *Four Quartets* as a response to catastrophe:

> These poems have a more than merely artistic importance in that they are the singularly candid and self-sacrificial response of a very sensitive, aware and representative consciousness to the full impact of an unparalleled crisis and catastrophe of spirit. [. . .] *Little Gidding* cannot be justly considered except in relation to the three poems which prelude it and to the background of world-catastrophe which conditions them all.[3]

Chaning-Pearce read *East Coker* as "a dirge upon a dead or dying order; the magnificent muffled beat of the third movement ('O dark dark dark') was a dead march over, not only France, but an age."[4] Stephen Spender agreed in *Horizon*, reading "O dark dark dark" as a response to "the contemporary situation."[5] F. O. Matthiessen wrote in the *Kenyon Review* that 'The content of *Little Gidding* is most apparently under the shadow of the war [. . .] the "dark dove" is the bird that haunts now all our skies; its "flickering tongue" is the airman's fire of destruction.'[6] *Four Quartets* was perceived to be as much a record of the Blitz as *Autumn Journal* was of Munich.

Eliot himself considered the *Four Quartets* to be war poems. In his 1942 article for *Common Sense*, "Poetry in Wartime," Eliot distinguishes between "patriotic" war poetry and war poetry arising from the experience of "cold, discomfort, or the boredom of waiting."[7] Peter Ackroyd has noticed that "in a draft version of 'The Three Voices of Poetry', he wrote that the last three quartets were patriotic poems; then he crossed out the remark."[8] This brilliant piece of research suggests that Eliot draws his poetry from the second well. Eliot is writing out of experience; his war poetry is about the boredom of waiting. In *East*

and that the reversion to the reading of CP in *Four Quartets*, published in 1944, indicated that Eliot felt that by then the word had become less loaded" (84). This is only the first half of her argument: but these complicated gyrations are not necessary, as the revised edition makes clear. "Appeasing" first appeared in 1944.

Coker, "the faith and the love and the hope are all in the waiting" (EC, 126); *The Dry Salvages* cries "Where is there an end of it" (DS, 49). *Little Gidding* enters a purgatorial world which is clearly a waiting world. The uneasy waiting of wartime London always finds its best expression in the myth of purgatory, and Eliot, no stranger to images of purgatory, follows suit. All four poems respond to a waiting world; Eliot's war poetry is purgatorial poetry. As Paul Goodman wrote in his review of *Little Gidding* for *The New Leader*, "Eliot is everywhere, but especially in this poem, the Poet of Purgatory."[9]

The myth of purgatory, for Eliot, like the myth of Odysseus for Joyce, is "a way of controlling, of ordering, of giving a shape and a significance to the immense panorama of futility and anarchy which is contemporary history."[10] Though Joyce had little Greek, the letter and the spirit of the *Odyssey* underlies his work: Dante is to Eliot as Homer is to Joyce.* The myth underpins *Four Quartets*; it provides both the subtext and the structure for *Little Gidding*. Though Eliot is primarily the poet of Dante's purgatory, he also calls upon the purgatories of St. John of the Cross, Shri Krishna, and Buddha. These latter converge upon the way down; Dante, for Eliot, takes the way up. Before turning to the more abstruse mystics in the second part of this chapter, Dante's force in *Little Gidding*, and especially in the second movement's dawn encounter, will be the focus of attention.

Reviewing Laurence Binyon's translation of the *Purgatorio* in 1938, Charles Williams wondered what would result if "some English poet, eschewing his own work, should read nothing but Dante for a number of years (except possibly theology and certainly murder stories) and should then rewrite the *Comedy*, reimagining it all in English style."[11] Theology and the murder story—these are peculiar prerequisites for a translator of Dante. But both Williams and Eliot fulfill these curious requirements. Williams read some four hundred murder stories for the *News Chronicle* while reviewing works of theology for *Time and Tide*; theology also meets the murder story in Eliot's *Murder in the Cathedral* (1935). And with the publication of *Little Gidding* in 1942, Williams' remark was answered.

---

*Eliot was often asked by various presses if he would translate the *Divine Comedy*. He always refused, disclaiming any qualifications for the task. After allowing for the smoke-screen of Eliot's modesty, this does seem to suggest that Eliot, like Woolf and so many other moderns, had at best a working knowledge of Dante's Italian.

The poem was immediately celebrated for its transposition of Dante into the world of wartime London. Delmore Schwartz wrote for *The Nation* that

> Especially the encounter with a dead master just before morning in London in war time strikes one with such astonishment and admiration that [. . .] one wishes to say, "At last Dante has been translated into English and into modern life."[12]

Eliot, like Williams, had been attempting to translate Dante "into English and into modern life" for decades; the war finally enabled this recreation.

Four particular lines from Dante's *Purgatorio* reappear throughout Eliot's literary career. At the top of Mount Purgatory, Dante meets the troubadour Arnaut Daniel, who has been refining his lust in the flames on the highest terrace. Just before he returns to the refining fire, he bids Dante a Provençal farewell:

> 'Ara vos prec, per aquella valor
>   que vos guida al som de l'escalina,
>   sovenha vos a temps de ma dolor!'
> Poi s'ascose nel foco che li affina. (26, 145–48)*

These lines, for Eliot, were "superb verses,"[13] and recur almost obsessively in his poetry. "Ara vos prec" provided the British title for Eliot's third book of poetry; "the summit of the stair" is reached in both "Ash Wednesday" and "La Figlia che Piange." "*Sovenha vos*" was excised from *The Waste Land*, only to resurface in "Ash Wednesday," and again in *The Dry Salvages*. Arnaut Daniel himself plunges back into the fire near the close of both *The Waste Land* and the *Four Quartets*. The insistent reappearance of this Arnoldian touchstone in Eliot's poetry is testament to a profound literary obligation. In "What Dante Means to Me," a lecture delivered at the Italian Institute in 1950, Eliot establishes the full extent of that debt: "I still, after forty years, regard his poetry as the most persistent and deepest influence upon my own verse."[14]

---

*" 'Now I pray you, by that Power guiding you to the summit of the stair, remember, in time, my suffering here!' Then he hid himself in the fire that refines." The Dante that Eliot knew and quoted, the Temple Classics facing-page translation, differs from the modern text of the *Commedia*, with "*gli affina*" for "*li affina*" and "*sovegna*" for "*sovenha*."

In the Second World War, and in *Little Gidding*, Eliot draws upon Dante's *Purgatorio* with a more concentrated purpose than ever before. The hallucinatory encounter in the second movement, where the speaker meets a familiar compound ghost during a dawn patrol, is Eliot's most deliberate reworking of Dante, "intended to be the nearest equivalent to a canto of the Inferno or the Purgatorio, in style as well as content, that I could achieve."[15] On 27 August 1942, Eliot sent to his friend and editor John Hayward a second revision of the dawn meeting, accompanied by a response to Hayward's comments upon the first. The letter explains that the primary subtext for the encounter is the *Purgatorio*:

> I wished the effect of the whole to be Purgatorial which is much more appropriate. That brings us to the reference to swimming in fire which you will remember at the end of Purgatorio 26 where the poets are found. The active co-operation is, I think, sound theology and is certainly sound Dante, because the people who talk to him at that point are represented as not wanting to waste time in conversation but wishing to dive back into the fire to accomplish their expiation. (HG, 65)

It is an autumn air raid because it *was* autumn; the reference is to *Purgatorio* 26 because it *was* purgatory.

One must examine how Eliot translated Dante before looking for the reasons why he felt it necessary to do so. For Eliot found the transposing of Dante into English style to be extremely problematic. "This austere Dantesque style is more difficult, and offers more pitfalls, than any other" (HG, 63–64), he writes to Hayward; eight years later he will say that "This section of a poem—not the length of one canto of the Divine Comedy—cost me far more time and trouble and vexation than any passage of the same length that I have ever written."[16] There are eighteen drafts of this section of *Little Gidding*, to only one extant draft of the whole of *Burnt Norton* and *The Dry Salvages*. The episode is in unrhymed terza rima; replacing the rhyme words, which Eliot felt drew too much attention to themselves in English, are alternating stressed and unstressed line-endings. As Eliot wrote later, "Dante *thought* in *terza rima*":[17] the challenge is to capture the rhythm and form of Dante. This Eliot does beautifully. The first line, "In the uncertain hour before the morning" (LG, 78), is not only a verbal echo of the line with which Dante begins his ascent of Mount Purgatory, *"Dianzi, nell'alba che procede al giorno"* (9, 52);* it perfectly

*"Earlier, in the dawn which precedes the day."

reproduces the rhythm of Dante's hendecasyllable line. Another verbal echo is heard at the close of the ghost's speech: "set a crown upon your lifetime's effort" (LG, 130) recalls Virgil's final words to Dante, *"per ch'io te sovra te corono e mitrio"* (27, 142).*

The structure of the dawn meeting mirrors that of the typical Dantean encounter. First, Eliot provides the setting:

> While the dead leaves still rattled on like tin
> Over the asphalt where no other sound was
> Between three districts whence the smoke arose
> I met one walking. (LG, 83–86)

(These are presumably the three districts of Kensington, Hammersmith, and Chelsea: Eliot told Hayward that the scene took place on "the Cromwell Road" [HG, 181].) Then, the moment of half-recognition: Eliot's speaker, as Dante often did, has an initial difficulty placing the encountered ghost:

> And as I fixed upon the down-turned face
> That pointed scrutiny with which we challenge
> The first-met stranger in the waning dusk
> I caught the sudden look of some dead master. (LG, 89–92)

"Pointed scrutiny" is a long reach to the fifteenth canto of the *Inferno*, where the Sodomites sharpen their brows towards Dante and Virgil, "as an aged tailor does at the eye of his needle."† The distant recollection of a lovely image brings *Little Gidding* into the seventh circle of Hell. There, both Dante and Eliot eventually recognize Ser Brunetto. In the *Commedia*, Dante has some trouble distinguishing the ghost's *"cotto aspetto,"* but finally addresses him with *"Siete voi qui, ser Brunetto?"*[8] In *Little Gidding*, Eliot's speaker does the same: he deciphers the ghost's "baked features" (LG, 94) and cries, in the early draft, "Are you here, Ser Brunetto?" (HG, 174).

---

*"For which I crown and mitre you over yourself." For a comprehensive listing of Eliot's echoes of Dante in this passage, see Julia Reibetanz, *A Reading of* Four Quartets, 153–65.

†*Inferno* 15, 20–21: *"e sì ver noi aguzzavan le ciglia, / come'l vecchio sartor fa nella cruna."* The tailor was singled out by Matthew Arnold for especial praise, as Eliot remarks in "Dante" (205).

The translation from *Inferno* 15 is exact.* But the final text simply reads "What! are *you* here?" (LG, 98); the direct reference to Ser Brunetto has been removed, and the mapping is lost.

When Hayward asked why, Eliot replied that the ghost could be readily identified as Yeats, and "I do not wish to take the responsibility of putting Yeats or anybody else into Hell and I do not want to impute to him the particular vice which took Brunetto there" (HG, 176). This joke, though a good one, is a blind, for the ghost cannot be restricted to Yeats, but is "one and many," a compound of a good dozen poetic sources. The shade echoes Tennyson, Arnold, Shelley, Auden, Owen, Williams, Mallarmé, Blake, Shakespeare, and Baudelaire, as well as Yeats and Dante. A detailed description of these echoes is provided in the appendix. Eliot removes "Ser Brunetto" because he is not writing Waste Land poetry any more: 'The intention of course, was the same as with my allusions to Dante in "The Waste Land": [. . .] But the method is different: here I was debarred from quoting or adapting at length."⁹ The many poets comprised in the compound ghost rest in the background; their influence is not foregrounded as it was in 1922. What is important now is a penumbra of reference. The surface gloss to *Inferno* 15 is debarred while the more oblique glance at the tailor's "pointed scrutiny" is retained. "Are you here, Ser Brunetto" would have broken the rhythm as much as a reference to the Cromwell Road; nowhere in this passage does Eliot narrow the reach of his poetry with a specific detail.

Following the moment of recognition, the encounter takes Dante's familiar course. The shade is invited to speak, his discourse occupies the greater part of the scene, and he departs, returning into the fire:

'From wrong to wrong the exasperated spirit
    Proceeds, unless restored by that refining fire
    Where you must move in measure, like a dancer.' (LG, 144–46)

Eliot has followed Dante's structure exactly—except that these are now purgatorial flames. Having left the flames of the *Inferno* the ghost is returning to a refining fire, to the flames at the summit of Mount Purgatory. An earlier prose version clearly marks this second fire as the flame

*For a meticulous examination of the parallels with *Inferno* 15, see J. A. W. Bennett, ' "Little Gidding": A Poem of Pentecost,' *Ampleforth Journal*, 79 (Spring 1974), 65–66, reproduced in the appendix.

which purifies the Lustful at the top of the mountain. The draft of the ghost's closing lines reads

> *Those who have known purgatory here know it hereafter--so shall you learn when enveloped by the coils of the fiery wind, in which you must learn to swim.* (HG, 186)

"Swim" is a straight translation, as Eliot admits in his letter to Hayward of 27 August 1942. Arnaut Daniel dives back into the flames like a fish at the end of *Purgatorio* 26: *"come per l'acqua il pesce andando al fondo"* (26, 135).* The ghost begins as Ser Brunetto and ends as Arnaut Daniel; Eliot appears to have conflated Hell and Purgatory.

This conflation is deliberate, for the ghost's fire is both infernal and purgatorial. Eliot allows the ambivalence of the flame; *Little Gidding* IV ends with the choice of being "Consumed by either fire or fire" (LG, 213). The meeting is intended to be "the nearest equivalent to a canto of the Inferno or the Purgatorio [. . .] that I could achieve," and it does not seem to matter which. As Matthiessen wrote of *Little Gidding* in 1943, "A characteristic of Eliot's poetic thought ever since *Ash Wednesday* has been to make free transitions from the *Inferno* to the *Purgatorio*."[20] This easy transition is best captured in the fourth part of *East Coker*, where "I must freeze / And quake in frigid purgatorial fires / Of which the flame is roses, and the smoke is briars" (EC, 164–66). Frigid fires are found in Cocytus, the circle of ice at the bottom of Hell, not in Purgatory. For Eliot, as for many others in the Second World War, Hell and Purgatory are parallel worlds.†

Eliot does distinguish between the two fires with some precision in his 1929 essay on Dante:

> The last "episode" at all comparable to those of the *Inferno* is the meeting with Dante's predecessors, Guido Guinizelli and Arnaut Daniel (Canto XXVI). In this canto the Lustful are purged in flame, yet we see clearly how the flame of purgatory differs from that of hell. In hell, the torment issues from the very

---

*"Like, through the water, a fish going to the bottom."

†Charles Williams' review of the *Four Quartets*, "A Dialogue on Mr. Eliot's Poem," touches upon this ambiguity. Eugenio, one of the four speakers in Williams' Platonic dialogue, talks of Eliot's purgatorial fires. He then quotes the compound ghost's speech in its entirety, and suggests that all of Dante's *Inferno* is contained within it: "Is not that a proper summary of the dark journey from Styx to Judecca?" (121). The ghost in *Little Gidding*, as Williams has seen, is a figure from the infernal as well as the purgatorial world.

nature of the damned themselves, expresses their essence; they writhe in the torment of their own perpetually perverted nature. In purgatory the torment of flame is deliberately and consciously accepted by the penitent.[21]

The flames are internal and inescapable in the *Inferno*; in the *Purgatorio*, they are external, offering the possibility of redemption. The dawn encounter is ultimately purgatorial, as the compound ghost is ultimately Arnaut Daniel. Dante must pass through Daniel's refining fire to reach Beatrice and Paradise; the Blitz offers Eliot hope. A draft of *Little Gidding* in Magdalene College, Cambridge has the following short lyric prefacing the encounter:

Fire without and fire within
Shall purge the unidentified sin.
This is the place where we begin. (HG, 168)

As John Bennett has written, these lines "would have provided the first hint that the destroying fire figured the purging fire of Pentecost."[22] In the Magdalene lyric, both the fires within and those without are purgatorial; Eliot sees the flames of London burning as the fire without, the contemporary and external equivalent of Dante's inner ordeal by fire.

In the second movement of *Little Gidding*, then, Eliot draws upon the *Purgatorio* to capture the experience of the home front, to distill it as Wilfred Owen's poetry presented "the pity war distilled" from the trenches.[23] Throughout the writing of *Little Gidding* Eliot speaks of his successive drafts as "recensions" (HG, 27). With each recension, Eliot attempts to bring together the internal and the external fire, mapping Dante's world onto the modern world. This superposition is best seen in the early prose draft with *"Those who have known purgatory here know it hereafter."* According to Helen Gardner, this particular draft is "the best example among the typescripts of Eliot composing on the typewriter" (HG, 189). Eliot types quickly and directly from immediate experience; he knows *"purgatory here."* As the spirit says, "the passage now presents no hindrance [. . .] Between two worlds become much like each other" (LG, 120–22). A "common wind" blows the ghost from Dante's *Purgatorio* into the real world; the two worlds of London and Purgatory confront each other "at this intersection time" (LG, 103; 105).

They have confronted one another before in Eliot's war work. Though *The Family Reunion* was published in March 1939, it is very much an anticipation of war. The chorus announces a catastrophic future: "And the past is about to happen, and the future was long since settled. / And the wings of the future darken the past, the beak and claws have desecrated / History."[24] The chorus adopts the mock-Tiresean voice found in the pre-war plays of MacNeice and Auden: "We must listen to the weather report / And the international catastrophes."[25] *The Family Reunion* is also a play of purgation. Agatha says to Harry:

> You are the consciousness of your unhappy family,
> Its bird sent flying through the purgatorial flame.
> Indeed it is possible. You may learn hereafter,
> Moving alone through flames of ice.[26]

These purgatorial flames of ice anticipate the frigid purgatorial fires of *East Coker*; "You may learn hereafter" leads directly to the ghost's lines in the early draft. *The Family Reunion* resounds with other pre-echoes of the ghost. Agatha speaks to the dying Amy in the ghost's words: "You and I, / My dear, may very likely meet again / In our wanderings in the neutral territory / Between two worlds."[27] The play's final speech echoes the close of *Four Quartets*:

> This way the pilgrimage
> Of expiation
> Round and round the circle
> Completing the charm
> So the knot be unknotted
> The crossed be uncrossed.[28]

At the end of *Little Gidding*, the "knot" of Dante's rose and St. John's "cross" will come together, and the pilgrimage of expiation will be complete. But Eliot, in 1939, has a long way to go until then.

First he must suffer through the Blitz. The air raids dramatically altered the course of *Four Quartets*: "they thrust themselves in as he wrote" (HG, 169). Eliot was an air-raid warden during the first Blitz of autumn 1940; he described his war work to W. T. Levy in 1948:

> "[. . .] during the Blitz the accumulated debris was suspended in the London air for hours after a bombing. Then it would slowly descend and cover one's sleeves and coat with a fine white ash. I often experienced this effect during long night hours on the roof."[29]

This memory leads straight to *Little Gidding*, yielding the incantation before the dawn patrol.

> Ash on an old man's sleeve
> Is all the ash the burnt roses leave.
> Dust in the air suspended
> Marks the place where a story ended.
> Dust inbreathed was a house—
> The wall, the wainscot and the mouse.
> The death of hope and despair,
>   This is the death of air. (LG, 54–61)

The diction is identical: "sleeve," "suspended," "ash." The second line originally read "Is all the dust the burnt roses leave" (HG, 166), in reference to *Burnt Norton*'s "Disturbing the dust on a bowl of rose-leaves" (BN, 16).* The dust the† burnt roses leave is displaced into the ash of the Second World War; the death of air is also a death by air. The dove descending that breaks the air with flame of incandescent terror is both the Holy Spirit, tongued with flame, and a German dive-bomber.

The dive-bomber is one of the most troubling and revealing images in Eliot's poetry. Eliot was not the first artist to depict the war planes as doves. In an article for *Vogue* magazine in March 1942, the painter Paul Nash describes the Whitley as a "dove of death."§ But Eliot's use of a Nazi fighter-plane as the vehicle for the Holy Ghost has disturbed many critics, some of whom dismiss the conjunction as puerile and perverse. A metaphor can never capture pure evil—Hitler and Auschwitz broke the

---

*Though the reference to *Burnt Norton* is discarded, Eliot retains the gloss on *East Coker*'s mouse in the wainscot, which is itself a reference to Tennyson's *Maud*— "the shrieking rush of the wainscot mouse" (I. vi. 71)—and "Mariana": "the mouse / Behind the mouldering wainscot shriek'd" (ll. 63–64).

†Hayward wanted to drop the definite article before "burnt roses," thinking to improve the rhythm of the line. But Eliot insisted on its retention, suggesting that these roses are specifically the flaming roses and smoking briars of *East Coker*'s "purgatorial fires." The scene thus enters deeper into a purgatorial world.

§Eliot came up with the image in 1941, but the parallels between Eliot and Nash are interesting nevertheless. Nash is still best known for his paintings of the First World War; in the Second, he was selected by the War Artists' Advisory Committee to paint for the R.A.F. This, according to Eric Newton, was "rather like asking T. S. Eliot to write a report on the Louis-Farr fight" (M. and S. Harries, *The War Artists*, 173–74).

vessels by which evil could be represented. The only possible presentation is stark and atomic, as in the sixteenth Sonnet of Auden's "In Time of War":

> And maps can really point to places
> Where life is evil now:
> Nanking; Dachau.[30]

The compressed line, though written in 1937, remains one of the few true expressions of the horror of the Second World War. Eliot is guilty of more than using a metaphor for World War Two; he is using World War Two as metaphor.

Eliot's aestheticizing of the Luftwaffe is almost certainly a mistake, but it is a necessary error. He is writing for an audience desperately needing to make sense of the Blitz. The perception of the flames as heaven-sent, offering relief and expiation, is a welcome medievalism. Moreover, the conflation of Holy Ghost and Nazi war-plane should not disturb those familiar with either Eliot's poetry or his theology. The two conflicting images are yoked by violence together in the best tradition of metaphysical poetry; this is nothing compared to the grotesque conceits of Richard Crashaw.[31] The fourth movement of each quartet creates these perverse juxtapositions in conscious imitation of the Metaphysical Poets. Secondly, religion in Eliot's poetry has always been a vast compendium of often conflicting sources. Eliot may "not know much about gods," but in the *Quartets* he brings together all he knows, and sometimes the pieces do not mesh. The synthesis of religions in the *Quartets* will be discussed later in this chapter.

With the alteration from "dust" to "ash," the old is discarded for the searing new. This progression is also witnessed in the ghost's speech. Originally, the ghost's lines included a twenty-four line sequence, cut from the final text. The lines expand upon "the rending pain of re-enactment," with a stream of painfully re-enacted memories:

> The wild strawberries eaten in the garden
> The walls of Poitiers, and the Anjou wine,
> The fresh new season's rope, the smell of varnish
> On the clean oar, the drying of the sails. (HG, 183)

As A. Walton Litz has written, 'Here there is "acute personal reminiscence" in abundance, memories of Cape Ann, of London in the autumn of 1940, and perhaps of the visit to the south of France made with the Pounds in the summer of 1919."[32] Eliot removes these biographical particulars because he no longer wants the personal experience that he has always found necessary to successful poetry to be the experience of memory. We cannot ring the bell backward, revive old factions, restore old policies, or follow an antique drum. The personal reference must be an immediate experience, not a recollection. The Anjou wine must go, replaced by the disfigured street.

Eliot's poetry has always been grounded in personal experience, from the marital conversations in *The Waste Land* to "Marina" and the five "Landscapes." The first editions of *The Dry Salvages* found an impossible hermit crab leaving its shell on the beach. Hermit crabs, having no shell, cannot do this, and four years after its publication, Eliot corrected the mistake. A letter to the *New English Weekly* requested its readers to "kindly make the alteration" to horse-shoe crab.[33] This concern for the accurate detail suggests not only Eliot's pedantry but his love of the Gloucester shore. The crab inhabits Eliot's rock-pool of childhood images, described in *The Use of Poetry*:

> There might be the experience of a child of ten, a small boy peering through sea-water in a rock-pool, and finding a sea-anemone for the first time: the simple experience [. . .] might lie dormant in his mind for twenty years, and re-appear transformed in some verse-context charged with great imaginative pressure.[34]

"Rhapsody on a Windy Night" draws from this reservoir of images: "The memory throws up high and dry / A crowd of twisted things; / A twisted branch upon the beach."[35] Eliot's discussion of impersonality in his 1940 Yeats lecture explains the importance of the rock-pool in his poetry:

> The second impersonality is that of the poet who, out of intense and personal experience, is able to express a general truth; retaining all the particularity of his experience, to make of it a general symbol.[36]

Eliot's poems retain "all the particularity of his experience"; it is essential to get these particulars right.

Gardner's study of the sources of *The Dry Salvages* concludes that Eliot brings together in that quartet the "shores of Asia and the Edgware Road" (HG, 57). Throughout the writing of *Little Gidding*, Eliot felt the absence of the Edgware Road. He would write that it lacked "some sharpening of personal poignancy" (HG, 173), "some acute personal reminiscence," adding that "I can *perhaps* supply this in Part II" (HG, 184). A comparison of the first and last versions of Part II shows the supplier to be the war. The closing lines originally read

> He turned away, and in the autumn weather
> I heard a distant dull report
> At which I started: and the sun had risen. (HG, 184)

Eliot's insistence upon the season—"it *was* autumn weather--it is supposed to be an *early* air raid" (HG, 184)—implies that the scene is rooted in real experience, that the hallucination may have actually happened to him. The lines in the final version bring the war even closer:

> The day was breaking. In the disfigured street
> He left me, with a kind of valediction,
> And faded on the blowing of the horn. (LG, 147–49)

The disfigured street is the Cromwell Road; the horn, the morning siren signalling the all-clear.

Eliot does not place the scene precisely in the Cromwell Road, any more than he permits the compound ghost to be precisely identified as Ser Brunetto. For to specify is to restrict, allowing a reader's distance. The war atmosphere cannot be so particularly described that detachment from the scene is possible. This is seen in the convolutions Eliot was forced to in order to reach "waning dusk" (LG, 91). Eliot was trying to replace "at dawn," which was impossible after "dawn wind" three lines earlier. The replacement cost him a great deal of mental effort.* "Antelucan" is too latinate for the speaker, though Eliot admits to liking the word and finding it otherwise perfect. "Black-out" is wrong because Eliot wants "something more *universal* than black-out" (HG, 178). "Black-out" limits the experience too much; World War Two must appear in the reader's mind, not on the page. The expression of a "general truth" from "intense and personal experience" is a condition of "impersonality": for a poem to be universal the personal must be suppressed.

---

*He writes to Hayward about his painstaking search for the *mot juste*, and talks of it in *"Charybde et Scylla,"* a lecture given at the *Centre Universitaire Méditerranéen* in 1952 and quoted *in extenso* by Christopher Ricks in "A Note on *Little Gidding*," 149–53.

In "A Note on War Poetry," a poem published in Storm Jameson's *London Calling* in 1942, Eliot outlines this paradoxical principle. What is needed in wartime is the private experience, "Not the expression of collective emotion / Imperfectly reflected in the daily papers."[37] Elizabeth Bowen writes in her preface to *Ivy Gripped the Steps* that "through the particular, in wartime, I felt the high-voltage current of the general pass."[38] But the expression must be abstract: Eliot calls poetry the "abstract conception / Of private experience at its greatest intensity / Becoming universal."[39] Only in the abstract can private experience become poetry; the concrete details of the black-out or the Cromwell Road prohibit the creation of a universal image. Eliot initially called his four poems *Kensington Quartets*. That he even considered this reductive title reveals how steeped in experience, and in particular the experience of Kensington in wartime, the poems are; that "Kensington" is replaced by a digit shows his need to universalize that experience. Eliot is debarred from a narrowing referentiality; his suppression of Kensington recognizes the paradox of private experience in poetry, its necessity and its impossibility. The war experience in *Little Gidding*, like that in *Between the Acts*, is suppressed. This is why so many readers today miss both messages of war. Eliot suppresses his war experience not, as in Woolf, to conceal it, but to allow it to be gradually revealed.

The dawn patrol scene draws from the personal record of a war, but Eliot's war work is not the only private experience underlying *Little Gidding*'s second movement. The strange meeting is also an encounter with God; the speaker meets the Holy Ghost as well as a more familiar one. If poetry is, for Eliot in 1942, "the abstract conception / Of private experience at its greatest intensity," that greatest intensity is religious, realized at the moment of purgation, of expiation. This moment's metaphor is found, for Dante, in the flames at the top of Mount Purgatory. For Eliot, the metaphor is found in the flames that are burning London down—but both conflagrations are merely metaphors. The emphasis, for both Dante and Eliot, is on the fire within. The whole of *Little Gidding* traces, through its five movements, the process of purification. The purgatorial effect which Eliot desired is "much more appropriate" not only to the poem's subject, but to the structure of the poem itself.

The first movement charts the entrance to the church in the village of Little Gidding: "If you came this way [...] It would be the same, when you leave the rough road / And turn behind the pig-sty to the dull façade / And the tombstone" (LG, 20–30). The movement concludes with the preparation for prayer: "You are here to kneel / Where prayer has been valid" (LG, 45–46). Kneeling in the church, the supplicant enters a hallucinatory purgatorial world that is both Dante's world and a world at war. The third movement returns the speaker to the church—"If I think, again, of this place" (LG, 169)—and closes, as the second movement did, with a supplication to enter the purifying fire: "And all shall be well and / All manner of thing shall be well / By the purification of the motive / In the ground of our beseeching" (LG, 196–99). The fourth movement is the prayer within the fire itself:

> The dove descending breaks the air
> With flame of incandescent terror
> Of which the tongues declare
> The one discharge from sin and error.
> The only hope, or else despair
>   Lies in the choice of pyre or pyre—
>   To be redeemed from fire by fire.
>
> Who then devised the torment? Love.
> Love is the unfamiliar Name
> Behind the hands that wove
> The intolerable shirt of flame
> Which human power cannot remove.
>   We only live, only suspire
>   Consumed by either fire or fire. (LG, 200–213)

After the prayer, with the fifth and last movement, comes pardon—"With the drawing of this Love and the voice of this Calling" (LG, 238)—and renewal: "And the end of all our exploring / Will be to arrive where we started / And know the place for the first time" (LG, 240–42). The renewal is a return to childhood, to "The voice of the hidden waterfall / And the children in the apple-tree" (LG, 247–48), and a return to Eliot's earlier work. The waterfall is half-heard in *The Dry Salvages* and *The Family Reunion*; the children laugh in *Burnt Norton* and "New Hampshire."

Eliot presents the war as a place of renewal, a necessary purgatory that anticipates Paradise. Paul Goodman's review of *Little Gidding* held that "Eliot is everywhere, but especially in this poem, the poet of Purgatory," but continued to ask "if there *can* be a great poet of Purgatory; a great poet not always attended by some angel of Paradise."[40] *Little Gidding*'s readers, with Goodman, concluded that Eliot was indeed attended by that angel. The poem is a five-part prayer in the time of war. To its readers, such a prayer, personal and universal, as all of Eliot's best poetry is, was badly needed. One reviewer even suggested that *Little Gidding*'s optimistic message was responsible for the "turn of the tide of war and morale which almost exactly coincided with its publication."[41] In *Little Gidding*, Eliot moves from the *Inferno* to the *Purgatorio* to intimations of the *Paradiso*, where "the fire and the rose are one" (LG, 259). The fires of hell transmuted to purgatorial flames are now the flames of Pentecost, which beatify as well as purge. Eliot's last quartet is the work Charles Williams looked for in 1938, the perfect reimagination of Dante in English style.

The Co-inherence of the Ways: The Way Down

> Dante and St. John of the Cross—what interpreters of poetry are these? Can this hell be rather the place of purgation?
>
> Williams.

Purgatory cannot be restricted to Dante's vision alone; the *Purgatorio* is not the only place of purgation in *Little Gidding*. Together with Dante underneath *Little Gidding* lies the purgatory of the sixteenth-century Spanish mystic, Juan de la Cruz. Purgation, for St. John of the Cross, was the withdrawing of the soul from the outside world. As St. John writes in *The Living Flame of Love*, "This purgation is sometimes as fierce in its way as that of Purgatory."[1] As Charles Williams wrote of Eliot in 1930, "Dante and St. John of the Cross—what interpreters of poetry are these? Can this hell be rather the place of purgation?"[2] These preternaturally appropriate lines appear in *Poetry at Present*, referring to the epigraphs to "Prufrock" ("*S'io credessi* [. . .]") and "Sweeney Agonistes" ("*Hence the soul cannot be possessed* [. . .]") respectively. As Williams foresaw, the hell Eliot experiences during the early years of the war is also a place of purgation. Eliot finds in St. John's teaching a complementary expression of a purgatorial world.

The writings of St. John of the Cross and Dante Alighieri present the *via negativa* and the *via positiva* respectively, the two separate ways through which the ascent into a medieval Christian heaven may be achieved. The negative way traces the progression of the soul, through introspection, towards complete detachment from the outside world. "It consists," in the words of Charles Williams, "in the renunciation of all images except the final one of God himself."³ The positive way, on the other hand, reaches God through the embracing of that outside world: "The other Way is the Way of Affirmation, the approach to God through these images."⁴ In the history of the Christian faith, the two ways have always co-existed. Both ways trace an ascent towards God.

The ascent to heaven is portrayed, in Dante, as a climb, terrace by terrace, up a mountain of purgation. In St. John's *Ascent of Mount Carmel*, a similar ascent is achieved upon a ladder of ten rungs—the very figure that Eliot describes in *Burnt Norton*: "The detail of the pattern is movement, / As in the figure of the ten stairs" (BN, 159–60).* The seven sins on Dante's forehead have their analogue in the ten rungs of St. John's ladder: in both, purgation is a stratified process. As Heraclitus observed long before either Dante or St. John, ὁδὸς ἄνω κάτω μία καὶ ὡυτή, "the road up and the road down are one and the same." This line provided an epigraph for *Burnt Norton*, and ultimately, in 1944, for all four poems. Though Eliot appropriated the Heraclitan epigraphs in 1936, he explores the way up and the way down most deeply during the war, finally bringing them together in *Little Gidding*.

To reduce Dante to a poet of the affirmative way is to blithely misread the *Commedia*. Many critics have found elements of the negative way in Dante. Lucy Redpath remarks upon Dante's dark night in Paradise before he sees God: "And what St. John of the Cross called 'the dark night of the soul', experienced by all great mystics, seems to be symbolized by the blindness which the poet had to endure for a time in the eighth heaven before reaching the goal of his pilgrimage."⁵ Dante is much more a poet of both paths: his dream of Leah and Rachel before he enters the earthly paradise presents the active and the contemplative sides in Jacob's two wives. However, it is Eliot's perception of Dante that is at issue here. Dante is generally taken by the moderns to be a poet of the affirmative way. For Williams, "The whole work of Dante is an exhibition of a process—the process of the preparation of the essence for its function—[. . .] a process according to the Affirmative Way."⁶ Dante, with Lady Julian and St. Athanasius, exemplifies the cataphatic route to a knowledge of God.

These three medieval mystics are complemented by their apophatic counterparts, St. John of the Cross, Dionysius the Areopagite, and the

---

*That some early copies of *The Ascent of Mt. Carmel* substitute the word "figure" for "ascent" further links Eliot's phrase to St. John.

author of the *Cloud of Unknowing*. Charles Williams again must take the credit for this massive generalization. His study of the history of the Spirit, *The Descent of the Dove* (1939), which Eliot reviewed for the *New Statesman*, divides early Christian philosophy into these two factions. Eliot agreed, in his review, with this summation, noting especially that the book "gives St. John of the Cross his due place."[7] For Williams, the Western ways to God are best represented by two books: "The first is the *Cloud of Unknowing*; the second is the works of Dante. The Way of the Rejection of Images and the Way of Affirmation of Images had hardly been better expressed before, nor perhaps since."[8] This remark, as Eliot must have realized, is something of a challenge. Four years after these words were written and reviewed, a work was finished which expressed the Way of the Rejection of Images and the Way of the Affirmation of Images with as much grace as either the *Commedia* or the *Cloud of Unknowing*. *Four Quartets*, and *Little Gidding* especially, directly responds to Williams' sweeping statement.

Eliot walked with the early practitioners of the positive and negative ways all his life. Dante recurs obsessively in Eliot's work; so too does his counterpart, St. John of the Cross. Bennett suspects that "he first learnt of the Spanish mystic in his Harvard days," supporting his claim with the imitation of St. John in *East Coker* III, which proves to be taken from Eliot's professor William James' translation in *Varieties of Religious Experience*.[9] Eliot turns to St. John early in 1926, prefacing "Fragments of a Prologue" with the heavily ironic epigraph: *"Hence the soul cannot be possessed of the divine union, until it has divested itself of the love of created beings."*[10] As Williams stressed in his 1930 study of contemporary poetry, *Poetry at Present*, this formulaic statement of the negative way expresses a strong commitment: "In an age plagued by facile and therefore false mysticisms the full harshness of that first extract is apt to be overlooked."[11] Eliot is disturbed by the Princeton humanist Paul Elmer More's neglect of St. John, and writes to him to tell him so on 17 February 1932.[12] He repeats this disagreement in a tribute to More in the *Princeton Alumni Weekly*: "In his treatment of Christian Mysticism (in *The Catholic Faith*) he seems to me to fail to appreciate the greatness of St. John of the Cross."[13]

The most complete study of this subject, Eloise Hay's *T. S. Eliot's Negative Way*, begins: "T. S. Eliot was the first English poet who fully explored the desert places of negativity as a new domain of poetry."[14] Critics from Louis Martz to Leonard Unger to Cleo Kearns have written of the negative way in Eliot's work, but have not found it necessary to remark that he followed the path of St. John in his life as in his poetry. The faith he discovers in 1927 is a way of profound emptiness, as he reveals to More in a letter of 2 June 1930.[15] The terrifying desert that Eliot finds in religion is St. John's "Dark Night of the Soul." A disciple of St. John, Eliot detaches himself from illusory affirmations, as Williams perceived in his review of *Four Quartets*: "Those who supposed him disillusioned spoke perhaps wiser than they knew, for he stood from the beginning on a bare solidity."[16] "From the beginning": even before his conversion, Eliot took the road less travelled by.

With his conversion, announced in 1928, the negative way assumes a dominant place in Eliot's poetry. An analysis of *Four Quartets*, quartet by quartet, shows the fire of the negative way undergoing a series of transformations before it is infolded into Dante's rose. The road down has many turns in it. The negative way begins as textbook St. John of the Cross, twists in *The Dry Salvages* to accommodate what Eliot sees as pre-Christian precursors of the negative way, only to leave Hinduism and Buddhism before co-inhering with Dante and the affirmative way at the close of *Little Gidding*.

Burnt Norton's entrance into the London Underground passes into the purgatory of St. John of the Cross. Eliot invites the reader down this apophatic path:

> Descend lower, descend only
> Into the world of perpetual solitude,
> World not world, but that which is not world,
> Internal darkness, deprivation
> And destitution of all property,
> Desiccation of the world of sense,
> Evacuation of the world of fancy,
> Inoperancy of the world of spirit. (BN, 114–21)

Besides being the entrance to the Tube Station, these lines present the doctrine of *Contemptus Mundi* at its simplest. Detachment from the worlds of sense, fancy, and spirit is the first act of a practitioner of the negative way. But this is only one of the purgatories of St. John.

Purgation in the negative way is two-fold, both active and passive. Two nights must be undergone, the night of the senses and the night of knowledge. The first involves the deprivation of worldly possessions, the second is the much harder act of the deprivation of being, of contemplating oneself out of one's very existence. As St. John writes in *The Dark Night of the Soul*, "this latter night is a more obscure and dark and terrible purgation."[17] The descent into the London Underground continues into this second night:

This is the one way, and the other
Is the same, not in movement
But abstention from movement; while the world moves
In appetency, on its metalled ways
Of time past and time future. (BN, 122–26)

"The other" of line 122 is the other negative way, the route of passive purgation, a way without movement, where even time ceases to have meaning. *Burnt Norton* has been brought into the timeless negative world of St. John. "The other / Is the same" because both ways are negative: one for the novice, and one for the proficient.*

This distinction between the active and passive nights is made in *East Coker*, in the space of one word. The third movement of *East Coker* reproduces verses written by St. John in the *Ascent of Mount Carmel*:

In order to arrive there,
To arrive where you are, to get from where you are not,
    You must go by a way wherein there is no ecstasy.
In order to arrive at what you do not know
    You must go by a way which is the way of ignorance.
In order to possess what you do not possess
    You must go by the way of dispossession.
In order to arrive at what you are not
    You must go through the way in which you are not.
And what you do not know is the only thing you know
And what you own is what you do not own
And where you are is where you are not. (EC, 135–46)

---

*Incidentally, the ways are also the same because they are the two ways to reach the train platform. The one way, the way of movement, is the staircase; the other, the way of abstention from movement, is the lift. This reading provides a concrete explanation for line 125's "metalled ways." Eliot's use of the Gloucester Road Tube Station as an exact analogue for St. John's two-part negative way not only shows Eliot's pawky humor at its best, it also reveals how much of *Four Quartets* is rooted in suppressed personal experience.

The lines do not follow the *Ascent* exactly: St. John renounces pleasure, knowledge, possession, and being in a different order.* And in the lines that renounce being, Eliot adds an important twist. As Charles Williams immediately recognized in his review of *East Coker*, "You must go through the way in which you are not" is beautifully ambiguous:

> "*In which you are not*"—there are two ways of reading that. The one is of the way in which you have not been moving; the other is of the way in which you seem to cease, as you, to exist.[18]

To move in a new direction is to take the active path; to move in no direction at all, to cease to exist, is to pass into the darker night, the night of knowledge.

East Coker completes the introduction to the negative way that *Burnt Norton* began, preparing the way for purgation in *Little Gidding*. But *East Coker* also confuses the issue, introducing unexpected travellers along the negative way. Before the doggerel that closes the third movement, Eliot paraphrases many passages in the *Ascent* in addressing his soul:

I said to my soul, be still, and wait without hope
For hope would be hope for the wrong thing; wait without love
For love would be love of the wrong thing; there is yet faith
But the faith and the love and the hope are all in the waiting.

---

*The lines in *Ascent of Mount Carmel* read:

In order to arrive at having pleasure in everything,
Desire to have pleasure in nothing.
In order to arrive at possessing everything,
Desire to possess nothing.
In order to arrive at being everything,
Desire to be nothing.
In order to arrive at knowing everything,
Desire to know nothing.
In order to arrive at that wherein thou hast no pleasure,
Thou must go by a way wherein thou hast no pleasure.
In order to arrive at that which thou knowest not,
Thou must go by a way that thou knowest not.
In order to arrive at that which thou possessest not,
Thou must go by a way that thou possessest not.
In order to arrive at that which thou art not,
Thou must go through that which thou art not.
(*The Complete Works of St. John of the Cross*, I, 59)

Wait without thought, for you are not ready for thought:
So the darkness shall be the light, and the stillness the dancing.
   (EC, 123–28)

The darkness of the soul, deprived of the affirmative acts of faith and love
and hope, is certainly the dark night of St. John of the Cross. But the
light, the stillness, and the dancing are all alien images to St. John's
purgatory.

These images have various and conflicting sources. They are drawn from
Dante: light is the blinding light of God in *Paradiso*, the stillness is Dante's,
"immobile" before entering the fire of *Purgatorio* 27. The dancing is also
Dante's: the ghost will dance in Dante's flame in *Little Gidding*. The light,
the stillness, and the dancing are not only Dantesque images, they also
derive from pre-Christian philosophy. Shiva dances in a wheel of fire. The
bodhisattva, or Buddhist master, enters a stillness to reach enlightenment:
this stillness is captured in *Burnt Norton*'s Chinese jar. The light is an
Eastern enlightenment, both Hindu and Buddhist, as well; Eliot here
conflates St. John's negative way with its origins in Eastern philosophy.

This conflation involves a series of misperceptions. For Schopenhauer,
Buddhism was part of a vaguely understood Eastern mysticism. He and
other German idealists allowed Buddhism to share in a Hindu *askesis*,
though Buddhism is in many ways anti-mystical, anti-ascetic. This essential
misprision passed to Eliot, filtered through F. H. Bradley. A further misprision common to the West is to see Buddhism and Hinduism as "pre-
Christian," as if teleologically destined towards Christianity. Eliot admits
to these deliberate misreadings in *After Strange Gods*:

> I came to the conclusion—seeing also that the 'influence' of Brahmin and Bud-
> dhist thought upon Europe, as in Schopenhauer, Hartmann, and Deussen, had
> largely been through Romantic misunderstanding—that my only hope of really
> penetrating to the heart of that mystery would lie in forgetting how to think
> and feel as an American or a European: which, for practical as well as sentimental
> reasons, I did not wish to do.[19]

Eliot's most compelling practical reason for a Romantic misunderstanding
of Hinduism and Buddhism was that he could thereby perceive the Eastern
philosophies as precursors of St. John's negative way. As Hay remarks,
"if Eliot had not first steeped himself in the negative way of Buddhism,

he would not have found his bearings toward the negative way of Christianity."*

Eliot has always been fond of such a panjandrum-like synthesis of beliefs. The last lines of *The Waste Land*'s "Fire Sermon," "O Lord thou pluckest / Burning," unite the fires of St. Augustine and Buddha with such stark simplicity that Eliot felt called upon to comment drily in his notes that "The collocation of these two representatives of eastern and western asceticism, as the culmination of this part of the poem, is not an accident."[20] This collocation is worked out fully in *The Dry Salvages*. The strong brown river is both the Thames and the Ganges, the god within it is both Hindu and Christian. *The Dry Salvages* takes place on "the shores of Asia, or in the Edgware Road" (DS, 198), and these Asian shores are both Hindu and Buddhist. In the third quartet, Eliot conjoins his familiar compendium of mysticisms.

On the Buddhist shore, *The Dry Salvages* continues *Burnt Norton*'s union of the lotos and the rose. The two flowers are parallel metaphors in Buddhism and Christianity. Dante's rose draws him up to Paradise; for the followers of Buddha, enlightenment is reached as a lotos reaches the surface of a river. The flower's roots are at the river bottom; it grows through the cess and blooms, above the water, in the open air. That cess is the drifting wreckage of the world, the endlessly flowing and endlessly changing cycle of material existence that Buddhism calls *samsara*. It is found in the second movement of *The Dry Salvages*:

> There is no end of it, the voiceless wailing,
> No end to the withering of withered flowers,
> To the movement of pain that is painless and motionless,
> To the drift of the sea and the drifting wreckage. (DS, 79–82)

---

*Hay, *T. S. Eliot's Negative Way*, 69. Cleo Kearns also describes this transformation:

> Rather Eliot was able to give the early Buddhist "heart of darkness" a turn toward "the heart of light" and to bring it into relation to certain expressions of the via negativa in the West. (This effect was achieved, for example, with both bravura and delicacy in the third section of "East Coker," where John of the Cross's dark night and a Buddhist sense of emptiness and stillness confirm and modify one another.) (Kearns, *T. S. Eliot and Indic Traditions*, 158)

Kearns gives a reasoned account of Eliot's distillations, arguing that Eliot distinguished between the various strands of Eastern religious thought with a scholastic precision.

Samsara is directly opposed to the philosophy of Heraclitus, whose epi-grams oversee the whole of the quartets. Πάντα ρεῖ, everything flows: by this Heraclitus means not that the cycle is unchanging but that recurrence is impossible, that one "never sets foot in the same river twice." Though the water image is common to both, the Christian and Buddhist ideas of the time process are directly opposed; Eliot nevertheless brings them together.

The Dry Salvages takes place primarily on the Hindu Shore. Krishna is invoked, at the moment of his admonition to Arjuna to fight, and thereby purge themselves: "Not fare well, / But fare forward, voyagers" (DS, 167–68). Krishna's words, after *Little Gidding*, are familiar: Krishna, the Fire God, both creator and destroyer, anticipates the creative and destructive voice of the Holy Ghost, descending in flames. Both the Hindu and the Christian God appear on the field of battle, the one at the Battle of Kurukshelra, the other in the Blitz. The two battlegrounds are purgatorial worlds, places of passage, proving grounds like Dante's flame. As Hay has written, 'Eliot treats purgation both as *askesis* (the discipline of purifica-tion), ridding the mind of all that is not ultimate, and as intuition of "the darkness of God." '²¹ The war is the ground upon which this two part purgation is possible, the place of purification and the place where one may glimpse *East Coker*'s "darkness of God" (EC, 113). That purification is both Hindu—"fare forward, voyagers"—and Christian: "the purification of the motive / In the ground of our beseeching" (LG, 198–99). That creative/destructive God is both Krishna and the Holy Ghost.

In *The Dry Salvages* Eliot begins, rather synthetically perhaps, to knot everything together. The way up, for the first time since the epigraphs, is equated with the way down: "And the way up is the way down, the way forward is the way back" (DS, 129). The various downward paths, Bud-dhist, Hindu, and Christian, appear to be combined. But the Eastern precursors of St. John of the Cross are discovered only to be discarded. There is a way out of the samsaric cycle of withered flowers, of drifting wreckage. The only possible relief is "the hardly, barely prayable / Prayer of the one Annunciation" (DS, 83–84). Eliot speaks through Krishna to a world at war. He also speaks to a waiting world, a world that is in desperate need of some kind of purgation. And the purgation will be a Christian one.

The second movement of *The Dry Salvages* begins, like the second movement of *Little Gidding*, in autumn weather, in London after an air raid:

Where is there an end of it, the soundless wailing,
The silent withering of autumn flowers
Dropping their petals and remaining motionless;
Where is there an end to the drifting wreckage,
The prayer of the bone on the beach, the unprayable
Prayer at the calamitous annunciation? (DS, 49–54)

The verse shares the diction of *Little Gidding*'s description of the Blitz in "the soundless wailing," "Dropping their petals," "wreckage." As in *Little Gidding*, the only hope, or else despair, lies in the calamitous annunciation, the destructive and purging flames of the Holy Ghost. The supplicants to the Queen of Heaven, Dante's "Figlia del tuo figlio,"* are waiting for her Annunciation in the middle of the Blitz. *The Dry Salvages* raises the Oriental philosophies which so thoroughly inform Eliot's religious thought, only to drop them for *Little Gidding*'s collocation of the two Christian ways. The hint half guessed to which *The Dry Salvages* moves is not one of the frequent incarnations of Krishna, but the unique Incarnation of Christ.

Little Gidding opens in the purgatory of St. John of the Cross. The midwinter spring is outside time's covenant, removed from the metalled ways of time past and time future. The "pentecostal fire / In the dark time of the year" (LG, 9–10) is St. John's *Living Flame of Love*, the purging fire of the negative way. The phrase "Zero summer" (LG, 19), which caused Hayward so much difficulty, can be understood in the terms of the negative way. "Zero" is the goal of the practitioner of the negative way: the frontispiece to the 1619 edition of St. John's work marks the route to *"Yenel monte nada"* with *"nada nada nada nada nada."* The version of *Little Gidding* published in the *New English Weekly* inserted a line before "Zero summer," so that the passage read: "Where is the summer, the unimaginable / Summer beyond sense, the inapprehensible / Zero summer?" (HG, 160). As Gardner argues, the omission of this additional line may be accidental but is certainly unfortunate: "Any future editor would have to consider seriously whether it should be restored" (HG, 161). With it, the sense of the zero summer as culmination of the negative way is clear. A zero summer is unimaginable in that imagination must be put aside, inapprehensible because it is beyond sense. God is attainable, according to the negative way, but incomprehensible. (The *Cloud of Unknowing* suggests this incomprehensibility in its title; the liturgy retains a

*DS, 177, from *Paradiso* 33, 1. "Daughter of your son."

trace of the negative way in the phrase "the peace which passeth all understanding.")

Entering the church at Little Gidding, the supplicant prepares for prayer. Before that prayer can be valid, he must undergo the two renunciations required by St. John: "If you came this way [. . .] you would have to put off / Sense and notion" (LG, 39–43). These are precisely the nights of sense and knowledge in the *Ascent of Mount Carmel* and *The Dark Night of the Soul*. The prayer that will follow in the fourth movement can be only performed when removed from the world, the mind, and the body. It must be without awareness of language: "And prayer is more / Than an order of words" (LG, 46–47). It must be without awareness of the self: "the conscious occupation / Of the praying mind" (LG, 47–48). It must be without awareness of the body: "or the sound of the voice praying" (LG, 48). The way to *Little Gidding* is not only St. John's negative way, it is the path of the proficient.

This path turns into a *cammin* at the intersection time. The speaker enters Dante's purgatory in the second movement of *Little Gidding*. The presence of Dante in that movement has already been well established. St. John is still there: Melville Chaning-Pearce ties the encounter to both Dante and St. John of the Cross. For him, the word that awaits the language of the new year is "the terrible but redeeming word of the *Divina Commedia* as of *The Dark Night of the Soul*."[22] And with the return from the hallucinatory world of real London, St. John of the Cross reenters the poem in earnest. The third movement of *Little Gidding* brings Dante and St. John into the same hedgerow.

In the hedgerow flourish the three separate branches of Eliot's religious thought:

There are three conditions which often look alike
Yet differ completely, flourish in the same hedgerow:
Attachment to self and to things and to persons, detachment
From self and from things and from persons; and, growing between
    them, indifference
Which resembles the others as death resembles life,
Being between two lives—unflowering, between
The live and the dead nettle. (LG, 150–55)

Attachment to self and to things and to persons states precisely the doctrine of the affirmative way, while detachment from self and from things and from persons perfectly describes the isolation of the traveller on the negative way. The former is represented in the live nettle, to be grasped with both hands. The latter is described by the dead nettle, or White Archangel, a flowering plant that does not sting. As Eliot wrote to Hayward: "You know as well as I do that the dead nettle is the family of flowering plant of which the White Archangel is one of the commonest and closely resembles the stinging nettle and is found in its company" (HG, 200).*

The conditions of attachment and detachment are represented by live flowers; dead between them lies the Oriental hybrid Eliot discarded in *The Dry Salvages*. The middle way of indifference in the hedgerow is a Buddhist way. As G. Schmidt has noted in 'An Echo of Buddhism in T. S. Eliot's "Little Gidding," ' "The lines recall Warren's chapter on fruitful and barren karma, as translated from the *Aṅguttara-Nikāya.*"²³ The *bodhisattva* purges himself by taking a middle path, or the *Majjhima Patipada*:

> The Fourth Noble Truth is that of the way leading to the Cessation of *Dukkha* (suffering). This is known as the 'Middle Path' (*Majjhima Patipada*), because it avoids two extremes: one extreme being the search for happiness through the pleasures of the senses, which is 'low, common, unprofitable and the way of the ordinary people;' the other being the search for happiness through self-mortification in different forms of asceticism, which is 'painful, unworthy and unprofitable.'²⁴

The middle way is achieved through the rejection of extremes; like the speaker in *East Coker*, he is "in the middle way [. . .] *entre deux guerres*" (EC, 172–73). Between the two wars, or the two extremes of passion, he enters a stillness which is itself very much like Eliot's still point.

The middle way is also a Hindu way: as Krishna says to Arjuna in the Second Book of the *Bhagavad Gita*, "Discipline is defined as indifference."²⁵ Krishna admonishes Arjuna to act without engagement, without investing an emotional commitment. The disciplined mind is indifferent, disengaged. Christopher Isherwood's appendix to his 1944 translation of the *Gita*, "The Gita and War," discusses the meaning of this indifference:

> The Christians call it 'holy indifference' and the Hindus 'non-attachment.' Both names are slightly misleading. They suggest coldness and lack of enthusiasm. [. . .] But the doer of non-attached action is the most conscientious of men.

---

*Actually, as Gardner points out, living up to her name, the flower is a confusion of the White Deadnettle (*Lamium album*) and the Yellow Archangel (*Galeobdolon luteum*) (HG, 200n).

Freed from fear and desire, he offers everything he does as a sacrament of devotion to his duty.[26]

This may sound like sensible advice during wartime, but this middle way is alien to Eliot. Whether Christian, Hindu or Buddhist, 'holy indifference' can never be, for Eliot, a way to enlightenment.

The way of indifference in Eliot's hedgerow leads us down the garden path. Eliot, in the Second World War, insists upon engagement: "indifference [. . .] resembles the others as death resembles life." He closes his "Last Words" in *Criterion* in 1939 with "This is not to suggest that I consider literature to be at this time, or at any time, a matter of indifference."[27] In 1940, his review of J. Middleton Murry's *The Betrayal of Christ by the Churches* inveighs against Murry's disinterested and condescending tone. When Murry writes that he is "quite willing" to admit apostolic succession, Eliot responds "What can *willing* here mean except that this is a matter of indifference?"[28] In the theological context, especially, indifference is intolerable. As he continues in this review: "I could accept a still more violent denunciation if it came from somebody who was definitely either *inside* or *outside*."[29] For Eliot in wartime, indifference is a loaded word, connoting a lack of commitment that he finds insupportable. The middle way is indifferent, and it is rejected because it is neither positive nor negative. In the religious sphere, indifference is a barren failure.

(Eliot can never reject Buddhism and Hinduism completely. It will always underpin the way he writes about Christianity, and its purgatory does manifest itself in *Little Gidding*. Each branch in the hedgerow, whether the *via positiva*, the *via negativa*, or an Eastern middle way, requires some sort of purification; each presents a separate purgatory. For Eliot, that purgatory was realized in the war around him. Only in the Eastern philosophies is the world a living purgatory as well as a preparation for it; in most forms of Christianity, purification is not possible upon earth. In this sense, and only in this sense, is the purgatorial world of the Second World War an Eastern one.)

As *Little Gidding* draws to a close, the two extremes of Christian mysticism begin to come together. Though Eliot leans towards the negative way—attachment has "little importance" (LG, 161)—he does not permit the dialectic to disappear. The lines from Lady Julian's *Revelations* restore the balance in their emphatic expression of the affirmative way: "Sin is Behovely, but / All shall be well, and / All manner of thing shall be well"

(LG, 166–68). Gradually the symbols for this dialectic begin to converge into the fire and the rose. Both are images of God's love. Both are images of His Purgatory. Dante unites them at the moment of his passage from purgatory into paradise.* Eliot joins them together in *East Coker*'s "purgatorial fires / Of which the flame is roses, and the smoke is briars" (EC, 165–66). At the close of *Little Gidding* he does so again.

The fire has been presented as an ambivalent, or more properly a multivalent flame, as infernal, purgatorial, and pentecostal, as both the Holy Ghost and the Luftwaffe. It is also both Dante's "fire that refines" and St. John's *Living Flame of Love*. All the flames are symbolic reinterpretations of the Blitz, attempts to aestheticize and thus in some way anaesthetize an unbearable reality. The rose, too, can be variously interpreted, but it always betokens the way of images. The fire and the rose ultimately represent the negative and the affirmative ways of reaching God. Dante's celestial rose is the gateway to Paradise, and the name itself implies an ascent, as in *Burnt Norton*'s "lotos rose" (BN, 36). St. John of the Cross describes love as "fire, which ever rises upward with the desire to be absorbed in the centre of its sphere."[30] With the last lines of *Little Gidding*, the tongues of St. John's flame are infolded into Dante's knotted rose. "The fire and the rose are one": these words are inscribed on Eliot's memorial in East Coker church.

Eliot has been trying to bring these two extremes together throughout his life. He tells More after his conversion that asceticism and sensuality are the two poles of his belief, which only Christianity can reconcile.[31] He speaks of the snobbery of both the purely intellectual Christian and the purely emotional Christian, and of the need to co-ordinate thought and feeling.[32] What is needed is reconciliation, co-ordination of the two extremes of the affirmative and negative ways. Eliot sets out to reconcile

---

*Dante surmounts his reluctance to enter the fire of *Purgatorio* 27 by recalling the image of the dying Pyramus:

> As Pyramus, about to die, heard Thisbe
>   utter her name, he raised his eyes and saw
>   her there, the day mulberries turned blood red—
> just so, my stubborness melted away:
>   hearing the name which blooms eternally
>   within my mind, I turned to my wise guide.
> (*Purgatorio*, trans. Musa, 27, 37–42)

The suggestions of flowers in Beatrice's name, "which blooms eternally," and in the white mulberry bush dyed red by Pyramus' blood, bring rose and fire together as symbols of purgatory.

them in the *Four Quartets*, prefacing the whole endeavor in 1936, even before he had conceived of the whole, with this directive: to make the way up and the way down the same.

Auden wrote in "Autumn 1940" that

The positive and negative ways through time
    Embrace and encourage each other
    In a brief moment of intersection.[33]

In the *Four Quartets*, this moment of intersection is reached. Williams' term for the co-ordination of the ways, introduced in *The Descent of the Dove*, is "co-inherence": "Both methods, the Affirmative Way and the Negative Way, were to co-exist; one might almost say, to co-inhere."[34] Eliot's term is "co-existence" (BN, 145), as in the co-existence of the stillness of the violin and its music in *Burnt Norton*. And to what end? Why would Auden, Williams, and Eliot, the three great religious poets of the war, seek this co-inherence? In *The Dry Salvages*, "the impossible union / Of the spheres of existence is actual" (DS, 216–17) only through the Incarnation. The Incarnation is the crossroads of the two ways, "the end of all our exploring" (LG, 240). The co-inherence of the ways at the close of *Four Quartets* makes possible this impossible union—which is why one travels along the ways at all.

V. The Inklings in the War: J. R. R. Tolkien, C. S. Lewis, and Charles Williams

"My 'purgatorial' story": J. R. R. Tolkien's "Leaf by Niggle"

> I tried to show allegorically how that might come to be taken up into Creation in some plane in my 'purgatorial' story *Leaf by Niggle*.
>
> Tolkien.

In Edmund Crispin's *Swan Song* (1947), Gervase Fen, the Oxford Professor of English Literature and sometime detective, sees a familiar figure entering the 'Bird and Baby': ' "There goes C. S. Lewis," said Fen suddenly. "It must be Tuesday." '* Lewis is on his way to his regular Tuesday lunch with the Inklings, an assortment of Oxford men whose membership at one time included Hugo Dyson, Owen Barfield, Emlyn Havard, and Colin Hardie, later Public Orator for the University. These men shared a willingness and ability to discuss any subject whether under the sun or not, and a common friendship with C. S. Lewis. Lewis was the lynch-pin of the group; the Inklings would meet in his rooms in Magdalen every Thursday or Friday evening. Lewis wrote to a Catholic ex-pupil in 1941 that "Williams, Dyson of Reading and my brother (Anglicans) and Tolkien and Havard (our doctor), your Church, are the 'Inklings' to whom my *Problem of Pain* was dedicated. We meet on Friday evenings in my rooms." The circle was first joined at an undetermined point between 1933 and 1938, and broke in 1949. The primary figures in the group, especially during the war, were Lewis, Charles Williams, and J. R. R. Tolkien.

*Edmund Crispin [Bruce Montgomery], *Swan Song*, 62. The Eagle and Child was just one of the Oxford pubs the Inklings frequented. They were also regulars at The Mitre, The White Horse, and The King's Arms.

The extensive bibliography on these three men—a partial list is given below—generally suffers on two counts.* All of it, except for Humphrey Carpenter's ground-breaking study, tends to the over-serious. A case in point would be Rossi's *The Politics of Fantasy*, in which the ecstatic conclusion of "Leaf by Niggle" elicits this reaction: "by then he is a lobotomized cipher, his freedom and creativity so hemmed and hampered that it is finally merely abstract."[2] Therein, one might suggest, the patient must minister to himself. Rossi's book, despite its promising title, does not mention the impact of World War Two on the writings of Lewis and Tolkien. This is a second problem with Inklings criticism: it fails to take into full account the effect of contemporary events on what is essentially a wartime group. Charles Williams moved from Oxford to London in Autumn 1939; he died before the end of the war in 1945. The writings of all three respond directly to the war, as, presumably, their conversations must have done. Carpenter's recreation of a typical Inklings meeting brings this out:

> 'Should we try, for instance, to be aware of what it's like, say, to be a fighter pilot being shot down in flames at this moment?'
> 'I should imagine Williams would think one ought to be very much aware of it indeed,' says Havard. 'Isn't that part of his "Co-inherence"?'[3]

At these Tuesday lunches and these evening meetings during the war, each of the three read from his respective work in progress. Tolkien records the readings in his letters. "I heard two chapters of a new novel by Charles Williams, read by him, this morning,"[4] he writes to his son Christopher on 10 November 1943, referring to *All Hallows' Eve*. C. S. Lewis read

*The Inklings bibliography includes: Carpenter, Humphrey, *The Inklings* (1978); Dowie, William John, "Religious Fiction in a Profane Time: Charles Williams, C. S. Lewis and J. R. R. Tolkien" (1970); Fuller, Edmund *et al.*, *Myth, Allegory, and Gospel; An Interpretation of J. R. R. Tolkien, C. S. Lewis, G. K. Chesterton [and] Charles Williams* (1974); Hillegas, Mark Robert, ed., *Shadows of Imagination; The Fantasies of C. S. Lewis, J. R. R. Tolkien, and Charles Williams* (1969); Kaufmann, U. Milo, "Aspects of the Paradisiacal in Tolkien's Work" in Lobdell, ed., *A Tolkien Compass* (1975); Plank, Robert, ' "The Scouring of the Shire": Tolkien's View of Fascism' in *A Tolkien Compass*; Rossi, Lee, *The Politics of Fantasy, C. S. Lewis and J. R. R. Tolkien* (1984); Swinfen, Ann, *In Defence of Fantasy* (1971); Urang, Gunnar, *Shadows of Heaven; Religion and Fantasy in the Writing of C. S. Lewis, Charles Williams, and J. R. R. Tolkien* (1971); Wright, Marjorie Evelyn, "The Cosmic Kingdom of Myth; A Study in the Myth-philosophy of Charles Williams, C. S. Lewis, and J. R. R. Tolkien" (1960).

from *The Great Divorce* some months later, under the title "Who Goes Home." Tolkien writes to Christopher of "a book on Hell, which I suggested should have been called rather 'Hugo's Home'."[5] And in 1940, Tolkien read from "Leaf by Niggle": "It was written (I think) just before the War began, though I first read it aloud to my friends early in 1940."[6] Though "Leaf by Niggle" is pre-war, it is still post-Munich; with *The Great Divorce* and *All Hallows' Eve*, it is very much a war work.

All three are quite consciously reimaginations of purgatory. *Descent into Hell* begins, and *All Hallows' Eve* continues, a modern *Commedia*: Carpenter writes that "*All Hallows' Eve* (as he named it) proved to be Williams' triumphant *Purgatorio*."[7] Carpenter also attests to Lewis' literary purgatory: "Lewis too was writing a story concerned with Purgatory, or at least with the point of balance between Heaven and Hell."[8] Carpenter does not mention, though, that Tolkien's "Leaf by Niggle" is also a purgatorial story. Tolkien expressly refers to it as such in his letter to Peter Hastings of 1954, quoted in the first chapter. The letter, a sermon on the nature of art as a form of Creation, bears quoting again:

> To conclude: having mentioned Free Will, I might say that in my myth I have used 'subcreation' in a special way (not the same as 'subcreation' as a term in criticism of art, though I tried to show allegorically how that might come to be taken up into Creation in some plane in my 'purgatorial' story *Leaf by Niggle* (Dublin Review 1945)) to make visible and physical the effects of Sin or misused Free Will by men.[9]

Tolkien did not send this letter, writing at its top: "It seemed to be taking myself too importantly."[10] The self-consciousness of this extraordinary document is seen especially in the word 'purgatorial.' The quotation marks surrounding the word suggest that the 'purgatorial' is deliberately attempted, perhaps as a result of conversation with Lewis and Williams.

Carpenter could be forgiven the omission of a short story written four years earlier from his discussion of the purgatories, were it not for the fact that he believes "Leaf by Niggle" to have been written in 1943–44, at about the same time as *The Great Divorce* and *All Hallows' Eve*. "Leaf by Niggle" can be dated by an altercation between Tolkien and Lady Agnew, a neighbor on Northmoor Road. The Great Tree in "Leaf by Niggle" was inspired by Tolkien's anxiety over a poplar tree:

> Of course some elements are explicable in biographical terms (so obsessively interesting to modern critics that they often value a piece of 'literature' solely

in so far as it reveals the author, and especially if that is in a discreditable light). There was a great tree - a huge poplar with vast limbs - visible through my window even as I lay in bed. I loved it, and was anxious about it. It had been savagely mutilated some years before, but had gallantly grown new limbs - though of course not with the unblemished grace of its former natural self; and now a foolish neighbour was agitating to have it felled."

Carpenter suggests in his biography of Tolkien that Lady Agnew wishes to cut it down in 1943–44." This cannot be so, for Tolkien read his fable to the Inklings in 1940. In the same letter which talks of Lady Agnew, Tolkien states that "Leaf by Niggle" was "written (I think) just before the war began."

Tolkien is uncertain about this, raising the possibility that his recollection is wrong. But supporting the premise that the work was written before the war is the gardener's limp. Mr. Parish, Niggle's neighbor, is "very critical about gardening" (198) and "had a lame leg, a genuine lame leg which gave him a good deal of pain" (201).* Tolkien wrote to Stanley Unwin on 19 December 1939 that "My accident just before the outbreak of war left me very unwell for a long while." A note to this explains that Tolkien injured himself while gardening. It was probably during the long recuperation from this gardening accident that Tolkien wrote "Leaf by Niggle." The story is thus a product of the pre-war twilight, the purgatorial period after Munich and before the fall of France.

Tolkien's short story is 'purgatorial' in the time of its writing, and in the condition of its writer during that time. A sick bed is a quintessential purgatory-on-earth, as one waits, suspended, to be declared healed. The story is also 'purgatorial' in its effect on the writer: "Leaf by Niggle" was written while the writing of *The Lord of the Rings* had stalled. Tolkien is concerned about more than a poplar tree: "Also, of course, I was anxious about my own internal tree, *The Lord of the Rings*. It was growing out of hand, and revealing endless new vistas - and I wanted to finish it, but the world was threatening." The tree which Niggle attempts to paint and which he finally sees after his death is rooted in Tolkien's internal as well as Northmoor Road's external tree. Niggle the artist, obsessed with precise detail, is very much a type for Tolkien himself; Tolkien writes of *The Lord of the Rings*: "I don't suppose there are many sentences that have not been

*J. R. R. Tolkien, "Leaf by Niggle," in *Poems and Stories* (London: Allen & Unwin, 1980), 201. References to this edition of "Leaf by Niggle" in this section will appear within the text.

niggled over."[15] "Leaf by Niggle" tells of an artist's life cut off before his life's work can be completed: writing "Niggle" cleaned the slate.

Writer's block, however, was not the only thing to be purged. "But the world was threatening": the slate had also to be cleaned of war. Tolkien writes of the fable's genesis:

> *Leaf by Niggle* arose suddenly and almost complete. It was written down almost at a sitting, and very nearly in the form in which it now appears. Looking at it myself now from a distance, I should say that, in addition to my tree-love (it was originally called *The Tree*), it arose from my own pre-occupation with *The Lord of the Rings*, the knowledge that it would be finished in great detail or not at all, and the fear (near certainty) that it would be 'not at all'. The war had arisen to darken all horizons.[16]

The last sentence is the first suggestion that the story's Minerva-like appearance, "suddenly and almost complete," was in any way triggered by the time of its writing. "Leaf by Niggle" was written in an attempt to brighten a horizon darkened by a host of contemporary events: Lady Agnew, a gardening injury, aporia, and the coming war.

That Niggle's purgatory is a response to war has gone unnoticed in Inklings criticism mainly because critics are looking for the war in the wrong place. The most common snare is to perceive *The Lord of the Rings* as an allegory of war. Tolkien did, after all, work on the book throughout the war. Robert Plank, in "The Scouring of the Shire: Tolkien's View of Fascism," suggests that Frodo returns to a fascist state. Tolkien's own disclaimer of this, which for some reason Plank quotes, sabotages his argument. Dr. Åke Ohlmarks prefaced the first Swedish translation of *The Lord of the Rings* in 1959 with an interpretation of the book as an allegory of contemporary geopolitics. Unfortunately for Dr. Ohlmarks, Tolkien read Swedish. His rebuttal to Ohlmarks' ludicrous commentary is a priceless caution to future biographers:

> *The Ring is in a certain way 'der Nibelungen Ring'* . . . .
> Both rings were round, and there the resemblance ceases. [. . .]
>
> *Here rules the personification of satanic might Sauron (read perhaps in the same partial fashion Stalin).*
> There is no 'perhaps' about it. I utterly repudiate any such 'reading', which angers me. The situation was conceived long before the Russian revolution. Such allegory is entirely foreign to my thought. The placing of Mordor in the east was due to simple narrative and geographical necessity, within my 'mythology'. [. . .]

There are reminiscences of journeys on foot in his own youth up into the Welsh border-regions.

As Bilbo said of the dwarves, he seems to know as much of my private pantries as I do myself. Or pretends to. I never walked in Wales or the marches in my youth. Why should I be made an object of fiction while still alive?[17]

In his foreword to *The Lord of the Rings*, Tolkien dismisses the presence of World War Two in his novel as a confusion of " 'applicability' with 'allegory.' "[18] As C. S. Lewis put it, talking of the trilogy, "These things were not devised to reflect any particular situation in the real world. It was the other way round; real events began, horribly, to conform to the pattern he had freely invented."[19]

But is this applicability completely an accident? One can respect Tolkien's resistance to allegorical interpretation of his text, for the book itself resists such interpretation at every turn, but surely the presence of the war affected Tolkien's writing, as it affected the work of every other major writer in the war. One need not fall into the trap of Joanna de Bortadano, who asked Tolkien in 1956 if the book was an allegory of Atomic Power.[20] The war quite possibly informs these lines from "The Shadow of the Past": "From there the power was spreading far and wide, and away far east and south there were wars and growing fear."[21] The placing of Mordor in the east may not be simply a matter of geographical necessity. Sometimes Tolkien protests too much. Writing of "The Shadow of the Past," "one of the oldest parts of the tale," he says that "It was written long before the foreshadow of 1939 had yet become a threat of inevitable disaster."[22] This must be a blind, for this chapter was written between February and March of 1938, by which time the coming war was obvious. Tolkien does admit to Stanley Unwin in 1938 that "The darkness of the present days has had some effect on it. Though it is not an 'allegory'."[23]

With "Leaf by Niggle" there is no smoke-screen; the story is quite clearly allegorical. Not of the war, but of Dante's *Purgatorio*. The progress of Niggle from the Northmoor Road to the earthly paradise is easily sketched. The story begins "There was once a little man called Niggle, who had a long journey to make" (195). Niggle begins this journey after catching his death of cold trying to help Parish, his neighbor, during a gale. Once dead, he is taken by a "Driver" to a "very large, dim railway station" (204), where he waits to be found worthy by a Court of Inquiry to advance to the next stage. The Driver, "tall, dressed all in black" (203), is, like Auden's scissor man, Conrad's cab-driver in *The Secret Agent*, and Lewis' Driver in *The Great Divorce*, Death. In Dante, he is both Charon and his purgatorial equivalent, the Angel that pilots the Ship of Souls. Neither does the railway station resist allegorical interpretation. Niggle waits there for centuries; the Court of Inquiry is "waiting for him to get better, and judging 'better' by some odd medical standard of their own" (206).

The railway station is not only a purgatory, it is particularly a war purgatory. The train careering helplessly towards war, an image so dear to British pre-war writers, comes to a sullen halt in 1940. Leonard Woolf describes the sheer boredom of war in *The Journey not the Arrival Matters* as "the feeling that one is endlessly waiting in a dirty grey railway station waiting-room, a cosmic railway station waiting-room, with nothing to do but wait endlessly for the next catastrophe."[24] In Charles Williams' *All Hallows' Eve*, Betty Wallingford reads the future in the newspaper in a railway station waiting-room: "She read one paper, finished it, folded it, laid it down, took up another, and so through all. She read the future, but the future was not known to her."[25] The pervasiveness of this image to describe the waiting of the early war may be attributable to the amount of time people were forced to spend in railway stations, waiting for trains which were few and far between.

Often, they were waiting for evacuees; in wartime, the railway station was more of an arrival than a departure platform. C. S. Lewis' *The Lion, the Witch, and the Wardrobe* (1950) is a story of four evacuees ("This story is about something that happened to them when they were sent away from London during the war because of the air-raids") and places the Professor's house "ten miles from the nearest railway station."[26] In *Prince Caspian*, the four children are whisked to Narnia from a railway platform. And in *The Last Battle*, the seven children of Narnia are killed on British Rail:

> "There *was* a real railway accident," said Aslan softly. "Your father and mother and all of you are—as you used to call it in the Shadow-Lands—dead. The term is over: the holidays have begun. The dream is ended: this is the morning."[27]

Escapist literature is set as far from the railway station as possible, distancing itself from the symbol of a purgatorial war world. To get to Narnia you have to get off the train.

When Niggle is finally permitted to leave the station he takes a one-coach engine to the next stage, the world of the painting he never finished:

Before him stood the Tree, his Tree, finished. If you could say that of a Tree that was alive, its leaves opening, its branches growing and bending in the wind that Niggle had so often felt or guessed, and had so often failed to catch. He gazed at the Tree, and slowly he lifted his arms and opening them wide.

'It's a gift!' he said. (212)

Carpenter closes his biography of Tolkien with these lines; they were read at a memorial service for Tolkien in California. Tolkien's Great Tree is many trees. It is Lady Agnew's poplar; it is his beloved *Pinus Nigra* in Oxford's Botanical Gardens, beside him in his last photograph. It is the "internal tree" of *The Lord of the Rings*, and all the trees within that book; it may also be the Fyfield elm of Arnold's "Thrysis":

> 'Tis done; and see
> Backed by the sunset, which doth glorify
> The orange and pale violet evening sky,
> Bare on its lonely ridge, the Tree! the Tree! (ll. 157–160)

The tree is a metaphor for his own life. Four days after the death of C. S. Lewis he writes: "So far I have felt the normal feelings of a man my age - like an old tree that is losing all its leaves one by one: this feels like an axe-blow near the roots."[28]

Above all, Niggle's tree is Dante's Tree of Knowledge at the top of Mount Purgatory. On reaching the earthly paradise, Dante sees the great tree burst into full blossom:

> *men che di rose e più che di vïole*
> *colore aprendo, s'innovò la pianta,*
> *che prima avea le ramora sì sole.* (32, 58–60)*

Niggle sees his Tree burst into the same flower: "The blossom on the Great Tree was shining like flame. All the birds were flying in the air and singing" (217). The fire and the rose are one once more; this is Tolkien at his most Dantesque. Dante compares his flames with the blossoms on Pyramus' mulberry tree, and when he first reaches *"la divina foresta spessa e viva"* (28, 2), he too hears the birds singing:

*"Showing less of the rose and more of the violet, the plant renewed itself, which before had such bare branches."

[...] li augelletti per le cime
[...] con piena letizia l'ore prime,
cantando, ricevieno intra le folgie. (28, 14–17)*

For both, the earthly paradise is a way-station, where the final purgation must be enacted before ascending to paradise. Before reaching the distant mountains, Niggle must drink from a Spring:

> They found the Spring in the heart of the Forest; only once long ago had Niggle imagined it, but he had never drawn it. Now he perceived that it was the source of the lake that glimmered, far away and the nourishment of all that grew in the country. The few drops made the water astringent, rather bitter, but invigorating; and it cleared the head. (215)

A spring, the river Eunoe, runs through Dante's paradise as well: *"ed ecco più andar mi tolse un rio"* (28, 25).† As Matilda plunges Dante into the water *"Asperges me"* is sung (31, 98); for both, the water is an invigorating and necessary purgation.§ After drinking from the spring, there remains only the ascent: Niggle is "going to learn about sheep, and the high pasturages, and look at a wider sky, and walk ever further and further towards the Mountains, always uphill" (217). Dante ends the *Purgatorio* coming from the waters, as a plant covered with new leaves, ready to climb to the stars:

Io ritornai dalla santissima onda
rifatto sì come piante novelle
rinovellate di novella fronda,
puro e disposto a salire alle stelle. (33, 142–45)‖

"Leaf by Niggle," then, is a " 'purgatorial' story" in every way a story can be purgatorial. It follows Dante's *Purgatorio* in its general structure

---

*"The divine forest thick and alive"; "The little birds in the treetops greeted the dawn with fullness, singing, among the leaves."

†"And suddenly, blocking my way, a river."

§"Purge me." For Dante the water is not bitter but surpassing sweet: *"a tutti altri sapori esto è di sopra"* (28, 133). There are, arguably, differences between "Leaf by Niggle" and *The Divine Comedy*. That Parish bids farewell to Niggle need not imply that Parish represents Virgil. As Tolkien writes to Jane Neave, "It ["Leaf by Niggle"] is not really or properly an 'allegory' so much as 'mythical' " (320).

‖"I returned from the holy waters remade as new plants are renewed with new leaves, pure and ready to climb to the stars."

and in its smallest detail. It is purgatorial in effect, allowing Tolkien to continue *The Lord of the Rings*. It responds to the purgatory of the time. Finally, it is purgatorial in that it is fantasy. Dante invokes the Muse of Fantasy in *Purgatorio* 17:

> *O imaginativa che ne rube*
> *tal volta sì du fuor, ch'om non s'accorge*
> *perchè dintorno suonin mille tube,*
> *chi move te, se'l senso non ti porge?*
> *Moveti lume che nel ciel s'informa,*
> *per sè o per voler che giù lo scorge.* (17, 13–18)*

That light, from a world outside the world, is received and celebrated in the wartime work of all three of Lewis' Inklings.

C. S. Lewis and the Perversion of Purgatory

> The meeting of the "Tragedian" with his wife is consciously modelled on that of Dante and Beatrice at the end of the *Purgatorio*: i.e. it is the same predicament, only going wrong.
>
> Lewis

In 1939, Mrs. Joan Bennett was perturbed about the unpalatable prospect of eternal damnation. C. S. Lewis wrote to reassure her:

> Residence in Limbo I am told is compatible with 'perishing everlastingly' and you'll find it quite jolly, for whereas Heaven is an acquired taste, Limbo is a place of 'perfect *natural* happiness'. In fact you may be able to realize your wish 'of attending with one's whole mind to the history of the human spirit'. There are grand libraries in Limbo, endless discussions, and no colds. There will be a faint melancholy because you'll all know that you have missed the bus, but that will provide a subject for poetry. The scenery is pleasant though tame. The climate endless autumn.†

---

*"O fantasy, which steals us at times from the outside world, so that man ignores the sound of a thousand trumpets, who moves you, if the senses do not? A light moves you that is made in heaven, either by itself or by a will directing it from above." These lines form the epigraph to Ann Swinfen's *In Defence of Fantasy*.

†C. S. Lewis, Letter to Mrs. Joan Bennett, 5 April 1939, *Letters*, 164. The absence of colds in Limbo was perhaps inspired by Lewis' influenza at the time.

Again, it is autumn in Limbo. MacNeice describes the autumn world of 1938 as "life rotating in an office sleep / As long as things are normal," in *Autumn Journal*.¹ Stephen Spender begins his wartime journal on 3 September 1939 feeling the weight of the season: "Sentences are covered with leaves, and I really cannot see the line of the branch that carries the green meaning."² Auden continues Lewis' idea of "endless autumn" in "Autumn 1940": "Returning each morning from a timeless world / The senses open upon a world of time."³ Eliot's cry, "it *was* autumn," resounds through the writings of the early war.

Lewis' perception of an autumnal world is, like Eliot's, both religious and intensely personal. His choice of climate provides a moving back-drop for his last letter: "Thanks for your note. Yes, autumn is really the best of the seasons; and I'm not sure that old age isn't the best part of life. But of course, like autumn, it doesn't *last*."⁴ Lewis died in autumn, the day John F. Kennedy was shot. He writes to Sister Penelope a month before his death, "When you die, and if 'prison visiting' is allowed, come down and look me up in Purgatory."⁵ Lewis passes from one autumnal world to another, from a November death-bed to the November world of Purgatory. His jocularity belies a deep-seated preoccupation with the middle ground between heaven and hell. In 1939, that middle ground is Limbo; during the war, it becomes Purgatory.

Lewis' wartime letters trace this progression. In May 1939, he calls *Romola* "a most purgative work on the *facilis descensus* because the final state of the character is so different from his original state and yet all the transitions are so dreadfully natural."⁶ *Facilis descensus averni*: Lewis is still looking downward, here into Virgil's Hell. But Tito Melema's downward path is interpreted as a cautionary, or purgative, tale. Two years later Lewis reaches the Ante-Purgatory, feeling himself liable to be incarcerated in "some sort of Borstal institution on the lower foot-hills of the mountains of Purgatory."⁷ As "mountains" indicates, Lewis is not strictly referring to Dante's *Purgatorio*. By the end of his life, Lewis considers himself destined for a purgatorial prison: "come down and look me up in Purgatory."

The transition from Limbo to Purgatory during the war parallels that of another converted Christian writer, Evelyn Waugh. C. S. Lewis' Limbo sounds remarkably similar to Ambrose Silk's in *Put Out More Flags*: "In Limbo one has natural happiness without the beatific vision; no harps; no communal order; but wine and conversation and imperfect, various humanity."⁸ By the end of the war, in *Brideshead Revisited*, the Limbo that

Silk looks forward to has been transformed into a Catholic Purgatory. Waugh wrote *Put Out More Flags* within a year of Lewis' letter to Mrs. Joan Bennett; *Brideshead Revisited* was written at the same point in the war as *The Great Divorce*. Both the latter books are concerned with Purgatory; neither refers precisely to the *Purgatorio*. As he suggests in the phrase "mountains of Purgatory," Lewis has his own ideas about the middle world between Heaven and Hell. Rather than bridge the gap between Heaven and Hell, Lewis' Purgatory widens the chasm. He begins the preface with a statement of perverse purpose: "Blake wrote the Marriage of Heaven and Hell [...] I have written of their Divorce" (5).*

The Great Divorce is anticipated in his letter to Mrs. Bennett: "You'll all know that you have missed the bus, but that will provide a subject for poetry." *The Great Divorce* elaborates upon this vision, dramatizing the bus-ride that those in Limbo miss. At the start of the book, the narrator stands waiting for the bus:

> I seemed to be standing in a bus queue by the side of a long, mean street. Evening was just closing in and it was raining. I had been wandering for hours in similar mean streets, always in the rain and always in evening twilight. (11)

This could be the beginning of a typical war novel. It is set in war twilight, in the same city streets as Philip Larkin's *Jill* (1940), Williams' *All Hallows' Eve*, or Patrick Hamilton's *Hangover Square*. The bus queue is a novel way of expressing a common waiting. With "I seemed" Lewis returns to the hallucinatory world of Wilfred Owen's "Strange Meeting": "It seemed that out of battle I escaped" (l. 1). But though *The Great Divorce* is certainly a response to war, it is scarcely a traditional one.

The dismal city occupies two worlds: it is London, and a "grey town" (17) inhabited by ghosts. A poet reveals in conversation on the bus that "He had jumped under a train . . ." (17). Parallel worlds, after *Little Gidding* and *Descent into Hell*, are familiar in 1943; the dead will walk through the city of London in *All Hallows' Eve*: "The two dead girls went together slowly out of the Park."⁹ Though the "grey town" is a standard evocation of a war world, its position in the other world is different. Neither precisely Hell, nor precisely Purgatory, the middle ground conflates the two. Throughout *The Great Divorce* Lewis stresses that the worlds of Hell and

*C. S. Lewis, *The Great Divorce* (New York: Macmillan, 1946), 5. References to this edition of *The Great Divorce* in this section will appear within the text.

Purgatory are separated only by perspective. Lewis writes in the preface: "I think earth, if chosen instead of Heaven, will turn out to have been, all along, only a region in Hell: and earth, if put second to Heaven, to have been from the beginning a part of Heaven itself" (7). George Macdonald, a Spirit encountered during the novel, puts this more succinctly: "If they leave that grey town behind it will not have been Hell. To any that leaves it, it is Purgatory" (67).

Little Gidding has presented a similar conflation, but Lewis goes one step further. He compresses Dante's structure: the mountain of Purgatory is collapsed into Dante's concentric Hell. The poet on the bus explains:

> "All the people you've met were living near the bus stop: but they'd taken centuries—of our time—to get there, by gradual removals."
> "And what about the earlier arrivals? I mean—there must be people who came from earth to your town even longer ago."
> "That's right. There are. They've been moving on and on. Getting further apart. They're so far off by now that they could never think of coming to the bus stop at all. Astronomical distances." (19)

Lewis outlines a Purgatory in reverse, where the challenge is not to climb upward but to stay in the same place. As Macdonald says later, speaking of Christ's love, "It is like when you throw a stone into a pool, and the concentric rings spread out further and further" (108). A sinner who treads water long enough, resisting the temptation to ripple away to the outer rings, will eventually catch the bus. The middle world becomes, in Lewis' system, a vivid waiting, a kinetic stasis. In this thoroughly original synthesis of Limbo and Purgatory, Lewis distills the essence of purgatorial waiting.

The grey town, then, is both Limbo and an Ante-Purgatory. The Driver of the bus is described as a contemporary version of *"l'uccel divino"* (2, 38) who pilots the Ship of Souls to the base of Mount Purgatory: "It was a wonderful vehicle, blazing with golden light, heraldically coloured. The Driver himself seemed full of light and he used only one hand to drive with" (13). And yet the actual destination of the bus seems to be the top of Mount Purgatory rather than its foot:

> We were mounting all the time. At last the top of the cliff became visible like a thin line of emerald green stretched tight as a fiddle-string. Presently we glided over that top: we were flying above a level, grassy country through which there ran a wide river. (26)

The bus brings the souls both to the foot of Purgatory and to the earthly paradise at its height, as the grey town was both the first circle in Hell and the first circle in Purgatory. *The Great Divorce* describes the leap to the earthly paradise; it also, at the same time, describes the step-by-step ascent towards it. Lewis' middle world embraces the gates of both Heaven and Hell.

In picturing the earthly paradise, Lewis follows Dante as closely as Tolkien. *The Great Divorce* shares a great deal with the story Tolkien read to his friends in 1940. The cab-driver in "Leaf by Niggle" was called "The Driver," who also conducted dead souls to a purgatorial world. These worlds share the same ground. In "Leaf by Niggle" the turf is "green and close; and yet he could see every blade distinctly."[10] In *The Great Divorce*, the earthly paradise is not merely a realistically painted world, but a world more real than earth, which the phantom visitors from the grey town cannot disturb: "I noticed that the grass did not bend under their feet: even the dew drops were not disturbed" (27). Lewis has reversed Dante once again. In the *Purgatorio*, the Shades gasp at Dante's shadow, evidence of his reality; in *The Great Divorce*, it is the visitors who are unreal: "I gasped when I saw them" (27). Every blade is distinct and, being heavenly matter, unbreakable: "The little flower was hard, not like wood or even like iron, but like diamond" (28); "The grass, hard as diamonds to my unsubstantial feet, made me feel as if I were walking on wrinkled rock" (31). Niggle's painted world has returned with a vengeance. Through both Tolkien's and Lewis' worlds there runs a stream, a conscious imitation of Dante's two-part stream. On one side the stream is called Lethe, washing away the memory of sin, and on the other Eunoe, in whose waters Dante is purified: "*Quinci Letè; così dall'altro lato / Eunoè si chiama*" (28, 130–31). The astringent waters of Niggle's river have been seen to parallel those of Eunoe; the speaker in *The Great Divorce* finds the water "Very cold and clear, between two green hills. A little like Lethe" (82).

As the direct reference to Lethe suggests, Lewis' writing is more strictly allegorical than Tolkien's. Tolkien always distrusted allegory, denying it in his own books and decrying it in others. *The Lion, the Witch, and the Wardrobe*, together with the whole Narnia series, came in for special rebuke under this light. Lewis is Tolkien's reverse in this respect; the mapping with the *Purgatorio* in *The Great Divorce* is deliberate.* In an otherwise

---

*What is more, his Dante is fresh: Lewis had read the *Commedia* aloud with Colin Hardie before the war. See Humphrey Carpenter, *The Inklings*, 194.

unpublished letter to Mr. W. Kinter of 29 September 1951, quoted in Carpenter's *The Inklings*, Lewis talks of *The Great Divorce*:

> 'The meeting of the "Tragedian" with his wife is consciously modelled on that of Dante and Beatrice at the end of the *Purgatorio*: i.e. it is the same predicament, only going wrong. I intended readers to spot these resemblances.'¹

As the letter to Kinter perhaps establishes, there are many such correspondences, all illuminating to varying degrees. Since Lewis "intended readers to spot these resemblances," they are well worth searching out.

The Great Divorce is divided into separate encounters between the Spirits of Heaven and the phantoms who have journeyed from the grey town. Sometimes the narrator meets a Spirit himself, sometimes he witnesses the encounter. As in Dante, each phantom, or Shade, represents a specific vice. As the book progresses the vices conform more closely to the seven sins on Dante's cornices; the book gradually becomes more clearly an analogue. The first encounters, then, are not richly allegorical. On the bus-ride, the narrator meets a Tousle-Headed Poet, who is, if anyone, Casella, in that he is the first encountered shade, and an artist. Beyond that, there is little to connect them. Similarly, the Intelligent Man, the second man the narrator meets, may or may not be Manfred: both explain to the traveller something of the structure of the place. Alighting from the bus, a fellow-traveller meets the Ghost of a man who murdered his friend. He is understandably upset: "If they choose to let in a bloody murderer all because he makes a poor mouth at the last moment, that's their lookout" (34). The narrator has reached the Late-Repentant, the last terrace on the Ante-Purgatory. Soon afterwards, two velvet-footed lions appear, perhaps the two guardians in the eighth canto, at the gate of Mount Purgatory itself.

With the entrance into Purgatory Proper, the allusions to Dante are more clear-cut. Finding the water hard enough to walk on, the narrator walks upstream until he discovers, as Niggle did, a glorious tree:

> Near the place where the fall plunged into the lake there grew a tree. Wet with the spray, half-veiled in foam-bows, flashing with the bright, innumerable birds that flew among its branches, it rose in many shapes of billowy foliage, huge as a fen-land cloud. From every point apples of gold gleamed through the leaves. (49)

This is "the Great Tree," Dante's Tree of Knowledge, around which birds also sang in "Leaf by Niggle." Dante's tree has apple blossoms as well:

"fioretti del melo / che del suo pome li angeli fa ghiotti" (32, 73–74).* And next to the tree in *The Great Divorce* is a "hawthorn bush" (49), whose red berries once again recall Dante's image of Pyramus and the mulberry, an image Beatrice herself recalls beside the tree in the thirty-third canto, calling Dante *"un Piramo alla gelsa"* (33, 69)† for his stained mind. We seem to have already reached, as in "Leaf by Niggle," the earthly paradise.

But this tree is not just the Tree of Knowledge, it is also the tree that tantalizes the gluttonous on the sixth terrace. In Dante's twenty-second canto, an enormous Fruit-Tree, *"con pomi a odorar soavi e boni"* (22, 132) grows beside a cascade: *"cadea dell'alta roccia un liquor chiaro / e si spandeva per le folgie suso"* (22, 137–38).§ As Dante and Virgil walk towards it, a voice forbids them to eat the fruit: *"Di questo cibo avrete caro"* (22, 141). Much the same thing happens in *The Great Divorce*. A man in a bowler hat reaches for windfall apples from the tree, only to find them a heavy burden: "I saw him rise staggering to his feet actually holding the smallest of the apples in his hands" (51). From the waterfall next to the tree comes a familiar cry: ' "Fool. Put it down," said a great voice suddenly' (51). Lewis compounds the two trees; the work is simultaneously an ascent up Mount Purgatory and a tour of the earthly paradise. (Incidentally, Dante also compounds the tree of avarice and the tree of knowledge. The injunction *"Di questo cibo avrete caro"* is addressed to Dante not only as a potential glutton but also as a Son of Adam.)

Herein after the shades begin to acquire specific sins. Leaving the Avaricious Man, the narrator meets "the Solid One" (60), who quite clearly represents Pride, or Vanity: "Do you really suppose I'm going out there among all those people, like *this*?" (60–61). An artist in the next chapter betrays Envy, differing from Pride only in that it includes fear: "Do you mean those damned Neo-Regionalists have won after all?" (83). A woman's tirade in the following chapter displays Anger, and a Man in the next is purged of Lust, represented by a Lizard on his shoulder. An Angel metamorphoses the Lizard into a stallion: "What is a Lizard compared with a stallion? Lust is a poor, weak, whimpering whispering thing compared with that richness and energy of desire which will arise when lust has been killed" (104–105). As in Dante, Lust is purged by fire—the

---

*"Apple blossoms which make the angels hungry for its fruit."

†"A Pyramus to the mulberry."

§"With apples having a sweet and good smell"; "there fell from the high rock a clear water which disappeared among the leaves."

Angel is called "the Burning One" (102)—and is the last sin to be en-countered before the earthly paradise. The next chapter introduces the Lady and the Tragedian, whose meeting, as Lewis wrote, is "consciously modelled on that of Dante and Beatrice at the end of the *Purgatorio*." The two planes have intersected; the narrator has finally reached the top of the mountain.

George Macdonald has been accompanying the narrator through these last chapters. Macdonald was to Lewis as Virgil to Dante: possibly the strongest poetic influence on his work. Lewis, on meeting Macdonald, drops his narrative persona and simply confesses a debt. In his confession he compares himself with Dante:

> I tried, trembling, to tell this man all that his writings had done for me. I tried to tell him how a certain frosty afternoon at Leatherhead Station when I first bought a copy of *Phantastes* (being then about sixteen years old) had been to me what the first sight of Beatrice had been to Dante: *Here begins the New Life.* (65)

But Macdonald is more Virgil than Beatrice: his are the academic discussions of the soul, the conclusions drawn from the sight of each sinner. Soon the narrator is calling Macdonald by Dante's name for Virgil: "my Teacher" (96).

The entrance of the Lady is preceded by a procession of Spirits:

> First came bright Spirits, not the Spirits of men, who danced and scattered flowers—soundlessly falling, lightly drifting flowers, though by the standards of the ghost-world each petal would have weighed a hundred-weight and their fall would have been like the crashing of boulders. Then, on the left and right, at each side of the forest avenue, came youthful shapes, boys upon one hand, and girls upon the other. If I could remember their singing and write the notes, no man who read that score would ever grow sick or old. Between them went musicians: and after these a lady in whose honour all this was being done. (106–107)

The writing of any Christian fabulist is inevitably inspired by Dante: here Lewis draws from the pageant which introduces Beatrice in the twenty-ninth canto.* The narrator continues with the strange meeting of the Lady

---

*There is also a suggestion, in the falling flowers, of *Little Gidding*'s "metal leaves" (LG, 87).

with a Dwarf holding a Tragedian by a chain.* She must convince the Dwarf to release the Tragedian within himself, an act as difficult for the Dwarf as Dante's passing through the fire: "I do not know that I ever saw anything more terrible than the struggle of that Dwarf Ghost against joy" (115). Eventually, he cannot relinquish his "death-line" (115), and the Dwarf and the Tragedian vanish. Lewis intended the resemblance, he also intended its perversion: "i.e. it is the same predicament, only going wrong." He raises the parallel of Beatrice's reunion with Dante only to present its monstrous inversion. Throughout *The Great Divorce* Lewis perverts the expected course of purgation. Except for the Lustful Man, all the ghosts fail the tests and return to hell. Only one man is purged; the *Purgatorio* is turned upside-down.

Lewis is a past master at twisting an expected paradigm inside out, as *The Screwtape Letters*, written for *The Manchester Guardian* during 1941, attests. This is not to say that he enjoyed doing so: in a later preface to *The Screwtape Letters* he says "though it was easy to twist one's mind into the diabolical attitude, it was not fun, or not for long."[12] Lewis always widens the chasm out of more than perversity; both *The Screwtape Letters* and *The Great Divorce* are responding to the time. Screwtape writes to his nephew: "Let us therefore think rather how to use, than how to enjoy, this European war."[13] The immense popularity of Screwtape when he appeared in 1941 was partly circumstantial: the public at the time had an invested interest in the workings of the diabolical mind. Lewis' presentation of a World Turned Upside Down in *The Great Divorce* is also, in a sense, a record of contemporary history.

From the opening in the grey town twilight, *The Great Divorce* is clearly a product of the war. Throughout the book Lewis uses military metaphor to suggest the diamantine hardness of the surroundings. The Ghost attempting to reach the apples faces a belt of lilies: "It might as well have tried to tread down an anti-tank trap as to walk on them" (50). The Hard-Bitten Ghost warns the narrator about the rain: "every raindrop will make a hole in you, like a machine-gun bullet" (57). The images are drawn from war because Lewis is tapping the collective imagination of a wartime audience. This in itself is Dantesque, for the *Purgatorio* is, with the whole *Commedia*, very much a war poem. The imagery in the earthly paradise,

---

*The image casts forward to *The Lion, the Witch, and the Wardrobe*, where the tragedian Edmund is roped to the Dwarf before the White Witch during the great thaw (97).

as Sinclair observes, comes from the parade ground: "in the whole account of the pageant there is a marked choice of expression more or less military—*pennons, standards, banners, leaders, file, array*, with *arms, squadron, soldiery, colours* in the thirty-second canto."[14] The *Commedia* was written of and for a wartime audience; the shades Dante meets are often veterans of the Guelf-Ghibbeline war. The Hard-Bitten Ghost, in *The Great Divorce*, is a veteran of both world wars: "And all through two wars what didn't they say about the good time coming if only I'd be a brave boy and go on being shot at?" (55).

Lewis hints at the wartime setting of *The Great Divorce* through such glances: the war world reappears dramatically at the close of the book. Lewis wakes from his Wonderland into a real nightmare:

> Next moment the folds of my Teacher's garment were only the folds of the old ink-stained cloth on my study table which I had pulled down with me as I fell from my chair. The blocks of light were only the books which I had pulled off with it, falling about my head. I awoke in a cold room, hunched on the floor beside a black and empty grate, the clock striking three, and the siren howling overhead. (128)

This siren, the final image of *The Great Divorce*, shatters a complacent reader's detachment, thrusting all that has gone before into the context of war. The purgatorial failures acquire a new immediacy; the book suddenly becomes a response to war. The air-raid siren is a favorite device of World War Two literature, a trump card that raises war writing to a new, more urgent level. Pauline hears a siren before meeting John Struther in *Descent into Hell*. Sirens wail throughout the war work of Henry Green, Patrick Hamilton, and Evelyn Waugh. *Little Gidding*'s dawn encounter closes with "the blowing of the horn."*

*Little Gidding and *The Great Divorce* have a great deal in common. They are both recreations of Dante, both conflate hell and purgatory, both are set in air raids in World War Two, and both end with a siren overhead. Eliot also filters into the twilight at the beginning of *The Great Divorce*, a strange light that can be considered either as deepening into night or, for the Intelligent Man, growing into daylight: "in this subdued and delicate half-light is the promise of the dawn" (24). This *ambage* is also distilled in Eliot's "waning dusk," as Christopher Ricks has writtten: "Eliot's imagination chose to add to 'dusk' exactly the adjective which would *not* clarify but dim any assurance as to which of the two dusks it was [. . .] the phrase—in its evocation of eerie process and in its uncoercive aptness to the haunting equivocation of the whole scene (the vision by night is an illumination, and daybreak is likely to bring disfigured obfuscation)—is a glory of the poem" ("A Note on *Little Gidding*," 152).

Sirens also sound through the dead city in Charles Williams' *All Hallows' Eve*, read to the Inklings at the same time as *The Great Divorce*. Lewis met Williams just before the war, and introduced him to the Inklings on his arrival in Oxford in 1939. Tolkien resented the intrusion, and dates the Inklings' fall by Williams' arrival. His clerihew on Charles Williams after the success of *The Figure of Beatrice* (1943) betrays this resentment:

> The sales of Charles Williams
> Leapt up by millions,
> When a reviewer surmised
> He was only Lewis disguised.[15]

His dislike of Williams was partly a reaction to Lewis' admiration for the newcomer, an adulation bordering on idolatry. Lewis' dedication to Williams of *A Preface to* Paradise Lost (1942) is Elizabethan in its indulgent eulogy: "You were a *vagus* thrown among us by the chance of war. [...] Apparently, the door of the prison [of Milton criticism] was really unlocked all the time; but it was only you who thought of trying the handle. Now we can all come out."[16] Lewis' *Preface* was begun soon after Williams' lecture on chastity in *Comus*, a lecture Lewis described to his brother in February 1940: "It was a beautiful sight to see a whole roomful of modern young men and women sitting in that absolute silence which can not be faked, very puzzled, but spell-bound."[17] That Lewis' *Preface* and Williams' lecture share a common subject is no coincidence. The war work of Williams and Lewis has not only Dante's but Milton's Hell in common.

In *A Preface to* Paradise Lost, Lewis examines Milton's Hell. His description of Satan's world sounds like a threat:

> To admire Satan, then, is to give one's vote not only for a world of misery, but also for a world of lies and propaganda, of wishful thinking, of incessant autobiography. Yet the choice is possible. Hardly a day passes without some slight movement towards it in each one of us. That is what makes *Paradise Lost* so serious a poem. The thing is possible, and the exposure of it is resented.[18]

The seriousness of *Paradise Lost* rests in its immediate relevance to the modern world. The same is true of Dante: the two hells are similar in their value as metaphor for a present evil otherwise beyond metaphor. The chapter from which this paragraph is taken has as its epigraph lines from the beginning of Dante's *Inferno*: *"le genti dolorose / c'hanno perduto il ben dell'intelletto."** Lewis also brings Milton and Dante together in *The Great Divorce*. George Macdonald quotes Milton to the narrator twice, once with the appearance of the Lady—*"A thousand liveried angels lackey her"* (107)—and once in a discussion of the damnation of souls: ' "Milton was right," said my Teacher. "The choice of every lost soul can be expressed in the words 'Better to reign in Hell than serve in Heaven' " ' (69). Lewis' interest in both Hells is in part an attempt to come to terms with Hitler, as his presentation and perversion of Purgatory in *The Great Divorce* is in part a response to war.†

Lewis and Williams share an interest in Dante's and Milton's Hell; they also share a life-long obsession with Purgatory. *All Hallows' Eve* continues along the passageway which connects the purgatorial world of London during the war and the middle ground between Heaven and Hell. Niggle enters the other world in death, Lewis in dream; Williams does not need to do so. Williams' last work superimposes the supernatural upon the real world. His setting is the City of London, in autumn, during the war, where ghosts and necromancers walk together with W.A.A.C. nurses and war painters. The novel draws on Williams' past work, especially *Descent into Hell*, on Eliot's work, especially *Little Gidding*, on Dante, and on the wartime writings of the Inklings. *All Hallows' Eve* will place the capstone upon the Literature of Experience.

---

*C. S. Lewis, *A Preface to* Paradise Lost, 94. The epigraph is from *Inferno* 3, 17–18: "the miserable people who have lost the benefit of intellect."

†Margery Allingham will be seen in chapter VII to make a similar conjunction in *The Tiger in the Smoke*, combining the Hells of Milton, Virgil, and Dante in the Canon Avril's confrontation with a man very much like Hitler.

Further Co-inherence: "The Significance of Charles Williams"

> It has certainly been thought, but the speculation is that of
> dreamers, that in the year of our great danger the grand attack
> of our enemies succeeded; that London and England perished;
> and that all we who then died entered it together and live there
> till we have wrought out our salvation—to enjoy (purgatorially)
> a freedom unpermitted on earth.
>
> Williams.

Charles Williams and T. S. Eliot first met each other between 1927 and
1934, at one of Lady Ottoline Morrell's Thursday afternoon teas at Gower
Street. Four different sources give four different dates for this encounter.
David Evans stakes the earliest claim: "When they met in 1927, both men
were a part of the checkered literary life of London, Williams as a staff
member of the Oxford Press, Eliot as editor of *The Criterion*."[1] According
to Eliot himself, in his introduction to *All Hallows' Eve*, the two men met
for the first time between 1928 and 1930: "It was in the late 'twenties, I
think, that I first met Charles Williams, and it was through the friend who
first called my attention to his work that the introduction was effected."[2]
Alice Hadfield's *An Introduction to Charles Williams* offers a third possibility: "They had met at a gathering of Lady Ottoline Morrell's soon after
the publication of *The Place of the Lion* in 1931."[3] Humphrey Carpenter
suggests that the meeting took place in 1934: "Eliot had been told to read
War in Heaven and *The Place of the Lion* by Lady Ottoline Morrell, and
shortly afterwards (in 1934) she invited Williams to one of her London
tea parties to meet Eliot."[4] 1927 is too early since Lady Morrell did not
set up her teas until the following summer; 1934 is too late since by 1931
she was already "a faded relic of a great hostess."[5] Since Eliot mentions
having read *The Place of the Lion* before Lady Morrell's invitation, even
his own opinion may be respectfully discounted. The right date is probably
1931.

It is extremely difficult to pinpoint when Charles Williams first met
T. S. Eliot; it is next to impossible to separate the literary influence of the
one upon the other. The exact moment of their meeting is of consequence
only to biographers; the precise nature of their literary meeting-points is
of critical importance. Ambiguity surrounds the friendship of Eliot and
Williams right from the start, and as their friendship progresses, it is harder

and harder to tell who is borrowing from whom. Eliot and Williams freely exchanged literary ideas in their works; the results of that correspondence will be assessed here.

Both men were in London before the outbreak of war. Charles Williams was editing and reviewing for Oxford University Press at Amen House, while Eliot worked his way up the ranks of Faber & Faber. Eliot did much in his capacity as director of Faber & Faber to further Williams' career. Beginning in 1937, Eliot, by his own admission to Mary Trevelyan, "launched" Williams.[6] He commissioned works for Williams to write: *Witchcraft* (1941) and *The Figure of Beatrice* were among the results of Eliot's attention. Williams sometimes resented this: he wrote to a friend that Eliot "is being a Pest" in asking him to rewrite the opening to *The Figure of Beatrice*.[7] The two reviewed each other's work throughout the war, which Williams did not see out. Eliot wrote an unsigned obituary for him in *The Times* of 17 May 1945.

In the works themselves the parallel lines run closer together. The Canterbury Festival presented Eliot's *Murder in the Cathedral* (1935) and Williams' play *Cranmer* (1936) in consecutive years. Auden compares the two in *Secondary Worlds*, discussing Williams' skeletal Figura Rerum and Eliot's Tempters as representatives of similar secondary worlds.[8] Eliot's plays, particularly *The Cocktail Party*, borrow considerably from Williams. Rossell Robbins has discussed *Descent into Hell* as "A Possible Analogue for *The Cocktail Party*," and Lois Thrash has unearthed traces of *The Greater Trumps* in that play as well.[9] The "dove descending" in *Little Gidding* may originate in Williams' *The Descent of the Dove*. *Descent into Hell* will be seen to provide much of the imagery for *Little Gidding*, which in turn leads directly into *All Hallows' Eve*.

The *locus classicus* for influence studies of Williams and Eliot is *Burnt Norton*'s still point:

> At the still point of the turning world. Neither flesh nor fleshless;
> Neither from nor towards; at the still point, there the dance is,
> But neither arrest nor movement. (BN, 62–64)

According to both men, the still point is borrowed from Charles Williams' *The Greater Trumps*: "Charles Williams told me, and Eliot confirmed, that the image of the dance around the 'still point' was suggested by Williams's novel *The Greater Trumps*" (HG, 85). Nancy Coningsby, watching a miniature cosmos in the dance of a pack of Tarot cards, sees the Fool standing motionless at its center: "It was still: it alone in the middle of all that curious dance did not move"; "The dance went on in the void; only even there she saw in the centre the motionless Fool."[10] Nancy experiences a familiar *Erhebung* from the perception of that still point: "The very dance itself seemed to have paused in her, so motionless her light form held itself, so rapt in its breathless suspension as the words sounded through her."[11] Again, "For an infinitesimal fraction of time the immortal dance stood still to receive the recollection of that ever-moving and never-broken repose of sovereign being."[12] Eliot's borrowing from these passages is straightforward: his still dance surrounds with "a grace of sense, a white light still and moving, / *Erhebung* without motion" (BN, 73–74). The still point, though, does not rest in Eliot's first quartet.

Charles Williams echoes the stillness of *Burnt Norton* one year later in *Descent into Hell*. Pauline Anstruther dances within it at the close of Peter Stanhope's play:

> She had had relation with her ancestor and with that other man more lately dead and with her grandmother—all the presently disincarnate presences which lived burningly in the stillness, through which the fire burned, and the stillness was the fire. She danced out of it, a flame flung up, a leaf catching to a flame. They were rushing towards the end of the play, an end, an end rushing towards the earth and the earth rushing to meet it. The words were no longer separated from the living stillness, they were themselves the life of the stillness, and though they sounded in it they no more broke it than the infinite particles of creation break the eternal contemplation of God in God. The stillness turned upon itself; the justice of the stillness drew all the flames and leaves, the dead and living, the actors and spectators, into its power. (186)*

Once more, there is dancing amid the burning leaves. On either side of the procession in *The Great Divorce*, "the undersides of the leafy branches had begun to tremble with dancing light."[13] Williams' vision, like that of Lewis, reimagines Dante's passage through the flame in *Purgatorio* 27, which also juxtaposes the flower and the flame. The moment clearly refers to Eliot's first quartet as well. The words of the play sounding in the stillness, turning upon themselves, are the words of *Burnt Norton* V:

> Words, after speech, reach
> Into the silence. Only by the form, the pattern,

*Charles Williams, *Descent into Hell* (1937; rpt. Grand Rapids: Eerdmans, 1985), 186. References to this edition of *Descent into Hell* in this section will appear within the text.

> Can words or music reach
> The stillness, as a Chinese jar still
> Moves perpetually in its stillness. (BN, 139–43)

Pauline's dance not only throws back to *Burnt Norton*, it looks ahead to *East Coker*: "So the darkness shall be the light, and the stillness the dancing" (EC, 128). The leaves burning in Williams' flame—"a leaf catching to a flame," "the justice of the stillness drew all the flames and leaves"— anticipate *East Coker*'s burning roses: "And quake in frigid purgatorial fires / Of which the flame is roses, and the smoke is briars" (EC, 165–66). Both Eliot and Williams recall the flames of Dante's twenty-seventh canto, and in that common reflection they mirror one another. The "stillness" has been interpreted earlier as a compilation of images taken from Dante, St. John of the Cross, Hinduism, and Buddhism. The "stillness" also draws from *Descent into Hell*. Eliot certainly read *Descent into Hell* before working on *East Coker*, accepting it for publication on behalf of Faber & Faber in 1937: "Eliot said that he did not find it as enthralling as Williams's earlier novels; but he liked it enough to want to see it in print."[14]

The still point, then, is passed from *The Greater Trumps* to *Burnt Norton* to *Descent into Hell* to *East Coker*. The question of influence does not stop even here, however, for "The still point of the turning world" appears in Eliot's "Coriolan," a poem published in 1931, a year before *The Greater Trumps*. And Williams provides only the dance: the dance around a motionless centre has a venerable legacy, going at least as far back as John Davies' *Orchestra*, and beyond Davies to neo-Platonism and the maypole. It is important to stress that one cannot discuss Eliot and Williams in terms of influence: the two poets are writing in the same key.

A common note sounding through the writings of Williams and Eliot is the occult. As David Evans is one of the few to point out, Eliot has always been a poet of the occult.[15] A reader of the *New English Weekly* claimed in a letter to Eliot that a true appreciator of poetry enters into the mind of the poet; Eliot responded in May 1939 with the following suggestive analogy: 'This reminds me of the investigator who, after an encounter with a ghost, reported that he "come as near to bein' strangled as made no difference." '[16] Poetry, for Eliot, is a ghost with a stranglehold upon the poet; such, in 1939, is the experience of the poet at the time of writing. Williams would certainly have agreed; the supernatural has him by the neck throughout his life. Eliot writes of Williams' *The Descent of the Dove* that "There is an element of wilfulness in Mr. Williams's expression—a temptation to which anyone is exposed who is trying to convey the beauty of colour to the colour-blind."[17] In a 1946 broadcast on "The Significance of Charles Williams," reprinted as the introduction to *All Hallows' Eve*, Eliot says "I have always believed that he would have been equally at ease in every kind of supernatural company; that he would never have been surprised or disconcerted by the intrusion of any visitor from another world."[18] Williams returns the compliment in a review of *East Coker*:

> Mr Eliot has been admired, times without number, for describing the disease. What his poetry has been (*"In my beginning is my end"*) always calling is the note of strange and beautiful health. But O that we should have to listen to it!*

Each poet celebrates the extra-ordinary, the super-natural qualities in the other's work, especially during the war. All of the reviews above were written between 1939 and 1946, when the spectre breathing down the neck of the poet is that of a hideously unreal war.

Williams' appreciation of the occult in Eliot is strongest in his review of *Four Quartets* for *The Dublin Review* in 1943. Besides its importance as a wartime review, and the light it affords on both poets, "A Dialogue on Mr. Eliot's Poem" is possibly the wisest thing ever written on Eliot's last quartet. The review takes the form of a dramatic conversation among four speakers, Eugenio, Nicobar, Sophonisba, and Celia. Each has read a quartet aloud to the others, which is the only valid way of explaining anything, according to Stanhope in *Descent into Hell* (15). The form owes something to Dryden's dialogues; it more nearly borrows from Henry James' review of *Daniel Deronda*, which begins with Pulcheria reading the last chapters of the novel to Theodora.† The conversation moves quickly to the supernatural. Nicobar considers "that this last poem peculiarly re-

---

*Charles Williams, "The Poetry of Health," rev. of *East Coker, Time and Tide*, 5 October 1940, 990. By this cryptic close Williams does not mean to disparage Eliot, but rather to disparage an age which requires a healing voice. Williams is always, and as Eliot says almost wilfully, oblivious to lower meanings.

†Henry James, "Daniel Deronda: A Conversation," *Atlantic Monthly*, XXXVIII (December 1876), 684–94. Theodora's only complaint about Pulcheria's reading is that "in some of the fine passages of this last book she took quite a false tone." Nicobar says much the same to Eugenio: "A precise judge could not complain of anything beyond, here and there, somewhat of a greater rhetorical emphasis than the poem requires" (114).

moves itself from mortality, and is more like the cry of a strange bird flying over that sea from a coast beyond it than anything in the sea itself."[19] Celia agrees, and feels the cry of that bird to be too near: "Let us draw the curtains. There may be birds from beyond another sea tonight whose rhetoric would be less quiet than Nicobar approves."[20] This is strange stuff for a book review, but characteristic Williams, who is always aware of the possible impingement of the supernatural world. Reading Eliot through his own propensities, Williams emphasizes the occult in *Little Gidding*, especially "the passage that presents no hindrance" (LG, 120) between the worlds.

It is in this passageway that Eliot and Williams meet each other most frequently. Eugenio, speaking for Williams, claims that "I have talked with the apparition in our poet's fourth poem."[21] So he has: that conversation took place in *Descent into Hell*. John Struther's ghost from *Descent into Hell* reappears in *Little Gidding*'s dawn encounter. Struther also converses with the apparitions in *The Family Reunion*. Williams suggests this very subtly in his review:

> *Sophonisba*: I am not as oracular as you. But I know that the greatest moments are those whose movement is within them—yes, even all our little bodily movements.
> *Nicobar*: "The last apparent refuge, the safe shelter". Those moments are not shelters, because of the interior dance.[22]

Nicobar is not quoting from *Four Quartets*. "The last apparent refuge, the safe shelter" is sought by Harry Monchensey in *The Family Reunion*. The line is critical to the play, for in it Eliot presents the passage between the worlds, the crossing from the spectral into the real. And in quoting it Williams inserts into his discussion of *Four Quartets* the one line in *The Family Reunion* that owes the most to Williams himself.

Harry says to Amy:

> [...] I have been in flight
> But always in ignorance of invisible pursuers.
> Now I know that all my life has been a flight
> And phantoms fed upon me while I fled. Now I know
> That the last apparent refuge, the safe shelter,
> That is where one meets them. That is the way of spectres ... [23]

Pauline Anstruther, in *Descent into Hell*, is chased by the same invisible pursuers. The spectres in *The Family Reunion* are most obviously the Eumenides, hidden in an embrasure behind the drawing-room curtain. In *Descent into Hell*, the ghosts are also the Eumenides: "Seize on him, Furies" (111). Trying to escape from her spectres, Pauline searches for "this one refuge where she might find shelter" (23). Common words, but Pauline's flight is a touchstone for Eliot during and after the war. The moment reappears in *The Family Reunion*, in *Little Gidding*, and in *The Cocktail Party*.

Pauline's and Harry's pursuers are both reflections of their victims. Pauline is afraid of herself:

> It was coming up at her pace—*doppelgänger, doppelgänger:* her control began to give . . . two . . . she didn't run, lest it should, nor did it. She reached her gate, slipped through, went up the path. If it should be running very fast up the road behind her now? (22)

The invisible pursuers in *The Family Reunion* are also *doppelgängern*. An earlier allusion to Henry James' "The Jolly Corner" establishes this:

> Yes. I mean that at Wishwood he will find another Harry.
> The man who returns will have to meet
> The boy who left. Round by the stables,
> In the coach-house, in the orchard,
> In the plantation, down the corridor
> That led to the nursery, round the corner
> Of the new wing, he will have to face him—
> And it will not be a very *jolly* corner.
> When the loop in time comes—and it does not come for
>   everybody—
> The hidden is revealed, and the spectres show themselves.[24]

In the original manuscript, Agatha continued: "I am sorry, Gerald, for making an allusion / To an author whom you never heard of."[25] Eliot italicizes "*jolly* corner" to throw back to James' short story, where Spencer Brydon feels "a strange *alter ego* deep down somewhere within me."* Harry ultimately meets the spectre of himself around the jolly corner.

*Henry James, "The Jolly Corner," in *The Complete Tales of Henry James*, vol. 12, 204. "The Jolly Corner" may also provide the title for Eliot's *After Strange Gods*: Brydon says "I've followed strange paths and worshipped strange gods" (205).

Williams' quotation of the line within the context of his review suggests more, implying that Pauline's moment reappears, via *The Family Reunion*, in *Four Quartets*. The jolly corner in the orchard, down the corridor that led to the nursery, where the man who returns meets the boy who left, this corner is turned in *Burnt Norton*'s rose-garden: "Quick, said the bird, find them, find them, / Round the corner" (BN, 19–20). This is the first coming of the "loop in time" in *Four Quartets*. That loop returns in *Little Gidding*, and then the spectres show themselves. Eliot's ghost at the antelucan hour, like Pauline's ghost, is ultimately the speaker's shadow. Eliot meets himself at the intersection time, and, as with Spencer Brydon, it is not a particularly jolly corner.

Pauline's *doppelgänger* also makes an appearance at *The Cocktail Party*. Pauline recites Shelley as she prepares to meet the ghost:

> *Doppelgänger*, the learned called it, which was no comfort.
> Another poet had thought of it; [...]
>   *The Magus Zoroaster, my dead child,*
>   *Met his own image walking in the garden.* (19)

In *The Cocktail Party*, Dr. Reilly describes his premonition of Celia Coplestone's death with the same lines from *Prometheus Unbound*:

> *The magus Zoroaster, my dead child,*
> *Met his own image walking in the garden.*
> *That apparition, sole of men, he saw.*
> *For know there are two worlds of life and death:*
> *One that which thou beholdest; but the other*
> *Is underneath the grave, where do inhabit*
> *The shadows of all forms that think and live*
> *Till death unite them and they part no more.*[26]

Rossell Robbins has traced other parallels between the two works: both Peter Stanhope and Harcourt-Reilly, for example, dismiss their interlocutors with the phrase "Go in peace."[27] Stanhope, Christian poet and playwright, is modelled very closely on Eliot himself. Stanhope rises to speak at the close of his play, as Eliot did after a performance of Williams' *Seed* *of Adam* (1936) earlier in the year.* Much of Williams' work deliberately echoes the poetry of his friend: in *The Cocktail Party* the echoes rebound. Both Eliot and Williams draw upon Shelley to express a spectral visitation, bringing *Descent into Hell* deeper into the penumbra of Eliot's playwriting. All these roads travelled by the *doppelgänger* lead eventually to *Little Gidding*.

After Nicobar's digression to *The Family Reunion*, Eugenio returns to the ghost in *Little Gidding*. His disquisition on *Little Gidding*'s ghostly encounter is one of the most illuminating critical pieces yet written on the passage:

> *Nicobar*: You spoke, Eugenio, of the apparition in the fourth poem, or rather in the fourth part of the whole poem. Will you not discourse to us on it at more length?
>
> *Eugenio*: I could say little that would make it more effective, and I might be too apt to catch the sad note of exposition, than which I can imagine nothing our poet—*poeta nostra*—would more dislike. We have not spoken of his allusions, which (if one knows them) enlarge his poem from within. But there is one here we must not altogether pass. "What! are *you* here?"—there is only one place in all Christendom where that cry was heard, and that was out of Christendom. Do you remember, Nicobar?
>
> *Nicobar*: I had forgotten—till now. *"Siete voi qui, Ser Brunetto?"* But why is the baked countenance of Brunetto Latini remembered here?
>
> *Eugenio*: There is fire in the distance here—in "three districts", as in that other place it fell from the dark skies; and here it is the time of "the recurrent end of the unending", much as the torments of Dante's hell in each moment become again recurrently unending. But we were not perhaps meant too closely to hunt out comparisons; or if, I am not the one to do it. Let us observe only how that terrible remembrance accentuates the cry, and how the dialogue between the poet and the apparition,
>
> > a familiar compound ghost
> > Both intimate and unidentifiable,
>
> however different, is awfully undershaken by the Italian. The whole passage, correctly or incorrectly—or I will say wisely or unwisely—seems to me full of infernal reminiscence, though the English poet is ostensibly speaking of time ending here and not of time unending there—and yet his words reverberate through the monotonous funnel of hell; indeed, the funnel is here. Listen:

*Alice Hadfield, *An Introduction to Charles Williams*, 134. Stanhope is Williams too, as Carpenter points out: "Williams himself used 'Peter Stanhope' as a *nom de plume* for his religious drama *Judgement at Chelmsford*, and the character of Stanhope in *Descent into Hell* resembles Williams in many particulars" (*The Inklings*, 107n).

[Then follow lines 126–49, from "Since our concern was speech" to "And faded on the blowing of the horn."]

Is not that a proper summary of the dark journey from Styx to Judecca? And is there anywhere a greater word for the deepening yet monotonous perpetuity of the lost than

> From wrong to wrong the exasperated spirit
> Proceeds?

> *Sophonisba*: I have seen it said somewhere that the last line—"And faded on the blowing of the horn"—has a relevance to *Hamlet*—"It faded on the crowing of the cock."
> *Eugenio*: It may well be so, for there has been a reference to the "refining fire" of that purgatory in which the ghost of the elder Hamlet dwelled.[28]

Eugenio's speech reveals a great deal about Williams' own work, his understanding of Eliot's work, and the relation between the two. The parenthetical "*poeta nostra*" suggests that, for Williams, Eliot is to the English as Dante is to the Italians. The ghost compresses the journey from Styx to Judecca, passing from the outermost to the innermost circle of hell. Eugenio compares the "torments of Dante's hell" to "fire in the distance here," emphasizing Dante's relevance in wartime. That relevance is both infernal and purgatorial: Williams enlarges upon the ghost's dwelling in purgatory as well as his journeying through hell. Williams has always been alive to purgatorial images in Eliot. He was one of the first critics to see purgatorial possibilities in Eliot's poetry of the twenties: "Can this hell be rather the place of purgation?"[29] Reviewing *The Family Reunion*, he underscores Agatha's 'obscure sense of the word "expiation," ' and writes that 'He has redeemed the word "expiation" from the classical scholars.'[30] Eliot has brought expiation into the modern world.

Williams is alive to these possibilities since he too has redeemed the word. His work is also concerned with purgatory, in the rigid sense of a place of expiation for sin, a place of hope and painful atonement. *Descent into Hell* descends into a purgatorial fire. Williams shies away from discussions of influence upon the dawn encounter: "But we were not perhaps meant too closely to hunt out comparisons, or if, I am not the one to do it." Williams is not the one to do it because he is Eliot's greatest point of comparison. Eugenio would be forced to bring up himself.

Descent into Hell and *Little Gidding* share, above all, the passageway between the two worlds. Eliot writes of Williams that "To him the supernatural was perfectly natural, and the natural was also supernatural."[31]

Shelley's "two worlds of life and death" coalesce in Eliot's and Williams' common idea of an intersection time. Eliot's encounter takes place at the "intersection time" (LG, 105) between these worlds; in *Descent into Hell*, Wentworth meets the ghost of Adela in "the interstices of time where she lived" (89). With Shelley, Eliot presents the real and the nether worlds as mirror-images, allowing intercourse between them:

> [. . .] the passage now presents no hindrance
> To the spirit unappeased and peregrine
> Between two worlds become much like each other. (LG, 120–22)*

Williams, five years before *Little Gidding*, does likewise:

> Sometimes where time varies place is stable; or where places intermingle time is secure, and sometimes the equilibrium of both, which is maintained in so many living minds, swings into the place of the dead. Sometimes the dead know it, and sometimes the living; a single clock ticks or a single door opens in two worlds at once. (132)

The table of contents for *Descent into Hell* alone suggests the easy passage from here to eternity: "Via Mortis / Quest of Hell / Junction of Travellers / The Tryst of the Worlds / The Sound of the Trumpet / The Opening of Graves." "The Tryst of the Worlds" begins:

> As if the world of that other life to which this in which Margaret Anstruther lay was but spectral, and it to this, renewed itself with all its force in the groan he heard, as if that groan had been but its own energy of freeing itself, the dead man found when it ceased that he was standing alone among the houses. (152)

This almost impossibly knotted opening sentence seems to suggest, if I have correctly parsed it, that the two worlds are spectral images of each other.

In *Descent into Hell*, as in the majority of Williams' novels, ghosts walk freely from one world to the next: "About her the familiar and transfigured personages moved; this was the condition and this the air of supernatural life" (151). As in Eliot, these are "familiar" ghosts. John Struther appears

---

The Family Reunion's anticipation of these lines may be recalled here: "You and I, / My dear, may very likely meet again / In our wanderings in the neutral territory / Between two worlds" (121).

to Pauline in the street at the end of an interminable night. As Pauline prepares herself to meet him, she thinks "a ghost in the fire was a ghost in the street" (161). He passes through a refining fire and appears with "the echo of the trumpet [...] or of a siren" (167). Eliot's ghost departs not with the sound of a trumpet or an air-raid siren but with both: "And faded on the blowing of the horn" (LG, 149). These startling pre-echoes of Eliot's encounter draw Struther into the pantheon of figures behind Eliot's compound figure. The more one studies *Descent into Hell* the more the book becomes an echo-chamber for Eliot, screaming *Little Gidding* from every page.

Descent into Hell presents the complementary fates of two men, Lawrence Wentworth and John Struther. Struther commits suicide at the beginning of the novel, only to reappear and be purged in a refining fire. Wentworth ends the book in hell. Wentworth's sin is the creation of an ideal other. His infatuation for Adela Hunt necessitates the rejection of her reality, and the embrace of a monstrous fantasy. He creates a mythical Adela in the face of all humanity, despite the advance of a "son of Adam":

> It still came on, [...] inexorably advancing as the glory of truth that broke out of the very air itself upon the agonized Florentine in the Paradise of Eden: "ben sem, ben sem, Beatrice"; the other, the thing seen, the thing known in every fibre to be not the self, woman or beggar, the thing in the streets of the City. (88)

From the streets of the City, from the Heavenly Kingdom, Beatrice's greeting to Dante calls Wentworth back. Beatrice is the glory of the affirmative truth, signifying everything not the self, an image of all the blessed. Williams quotes from Dante's confrontation with Beatrice to underscore Wentworth's monstrous reversal of that encounter. Wentworth rejects this affirmative path, leaving the City for a nightmare wilderness of his own creation: "No, no; no canvassers, no beggars, no lovers; and away, away from the City into the wood and the mist, by the path that runs between past and present, between present and present, that slides through each moment of all experience, twisting and twining, plunging from the City and earth and Eve and all otherness, into the green mist that rises among the trees." (88–89)

Wentworth wanders down a markedly Eliotic path: "the path that runs between past and present, between present and present" leads, in *Burnt*

Norton, to the rose-garden.* But Wentworth's plunge into the green mist is not just a journey down the garden path. *Burnt Norton's* trip to the rose-garden becomes, in *East Coker*, a descent into hell:

> In the middle, not only in the middle of the way
> But all the way, in a dark wood, in a bramble,
> On the edge of a grimpen, where is no secure foothold,
> And menaced by monsters, fancy lights,
> Risking enchantment. (EC, 89–93)

These lines owe something to *The Hound of the Baskervilles*; they also recall *Descent into Hell*. For Wentworth takes this route as well. Wentworth risks enchantment through the creation of a great strangling she-beast named Lilith, to whom he does eventually succumb.† Wentworth displays Eliot's folly of old men, "their folly, / Their fear of fear and frenzy, their fear of possession / Of belonging to another, or to others, or to God" (EC, 94–96). Wentworth, an old man, risks enchantment, is menaced by monsters in a dark wood, and fears, frenziedly, of belonging to others, or to God. Later he will catch a "feverish chill" (176): "The chill ascends from feet to knees / The fever sings in mental wires" (EC, 162–63). His damnation clearly informs *East Coker's* hell.

Struther, on the other hand, is saved. After his suicide, he comes before Pauline to re-enact Dante's reconciliation with Beatrice. He cries, with Dante, "Lord God, I cannot bear the fear of the fire" (169). He passes through the fire saying "I have seen the salvation of my God" (170). His words are not only Dante's; Pauline's ancestor, also called Struther, died a martyr crying *"I have seen the salvation of my God"* (55) in the midst of the fire. Struther's parallel fate establishes him as the ghostly double Pauline feared to meet earlier in the novel: he, like Eliot's ghost, is a *doppelgänger*. Struther can only pass through the fire with the encouragement of Pauline, who has been taught by Stanhope to carry his metaphysical weight: "Give it to me" (170), she says. Stanhope's Doctrine of Substituted Love, requiring a complete identification with and assimilation of the burdens of

*As Rossell Robbins has observed, Eliot's double sense of the word "present" appears elsewhere in *Descent into Hell*: "But if the past still lives in its own present beside our present" (25).

†Lilith makes a rare literary appearance in the work of the Inklings, probably as a result of George Macdonald. The White Witch is a daughter of Lilith (*The Lion, the Witch, and the Wardrobe*, 65).

another, is Eliot's attachment to self and to things and to persons; both are manifestations of the affirmative way. Pauline then experiences "beatitude" (171) and rejoices in "their meeting and their reconciliation" (170). Williams' recreation of Dante's purgation upon the affirmative way is exact.

Struther's salvation is not only a reconciliation with Pauline; it is also "a meeting and a reconciliation" of the two ways. He travels on the negative way as well, again with express reference to its early practitioner. His ascent on the ladder of bone, leaving behind crowds of familiar faces as he climbs into the void, is the act of a contemplative:

> The living death crowded round the ladder of bone, which it could not ascend. White faces of unvitalized, unsubstantial, yet real, existence, looked up at him mounting. Nothingness stared and panted, with false breath, terrible to those who live of choice in its phantasmal world. But for him, who rose above them [. . .] there entered through the grasp he had on the ladder shafts an energy. (154)

The ladder is St. John's image: the ascent of Mount Carmel is achieved upon a ladder of ten rungs. Struther passes through St. John's "Nothingness." Struther's purgation is a conjunction of the negative and the affirmative ways; he must both ascend the ladder of bone and pass through the flame to reach a state of grace. As in Eliot, the healing flame is both Dante's and St. John's.

The flames in *Little Gidding* burn along the *via positiva* and the *via negativa*; they also burn in hell and purgatory. These two fires burn in *Descent into Hell* as well, with the damnation of Lawrence Wentworth and the salvation of John Struther. In the most hair-raising depiction of hell since Stephen Dedalus' retreat, Wentworth descends at the close of the book into an infernal flame. Daydreaming in his armchair, he loses hold of a "million-mile-long rope," and enters an abyss "where there is no measurement because there is no floor" (218). He enters Dante's hell, where he sees "the Gorgon's head that was hidden from Dante in Dis" (214). His descent is a rejection of a purgatorial flame; hatred for Sir Aston Moffat precludes his feeling "a touch of the fire in which the Marian martyr had gone to his glory, and still been saved" (219). Wentworth cannot suffer Cranmer's fire (though there were three Marian martyrs, Williams' play *Cranmer* singles the archbishop out here), but must endure the terror of tiny pricks of flame. *Descent into Hell* ends with some of Williams' headiest writing:

[. . .] small burning flames flickered down on his soul. His eyes opened again in mere despair. A little hopeless voice came from his throat. He said, and rather gasped than spoke: "Ah! ah!" Then everything at which he was looking rushed together and became a point, very far off, and he also was a point opposite it; and both points were rushing together, because in this place they drew towards each other from the more awful repulsion of the void [. . .]. He was sitting at the end, looking up an avenue of nothingness, and the little flames licked his soul. (221)

Wentworth's nothingness is the inverse of Struther's: Struther does experience Cranmer's fire. The flame surrounding Pauline as she brings him to his salvation is a positive, redeeming force: "the very fire her ancestor had feared was a comfort to her now" (170); "The air was fiery to her sense" (161). Fire has been seen to have this power in both Dante and St. John. The Refiner's fire burns along both paths; Struther passes through it twice before completing his purgation. He enters the fire on the road outside Wentworth's house; Wentworth descends to hell sitting in his armchair. In having the metaphysical conflagrations take place within sight of each other, Williams suggests, with Eliot, that a fire can be at once infernal and purgatorial.

Eliot's flame is inherently ambivalent; in Williams, the fires are not simultaneous, but separated only by a window and a hedge. The communication of the dead is tongued with flame in both Eliot and Williams, and that flame can be either damning or healing. In both, hell and purgatory are compounded, as are the philosophies of the negative and affirmative ways exemplified in St. John and Dante. The chapter in which Struther's purgation takes place is entitled "The Tryst of the Worlds," referring both to the natural and the supernatural worlds, and to the twin worlds of the two ways. In *Descent into Hell*, "holy love" frees mankind through "its revelation of something ever alien from and conjoined with the self" (132). The love of God is both negative and positive, detached and attached, alien and conjoined. In *Descent into Hell*, Williams presents the further co-inherence of the ways.

The two ways, for Williams as for Eliot, are particularly represented in Dante and St. John. Williams' two major studies of the *Commedia, Religion and Love in Dante* (1941) and *The Figure of Beatrice*, both written in wartime, emphasize Dante as a poet of the affirmative way. Beatrice is viewed as a mediating figure between God and man, an image through which the existence of God can be affirmed. Williams considered *"Guardaci ben! Ben son, ben son Beatrice"* (30, 73), Beatrice's summons to Dante, to

be the greatest line in European poetry.* This was perhaps for its impli-
cation that only through the act of seeing, through the identification with
and subsequent transcendence of images of the outside world, can Dante
enter into Paradise. Anne Ridler writes in her excellent introduction to
The Image of the City: "as Charles Williams was a poet and a married man,
his life was lived along the *Via Positiva*."[32] Dorothy Sayers recognized
Dante's importance in Williams' affirmative way, dedicating the first two
books of her translation of the *Commedia* "To The Dead Master Of The
Affirmations, Charles Williams."[33]

Williams is also a Master of the Negations, travelling on the negative
way. Williams confided in Alice Hadfield that "At bottom a darkness has
always haunted me"—surely the darkness of the negative way.[34] T. S. Eliot
confided in Hadfield that he saw in Williams a fellow-traveller: "He was,
Mr. Eliot said, a genuine Anglican, and no Papalist. Mr. Eliot, himself a
solitary, felt the central solitude and the darkness in C. W.'s vivacity."[35]
In 1942, the five hundredth anniversary of St. John's birth, Williams voices
through St. John a conviction Eliot shares:

> "The soul must be in darkness with regard to everything that enters through
> the eye and by the ear, or which can be imagined by the fancy (or imagination)
> and comprehended in the heart."[36]

The quincentenary article closes with Saroyan's affirmative interpretation
of the love of God, and the conclusion that "It is this meaning or St.
John's; there is, in the end no other choice."[37]

These two choices are everywhere in Williams' work. In Charles Williams' *War in Heaven* (1930), the Archdeacon of Castra Parvulorum's
ascent to heaven is anticipated by two books in his library. John Davenant
has been reading the *Ascent of Mount Carmel*, together with the *Revelations*
of Lady Julian.[38] As Williams implies in the Archdeacon's readings before
his apotheosis, both paths lead to God. *The Descent of the Dove* is dedicated
to "the Companions of the Co-inherence," Williams' term for his disciples
at the London County Council's Evening Institute before the war. *The
Descent of the Dove* has as its frontispiece Lodovico Brea's *Paradise*, which
depicts, in Williams' words, "travellers upon one or other of the Ways.

---

*Charles Williams, *Religion and Love in Dante*, 29. "Look well! We are, we are
indeed Beatrice." As with Eliot, the modern text of the *Commedia* differs slightly
from the Dante Williams knew. In *Descent into Hell*, for instance, Williams has
"ben sem, ben sem" (88) for *"Ben son, ben son."*

But the painting, above and below, is of the co-inherence of the whole redeemed City."³⁹ St. John's penchant for asparagus best expressed, for Williams, this co-inherence:

> (And even he, towards the end, was encouraged to remember that he liked asparagus; our Lord the Spirit is reluctant to allow either of the two great Ways to flourish without some courtesy to the other.)⁴⁰

For Lewis, co-inherence was standard Christian doctrine: both Lewis and Tolkien are among Williams' Companions. There is a suggestion of Williams' co-inherence in the final lines of "Leaf by Niggle," when Niggle and Parish discover, to their great delight, that their way-station has been renamed "Niggle's Parish."⁴¹ Eliot is one of these Companions as well; throughout the *Four Quartets* the way up and the way down co-inhere. "Attachment to self and to things and to persons" (LG, 152) states precisely Stanhope's Doctrine of Substituted Love, while "detachment / From self and from things and from persons" (LG, 152–53) perfectly describes the isolation of Struther on his ladder of bone. Williams and Eliot walk with Dante and St. John throughout their lives; and above all, they walk together. In *Descent into Hell* and *Four Quartets* all four voices resolve into one resounding chord. As Pauline perceives at the end of Stanhope's pageant:

> [. . .] from the edge of eternity the poets were speaking to the world, and two modes of experience were mingled in that sole utterance. (186)

The two poets speak from that edge, "trying to convey the beauty of colour to the colour-blind."⁴² Their work conjoins the "two modes of experience," the road up and the road down. In that conjunction lies their co-inherence: *Descent into Hell* and *Four Quartets* echo each other so strangely that they may be considered, in Pauline's words, a "sole utterance."

Descent into Hell is not a war novel. But *All Hallows' Eve* is: Williams read the first chapters of it to the Inklings in Autumn 1943, some months before Lewis read from *The Great Divorce*. In fact, the beginning of *All Hallows' Eve* sounds very much like the opening of *The Great Divorce*:

> She was standing on Westminster Bridge. It was twilight, but the City was no longer dark. [. . .]

> Lester Furnival stood and looked at the City while the twilight deepened.
> The devastated areas were hidden; much was to be done but could be. (1)*

It is twilight in the grey town once more; Lester stands, like Lewis' narrator, in the streets of wartime London. She is waiting, not in a bus-queue, but on a bridge. Like the shades in *The Great Divorce*, Lester Furnival is dead. She walks through the disfigured streets of London, a ghost revisiting a twilight world.

Lester's encounters, with her school-friend Evelyn and her husband Richard, draw quite consciously from the dawn encounter in *Little Gidding*. She greets Evelyn with the startled cry heard twice before: 'She said, "So you're here!" ' (12). They descend into the London Underground, which Lester sees as the entrance to the first circle of Hell:

> There was the entrance; they had meant to go—yes, but there could not now
> be any Tube below; or it would be as empty as the street. A medieval would
> have feared other things in such a moment—the way, perhaps, to the *città
> dolente*. (13)

Though this is Leicester Square rather than Gloucester Road, Eliot's "Descend lower" (BN, 114) is nevertheless brought to mind on the Piccadilly Line.

Lester's meeting with her husband calls upon *Little Gidding* directly. Together they suffer "the awareness / Of things ill done" (LG, 141)—"Darling, did I neglect you?" (46)—and "the rending pain of re-enactment" (LG, 138): "As she remembered, she felt a sudden renewal of the pain and of the oblivion" (11). Later Lester will feel "the pain of the rending flesh" (246): throughout *All Hallows' Eve* Williams expressly quotes Eliot's diction. When Richard finally meets Lester, recognizing her across the passageway between the worlds, "He thought almost he saw her suspire with a relief beyond joy" (48). As in *Little Gidding*, the meeting is both strange and familiar: "But the strangeness, for all the familiarity, had never quite gone" (47). The still point is here: "Lester was not smiling any recognition; the recognition was in her stillness" (48). So are the four elements of Eliot's quartets: Lester is "More stable than rock, more transient in herself than rivers [. . .] more pleasant than wind, more dangerous

*Charles Williams, *All Hallows' Eve* (1948; rpt. Grand Rapids, Eerdmans, 1985), 1. Subsequent references to this edition of *All Hallows' Eve* in this section will appear within the text.

than fire" (48). At the close of the meeting, Williams permits himself a punning confession of his source: "He was giddy with too much apprehension; he waited to recover; then he crossed the by-way and he too went on" (49).

A third tryst of the supernatural and natural worlds involves Betty Wallingford, forced into the ghostly City by Simon the Clerk. She walks through "spectral streets" (76) on a windy autumn night in the hours before dawn: "It was again October and a fresh wind was blowing" (84). Betty finds herself quite comfortable in this nightmare version of war-torn London: "The world was as familiar as this world and to her less terrifying. It lay there, as it always does—itself offering no barriers" (77). In Eliot's early versions of *Little Gidding*, *"the passage now presents no barrier"* (HG, 191); for both Eliot and Williams, the barrier between the worlds collapses during the war. Owen's "profound dull tunnel" into the netherworld was groined by "titanic wars." In *All Hallows' Eve*, Williams explains how such a passageway comes to be carved by war:

> It has certainly been thought, but the speculation is that of dreamers, that in the year of our great danger the grand attack of our enemies succeeded; that London and England perished; and that all we who then died entered it together and live there till we have wrought out our salvation—to enjoy (purgatorially) a freedom unpermitted on earth; and that our conquerors live on that earth, troubled and frenzy-driven by a mystical awareness of our presence. More justly, it is held by learned doctors that in times of much bloodshed that world draws closer (so to call a neighbourhood we cannot define) to this, that chance entry for the living is easier. (77–78)

This passage unlocks the book, revealing, albeit within an occult construct, how and why these ghosts walk through London at all. The war causes the two worlds to come together: "in times of much bloodshed that world draws closer." The passage explains the insistent recurrence of purgatorial situations in *All Hallows' Eve*. Lester begins the book waiting on a bridge, sensing the whole City held in abeyance:

> If she lost it, she would be left in the midst of this—this *lull*. She knew the sudden London lulls well enough, but this lull was lasting absurdly long. All the lulls she had ever known were not as deep as this. (3)

Richard waits in Father Simon's waiting-room with a once-paralyzed secretary (100). The railway station waiting-room makes an appearance soon after Betty's dissertation on the impingement of the supernatural in wartime. There Betty reads of current events: "She went in the waiting-room and sat down to read" (83). *All Hallows' Eve* is full of purgatories-on-earth: the theory of the "learned doctors" accounts for these purgatories.

These doctors include Eliot, Tolkien, and Lewis, all of whom write of parallel worlds. The passage is the key to the Literature of Experience, explaining the repeated connection between the modern world and a purgatorial other world. For all four, the war has created a purgatory of the real world, breaching the passageway to its spectral mirror-image. Tolkien's other world is a joyful recreation of the painted world in Niggle's shed. Lewis' earthly paradise is an escape from a wartime nightmare. Both must travel, by train or by bus, to a glorious purgatory, with heaven in the distance. Eliot and Williams bring the other world straight into the blitzed streets of London. Eliot's ghost only occasionally describes his world in his speech; unlike Tolkien and Lewis, he affords no glimpses of an earthly paradise. Williams' purgatorial world is the bleakest of all. Hitler has won, we all have died, neither London nor the Blitz is real. *Manent* only the purgation of sin and the expectation of our salvation.

VI. Waugh's War: From Limbo to Purgatory

Four Works Suspended in *Work Suspended*

> "And this here *Purgatorio* doesn't look right to me, so that stays behind, pending inquiries."
>
> *Vile Bodies.*

At the beginning of *Vile Bodies* (1930), Adam Fenwick-Symes loses his copy of the *Purgatorio*, together with the only draft of his memoirs, to an over-zealous Customs officer. At the end of *Vile Bodies*, Waugh presents one of British literature's earliest anticipations of the Second World War. Fenwick-Symes is reunited with the drunk Major, now a General, and with Chastity, now a whore, in a Daimler stuck "in the biggest battlefield in the history of the world."' This surreal prevision, nine years before war, is in some respects startlingly accurate: Nina writes from the home front of the success of a *"Sword Unsheathed"* series of war poets, and of *"a new Government order that we have to sleep in gas masks because of the bombs, but no one does."* *Vile Bodies'* bizarre epilogue marks the beginning of Waugh's comprehensive literary record of World War Two. *Work Suspended*, begun in the summer of 1939, covers the pre-war world of Fitzrovian London. *Put Out More Flags*, written during his return from a military fiasco in Crete in the summer of 1941, is set in the phoney war. *Brideshead Revisited*, written in the first six months of 1944, begins and ends in the war, and *Sword of Honour* remembers the war a decade later. More than any writer, Evelyn Waugh traverses in these four very different works the whole gamut of British literary responses to the Second World War.

Work Suspended's title most obviously refers to the narrator's latest thriller, *Murder at Mountrichard Castle*. As John Plant begins his narrative, the book is very near completion: "my book, *Murder at Mountrichard*

Castle, was within twenty thousand words of its end" (106).* But the work is stuck between two chapters of Plant's life, between the death of his father and the birth of his love for Lucy. *Murder at Mountrichard Castle* is so much caught between these two worlds that Plant refers to it as two separate books: "Neither book - the last of my old life, the first of my new - was ever finished" (191). Plant's inability to complete his almost completed murder mystery is not only a personal problem; it is an inevitable side-effect of war. With the coming of war, the detective novel becomes next to impossible.

War is declared, and with it a hiatus in an entire genre. Very few murder mysteries were actually written in Britain between 1939 and 1945, and only a fraction of these have a wartime setting. The *grandes dames* of the British mystery, Sayers, Allingham, and Christie, went underground until the smoke cleared. Dorothy Sayers turned from mysteries to mystery plays, writing liturgical dramas for the BBC. Caught unawares by an air raid early in the war, she pulled a book at random from the shelf and found herself trapped in her basement reading Dante's *Inferno*. Instantly hooked, she proceeded to translate the *Commedia* throughout the war. Agatha Christie wrote some of her best work during the Second World War, but again, surprisingly little of it keeps the war in the foreground. Her wartime novels are in large part "murders in retrospect," set in the golden age of the detective story, the thirties. *Ten Little Indians* (1939), *The Body in the Library* (1942), and *The Moving Finger* (1943) hardly glance at the war at all. Christie also wrote Miss Marple's and M. Poirot's final cases during the Blitz, but both *Sleeping Murder* and *Curtain* deliberately withhold any contemporary detail that would betray the circumstances of their writing. Margery Allingham writes a fascinating sociological study of her village in wartime, *The Oaken Heart* (1941), but no detective novels. *Traitor's Purse*, her tale of counterfeiting by Fifth Columnists in the Potteries, is more a pot-boiled thriller than an essay in detection.

The illustrious group of pseudonymous academics, Innes, Blake, and Crispin among them, all left the war well alone in their wartime novels. Nicholas Blake sets *Malice in Wonderland* (1940) in a pre-war Amusement Park, and *The Case of the Abominable Snowman* (1941) is set in a girls' school. Though Michael Innes writes of German spies in *The Secret Van-*

---

*Evelyn Waugh, "Work Suspended," in *Work Suspended and Other Stories* (Harmondsworth: Penguin, 1982), 106. References to this edition of *Work Suspended* in this section will appear within the text.

guard, the war is kept firmly at a distance. Philip Ploss, the espionage ring's first victim, dies with a familiar book by his side:

> "There is something moving and mysterious—if you'll believe me—about a half-smoked cigarette lying beside a murdered tart. When its place is taken by the thirtieth canto of the *Purgatorio*—"
> "Quite so."[3]

Edmund Crispin's *Holy Disorders* (1946) mentions the war only in passing, while *The Moving Toyshop*, one of the best reads in all detective fiction and the Ur-text for the academic mystery, avoids the war entirely. Written in 1946, it is set firmly in 1938. British detective fiction is the dog that doesn't bark, marked by its singular and telling absence during the war years.* For Orwell in 1946, the best time to read a murder mystery was on a "Sunday afternoon, preferably before the war."[4] Orwell is echoing a widespread sentiment that the war has rendered the mystery novel temporarily obsolete.

The bomb-torn streets of London might seem a particularly inviting setting for a locked-door mystery, but not for those undergoing the air raids themselves. Violent and unexpected death was no longer an escape for the readers in the Blitz; only after the war could wartime London be effectively used as the setting for a detective novel. Only in 1947, with *Minute for Murder*, is it discovered that Nigel Strangeways' wife has died driving an ambulance in an air raid. *There is a Tide* is the first of Christie's novels to give the Blitz a significant role: Rosaleen Underhay loses her second husband in an air raid in the novel's first scene. Margery Allingham's *Coroner's Pidgin* (1945), a fancifully plotted exercise involving Nazi relocation of British treasures, is set in an England that has "just about won this war."[5] (Ricky, the boy whose concern for his puppet-theatre leads to the incriminating evidence of the three missing bottles of priceless wine, has had a revealing war experience: "Poor Ricky, [. . .] If this army is anything like the last he must be in purgatory.")[6] Allingham's *The Tiger in the Smoke* (1952) approaches an allegory of war, but again, such an allegory is impossible during the war itself.

---

*It should be always borne in mind that this phrase never actually appears in Conan Doyle. Sherlock Holmes merely draws attention, in "Silver Blaze," "to the curious incident of the dog in the night-time": ' "The dog did nothing in the night-time." "That was the curious incident." ' Incidentally, *The Adventures of Sherlock Holmes*, with Basil Rathbone in the title role, was released in 1939.

Julian Symons, in *Bloody Murder*, offers a convincing explanation for this studied avoidance of World War Two in contemporary detective fiction. For Symons, "The War was a watershed in the history of the crime story."[7] The Great Detective disappears with the collapse of the world of the guilty vicarage, the poisoned sherry, and the hump-backed bridge:

> This world was heavily eroded by the slump years, and had pretty well vanished by 1939, but detective story writers pretended that it was still there. [. . .] By the end of World War II the reassurances offered by the classical kind of detective story had become very shaky indeed.[8]

The British mystery was and is a leisure time activity, written by and for a leisured class. Leisure time disappeared in the waiting world of 1939–1945: the armchair mystery could not be read in an air-raid shelter. Symons argues that Wimsey and his kind failed in 1939. Great Detectives were never particularly good at prevention, usually presenting a belated but much appreciated cure. They could be forgiven the occasional second murder, which served to reinforce suspense and eliminate suspects,* but they could never be forgiven the war.

> The great problem for established writers was what could be done with the Great Detective, who in a symbolic sense had failed to prevent the War and in a realistic one appeared more absurd as scientific and forensic aids to detection became more refined and more important.[9]

John Plant's *Murder at Mountrichard Castle*, then, is a ludicrous anomaly in 1939. Plant ultimately cannot even bear to look at it: "The head of foolscap began to disgust me. Twice I hid it under my shirts, twice the club valet unearthed it and laid it in the open" (131). Waugh stresses the anomalous position of detective fiction in wartime in *Sword of Honour*. James Hadley Chase's 1939 detective thriller, *No Orchids for Miss Blandish*, is ridiculed twice in the trilogy. Guy dismisses the book as "Unreadable" on the Isle of Mugg;[10] the book then resurfaces among the hideous paraphernalia of Dr. Akonanga:

> Virginia shifted her gaze from the headless fowl to the unfamiliar assembly of equipment. She noticed a copy of *No Orchids for Miss Blandish*.

---

*John Plant, however, finds the second murder an unpardonable lapse: "I had always been a one-corpse man" (106).

'Dr Akonanga,' she asked, 'what can you think you are doing that is more important than me?'

'I am giving Herr von Ribbentrop the most terrible dreams,' said Dr Akonanga with pride and gravity."

This gratuitous assault on an admittedly offensive book emphasizes the place of the detective novel in Evelyn Waugh's hierarchy by the end of the war.*

John Plant's father also leaves a work suspended in 1939. Upon John Plant Senior's easel in the first versions of *Work Suspended* sits a harmless painting of a shipyard:

> He died with his 1932 picture still unfinished. I saw its early stage on my last visit to him; it represented an old shipwright pondering on the idle dockyard where lay the great skeleton of the Cunarder that was later to be known as the *Queen Mary*. It was to have been called 'Too big?' My father had given the man a grizzled beard and was revelling in it. That was the last time I saw him."

In the revised version of *Work Suspended* for the uniform edition of 1949, the ocean liner has suffered a sea change:

> He died with his 1939 picture still unfinished. I saw its early stage on my last visit to him; it was to have been called 'Again?' and represented a one-armed veteran of the First World War meditating over a German helmet. My father had given the man a grizzled beard and was revelling in it. That was the last time I saw him. (117)

The 1949 version jolts *Work Suspended* out of idle reminiscence into anxious prophecy. John Plant Senior dies seven years later, now under the shadow of World War Two. Through a flagrant abuse of the benefits of hindsight, the book now looks ahead to the coming war.

Work Suspended, like most of Evelyn Waugh's later work, has a complicated writing history. When it was first sketched in the months before war, the story was set in the early thirties. With the outbreak of war, Waugh found himself unable to continue an immediately dated work. The first two chapters were published in 1942 without any mention of the war, save in the dedicatory letter's admission that "the world in which and

---

*In his criticism of *No Orchids for Miss Blandish*, Waugh reaches a rare point of agreement with George Orwell. Orwell's attack in *Horizon*, "Raffles and Miss Blandish," can be found in *Collected Essays*, III, 212–24.

for which it was designed, has ceased to exist."[13] Although it was unfinished, Waugh thought well of the piece, announcing to his father the arrival of a "major work": "My major work, unfinished in 1939, appears shortly as a fragment in Penguin. A fragment of this fragment is in this issue of *Horizon*. It is about a father with whom you will be unable to trace any similarities."[14] The *Horizon* fragment, titled "My Father's House," is a truncated version of the first chapter. In it, the Gothic side to the narrator's profession—"I would kill an animal in atrocious circumstances," "Lord George Vanburgh, in *Death in the Dukeries*, was decapitated"—is cut, never to reappear in subsequent editions.[15] In fact, no mention is made of John Plant's detective novels at all: the narrator all but disappears in his elegy to his dead father. But the changes for *Horizon* are minor compared with Waugh's revisions in 1949.

Robert Murray Davis has rung the changes in the uniform edition:

> For example, he moves the date of the action from 1932 to 1939, changes the subject of Plant senior's Academy picture from shipbuilding to war, and replaces the Red Chinese Army with the Spanish Republic as an object of left-wing fund raising. Further, he removes references to later developments in the action [p. 135] and even changes tense to place the book's action irrevocably in the past [p. 5]. Another type of change accommodates historically conditioned shifts in connotation: both the Iron Curtain and news of the extent of Hitler's persecution of the Jews came between the first and second editions; thus the designation of some characters' political allegiance is changed from "communist" to "Socialist" and a half-dozen references to Jews that might be regarded as anti-Semitic have been removed entirely.[16]

The father's anti-Semitic slur, "I could tell they were Jews by the smell of their notepaper," is excised;[17] his support of "the Jewish cause" (113) in letters to *The Times* is inserted. Waugh appends a postscript to the later edition which hauls his story into the Second World War: "The date of this child's birth was 25 August, 1939, and while Lucy was still in bed the air-raid sirens sounded the first false alarm of the second World War. And so an epoch, my epoch, came to an end" (191). Both the elder Plant's death and the young Simmonds' birth are suddenly harbingers of the war. As in *Vile Bodies*, the Second World War brings his novel to an end. But in *Work Suspended* the war is a *post hoc* excuse, tacked on to cover the holes in an unfinished work. Technically, *Work Suspended* belongs to the Literature of Reimagination, though the bulk of the book was written in 1939.

Three artists, the narrator, the narrator's father, and the author, suspend their work in 1939. The narrator cannot finish his detective story. John Plant Senior dies leaving a work figuratively and literally suspended, both unfinished and upon an easel. Waugh's novel itself is aborted by the coming of war. Plant's excuse to his publisher suggests that his inability to complete his novel may have even wider implications: " 'I have been writing for over eight years,' I said, 'and am nearing a climacteric' " (130). 1939 is a climacteric for an entire generation, a generation that has failed to prevent the war. The world of Fitzrovia, like the world of Mountrichard Castle, is being pushed out of sight:

> No one of my close acquaintance was killed, but all our lives, as we had constructed them, quietly came to an end. Our story, like my novel, remained unfinished - a heap of neglected foolscap at the back of a drawer. (191)

Work Suspended concludes with these lines, intimating that a fourth work has been suspended by the war. The lives of a generation have been "constructed," like the son's last mystery novel, like the ship in the father's last painting, like the author's last pre-war novel. All these constructions are suspended.

Sitting in Limbo: *Put Out More Flags* and *Between the Acts*

> But Limbo is the place. [...] Limbo for the unbaptized, for the pious heathen, the sincere sceptic.
>
> *Put Out More Flags.*

Waugh's 1939 world hangs suspended, like Miss La Trobe's audience in *Between the Acts*:

> All their nerves were on edge. They sat exposed. The machine ticked. There was no music. The horns of cars on the high road were heard. And the swish of trees. They were neither one thing nor the other; neither Victorians nor themselves. They were suspended, without being, in limbo. (124)*

*Virginia Woolf, *Between the Acts* (Harmondsworth: Penguin, 1953), 124. References to this edition of *Between the Acts* in this chapter will appear within the text.

Ambrose Silk rejoices in limbo at the end of Evelyn Waugh's second wartime novel, *Put Out More Flags*. Condemned to a sea-side oubliette, he finds himself unexpectedly content:

> But Limbo is the place. In Limbo one has natural happiness without the beatific vision; no harps; no communal order; but wine and conversation and imperfect, various humanity. Limbo for the unbaptized, for the pious heathen, the sincere sceptic. (60)*

In Waugh, limbo is a final resting-place, in Woolf, a restless way-station. The suspended worlds of Pointz Hall before the war and Mayfair during the twilight war do nevertheless share some common ground. Both are isolated, savage, and godless worlds: it is worth remembering that Limbo is, in Dante, the first circle in Hell. Woolf and Waugh present, in their parallel visions of limbo, a static, or secular equivalent for the myth of purgatory.

To yoke the works of Evelyn Waugh and Virginia Woolf together seems at first to do both authors a violent disservice. Mrs. Dalloway and Lady Metroland could surely have given dinner parties on the same evening; Septimus Smith would have cut a poor figure as a Halberdier. Even so, the comparison of *Put Out More Flags* with *Between the Acts* need be neither forced nor fanciful. Both works were published for a reading public as uncertain of the successful outcome of the war as the authors themselves, and so reflect many common preoccupations of the Chamberlain years. Woolf worked on *Between the Acts* intermittently for three years, from April 1938 until her death in 1941; Waugh dashed off *Put Out More Flags* sailing back from Abyssinia, beginning in July 1941.

Like the works themselves, the circumstances of their composition have more in common than may appear at first blush. In his preface to the 1967 edition of *Put Out More Flags*, Waugh writes of the seclusion of his working environment: "I had comfort and leisure and negligible duties, a large cabin with a table and a pile of army stationery. I wrote all day, and the book was finished in a month."[1] Woolf's diaries express a comparable serenity. Ten days after Hitler's invasion on March 12, she records "just as in private crises, a sudden lull"; on May 24 she writes "The 4th of August may come next week. At the moment there is a lull."[2] On August

---

*Evelyn Waugh, *Put Out More Flags* (Harmondsworth: Penguin, 1942), 60. References to this edition of *Put Out More Flags* in this section will also appear within the text.

7, "Harold [Nicolson] is very dismal, Vita says: predicts war, but not this week. A lull at the moment."³ *Between the Acts* was begun on the second of April, 1938, in the midst of this lull. Both Monks House and the *Duchess of Richmond* were sheltered from current events; these comfortable removes permitted the detached and unimpassioned presentation of life before and during wartime. Waugh and Woolf write in a similar seclusion, for a similar public, about a strangely similar limbo.

Neither limbo has a place for God: the limbo Ambrose envisions has "no harps." In voicing a desire for a world "without the beatific vision," Ambrose Silk speaks not only as the future representative of Atheism, but for the author as well. Waugh, though he officially joined the Roman Catholic church in 1930, is a long way from the religious conviction upheld in the conclusion to *Brideshead Revisited*. In *Brideshead Revisited* and *Sword of Honour*, purgatory will acquire its full and terrifying meaning; in *Put Out More Flags* the force of religion is gleefully denied at every turn. A victim must be found for the little lunatic wandering through the War Office with a suitcase full of bombs, and the Chaplain General is selected. Ambrose's flight into Ireland disguised as Father Flanagan prompts the following exchange with Basil Seal:

> 'Have you got a breviary?'
> 'Of course not.'
> 'Then read a racing paper.' (195)

Sir Joseph Mainwaring's purgation at the outbreak of war is not metaphysical but physiological:

> [...] on this Sunday morning, however, it would not have been fantastic to describe his spirit as inflamed by something nearly akin to religious awe. It *would* be fantastic to describe him as purged, and yet there had been something delicately purgative in the experiences of the morning and there was an unfamiliar buoyancy in his bearing as though he had been at somebody's Eno's. (21)*

*Mainwaring's new religious zeal was not uncommon. Churchill seems to have experienced a similar apotheosis:

> I felt a serenity of mind and was conscious of a kind of uplifted detachment from human and personal affairs. The glory of Old England, peace-loving and ill-prepared as she was, but instant and fearless at the call of honour, thrilled my being and seemed to lift our fate to those spheres far removed from earthly facts and physical sensation. (*The Gathering Storm*, 409)

Though *Between the Acts* is not as godless a work, the value of religion is still subjected to rigorous examination. The chapel at Pointz Hall is now a pantry: "the chapel had become a larder, changing, like the cat's name, as religion changed" (27). For Bartholomew, Lucy's recourse to religion is a renunciation of reality: "How imperceptive her religion made her! The fumes of that incense obscured the human heart" (141). Her crucifix confronts Bart's umbrella (21); his growls of "Superstition" (22) deny her religion validity in the modern world. The question of the contemporary value of faith is further debated as the audience disperses:

> But I was saying: can the Christian faith adapt itself? In times like these...At Larting no one goes to church...There's the dogs, there's the pictures...It's odd that science, so they tell me, is making things (so to speak) more spiritual. (138)

That Reverend Streatfield smokes tobacco is at first reassuring only to Bart—"A good fellow, who smoked cigars in the vestry" (22)—but as he rises to interpret the pageant, this one concession to reality relieves his entire audience: "One fact mitigated the horror; his forefinger, raised in the customary manner, was stained with tobacco juice" (132).

Religion and reality stand in direct opposition throughout Waugh's war writing. John Plant Senior speaks of the "first absurdities" of the Roman Catholic faith; even Lady Marchmain admits to "the poetry, the Alice-in-Wonderland side, of religion."[4] Barbara Seal, like Lucy Swithin, returns to her first faith:

> [...] as a cult will survive centuries after its myths have been exposed and its sources of faith tainted, there was still deep in her that early piety, scarcely discernible now in a little residue of superstition, so that this morning when her world seemed rocking about her, she turned back to Basil. (15)

Barbara worships not God but Basil; Waugh's mockery of religious superstition is more extreme. But the terms are the same: the war rocks Barbara back to a primitive faith in her brother, a faith dismissed as superstition. In both novels, this reversion is decried: there is little room for religion in the contemporary world.

Silk's limbo is not a place of "communal order": both novels stress the isolation of the individual. The dynamic between the individual and the community in Woolf's novels is always a restless one; it is never more restless than in *Between the Acts*. *Between the Acts* is the grimmest of Woolf's novels, the least remitting in its dissection of human relations. In *Mrs. Dalloway*, the bond of human contact is a fine thread: Richard Dalloway perceives "that spider's thread of attachment between himself and Clarissa," and those departing from Lady Bruton's are "attached to her by a thin thread (since they had lunched with her)."⁵ These filaments reappear in *Between the Acts*, but they fail to establish any such intimacy. Though Isa may recall Rupert Haines' brief exchanges with her hanging "between them like a wire, tingling, tangling, vibrating" (15), she can never reinforce this bond: "But, she was crying, had we met before the salmon leapt like a bar of silver . . . had we met, she was crying" (144). Isa does establish a bond with Rupert Haines—"The words made two rings, perfect rings, that floated them, herself and Haines, like two swans downstream"—only to quickly and brutally undercut the image herself: "But his snow-white breast was circled with a tangle of dirty duckweed; and she too, in her webbed feet was entangled, by her husband, the stockbroker" (8). The words which make this bond, "So we'll go no more a-roving by the light of the moon" (8), countervail Isa's image of floating downstream. And the bond is soon to be destroyed by Mrs. Haines: "she would destroy it, as a thrush pecks the wings off a butterfly" (9). Threads do not so much attach as strap her to her husband: " 'Oh,' she sighed, pegged down on a chair arm, like a captive balloon, by a myriad of hair-thin ties into domesticity" (17).

Mrs. Dalloway's filaments of communication unravel in *Between the Acts* and they do so because of the war. Miss La Trobe, eavesdropping upon a stray conversation, senses "invisible threads connecting the bodiless voices" (106), but the nature of that conversation belies the positive value of such filamented communication:

> 'It all looks very black.'
> 'No one wants it - save those damned Germans.'
> There was a pause. (106)

The fine balance between isolation and intimacy achieved in the earlier novels has been thrown out of kilter. Those who do not go to church after the pageant remain at Pointz Hall as bitterly isolated as they began. With the departure of Mrs. Manresa, Bart feels that "Solitude had come again" (142); he is left "with the ash grown cold and no glow, no glow on the log" (140). Lucy, gazing into the pond, sees that the fish have retreated: " 'All gone,' she murmured, 'under the leaves' " (142). She attempts to speak to Bart but he has withdrawn to the house; William Dodge's name still escapes her. For Isa, the play, which she misquotes, slowly disappears: " 'Orts, scraps, and fragments,' she quoted what she remembered of the vanishing play" (149). She has lost Rupert Haines, and hears the church-bell chimes come to a halt: "There was not going to be another note" (144). Miss La Trobe, too, ends loverless, and must experience "the horror and the terror of being alone" (146). A proleptic communion is permitted to offset this bleak catalogue of divorced couples, but Isa and Giles have a long way to go before they will embrace.

Isa hammers in the final nail with her response to Lucy:

> 'Did you feel,' she asked 'what he said: we act different parts but are the same?'
> 'Yes,' Isa answered. 'No,' she added. It was Yes, No. Yes, yes, yes, the tide rushed out embracing. No, no, no, it contracted. The old boot appeared on the shingle. (149)

Lucy raises her hands to her cross in defence at Isa's answer, for Isa has decided that an individual's disparity cannot be unified, like a piece of a jigsaw, into an overarching system of common identity. The image that surfaces with this decision, the old boot on the shingle, refers to Streatfield's appearance on the soap-box (132), and to one of Isa's earlier poems: " 'Dispersed are we,' Isabella followed her, humming. 'All is over. The wave has broken. Left us stranded, high and dry. Single, separate on the shingle' " (70). Woolf leaves the main characters in *Between the Acts* stranded, high and dry. The battle between isolation and intimacy lost, they end separated in a world without communal order.

Put Out More Flags ends with the principal characters equally alone. Alastair leaves Sonia, and Basil, Angela. Rampole is forced to sit out the war in a comfortable cell; Ambrose's isolation in Ireland is complete: "The days passed and he did absolutely nothing" (218).* But the charges on the poles of isolation and intimacy are reversed: the isolation Ambrose and Rampole experience has a positive force. For Waugh, the limbo world

---

*The serenity of Waugh's own surroundings may have contributed to the presentation of Ambrose's hermitage. The *Duchess of Bedford* returned to Liverpool via Iceland, travelling all the way up the Atlantic, which perhaps resulted in this description: "Only the wide, infested Atlantic lay between him and Parsnip. He had taken rooms in a little fishing town and the great waves pounded on the rocks below his windows" (218).

of Twilight War is a fine and private place: "This was February 1940, in that strangely cosy interlude between peace and war" (108–109). Ambrose expressly rejects the values of community propounded by Woolf's gramophone, proclaiming that "European culture has become conventional; we must make it cenobitic" (176).

Though both write of human contact and its ultimate failure, Waugh exults in man's ability to transcend the atrophy of human relations. Cedric registers this exultation, walking towards his death:

> As he walked alone he was exhilarated with the sense of being one man, one pair of legs, one pair of eyes, one brain, sent on a single intelligible task; one man alone could go freely anywhere on the earth's surface; multiply him, put him in a drove and by each addition of his fellows you subtract something that is of value, make him so much less a man; this was the crazy mathematics of war. (207–208)

Still walking, Cedric completely overturns Woolf's insistence on the paramount importance of community: "No one had anything against the individual; as long as he was alone he was free and safe; there's danger in numbers; divided we stand, united we fall, thought Cedric" (208). As the narrator points out, Cedric's exhilaration in his new-found isolation mirrors the antisocial stirrings in Ambrose Silk: "He did not know it, but he was thinking exactly what Ambrose had thought when he announced that culture must cease to be conventual [sic] and become cenobitic" (208). Cedric's unnecessary and unsuccessful attempt to connect with A company leads to his death: in Waugh's war, communication is intensely dangerous.

It is also undesirable: the communion so earnestly desired in *Between the Acts* is barren and unfulfilling in *Put Out More Flags*. Barbara and Freddy Sothill suffer "the atrophy endemic to all fruitful marriages" (10). A similar disease paralyzes the union of Cedric and Angela Lyme. Cedric's attempted farewell is a catastrophe:

> 'I'm afraid I'm tiring you.'
> 'Well, I'm not feeling terribly well to-day. Did you want to see me about anything special?'
> 'No, I don't think so. Just to say good-bye.' (172)

Sonia Trumpington's early married life was spent entertaining men in her bath; Angela counts the rings on her telephone. The only intimate union in *Put Out More Flags* is incestuous, as Waugh admits in a letter to his father: "it has good bits, such as the half incestuous relationship of Basil and Barbara."* Human contact in *Put Out More Flags* is either aborted or perverse: Ambrose retreats from these stunted intimacies into an antisocial peace. Ambrose, Cedric, and Basil rejoice in their escape from the masses of society, ending the book alone. The principal characters of both novels are ultimately disconnected; in Waugh, this singularity is their strength.

In both novels, the catalyst for this disconnection is the war. Woolf's original decision to end *Pointz Hall* with an invocation to the ideal of community cannot stand up in 1940. The wartime world is violently at odds with the pageant's past: "The young, who can't make, but only break; shiver into splinters the old vision; smash to atoms what was whole" (128). The threatened disruption prevents the translation of the pageant's unity into the modern world, as the audience's reaction to the aeroplanes makes clear: "And if one spirit animates the whole, what about the aeroplanes?" (137). If the characters in *Between the Acts* revert from a fulfilling community to a barren individuality due to the disruptive effect of the coming war, the situation in Waugh is exactly reversed. The war compresses individuals into types; the character's isolation is a reaction against the war's eradication of individuality rather than a natural consequence of its fragmentation of society.

In *Put Out More Flags*, war stamps out personality. Mrs. Seal says to Joseph Mainwaring: "In war time individuality doesn't matter any more. There are just *men*, aren't there?" (23). Christopher Sykes has argued that Ambrose Silk and Basil Seal are the two heroes of the book;[6] that heroism may be measured in their respective ability to assert their individuality in the midst of war. Sir Joseph answers Lady Seal: "Yes. Basil's individuality has always been rather strong, you know" (23). Ambrose's wartime sense of self is equally strong: "Here is the war, offering a new deal for everyone;

---

*Evelyn Waugh, Letter to Arthur Waugh [5 December 1941], *Letters*, 158. In *Basil Seal Rides Again*, a short sequel written in 1960, Waugh plays this theme to the hilt. Basil's relation with his daughter, also named Barbara, leaves little to the imagination: "Two arms embraced his neck and drew him down, an agile figure inclined over the protruberance of his starched shirt, a cheek was pressed to his and teeth tenderly nibbled the lobe of his ear" (*Basil Seal Rides Again*, 13). The incest is compounded when Basil pretends to be his daughter's fiancé's father in order to break an undesirable marriage. However, Sonia Trumpington's explicit statement in the sequel, "You Seals are so incestuous" (42), has been fairly obvious since Basil's scuffle with Barbara in front of Doris Connolly at Malfrey.

I alone bear the weight of my singularity" (61). Ambrose falls shy of the Nietzschean superman in many respects, but the following reverie begs that comparison:

> [...] if I were not a single, sane individual, if I were part of a herd, one of these people, normal and responsible for the welfare of my herd, Gawd strike me pink, thought Ambrose, I wouldn't sit around discussing what kind of war it was going to be. I'd make it my kind of war. I'd set about killing and stamping the other herd as fast and as hard as I could. (73)

The cenobitic life Ambrose advocates turns into an explicit rejection of war:

> 'Invasions swept over China; the Empire split up into warring kingdoms. The scholars lived their frugal lives undisturbed, occasionally making exquisite private jokes which they wrote on leaves and floated downstream.' (176)

Waugh, writing in "the happy circumstances" of complete physical isolation on the *Duchess of Bedford*, gives that isolation a positive value in *Put Out More Flags*.[7] Woolf, "out of things" in Monks House, does not permit her characters the pleasures of solitude, only the pain.[8] The isolation within Pointz Hall brings little cause for rejoicing.

Limbo has a third common characteristic: the inhabitants of Pointz Hall and Malfrey regress to a savage state. In *Put Out More Flags*, the savagery of the Connolly children sets the standard for a general reversion to an animalistic childhood.* With the coming of war, Barbara and Basil return to their childhood, to a first world Freddy finds ominously primitive:

> [...] it was very rarely, now, that the wild little animal in her came above ground; but it was there in its earth, and from time to time he was aware of

*The Connolly atrocities are scarcely an exaggeration. The evacuees at Piers Court seem to have been equally unthinkable: "We ate (and helpers) in the hall making a fine target for the children's spittle from the top landing" (Evelyn Waugh, *Diaries*, 444). The best story to come out of the evacuation, though, was that of a London boy sent to a beautiful country house in Wiltshire. Waking up in the morning, he went down for breakfast, where the Duchess was waiting for him. They waited for some time, among the silver, until the boy, unable to stand it any longer, cried: "Butler! Where's my bloody breakfast?" The Duchess turned to him and said: "Thank God. I've been wanting to say that for years!" (E. S. Turner, *The Phoney War*).

it, peeping out after long absences; a pair of glowing eyes at the twist in the tunnel watching him as an enemy. (15)

The wild animal resurfaces to join Basil "in the world where once they had played pirates," a world of incest, and of insults drawn from the language of the jungle: "Slimy snake," "Crawly spider," "Artful monkey" (102). The animal imagery is much less playful in *Between the Acts*. Mrs. Haines gobbles in the gutter and pecks the wings off butterflies; Isa is at once that mauled butterfly and a tangled swan. George, grouting pig-like in the grass, perceives his grandfather as "a terrible peaked eyeless monster" (13). For both writers, this general reversion is symptomatic of the larger retreat of society as a whole before the onslaught of war. The war heralds a return to a first world:

> Thus, when earthquake strikes a modern city and the pavements gape, the sewers buckle up and the great buildings tremble and topple, men in bowler hats and natty, ready-made suitings, born of generations of literates and rationalists, will suddenly revert to the magic of the forest and cross their fingers to avert the avalanche of concrete. (15)

The language above is Waugh's, but the sentiment is shared: both Woolf and Waugh witness a society retreating to the magic of the forest.

Ambrose's wartime limbo is a primitive place, where the prints of animals mingle with those of barefoot children, where "mist and smoke never lifted" (203), where he witnesses the people of England "quietly receding into their own mists" (218). The war creates the cloud: "when mist came rolling in from the sea one evening, the corporal in command of Alastair's section reported an enemy smoke screen, and for miles round word of invasion was passed from post to post" (216). The war also brings the blackout and the "strange jungle process" (215) of military communication. In *Men At Arms*, the war transforms Belgravia into a two-thousand-year-old swamp:

> At length Guy and Box-Bender joined a group walking to Belgravia. They stumbled down the steps together and set out into the baffling midnight void. Time might have gone back two thousand years to the time when London was a stockaded cluster of huts down the river, and the streets through which they walked, empty sedge and swamp.[9]

The image of the modern world suddenly dropped back centuries into swampland was dear to both authors well before the coming of World

War Two. "We are in a swamp now; in a malarial jungle," Bernard imagines in *The Waves*.[10] In his bath with a rubber sea-serpent, *Black Mischief*'s Sir Samson regresses to a primitive world:

> Soon he was rapt in daydream about the Pleistocene age, where among mists and vast, unpeopled crags, schools of deep-sea monsters splashed and sported; oh, happy fifth day of creation, thought the Envoy Extraordinary, oh, radiant infant sun, newly weaned from the breasts of darkness, oh, rich stream of the soggy continents, oh, jolly whales and sea-serpents frisking in new brine [. . .].[11]

Mrs. Dalloway recalls a primeval London with the street woman's singing: "Through all ages—when the pavement was grass, when it was swamp, through the age of tusk and mammoth, through the age of silent sunrise— the battered woman [. . .] stood singing of love."[12] But with the war the images of swamp acquire an insistent, bitter edge for both writers. The opening of *Men at Arms* stands in stark contrast to the Envoy's daydream; Mrs. Dalloway's wistful evocation of a primitive world would be out of place in *Between the Acts*. The characters in Pointz Hall retreat to a far more violent and savage place.

The swamp in *Between the Acts* is "that deep centre," "that black heart" (35), a repository of human desires from which all emotions surface. Mrs. Manresa's "spring of feeling bubbled up through her mud" (36); the image of Lucy Swithin's brother "rose from the depths of her lily pool" (143). Once in *Put Out More Flags* a pool fulfills a similar metaphoric function, as Ambrose waits for dawn: "mournful and black eyes open, staring into the blackness. From the fishy freight below him water oozed slowly on to the pavement making a little pool, as though of tears" (197). Woolf's swamp is not, however, a place of mist and tears. The lily pond, the river where Lucy remembers catching a fish—" 'Oh!' she had cried - for the gills were full of blood" (19)—and the salmon brook where Isa and Giles first cross wires, all are images of this primeval world.

The last scene of *Between the Acts* takes place in the heart of the swamp. Lucy's *Outline of History* provides the set:

> 'England [. . .] was then a swamp. Thick forests covered the land. On the top of their matted branches birds sang [. . .] Prehistoric man, half-human, half-ape, roused himself from his semi-crouching position and raised great stones.' (151–52)

Two violent images of the day return. The bloody rape Isa extrapolates from the article in *The Times* resurfaces with the second post. Isa looks down at Giles' presumably changed shoes, recalling his destruction of the snake-toad. Then Giles turns out the light, plunging the Olivers into pitch darkness:

> It was night before roads were made, or houses. It was the night that dwellers in caves had watched from some high place among rocks.
>   Then the curtain rose. They spoke. (152)

These words will raise Isa and Giles from the heart of darkness, breaking down their isolation and bringing them to an embrace. "The primeval voice sounding loud in the ear of the present moment" (99) is the voice of Eros. But though Miss La Trobe hears these words, the reader cannot. Waugh wrote of *A Handful of Dust* (1934) that though it began as "a short story about a man trapped in the jungle, [...] the thing grew into a study of other sorts of savage at home and the civilized man's helpless plight among them."[13] *Put Out More Flags* continues that study; with the coming of war, both Waugh and Woolf present the savagery of civilized man with a heightened urgency. As 1939 drags on into 1940, the suspension of *Work Suspended* becomes more acute. The narrators of *Between the Acts* and *Put Out More Flags* inhabit the same jungle as the society they present. Waugh and Woolf savagely undercut their characters, and in that savagery implicate themselves in the primitive state to which phoney war society has returned. Both narrate from an Ozymandian distance, monarchs of all they survey, thereby contributing to the isolation in which every central character ends. The narrators reflect a world without room for the values of faith, communion, and civilization. Both question the possibility of saving grace, a grace it will be left to *Brideshead* to provide.

The Operation of Divine Grace in *Brideshead Revisited*

> Perhaps in the mansions of Limbo the heroes enjoy some such compensation for their loss of the Beatific Vision; [...] I, at any rate, believed myself very near heaven, during those languid days at Brideshead.
>
> *Brideshead Revisited*

Limbo may be the place for Ambrose Silk in 1940; by 1943 Lord Marchmain's place is purgatory. Waugh's writing undergoes a profound spiritual change from *Put Out More Flags* to *Brideshead Revisited*. Waugh shows an unprecedented concern for the book as it goes to press, calling it his *magnum opus* throughout 1944, and admitting to Nancy Mitford in 1945 that "For the first time since 1928, I am eager about a book."[1] The book is more than a watershed; it represents for Waugh a new beginning: "it is the first of my novels rather than the last"; "Thank God I think I am beginning to acquire a style."[2] Certainly *Brideshead* is written very differently from any earlier work; but the revolution is not just stylistic, it is moral. In *Vile Bodies*, the *Purgatorio* is taken for a French novel, "and pretty dirty, too, I shouldn't wonder."[3] By the end of *Brideshead Revisited*, Ryder prays for Lord Marchmain to make the sign of contrition which will send him to purgatory: by the end of *Brideshead Revisited*, purgatory has become a very real place. In Waugh's writing in the twenties, everything was "too divine"—by 1943 divinity has a very palpable force.

Waugh is progressively more explicit about the force of religion in *Brideshead Revisited*. "He can call it 'A Household of the Faith' if he likes," he writes of his publisher in 1944; to Nancy Mitford he explains that "the book is about God."[4] In a 1946 interview with *Life* magazine, he makes the new direction in his work quite clear:

> So in my future books there will be two things to make them unpopular: a preoccupation with style and the attempt to represent man more fully, which, to me, means only one thing, man in his relation to God.[5]

Brideshead Revisited, by the time of the 1960 preface, has one central theme: "the operation of divine grace on a group of diverse but closely connected characters."[6] In *Brideshead* there is finally room for the Beatific Vision which Ambrose Silk decries.*

Charles receives this vision with his first sight of Brideshead Castle:

> Perhaps in the mansions of Limbo the heroes enjoy some such compensation for their loss of the Beatific Vision; perhaps the Beatific Vision itself has some remote kinship with this lowly experience; I, at any rate, believed myself very near heaven, during those languid days at Brideshead. (79)†

---

*The appearance of Beatrice at the end of the *Purgatorio* should not be confused with Dante's vision of her in *Paradiso* 30. The former vision is the material representation of the latter, as Brideshead is, for Charles, the material representation of Paradise.

†Evelyn Waugh, *Brideshead Revisited* (Boston: Little, Brown & Company, 1945), 79. References to this edition of *Brideshead Revisited* in this section will appear within the text.

This magnificent passage reiterates a point stressed throughout the literature of the Second World War: limbo and purgatory are mirror-images of one another. Here, Waugh makes the leap from the limbo of *Put Out More Flags* into the purgatory of *Brideshead* and beyond. Brideshead Castle is established as the earthly paradise, the place of the first vision of Beatrice, a place "very near heaven." "Et in Arcadia Ego," the title of this first section of *Brideshead Revisited*, alludes to the pastoral tradition of Sidney, Sannazaro and Montemayor, a tradition to which the last cantos of the *Purgatorio* belong. At the center of every Arcadia is found a grove, where rises a sacred spring. Charles finds his transcendent center before the fountain:

> [. . .] here, as I passed through those arches and broken pediments to the pillared shade beyond and sat, hour by hour, before the fountain, probing its shadows, tracing its lingering echoes, rejoicing in all its clustered feats of daring and invention, I felt a whole new system of nerves alive within me, as though the water that spurted and bubbled among its stones was indeed a life-giving spring. (82)

In the fountain Charles' original suspicion is confirmed. The fountain is "indeed a life-giving spring": Eunoe, Dante's river of life, running through the earthly paradise. Charles' beatific vision is complete; Brideshead becomes his Beatrice.

Charles begins an atheist and ends a Catholic; his road to purgatory is a difficult one. Ryder, like Plant in *Work Suspended*, has been brought up to treat religion with cynical indifference: "The view implicit in my education was that the basic narrative of Christianity had long been exposed as a myth, and that opinion was now divided as to whether its ethical teaching was of present value" (85–86). His detached attitude devolves from John Plant Senior's line on Catholicism: "Grant them their first absurdities and you will find Roman Catholics a reasonable people - and they have civilized habits." These reasonable and civilized Roman Catholics become the Marchmains; *Work Suspended* is in many ways a dress rehearsal for *Brideshead Revisited*. John Plant the younger is the only other first person narrator in Waugh's fiction. Both men are prigs, though Ryder is less drily so; both men are self-conscious, though Ryder is less dully so. And Charles shares, initially, Plant's disdainful and grudging respect for religion.

Charles has always perceived the Catholic faith to be built on illusion. Lady Marchmain admits that religion has its "Alice-in-Wonderland side"

(127), a side that utterly bewilders Rex Mottram in his thwarted attempt to convert to Catholicism. Rex swallows Cordelia's pack of lies about the Catechism whole, unable to distinguish between absurdities (194). In leaving Brideshead for the first time Charles thinks "I have left behind illusion," but he has drowned his book prematurely: "I have since learned that there is no such world" (169). Though he leaves the "Young Magicians Compendium" (169) behind him, he will always play Prospero before the "insubstantial pageant" (110) of his story. And at the close of the book, after denouncing Catholicism as "superstition and trickery," "witchcraft and hypocrisy" (324; 325), Charles finds himself praying for Marchmain's redemption. The master of illusions falls prey to the greatest mirage of all. But for Charles, and for Waugh, Catholicism is no longer a mirage.

His awakening is simultaneous with Lord Marchmain's:

> I suddenly felt the longing for a sign, if only of courtesy, if only for the sake of the woman I loved, who knelt in front of me, praying, I knew, for a sign. It seemed so small a thing that was asked, the bare acknowledgment of a present, a nod in the crowd. All over the world people were on their knees before innumerable crosses, and here the drama was being played again by two men—by one man, rather, and he nearer death than life; the universal drama in which there is only one actor.
>
> The priest took the little silver box from his pocket and spoke again in Latin, touching the dying man with an oil wad; he finished what he had to do, put away the box and gave the final blessing. Suddenly Lord Marchmain moved his hand to his forehead; I thought he had felt the touch of the chrism and was wiping it away. "O God," I prayed, "don't let him do that." But there was no need for fear; the hand moved slowly down his breast, then to his shoulder, and Lord Marchmain made the sign of the cross. Then I knew that the sign I had asked for was not a little thing, not a passing nod of recognition, and a phrase came back to me from my childhood of the veil of the temple being rent from top to bottom. (338–39)

As Waugh makes clear in a letter to Ronald Knox, the book depends on this scene, drawn from the death of Hubert Duggan:

> It was, of course, all about the death bed. I was present at almost exactly that scene, with less extravagant decor, when a friend of mine whom we thought in his final coma and stubbornly impenitent, whose womenfolk would only let the priest in because they thought him unconscious, did exactly that, making the sign of the cross. It was profoundly affecting and I wrote the book about that scene.[8]

Here Waugh has a double purpose. The drama is indeed played by "two men," and not just by Marchmain and the priest. The fight to worm Marchmain into purgatory is also a fight for Charles' soul.

Charles' indignant discussion with the Flyte family on the necessity of the chrism clearly marks Lord Marchmain's destination as purgatory. His family realize they cannot send him straight to heaven: "Having a requiem doesn't mean you go to heaven necessarily" (329). They just "want to keep him out of hell" (329). Marchmain is destined for the Ante-Purgatory at the foot of the mountain. But with Marchmain's death, *Brideshead Revisited* becomes the story of Charles' conversion as well. Father Brown's "twitch on the thread" (220) which Sebastian resists is felt first by Julia, then by Marchmain, and finally by Charles. Lord Marchmain's entrance into the ranks of the Late-Repentant opens the way for Charles' repentance, conversion, and revision of his past.

By the end of the book, then, Charles Ryder has matured to a new level of religious awareness. His narrative shows it: Ryder repeatedly stresses the religious theme after the fact. On his way to his first Sunday brunch with Sebastian Flyte, he thinks "So through a world of piety I made my way to Sebastian" (60). The remark is a *post hoc* reflection; Ryder recasts his memory in a religious frame. Stray details like Nanny Hawkins' rosary are highlighted by the narrator:

> Sebastian's Nanny was seated at the open window; the fountain lay before her, the lakes, the temple, and, far away on the last spur, a glittering obelisk; her hands lay open in her lap and, loosely between them, a rosary; she was fast asleep. (35)

The sentence balances obelisk and rosary, a witness to Charles' new preoccupation with religion. He occasionally admits to this curious form of hindsight, throwing forward to his present perspective: "Sebastian's faith was an enigma to me at that time" (85). On learning that Ryder has never seen a game of cricket, Father Graves "looked at me with the expression I have seen since in the religious" (85). "At that time" and "since" disrupt the narrative: Brideshead is revisited under Christian eyes.

Charles Ryder, like *The Good Soldier*'s John Dowell, is an unreliable narrator: unreliable not because he is a liar but because he is a Catholic. The two narrators have a great deal in common. Waugh wrote to Mitford of Ryder that "he is dim, but then he is telling the story, and it is not his story."⁹ This comment really applies better to John Dowell. Ryder is not dim, just aware of his limitations: "I knew it was good chance that had made my landscape, and that this elaborate pastiche was too much for me" (83). He and Julia, unlike Dowell and Florence, do manage to consummate their love on a transatlantic ocean liner. And though it is not initially Charles' story—he enters Brideshead by the back door—he need not be so rudely relegated to a sixpenny seat in the side-show. Dowell, on the other hand, is more than a bit dim, and the saddest story is not his story. In both novels, the religious theme becomes deadly serious by the end. As in *Brideshead*, Catholicism begins as a smoke-screen in *The Good Soldier* with Leonora's outburst: "don't you know that I'm an Irish Catholic?"[10] Julia decides, if she has a child by Rex, to "have it brought up a Catholic" (259), as Leonora does: "The child is to be brought up as a Romanist."[11] Charles is transformed, and Brideshead is revisited from his converted perspective. Dowell remains a Quaker to the end; the integrity of his retrospective is compromised not by religious faith but by a broken faith in humanity.

The second point of Charles' matured perspective is, more obviously, the war. A transformed Charles revisits a Brideshead changed utterly by World War Two. The presence of war in *Brideshead Revisited* moves beyond the frame of time and space provided by the prologue and epilogue. The coming war, as well as the coming conversion, is presaged in Charles' remembrance of the thirties' world. The opening chapters of Ryder's narrative open an unbridgable gulf between the past and present levels of narration. The first chapter ends with the present Ryder in tears: "This is the full account of my first brief visit to Brideshead; could I have known then that so small a thing, in other days, would be remembered with tears by a middle-aged captain of infantry?" (40). The third chapter also pulls sharply into the present to remind the reader that this is more than idle retrospective: "I felt a sense of liberation and peace such as I was to know years later when, after a night of unrest, the sirens sounded the All Clear" (78).

The present Ryder fades out as the story progresses; by the closing chapters the war surfaces in a different way. The past Ryder senses the rumblings of a coming avalanche:

> Quite silently a great weight forming against the timber; the bolt straining in its socket; minute by minute in the darkness outside the white heap sealing the door, until quite soon, when the wind dropped and the sun came out on the ice slopes and the thaw set in, a block would move, slide and tumble, high above, gather way, gather weight, till the whole hillside seemed to be falling,

and the little lighted place would crash open and splinter and disappear, rolling with the avalanche into the ravine. (310–11)

This passage, with Anthony Powell's Ghost Railway at the end of *Casanova's Chinese Restaurant*, is one of the most terrifying descriptions of the lowering of war. The metaphor is extended until the end of the narrative: the day before Marchmain's death, "the snow was beginning to shift on the slopes" (326), after his death "The avalanche was down, the hillside swept bare behind it; the last echoes died on the white slopes; the new mound glittered and lay still in the silent valley" (341). Marchmain's conversion also anticipates the coming war: his "struggle to keep alive" (331) will soon be everybody's struggle. Julia's struggle to keep Charles, her little sin, will be over in September 1939. "Julia would be free in September" (330)—that war is also lost.

With the coming of war, the savagery of *Put Out More Flags* returns. To the War Office, war is "something coming out of the waters, a monster with sightless face and thrashing tail thrown up from the depths" (331). Lady Marchmain's brother's book impresses on Ryder the necessary savagery of war:

> These men must die to make a world for Hooper; they were the aborigines, vermin by right of law, to be shot off at leisure so that things might be safe for the travelling salesman with his polygonal pince-nez, his fat wet hand-shake, his grinning dentures. (139)

The inhabitants of Brideshead retreat to a primitive world. After Kurt's suicide by hanging in a concentration camp, Sebastian "conceived the idea of escaping to the savages" (307). The Spanish Civil War returns Cordelia to a primitive state: 'when she said, "It's wonderful to be home," it sounded to my ears like the grunt of an animal returning to its basket' (301). Ryder imagines a team of archaeologists stumbling on his Company's camp and pronouncing it evidence of "tribal anarchy," of a civilization "overrun by a race of the lowest type" (7). His unspoken lament for Brideshead castle, *"Quomodo sedet sola civitas,"* was last sung by "a half-caste choir in Guatemala" (237) during his trip to South America. Brideshead, like Pointz Hall and Malfrey, returns to a primitive world as the war threatens.

Ryder's revisiting of Brideshead from a war perspective, filtering his experience through his knowledge of the coming avalanche, once again recalls *The Good Soldier*. John Dowell cannot do so, for the novel is pre-war on all narrative levels, but Ford, rewriting *The Good Soldier* in 1915, allows the book to anticipate the coming war. Florence is born, begins a world cruise with her uncle, sleeps with Jimmy, marries Dowell, meets Edward for the first time, witnesses Maisie's death, and dies, all on August fourth. As Frank Kermode has pointed out, the date was added after the war broke out. Virginia Woolf also reworks her novel during the second war, but reverses Ford by writing the war out. Waugh's revisions are different still. Evelyn Waugh, in 1960, neither increases nor decreases the pressure of war. The revised version of *Brideshead Revisited* heightens the pressure and the presence of Catholicism.

The book revolves around the death-bed conversion of Lord Marchmain and the narrator's simultaneous epiphany: "I wrote the book about that scene." With the frame of the war and the countless diversions *Brideshead Revisited* offers along the way, this point is easy to miss. In the 1960 version Waugh drives the point home. All the chapters gain running titles; the final chapter is subtitled "Lord Marchmain at home - death in the Chinese drawing room - the purpose revealed."[12] "The purpose revealed" frames the novel as much as the prologue and epilogue, and with an equally jarring effect. The novel is suddenly afforded a moral; Charles' narrative acquires a teleological force. Waugh also slightly rewrites the scene itself. The sentence

> All over the world people were on their knees before innumerable crosses, and here the drama was being played again by two men—by one man, rather, and he nearer death than life; the universal drama in which there is only one actor. (338)

is replaced with

> I prayed more simply: 'God forgive him his sins' and 'Please God, make him accept your forgiveness.'
>   So small a thing to ask.*

Charles becomes more directly implicated in Marchmain's conversion, praying for God's forgiveness.

Waugh's revisions reach beyond the final scene; as P. A. Doyle writes

*Evelyn Waugh, *Brideshead Revisited*, 1960 edition, 371. The revision recollects Ryder's tears in the prologue: "could I have known then that so small a thing, in other days, would be remembered with tears by a middle-aged captain of infantry?" (40).

in the *Catholic Book Reporter*: "No longer can a critic maintain that Ryder's Catholicism is hidden from the reader until the very end of the book."[13] Early in the novel, Charles outlines a derisive synopsis of the advantages and drawbacks of Christianity:

> The view implicit in my education was that the basic narrative of Christianity had long been exposed as a myth, and that opinion was now divided as to whether its ethical teaching was of present value, a division in which the main weight went against it; religion was a hobby which some people professed and others did not; at the best it was slightly ornamental, at the worst it was the province of "complexes" and "inhibitions"—catchwords of the decade—and of the intolerance, hypocrisy, and sheer stupidity attributed to it for centuries. No one had ever suggested to me that these quaint observances expressed a coherent philosophic system and intransigeant historical claims; nor, had they done so, would I have been much interested. (85–86)

This bald and dispassionate statement of the modern understanding of religion appears only in the 1944 edition: in 1960, Waugh wrote these lines out. Waugh, like Auden and Woolf, is unafraid to revise a sentiment which he can no longer accept. Finding such surgical exposure of a deeply-held religious faith intolerable in 1960, Waugh replaces the lines with a much more diluted criticism:

> The masters who taught me Divinity told me that biblical texts were highly untrustworthy. They never suggested I should try to pray. My father did not go to church except on family occasions and then with derision. My mother, I think, was devout. It once seemed odd to me that she should have thought it her duty to leave my father and me and go off with an ambulance, to Serbia, to die of exhaustion in the snow in Bosnia. But later I recognized some such spirit in myself. Later, too, I have come to accept claims which then, in 1923, I never troubled to examine, and to accept the supernatural as the real. I was aware of no such needs that summer at Brideshead.*

Ryder here is a mouthpiece for Waugh's personal declaration that religion has become more than a useful myth. Ryder comes to "accept the super-natural as the real": Catholicism, like Eliot's rose-garden, is a refuge for those who cannot bear too much reality.

*Evelyn Waugh, *Brideshead Revisited*, 1960 edition, 98. The fate of Charles' mother is not as random as it seems; Claire Hirshfield has shown that her fate was modelled on Katherine Harley's. Her death, like Lord Marchmain's, is drawn from life. See Hirshfield, "The Strange Death of Mrs. Ryder," *Evelyn Waugh Newsletter*, 18, #2 (Autumn 1984), 1–3.

The 1960 edition is a whitewash: Waugh paints over the gray areas in his attempt to press home his theme, "the operation of divine grace on a group of diverse but closely connected characters."[4] The goal is clarity of purpose, but the cost is a loss of ambiguity. In the first version religion is not the only ultimately necessary illusion. Ryder's war also has its Alice-in-Wonderland side. Disturbed by a commanding officer on the way to Brideshead, Charles placates him with the preposterous assertion that they are under enemy attack: ' "we are being sprayed with liquid mustard-gas," I said. "See that the windows are shut" ' (14). The war begins as real as Rex's canvas military convoy:

> "Couldn't stop, drove right into it, smack into a tank, broadside-on. Gave himself up for dead.... Hold on, this is the funny part."
> "This is the funny part."
> "Drove clean through it, didn't scratch his paint. What do you think? It was made of canvas—a bamboo frame and painted canvas." (293)

Ryder is thoroughly disillusioned with the army: "I knew it all, the whole drab compass of marital disillusion; we had been through it together, the army and I" (6). But some illusions, in the 1944 version, do remain. When he confronts Brideshead for the second time he stands "awed and bemused between two realities and two dreams" (15). The unreality of war melds with the unreality of the Arcadian world of Brideshead into one grand illusion: "Which was the mirage, which the palpable earth?" (16). In the 1960 version both these lines are cut.

To Charles in 1944, war is also a dream world, an escape from reality. War is not the villain of the peace; the real enemy is Hooper, for whose sake wars are fought: "These men must die to make a world for Hooper" (139). Hooper lives in a modern world free of illusions: "Hooper had no illusions about the army"; "Hooper was no romantic" (8; 9). Samgrass is of his kind: "it was Mr. Samgrass who was real, the rest were an insubstantial pageant" (110). Rex Mottram is the crowning example of the age of Hooper: "he was something absolutely modern and up-to-date that only this ghastly age could produce" (200). The age of Hooper is the real villain; Rex Mottram is potentially more destructive than any war.* A death's head grins in Poussin's "Et in Arcadia Ego," reality triumphant in

*Elizabeth Verney, in Waugh's 1947 short story "Tactical Exercise," replaces Mottram as "the archpriestess and maenad of the century of the common man" (*Tactical Exercise [and Other Stories]*, 240).

a pastoral world.* In *Brideshead*, that skull is Hooper's, not the war's. To Charles in 1960, war is no longer a dream world. Reality is the enemy; originally the fantasy worlds of war and religion offered separate escapes. But in the revised version Waugh has no more room for an unreal war. War is subsumed into the age of Hooper; it is quite clear which is the mirage, and which the palpable earth. There is only one reality and one dream: religion is the only way out.

Waugh widens the gap between reality and dream, between the natural and the supernatural worlds. The more fantastic passages in Charles' reminiscence, his rapturous celebrations of the Burgundy—"The Pathetic Fallacy resounds in all our praise of wine" (175)—and of Brideshead—"the sun standing still in the heavens and the earth throbbing to our own pulse" (79)—are excised. The real world is made more real: Julia and Charles' maritime encounter is made appallingly matter-of-fact. Originally, the meeting is joined with all the passion of a tribal ritual:

> So at sunset I took formal possession of her as her lover. It was no time for the sweets of luxury; they would come, in their season, with the swallow and the lime-flowers. Now on the rough water, as I was made free of her narrow loins and, it seemed now, in assuaging that fierce appetite, cast a burden which I had borne all my life, toiled under, not knowing its nature—now, while the waves still broke and thundered on the prow, the act of possession was a symbol, a rite of ancient origin and solemn meaning. (261)

Waugh's rescription is much more clinical:

> Now, on the rough water there was a formality to be observed, no more. It was as though a deed of conveyance of her narrow loins had been drawn and sealed. I was making my first entry as the freeholder of a property I would enjoy and develop at leisure."

In 1944, Waugh felt this scene to be inadequately descriptive: "I should like to give as much detail as I have of the meals, to the two coitions - with his wife and Julia. It would be no more or less obscene than to leave them to the reader's imagination, which in this case cannot be as acute as mine. There is a gap in which the reader will insert his own sexual habits instead of those of my characters."[16] One must presume that the 1960

---

*The subject is also treated by Guercino and Reynolds. For a discussion of all three paintings, see E. Panovsky, "Et in Arcadia Ego," in *Meaning and the Visual Arts*, 295–320.

revision draws a fuller representation of the sexual habits of his characters, and thus that the introduction of Charles' callousness is no accident. The *Times Literary Supplement*, reviewing the new version of the novel, found this twist "sordid and prosaic," one of "The real grossnesses of the novel."[17] But it follows from Charles' earlier description of the motives behind Rex and Julia's engagement: "Certainly the fact of his being Brenda Champion's property sharpened Julia's appetite for him [. . .] He knew of Julia; she was by all accounts top débutante, a suitable prize" (184–85). It follows from the age of Hooper; reality is as cold and dehumanized as the modern bathroom, "the uniform, clinical little chambers, glittering with chromium plate and looking-glass, which pass for luxury in the modern world" (153–54).

The supernatural world, on the other hand, is allowed to remain fantastic. The surreal outbursts from Julia and her father are preserved almost intact, since they are encounters with their God.* Waugh writes of the difference in his preface:

> These passages were never, of course, intended to report words actually spoken. They belong to a different way of writing from, say, the early scenes between Charles and his father. I would not now introduce them into a novel which elsewhere aims at verisimilitude. But I have retained them here in something near their original form because, like the Burgundy (misprinted in many editions) and the moonlight they were essentially of the mood of writing.†

Waugh's editing of the surreal is not only in the interests of verisimilitude; in his revision he allows religion to become the only, saving surreality.

Guy Crouchback, in a passage written between the first and the second versions of *Brideshead Revisited*, expounds his philosophy of religion to a chaplain over dinner:

> ' . . . Do you agree,' he asked earnestly, 'that the Supernatural Order is not something added to the Natural Order, like music or painting, to make everyday

---

*Julia's personification of sin, though, is struck out: "*Living in sin*, with sin, by sin, for sin, every hour, every day, year in, year out. Waking up with sin in the morning, seeing the curtains drawn on sin, bathing it, dressing it, clipping diamonds to it, feeding it, showing it round, giving it a good time, putting it to sleep at night with a tablet of Dial if it's fretful" (287).

†1960 edition, 9–10. The undrinkable Clos de Bère (172) becomes the more familiar Clos de Bèze. There is some question whether this was originally a misprint or a mistake. Auberon Waugh's article in the Winter 1986 *Evelyn Waugh Newsletter* has drawn attention to his father's truculent disinterest in wine.

life more tolerable? It *is* everyday life. The supernatural is real; what we call "real" is a mere shadow, a passing fancy. Don't you agree, Padre?'
    'Up to a point.'[8]

Charles, in 1960, comes round to Guy's view that "The supernatural is real": "Later, too, I have come to accept claims which then, in 1927, I never troubled to examine, and to accept the supernatural as the real." Waugh's revisions serve to accentuate the difference between the natural and the supernatural orders, and to strengthen Ryder's final reconciliation of the two. In revisiting Brideshead, Charles transforms his story into religious parable. In revisiting *Brideshead*, Evelyn Waugh does the same.

Soldiers Three: *Sword of Honour, Parade's End*, and *A Dance to the Music of Time*

> 'Not long for purgatory,' his confessor had said of Mr Crouch-back [. . .] His father had been worried, not by anything connected with his worldly progress, but by his evident apathy; he was worrying now perhaps in that mysterious transit camp through which he must pass on his way to rest and light.
>
> *Sword of Honour*

Sword of Honour, Waugh's last major work, sets a crown upon his lifetime's effort; it also holds a central place in the literature of its time. The trilogy completes the sequence of Waugh's own war writing, in replacing limbo with purgatory as figure and ground, and provides a preliminary focus for the Literature of Reimagination. In *Sword of Honour* art imitates life, as Waugh transforms his own experience of war; it also imitates art. Major Ludovic, in *Unconditional Surrender* (1961), is unaware that he is but one of the half dozen English writers who, as Waugh puts it, are "composing or preparing to compose books which would turn from the drab alleys of the thirties into the odorous gardens of a recent past transformed and illuminated by disordered memory and imagination" (532).* The study of *Sword of Honour* leads to at least a half dozen other products of "memory and imagination"—in particular, to the *recherches* of Ford Madox Ford

---

*Evelyn Waugh, *The Sword of Honour Trilogy* (Harmondsworth: Penguin, 1984), 532. References to this edition of *Sword of Honour* in this section will appear within the text.

and Anthony Powell. These grand old men revisit war as Charles revisited Brideshead, from a half-disillusioned, semi-detached perspective.

Crouchback, reversing Ryder, comes to accept not the supernatural as the real, but the real as the supernatural. By the time Waugh writes *Sword of Honour*, the poles of the natural and the supernatural orders have been reversed. Crouchback enters a fantasy world, an enchanted garden where Most Secret intelligence is "mostly about ground-nuts" (170), and where Congreve, a polo-player in Truslove's regiment, will turn up "elaborately disguised as an Afghan merchant with the keys of the Pathan fortress where Truslove himself awaited execution by torture" (171). Surreality, for Waugh, is reality taken to its logical extreme. The scorpions anxiously awaited by Dr. Akonanga so that he may give Von Ribbentrop nightmares do eventually arrive to send Crouchback's ward-mate into delirium (472). The Grace-Groundling-Marchpole file on Crouchback's alleged espionage activity—"The Box-Bender case." "I remember. *And* the Scottish nationalists." "And the priest in Alexandria" (484)—is a hilarious compilation of misinterpretations of reality, an attempt to inflict order upon chaos. In *Books Do Furnish A Room* (1971), Powell's novelist X. Trapnel dresses with "that touch of surreality which redeems from complete absurdity";* Crouchback's war, like Trapnel's costume, never quite shrugs off reality to become unbelievably absurd.

The Wonderland side of war in *A Dance to the Music of Time* is brought out in Jenkins' search for an overcoat at the beginning of *The Soldier's Art*. Standing before a looking-glass, he imagines himself passing through it:

> In a three-sided full-length looking-glass nearby I, too, critically examined the back view of the coat's shot-at-dawn cut, aware at the same time that soon, like Alice, I was to pass, as it were by virtue of these habiliments, through its panes into a world no less enigmatic. (SA, 2)

The shop assistant takes Jenkins for a stage actor performing in *The War*, an obscure London theatrical. Jenkins sees rich possibilities in the misunderstanding:

> Now that the curtain had gone up once more on this old favourite—*The War*— in which, so it appeared, I had been cast for a walk-on part, what days were

---

*Anthony Powell, *Books Do Furnish A Room*, vol. 10 of *A Dance to the Music of Time* (New York: Popular Library, 1976), 107. References to volumes in this edition of *A Dance to the Music of Time* in this section will appear within the text, prefaced by the appropriate initials.

left before joining my unit would be required for dress rehearsal. Cues must
not be missed. The more one thought of it, the more apt seemed the metaphor.
(SA, 3)

He returns to the metaphor throughout the war, seeing a phosphorescent
midnight raid as a "spectacle," a "set-piece," "theatrical yet sinister" (SA,
11–12). Demobilized, Jenkins leaves the theatre of war, passing back out
of Wonderland: "I almost expected the greatcoat, six years before seeming
to symbolize induction into this world through the Looking Glass, would
be ceremonially lifted from my shoulders" (MP, 241). Jenkins and Crouchback meander through a sham, absurdist, "tailor's war" (MP, 185).

The real has clearly become surreal; the supernatural order is real to
Crouchback from the start. For Charles Ryder, the reality of the saving
grace of faith is not revealed until the rending of the temple's veil. Not
so for Guy Crouchback, who begins *Men at Arms* "possessed of nothing
save a few dry grains of faith" (27). The distinction between limbo and
purgatory, collapsed by Ambrose Silk in *Put Out More Flags* and by Charles
on his first visit to Brideshead, is in *Sword of Honour* made absolute. Limbo
is consigned to the oubliette, the dead-end; purgatory becomes the only
way out. Waugh has always excelled at oubliettes, from Paul Pennyfeather's
stint in Llanabba Castle to Tony Last's exile, reading Dickens to Mr. Todd
in darkest Georgetown. Limbo can sometimes be a blessed relief: Ambrose
Silk rather enjoys his solitude in Ireland, and Sebastian ends up in Morocco
by choice. But Guy, recuperating from a botched parachuting exercise,
finds the stasis of the aerodrome's Emergency Ward acutely uncomfortable
(476); Bari in 1944 is equally intolerable: "In this limbo Guy fretted for
more than a week" (517). Purgatory, for Guy, is no joking matter either:

> It was All Souls' Day. Guy walked to church to pray for his brothers' souls
> - for Ivo especially; Gervase seemed far off that year, in Paradise perhaps, in
> the company of other good soldiers. Mr Goodall was there, popping in and
> down and up and out and in again assiduously, releasing *toties quoties* soul after
> soul from Purgatory.
> 'Twenty-eight so far,' he said, 'I always try and do fifty.'
> The wings of the ransomed beat all about Mr Goodall, but as Guy left
> church he was alone in the comfortless wind. (223)

Mr. Goodall's high spirits are lost on Guy, "alone in the comfortless wind."
Crouchback's crutch is his Catholicism: his few dry grains of faith have
blossomed into a real concern for a soul's spiritual progress.

For Guy Crouchback, purgatory has an overwhelming significance.

Virginia Troy is killed by a stray bomb during the second Blitz, "at the one time in her life when she could be sure of heaven - eventually" (542). Virginia will join Lord Marchmain among the Late-Repentant on the foothills of purgatory. Gervase enters purgatory at a higher level: the priest reassures Guy with "I don't think your father has got long for purgatory" (435). Guy, like Ryder before him, is genuinely concerned for the afterlife of the old man. He repeats the priest's words later in the funeral: " 'Not long for purgatory,' his confessor had said of Mr Crouchback" (436). His father has gone to "that mysterious transit camp through which he must pass on his way to rest and light" (437). With this line the waiting worlds of this life and the after-life co-inhere. Purgatory is a transit camp and *vice versa*. The war becomes a way-station on the way to rest and light. Guy's perception of purgatory is filtered by his experience of war; his perception of war, like the many different perceptions of war studied in these pages, is itself filtered by the myth of purgatory.

The filtering, or transformation, of wartime experience defines the Literature of Reimagination, and lies behind all three volumes of *Sword of Honour*. Waugh dedicates *Officers and Gentlemen* to Major General Laycock with the words: *"He will recognize this story as pure fiction: that is to say of experience totally transformed"* (195). The translation of Layforce into Crouchback's Hookforce is fairly straightforward; many scenes in *Sword of Honour* originated in Waugh's own war. Crouchback organizes a debate on marrying young (162), as does Waugh in 1940: "Debate on 'Any man who marries under thirty is a fool.' Lost by overwhelming majority."[1] The Halberdiers' peculiar dinner-table conversation, "a ritual dialogue under the names of 'Silly Bean', 'Black Bean' and 'Awful Bean' " (162) draws from the same entry in Waugh's diary: "A very curious performance by the sergeants who formed a ceremonial party with names of beans - 'Silly Bean', 'Black Bean', 'Awful Bean', etc."[2] Ritchie-Hook is clearly modelled on St. Clair Morford, "who looks like something escaped from Sing-Sing and talks like a boy in the Fourth Form at school - teeth like a stoat, ears like a faun, eyes alight like a child playing pirates, 'We then have to biff them, gentlemen.' "[3] Reading *Sword of Honour* concurrently with Waugh's wartime diaries, one realizes how much of his work is autobiographical, and the extent to which that experience is recast.

The *clefs* to Waugh's *romans* are never very difficult to find: Waugh often unlocks the novels himself. Llanabba Castle, in *Decline and Fall*, rises from Waugh's own "purgatorial interlude of schoolmastering," as Anthony Powell describes it.[4] Atwater, the man who runs over Plant's father in

Work Suspended and then touches the son for money for a wreath, is probably Henry Rhodes: "Worked well at novel. I have introduced the character who came here to beg, saying he was on the *New Statesman* and an authority on ballistics, as the driver who killed the father."⁵ The double embarkation onto the *Duchess of Cumberland* in *Put Out More Flags* was an ignominy actually suffered by Waugh on the *Ettrick* at Birkenhead.⁶ The escape of the poets Parsnip and Pimpernell to America stems from the highly-publicized flight of Auden and Isherwood in 1939. *Brideshead*'s deathbed scene was inspired by the death of Hubert Duggan. The prologue and epilogue occasionally ring uncomfortably of autobiography: Charles "felt as a husband might feel, who, in the fourth year of his marriage, suddenly knew that he had no longer any desire, or tenderness, or esteem, for a once-beloved wife"⁷ Charles is thirty-nine; Waugh, in 1942, was also thirty-nine and had been married to Laura for four years. Despite the *caveat* that begins *Brideshead*, "I am not I; thou art not he or she; they are not they," Waugh's figures are frequently drawn from life.

Less frequently they are drawn from art. Everard Spruce mourns the passing of Virginia Troy with an elegy from *Antic Hay*:

> 'Virginia Troy was the last of twenty years' succession of heroines,' he said. 'The ghosts of romance who walked between the two wars.'
>
> He took a book from his shelves and read: '*She crossed the dirty street, placing her feet with a meticulous precision one after the other in the same straight line as though she were treading a knife edge between goodness only knew what invisible gulf. Floating she seemed to go, with a little spring in every step and the skirt of her summery dress - white it was, with a florid pattern printed in black all over it - blowing airily round her swaying march.* I bet neither of you know who wrote that. You'll say Michael Arlen.' (541)

Here comparison is invited with what has long been a source book for Waugh. Simon Balcairn's false beaver in *Vile Bodies* grows from Gumbril's beard.⁸ Rex Mottram's severity over the brandy at Paillard's recalls Mr. Bulver's indignation:

> "Do you mean to tell me," he shouted in a perfect frenzy of righteous anger, "that you don't yet know how brandy ought to be drunk?"
>
> Perhaps it was only last week that he himself, Gumbril reflected, had learned to aerate his cognac in Gargantuan beakers.⁹

Anthony Blanche buys a copy of *Antic Hay* since "it's so banal saying you have not read the book of the moment, if you haven't."¹⁰

Everard Spruce's panegyric continues to hold Mrs. Viveash responsible not only for Virginia Troy but for an entire literary type:

> 'Anyway the passage I read, believe it or not, is Aldous Huxley 1922. Mrs Viveash. Hemingway coarsened the image with his Bret, but the type persisted - in books and in life. Virginia was the last of them - the exquisite, the doomed, and the damning, with expiring voices - a whole generation younger. We shall never see anyone like her again in literature or in life and I'm very glad to have known her.' (541)

We have not seen the last of her: the character persists beyond *Unconditional Surrender*, reaching an icy peak in Powell's Pamela Flitton. Her prototype is Helen of Troy. In the hospital after his escape from Crete, Guy feels the wind "which long ago delayed Helen and Menelaus on that strand" (372); at the end of the scene, as Mrs. Stitch drops the unknown soldier's identity disc into the waste-paper basket, "Her eyes were one immense sea, full of flying galleys" (386). Virginia Troy's analogy with Helen of Troy is less Homeric and more obvious: "Yes. Exactly. Like Helen of Troy. A very striking woman" (489).

Mrs. Viveash is Becky Sharp grown old, still beautiful, still cold and calculating, but now a tired and essentially sympathetic character. Her closest twin is Ford Madox Ford's Sylvia Tietjens. Sylvia delights in "pulling the strings of shower-baths,"" in wreaking, with one spirited and impulsive action, glorious havoc in Christopher's life. In *Some Do Not...* she is evil enough to require the threat of exorcism and vulgar enough, in one breakfast-table scene, to throw salad-dressing at her husband, taunt his now crippled memory, and question the paternity of his son. At the close of *No More Parades*, however, as she drunkenly and desperately attempts to seduce her husband, one feels a sudden shock of sympathy for Sylvia. And in *The Last Post* the two sides of Sylvia come together in her conversion before the shadow of Father Consett and her reversion upon her chestnut mare. Ford allows both criticism and sympathy for Sylvia Tietjens, inviting the reader to admire and to condemn.

The same delicate balance is struck in Virginia. Virginia Troy is a cross between Huxley's Myra Viveash and Ford's Sylvia Tietjens; Waugh's trilogy could not have been written without *Parade's End*. Peregrine initially despises her: "Virginia was a Scarlet Woman; the fatal woman who had brought about the fall of the House of Crouchback" (488). He reads aloud to her from *"Can You Forgive Her?"* (510), but eventually decides that he can. Even Angelica Box-Bender admits "One couldn't help liking her" (542); after her ordeal by Dr. Akonanga one can forgive her anything:

> What dreams troubled Ribbentrop that night, Virginia could not know. She dreamed she was extended on a table, pinioned, headless and covered with blood-streaked feathers, while a voice within her, from the womb itself, kept repeating: 'You, you, you.' (452)

Guy's first thought, his first New Year's Day in barracks, is of Virginia (65). His wartime obsession with his wife mirrors Christopher's in *No More Parades*, whose thoughts could be carbon copies of Guy's: "Sylvia Tietjens had been excruciatingly unfaithful, in the most painful manner. He could not be certain that the child he adored was his own. . . . That was not unusual with extraordinarily beautiful—and cruel!—women. But she had been haughtily circumspect."[12]

The connection between *Sword of Honour* and *Parade's End* is a well-attested one. Randall Stevenson compares Guy and Christopher at some length:

> Like Ford's Christopher Tietjens, Waugh's partly-autobiographical hero Guy Crouchback is a rare attempt at the portrayal of an exceptionally good man. Like Tietjens, Crouchback remains committed to his honour despite the manifest readiness of the wartime world to reward most highly the least honourable action. Like Tietjens, he finds the chaos and disturbing immorality of this world made painfully immediate by the spectacular, sustained infidelities of his wife.[13]

Guy's "unbroken silence" after the Cretan debacle—"This silence was Guy's private possession, all his own work" (375; 372)—recalls the stubborn silence at the end of the war of the other perfect English gentleman in *Parade's End*, Christopher Tietjens' brother Mark. The houses of Crouchback and Tietjens both search for an heir and end up with a bastard. Gervase Crouchback's concern for the *"Fin de Ligne"* simply puts an old line into a new bottle.

Guy Crouchback and Christopher Tietjens are detached from and disillusioned by war; their separate wars are reconsidered from a distanced perspective. A self-possessed, literate observer records the events of *A Dance to the Music of Time* through similarly dispassionate eyes. Nicholas Jenkins maintains his detachment throughout twelve volumes of first-person narration. Like Waugh's first-person narrators, Plant and Ryder, Jenkins is a reticent man. Ryder keeps the details of Celia's infidelity to himself; Jenkins reveals next to nothing about his wife—"Isobel has just had a miscarriage" (CCR, 99)—or himself—"I revealed my age" (SA, 95). This reticence permits the narrative distance which is the hallmark of the Literature of Reimagination. But Waugh and Powell have a great deal more than reticence in common. They share a central subject, similar attitudes towards that subject, and a whole cast of characters.

To take the cast first: Everard Spruce may claim that the mould was broken which made Virginia Troy (541), but Pamela Flitton is very much cast in her image. Sylvia Tietjens, the original for both women, is frequently compared with a thoroughbred: Gunning claims that Sylvia is "as full of vice as a mare that's a wrong 'un."[4] Pamela gives Jenkins the impression during an air raid, of "being thoroughly vicious, using the word not so much in the moral sense, but as one might speak of a horse - more specifically, a mare" (MP, 125). In Pamela Flitton, fascinating, farouche, and thoroughly nasty, the *femme fatale* persists. On a smaller level, Harold Acton, the source for Anthony Blanche in *Brideshead*, becomes the aesthete Ralph Barnby in *The Music of Time*, still reading from the same poem: " 'What do you expect to do?' he asked. 'Give readings from *The Waste Land*?' " (CCR, 33).

The central character in the twelve books, whose death ends the dance and whose childhood begins it, is Kenneth Widmerpool. His type must have been prevalent in the 1940's, for the following assessment by Keith Douglas of his squadron-leader, nicknamed "Sweeney Todd," describes him perfectly:

> For Sweeney is the true bull in a china-shop. Tactless, good-hearted, and perfectly unimaginative, he could infuriate more people in less time than anyone else I know. But all this without the least ill-will towards them, and without a suspicion that all is not well. His lack of imagination makes him shyer than the most sensitive youth: the converse of the man who didn't know much about art, Sweeney likes what he knows, and distrusts what does not come within the range of his experience. He mistrusts jokes, too many of which he does not understand. When someone makes a humorous remark which escapes him he looks as unhappy as a great dog who is being laughed at. He enjoyed very much being placed in charge of men and I believe experienced the same sort of pleasure as a small boy who sets out lead soldiers, altering and replacing them exactly in the order he wants. He is afraid of intellectual conversation, of music and of painting.[5]

The description also fits Crouchback's fellow Uncle in *Men at Arms*: Widmerpool bears, at least when in uniform, a marked resemblance to Apthorpe.

The subject of *A Dance to the Music of Time*, if it can be said to have one, is the Second World War. The middle sextet, from *At Lady Molly's* to *The Military Philosophers* (1968), revolves around the war. As John Russell points out in "A Music of Time: War," the narrative is weighted disproportionately to the first two years of war: "Clearly, the psychological strain undergone while the Germans had the initiative is what Powell remembers as *the* collective ordeal of the British in the war: the first two years deserve the attenuation they get because they collect the weight of decades as decisive action remains postponed."[16] This weight is not lifted until the end of the fifth book in the sextet, *The Soldier's Art*, with Germany's invasion of Russia: "An immediate, overpowering, almost mystic sense of relief took shape within me. I felt suddenly sure everything was going to be all right" (SA, 227). Russell observes that Powell's reaction to the invasion is diametrically opposite to Waugh's:

> The second volume of Waugh's trilogy also happens to pivot on the German invasion of Russia, only in a revealingly opposite way. The breach of faith between Germany and Russia *destroys* Guy Crouchback's vision of a holy war against Fascism and Communism. Now the detestable Communists must become allies. Nothing could demonstrate more powerfully the unideological basis of Powell's writing.[17]

Crouchback begins the war caught up in the vision of the Just Cause: "But now, splendidly, everything had become clear. The enemy at last was plain in view, huge and hateful, all disguise cast off" (11). Jenkins has never shared in this simplifying vision; or if he has, he has clouded his politics as he clouds all his deepest motivations.

There are similarities, though, in the narrators' attitudes to war. Waugh and Powell write an old war. They, like their main characters, are too old for World War Two; in their descriptions of war they repeatedly revert to World War One. Gervase's medal of Our Lady of Lourdes, sent back after his death in the first war, hangs around Guy's neck. Trying to work his way into the war, Guy is repelled by recollections of 1914: "we learned our lesson in 1914 when we threw away the pick of the nation"; "All that sort of thing happened in 1914 - retired colonels dyeing their hair" (20; 17). In *A Dance to the Music of Time*, the whole of the second trilogy slowly builds towards the Second World War. With war still undeclared, Jenkins compares this gradual three-volume crescendo to the thunderclap of August 1914:

Unlike the Stonehurst epoch, when, whatever jocular references to a German invasion might be made by persons like Bracey, war had come for most people utterly without warning - like being pushed suddenly on a winter's day into a swirling whirlpool of ice-cold water by an acquaintance, unpredictable perhaps, but not actively homicidal - war was now materialising in slow motion. Like one of the Stonehurst 'ghosts', war towered by the bed when you awoke in the morning; unlike those more transient, more accommodating spectres, its tall form, so far from dissolving immediately, remained, on the contrary, a looming, menacing shape of ever greater height, ever thickening density. The grey, flickering sequences of the screen showed with increased persistence close-ups of stocky demagogues, fuming, gesticulating, stamping; oceans of raised forearms; steel-helmeted men tramping in column; armoured vehicles rumbling over the *pavé* of broad boulevards. Crisis was unremitting, cataclysm not long to be delayed. (KO, 86–87)

The title *At Lady Molly's* has a past and a present referent, describing both the Sleaford establishment at Dogdene during the first war and the Jeavons' Kensington home in 1934. Both Jenkins and Jeavons bring Dogdene into the present day: Jenkins in his remembering, and Jeavons in his rekindling of the 1916 romance with Mildred Blaides. *The Kindly Ones* refers to the Furies, last seen as Eliot's Eumenides in *The Family Reunion.** As in Eliot, they hide in a haunted country seat, and herald its desolation. They are arriving for a second time; Jenkins remembers their appearance in 1914:

'They've just assassinated an Austrian archduke down in Bosnia. Did it today. Only happened a few hours ago.'
Uncle Giles muttered, almost whispered these facts, speaking as if he were talking to himself, not at all in the voice of a man announcing to the world in general the close of an epoch; the outbreak of Armageddon; the birth of a new, uneasy age. He did not look in the least like the harbinger of the Furies. (KO, 69–70)

Jenkins inhabits the childhood world of Stonehurst through most of *The Kindly Ones*; the trilogy ends when both wars begin: "Another stage of life was passed, just as finally, just as irrevocably, as on that day when childhood had come so abruptly to an end at Stonehurst" (KO, 254). Talking with Stonehurst's cook, Albert, Jenkins "found myself invoking the past. This seemed the only avenue of escape [. . .] I was now determined to re-create Stonehurst" (KO, 150–51). In preparing for a second War

*They will be seen again, pursuing Pynchon's Tyrone Slothrop in 1973.

Jenkins returns to his other war, to his childhood days at Stonehurst and Dogdene.

For Crouchback, too, war is both a fantasy world and a childhood world. The war triggers a return to childhood, as it did for Basil and Barbara Seal in *Put Out More Flags*. For Ritchie-Hook the war is a schoolboy's practical joke: "For this remarkable warrior the image of war was not hunting or shooting; it was the wet sponge on the door, the hedgehog in the bed; or, rather, he saw war itself as a prodigious booby trap" (57). Training at Kut-al-Imara, the Halberdiers are subjected to these fourth-form pranks and regress completely:

> There was no bugler at Kut-al-Imara and Sarum-Smith one day facetiously rang the school bell five minutes before parade. Major McKinney thought this a helpful innovation and gave orders to continue it. The curriculum followed the textbooks, lesson by lesson, exercise by exercise, and the preparatory school way of life was completely re-created. They were to stay there until Easter - a whole term. (89)

Later in *Unconditional Surrender*, De Souza remarks that "All army courses are like prep schools" (462). At the beginning of the war, Crouchback and Jenkins are schoolboys in a surreal world.

This backward-looking reaction to the coming war is characteristic of the Literature of Anticipation: MacNeice, Woolf, and Orwell all attempt to recapture the past to face the present. *The Soldier's Art* draws its title from Browning's "Childe Roland":

> 'Think first, fight afterwards - the soldier's art;
> One taste of the old time sets all to rights.' (SA, 221)

The soldier must look back and assess his past to understand what he is fighting for; the writers before the Second World War throw back to a past world to understand what they are writing to preserve. But neither *Sword of Honour* nor *A Dance to the Music of Time* is part of the Literature of Anticipation. The search for a vanishing past comes at a double remove; anticipation is reimagined, not experienced. *The Kindly Ones* is a remembrance of a remembrance of things past.

The Literature of Reimagination, for the most part, is Proustian at only one remove. Powell remembers, in *To Keep the Ball Rolling*, his first confrontation with the works of Proust: "Yorke and I had shared the discovery of Proust at Oxford, where we spend a good deal of time discussing *A la*

Recherche."[18] Green [Henry Yorke] remembers these discussions his 1939 autobiography *Pack My Bag*: "At the same time the last volumes of '*A La Recherche du Temps Perdu*' were coming out and anyone who pretended to care about good writing and who knew French knew his Proust."[19] These discussions have obvious results in each author's work. Green includes a long passage from Proust in *Back*, and in Powell's *The Military Philosophers*, the name Cabourg transforms the Normandy village into Proust's Balbec: "It all came back - like the tea-soaked madeleine itself - in a torrent of memory ... Cabourg ... " (MP, 167).

The torrent of memory runs far beyond Waugh and Powell. If it is true, as Eliot wrote during the war, that "You cannot understand war [...] while you are in the midst of it,"[20] then by the fifties, English writers were ready to come to terms with their experience of war. Keith Douglas has insisted that poets require time and distance to distill that experience: "the whole body of English war poetry of this war, civil and military, will be created after war is over."[21] The same is true of the war novel. Many writers after World War One found themselves unable to assess the impact of war on their lives until a decade had passed; the late twenties witnessed in the works of Sassoon, Ford, Graves, and others the sudden flowering of a new genre of war literature. *Parade's End* provided Waugh and Powell with a model for their own retrospectives. *Sword of Honour* and *A Dance to the Music of Time* are the two works most closely allied with their counterparts after World War One; but there are many different writers remembering very different wars. The last chapter will look at some of them. But the sword of Sir Roger de Waybroke, so often touched by the villagers that its edge is always bright, hangs in the center of these re-imaginings of war.

VII. Coda: The End of All Our Exploring

> We shall not cease from exploration
> And the end of all our exploring
> Will be to arrive where we started
> And know the place for the first time.

Eliot.

> Purgatory possessed no cocktail cabinets, television sets, jockeys, Bentleys or neverwozzers, and served bread and margarine instead of buttered toast.

Le Carré.

The Literature of Reimagination is an enormous subject, and one which I am thoroughly unqualified to address. I was born in 1961, and have not fought in any war. My only memory of World War Two is a story my father tells of his father, to whom this book is dedicated. K.G.J.C.K. was an air-raid warden in Nottingham during the war, and came back from work one evening covered in bandages. He put the second movement of Beethoven's Fourth Piano Concerto on the gramophone and stamped around the room, frightening the daylights out of his two children. He was acting out both piano and orchestra, playing both Orpheus and the beasts. I've probably got this story wrong; like *The Kindly Ones*, it's a memory of a memory. My grandfather is dead now; as people die and historical documents lose their color and fade, only the literature is left. The butchers of the forties now run flower shops and garages in little towns, hounded only by those who cannot forget. The war is in danger of becoming a forgotten time; its literature ensures that it will never be so.

This last section centers on writers who perceive the war as a literary text, who apprehend the meaning long after the experience. As Eliot puts it in *The Dry Salvages*:

We had the experience but missed the meaning,
And approach to the meaning restores the experience
In a different form, beyond any meaning
We can assign to happiness.[1]

It takes time for that approach, time for the resistance to memory to wear away. This was true of World War One; it was true of Vietnam. Wilfred Owen's poems were introduced by Sassoon in 1920 without success; only in 1931 was the public ready for Edmund Blunden's edition of the collected poems. Oliver Stone had a similar problem finding backing for *Platoon*; though the film was shot in the seventies, it had to wait for its audience. There is a danger in remembering too soon. Orpheus must surface from hell before looking back.

Those who reach the end of all their exploring, who return to the war and know the place for the first time, proceed to create an aftermyth of war. The literature after World War Two is more diffuse than the battery of war works that appeared after World War One; the aftermyth of war is less clearly defined. It is possible, though, to speak generally of the Literature of Reimagination. Eliot lays out the principles of return as early as "Tradition and the Individual Talent":

> Consequently, we must believe that "emotion recollected in tranquillity" is an inexact formula. For it is neither emotion, nor recollection, nor, without distortion of meaning, tranquillity.[2]

It is not emotion as much as a concentration, an energy. It is not recollection; the poet doesn't return to a memory as much as the memory floods into the present. And it is not tranquil as much as it is detached. This may seem like semantics, but Eliot is a poet of reticence rather than tranquillity. So it is with the Literature of Reimagination. *Gravity's Rainbow* (1973) and *The Naked and the Dead* (1948) are much less serene in their presentations of war than *Sword of Honour* and *A Dance to the Music of Time*. But British post-war literature is anything but disinterested. Churchill's stance in the following description, from *The Second World War*, is as passionate as anything in Mailer:

> Thereafter mighty forces were adrift; the void was open, and into that void after a pause there strode a maniac of ferocious genius, the repository and expression of the most virulent hatreds that have ever corroded the human breast - Corporal Hitler.[3]

A remembered waiting is never as acute as the experience itself. But two of the most powerful descriptions of wartime London come after the war, from Elizabeth Bowen and Margery Allingham. Margery Allingham, in *The Tiger in the Smoke*, describes the Blitz as follows:

> 'Remember V 2's? The whole city waiting. Silent. People on edge. More waiting. Waiting for hours. Nothing. Nothing to show. Then, strike a light! Suddenly, no warning, no whistle, wallop! End of the ruddy world! Just a damned great hole and afterwards half the street coming down very slowly, like a woman fainting.'[4]

For Elizabeth Bowen, in *The Heat of the Day*, the Blitz is not a fainting spell but a rape. Robert and Stella, on the brink of announcing their love, are transfixed by a passing plane:

> Overhead, an enemy plane had been dragging, drumming slowly round in the pool of night, drawing up bursts of gunfire—nosing, pausing, turning, fascinated by the point for its intent. The barrage banged, coughed, retched; in here the lights in the mirrors rocked. Now down a shaft of anticipating silence the bomb swung whistling. With the shock of detonation, still to be heard, four walls of in here yawped in then bellied out; bottles danced on glass; a distortion ran through the view. The detonation dulled off into the cataracting roar of a split building: direct hit, somewhere else.
> It was the demolition of an entire moment: he and she stood at attention till the glissade stopped.[5]

From *The Death of the Heart* (1936) to *The Heat of the Day*, the war hangs as an almost invisible backdrop behind Bowen's work. Major Brutt's jigsaw puzzles in *The Death of the Heart* gradually come to symbolize the coming war as Portia pieces them together. The first puzzle is revealed to have a military theme: Anna does "a bit of sky with an aeroplane on it"; Phyllis upsets "some sky and part of the officers."[6] With the arrival of the second jigsaw, "a magnificent air display," the war emerges from the background:

> The planes massing against an ultra-marine sky began each to take a different symbolic form, and as she assembled the spectators she came to look for a threat or promise in each upturned face. One evening Dickie offered to help her: the table was moved in to under a lamp, and Dickie completed an ambulance she had dreaded to tackle.[7]

Like Portia, Bowen dreads to tackle the scenery of war. Her short stories in *Ivy Gripped the Steps* make little reference to the war during which they were written, as Bowen concedes in her preface: 'I am sorry that the stories [...] do not contain more "straight" pictures of the British wartime scene.'[8] In the appropriately named *Afterthought* (1962), Bowen explains why: "The outside world war news was stupefying: headlines and broadcasts came down and down on us in hammer-like chops, with great impact but oddly little reverberation. The simple way to put it was: 'One cannot take things in.' "[9] Bowen is incapacitated by experience; only after the war can she "take things in." Unable to register her experience of war immediately, Bowen suppresses the subject until *The Heat of the Day*.

Four years after *The Heat of the Day*, Margery Allingham also returns to the Blitz in *The Tiger in the Smoke*. Though the book is set in contemporary 1952, 1942 again provides the backdrop. The 'smoke' is slang for the London Metropolis, as a prefatory note explains; it is also London's fog, celebrated since *Bleak House*. (By 1952, that fog had become so thick with anthracite as to be positively Dantesque: Dorothy Sayers, in her wartime translation of the *Purgatorio*, calls the smoke that surrounds the Wrathful on the third cornice of Mount Purgatory a 'Purgatorial "London Particular." ')[10] The smoke also refers both literally and metaphorically to the war.* The unmistakable presence of the war lies beneath *The Tiger in the Smoke*; the book is such a vivid re-vision of the war that it reaches the level of allegory. The discovery of its allegory is the true work of detection demanded from the reader. Without it, the book is merely a novel of suspense. With it, *The Tiger in the Smoke* becomes a profound response to the Second World War.

In that smoke, Allingham recreates the nightmare world of London burning through the Blitz. Through the fog in 1952 a band of ex-servicemen march, an albino, a dwarf, a thug, and a lunatic, rattling their money boxes and accidentally kicking men to death. One of the marching band masquerades as Major Elginbrodde, killed in action during the war. The smoke permits the illusion that the Major is still alive, that the war is still real. The band is searching for Major Elginbrodde's buried treasure, which they last heard of while on a raid with Elginbrodde to Brittany in 1942. Their efforts culminate in a final re-enactment of their original raid, sailing an appropriated fishing smack across the Channel. As a policeman says to Charlie Luke, "Chief, *suppose those lads tried to stage the raid again*."[11]

---

*"The fog of war has descended" (VB, 86) is a favorite phrase of Powell's Roland Gwatkin; Christianna Brand's detective novel *London Particular* (1952) begins "The dank grey fog was like an army blanket" (9).

The Tiger in the Smoke is a time warp back through the smoke, returning to the world of World War Two.

The leader of the war veterans, slashing his way through London towards the treasure of Saint-Odile-sur-Mer, is Jack Havoc, one of the purest distillations of evil since Iago. Havoc escapes from Parkhurst by feigning a compulsive neurosis about the number thirteen. A Harley Street doctor who specializes in criminal triskaedaphobia examines him and gets his throat cut. In his search for the Elginbrodde marbles, Havoc returns to his parish. The Canon Avril, his old pastor, hears him rummaging in the church at midnight, and feels compelled to go down and talk with him: " 'Johnny Cash,' he said in exactly the same voice which he had used so many years before, 'come out.' "[12] The man in black and the priest, sitting in the church with Havoc in the pew behind, then have an unlikely conversation which touches on Dante, Virgil, Milton, Sartre, and the nature of the soul.

Their extraordinary confrontation also explains whom Jack Havoc represents:

> 'That's it,' said Havoc, and his voice was natural. 'That's it. The same thing happened to me. Do you know what that is, you poor old bletherer? That's the Science of Luck. It works every time.'
>
> Now it was Avril's turn to understand and he was frightened out of his wits.
>
> 'The Science of Luck,' he said cautiously. 'You watch, do you? That takes a lot of self-discipline.'
>
> 'Of course it does, but it's worth it. I watch everything, all the time. I'm one of the lucky ones. I've got the gift. I knew it when I was a kid but I didn't grasp it.' The murmur had intensified. 'This last time, when I was alone so long, I got it right. I watch for every opportunity and I never do the soft thing. That's why I succeed.'
>
> Avril was silent for a long time. 'It is the fashion,' he said at last. 'You've been reading the Frenchmen, I suppose? Or no, no, perhaps you haven't. How absurd of me.'
>
> 'Don't blether.' The voice, stripped of all its disguises, was harsh and naive. 'You always blethered. You never said anything straight. What do you know about the Science of Luck? Go on, tell me. You're the only one who's understood at all. Have you ever heard of it before?'
>
> 'Not under that name.'
>
> 'I don't suppose you have. That's my name for it. What's its real name?'
>
> 'The Pursuit of Death.'
>
> There was a pause. Curiosity, fear, impatience bristled behind Avril. He could feel them.
>
> 'It's a known thing, then?'

'You did not discover it, my son.'

'No, I suppose not.' He was hesitating, a torn and wasted tiger but still inquisitive. 'You've got it right, have you? You have to watch for your chances and then you must never go soft, not once, not for a minute. You mustn't even think soft. Once you're soft you muck everything, lose your place, and every-thing goes against you. I've proved it. Keep realistic and you get places fast, everything falls right for you, everything's easy. Is that it?'

'That's it,' said Avril humbly. 'It is easier to fall downstairs than to climb up. *Facilis descensus averno.* That was said a long time ago.'

'What are you talking about?'

'The Science of Luck.' Avril bent his head. 'The staircase has turns, the vine climbs a twisted path, the river runs a winding course. If a man watches he can see the trend and he can go either way.'

'Then you know it? Why are you soft?'

'Because I do not want to die. A man who pitches himself down a spiral staircase on which all his fellows are climbing up may injure some of them, but, my dear fellow, it's nothing to the damage he does to himself, is it?'

'You're crazy! You're on to a big thing, you can see what I see, and you won't profit by it.'

Avril turned round in the dark. 'Evil be thou my Good, that is what you have discovered. It is the only sin which cannot be forgiven because when it has finished with you you are not there to forgive. On your journey you certainly "get places". Naturally; you have no opposition. But in the process you die. The man who is with you when you are alone is dying. Fewer things delight him every day. If you attain the world, you cannot give him anything that will please him. In the end there will be no one with you."[13]

Allingham's perception of the workings of the truly evil mind is a very literate one. (Though the Canon misquotes the *Aeneid*—it should be *"av-erni"*—he is under considerable stress.) Avril speaks for "the Frenchmen," Camus and Sartre, who are possessed in the forties and fifties with the power to do evil, with the question of necessary violence. Avril speaks against Milton's Lucifer, whose credo, "Evil be thou my Good" is taken up in the twentieth century not only by Jack Havoc but by Adolf Hitler. In *The Oaken Heart*, Margery Allingham writes of the Nazis' plan for world domination as "the most gigantic and most naively mistaken project since Lucifer got himself kicked out of heaven."* Avril's probing of Hav-oc's mind amounts to an attempt to explain how an evil as undistilled as Adolf Hitler can possibly exist.

*Margery Allingham, *The Oaken Heart*, 166. The title of Margery Allingham's social history of her village in wartime is probably taken from John Till Allingham's Restoration comedy, *Hearts of Oak*.

The Oaken Heart makes it clear that Havoc is a type for Hitler. His Science of Luck is, for Canon Avril, a downward spiral into oblivion, the Pursuit of Death. *The Oaken Heart* describes the Nazis' rise to power in exactly the same terms:

> It was later on in the next year (1940) that we ordinary people really saw the new German experiment for what it manifestly is, the plainest and most elementary attempt to gain the world by laboriously and meticulously backing the downward drive in the universal equilibrium.[14]

Havoc, more than mere psychopath, the leader of a pack of killers, is a powerful re-creation of the central figure of the war. Both hurtle down the same staircase. Both, alarmingly, are modernists. When Havoc finally finds the treasure at Saint-Odile-sur-Mer, he is bitterly disappointed, but consoles himself with the thought that "He was a modern."[15] So, for Allingham, was Hitler: "Hitler wanted the modern world. Well, I mean to say, Campion, *look* at the modern world!"[16] *The Oaken Heart* provides one further parallel. Allingham shared the national feeling that Chamberlain had betrayed England in 1940 with his false optimism over Scandinavia.

> When [...] Mr. Chamberlain winked at the country, when he gave it the little encouraging personal dig in the ribs for which it had been waiting so long and murmured the untranslatable "he's missed the bus," it was assumed by many simple people, and with immense relief, that there was a bag waiting for the tiger.[17]

But of course the tiger got out of the bag and leapt for Norway. As Allingham writes, in italics: "*There had been no tiger trap*. The wink meant nothing."[18] Hitler is the tiger in the smoke.

Neither Bowen nor Allingham remembers the war as particularly purgatorial. After the war, the purgatorial flame dies out. Embers of the flame still linger. Lord Angus Holden's *Purgatory Revisited* (1949), an encounter with the shades of various eminent Victorians, was inspired by the war: "It was during the first months of the second war against Germany that, in the gathering darkness of Brompton Oratory, I was considering the desirability of being shriven."[19] Returning to Oxford after the war, Nicholas Jenkins carries with him a fictional post-war memoir entitled *Purged Not in Lethe* (BDFR, 3). A Roman McDougald thriller of 1946, centering upon an impersonator, is called *Purgatory Street*. Isherwood describes

Down There on a Visit, the second half of which covers the years 1938 to 1940, as "a conducted tour, similar to Dante's tour of the Inferno. But this Inferno is more of a Purgatorio, because nobody in it is permanently damned—only temporarily self-detained."[20] In John Le Carré's *A Perfect Spy*, Magnus Pym remembers the period after the arrest of his father as purgatory. The war breaks out two pages after this passage:

> After the Fall came, very properly, Purgatory, and Purgatory possessed no Lippsies—I guess she was trying to make one of her breaks from me, using Rick's absence to cut herself off. Purgatory was where Dorothy and I served out our sentence, Tom, and Purgatory is just over the hill from here, a few of Rick's fare-stages along the coast, though the new time-share apartments have removed much of its sting. Purgatory was the same wooded hollow of clefts and chines and dripping laurels where Pym had been conceived, with red windswept beaches always out of season, and creaking swings and sodden sandpits that were closed to enjoyment on the sabbath and for Pym on any other day as well. Purgatory was Makepeace Watermaster's great sad house, The Glades, where Pym was forbidden to leave the walled orchard if it was dry or enter the main rooms if it was raining.[21]

But Le Carré's purgatory is postlapsarian, following the expulsion from Eden rather than preceding the entrance into Paradise.

Purgatory is a place of anticipation and ascent, where all the shades, excluding Virgil, have something to look forward to. Post-war writing leaves that waiting world behind: the Literature of Reimagination begins to look ahead in its remembering of war. As the Literature of Anticipation looked back to the past, putting history under glass to prepare for the future, so British post-war writers put the war behind them, to prepare for what lies ahead. But now the anticipation is no longer apprehensive. Each period of the literature of the Second World War has its particular tone. The Literature of Anticipation is Tiresean, regretful; the Literature of Experience is direct, immediate. The Literature of Reimagination is detached, and, finally, optimistic. Nick Carraway, whom Nick Jenkins very much resembles, may be borne ceaselessly into the past, but his boat is beating upstream. The end of all our exploring is to fare forward. Orpheus can leave the beasts behind.

On D-day in *The Heat of the Day*, Baby Victor is born. At the end of *Back*, with Henry weeping with happiness upon her, Nancy looks ahead to "what she had taken on."[22] In Greene's *The End of the Affair* (1951), Sarah's affair with Maurice ends as her love of God begins. Arthur Rowe speaks for the Literature of Reimagination in Greene's *The Ministry of*

Fear. Rowe has his fortune told at a charity fête, and becomes the unwitting center of a spy ring by accidentally hitting upon the group's password. Hearing the password, the fortune teller then gives him the false weight of a cake in an adjacent booth. He guesses the weight, is given the cake with the roll of film in it, and the story begins. The password which has set off this rather improbable chain reaction is something anyone might say, certainly anyone writing immediately after the war. Holding his palm before Mrs. Bellairs, he says: "Don't tell me the past. Tell me the future."[23]

Appendix: Figures in the Compound Ghost

The half-stranger encountered in the antelucan hour is "a familiar compound ghost," both "one and many" (LG, 95; 94). The ghost is an amalgam of Eliot's masters; through him speak over a dozen poetic voices. The figure is a crucible for the tradition from which his poetry devolves, to which his poetry responds. Leonard Unger's book, *Eliot's Compound Ghost*, has raised the question of Eliot's sources for the figure. An alphabetic catalogue of the principal poets comprised within the compound ghost follows. There are, of course, other figures behind the ghost, such as Arthur Hugh Clough, or the soldier that closes Book IV of *The Prelude*. This collection does not venture into the darker shadows of Eliot's penumbra.

Arnold. Woolf feels herself "hovering between 2 worlds" in 1938.[1] This Dantesque suspension is more directly a reference to Matthew Arnold's "Stanzas from the Grande Chartreuse":

Wandering between two worlds, one dead,
The other powerless to be born. (ll. 85–86)

The spirit's wandering "Between two worlds become much like each other" (LG, 122) almost certainly owes something to Arnold's two worlds as well. *The Family Reunion* fashions the missing link between "The Grande Chartreuse" and *Little Gidding*:

You and I,
My dear, may very likely meet again
In our wandering in the neutral territory
Between two worlds.[2]

Auden. Eliot was director of Faber & Faber during the war, the publishing company that owned the contractual rights to all of Auden's works.

In 1940, Eliot read Auden's *The Double Man*, published in England as *New Year Letter*. In the epilogue, he came across this quatrain:

> Time remembered bear witness to time required,
> The positive and the negative ways through time
>   Embrace and encourage each other
>   In a brief moment of intersection.[3]

These lines lead directly to *Little Gidding*'s intersection time, a loop in time at the conjunction of the positive and negative ways. Auden's poem begins: "Returning each morning from a timeless world."[4] Both Auden's epilogue and Eliot's dawn encounter begin at dawn after a "timeless" or "interminable" night (LG, 79).

Eliot himself provided the English title for Auden's work. The switch from *The Double Man* to *New Year Letter* emphasizes Auden's distance from England, and avoids the *doppelgänger*, an overused trope for writers in the Second World War. The new title necessitated an additional change: "a sorrow from the Double Man" is revised by Eliot to "a sorrow from the invisible twin."[5] Eliot is refashioning Auden in his own image, for the ghost in *Little Gidding* is in a sense Eliot's invisible twin.

Baudelaire. "Sept Vieillards," Eliot's touchstone poem from *Les Fleurs du Mal*, begins with a very similar supernatural encounter:

> *Fourmillante Cité, cité pleine de rêves,*
> *Où le spectre en plein jour raccroche le passant!*[6]

In "What Dante Means to Me," Eliot quotes these lines just prior to a discussion of the dawn encounter in *Little Gidding*, reinforcing the sense of Baudelaire in that passage. Eliot often talks of Baudelaire and Dante in the same breath. "Unreal city" prefaces the infernal encounter on King William Street in *The Waste Land*. Baudelaire's "mon semblable, mon frère," the cry which ends the Waste Land encounter, rings through the dawn meeting in *Little Gidding*.

Blake. Neither Dante nor Arnaut Daniel does actually "move in measure, like a dancer" (LG, 146) when passing through the fire at the top of Mount Purgatory. However, a drawing by Blake, which Eliot would certainly have known, has Dante assuming a balletic stance as he passes through these flames to reach Beatrice. Eliot almost certainly did not know that Blake's illustration was also the psychic inspiration for the dancing in "Byzantium," as Lawrence Lipking reveals in *The Life of the Poet.*[7] Eliot's closing lines also borrow from the image of the dance in Yeats' poem; Blake filters in on two removes. As Litz has said, "it seems entirely fitting that Eliot should have inherited this Romantic image from Yeats and used it to recreate that moment in the *Divine Comedy* which had obsessed him throughout his poetic life: Arnaut Daniel's willing acceptance of the purifying flames."[8]

Dante. The ghost has the *"cotto aspetto"* of Brunetto Latini, and burns in the *"foco che li affina"* (26, 148) of Arnaut Daniel. Eliot's speaker addresses him in Dante's words: *"Siete voi qui, ser Brunetto?"*,[9] "are *you* here?" (LG, 98). The ghost echoes Virgil's last words before returning to hell, *"per ch'io te sovra te corono e mitrio"* (27, 142), in "To set a crown upon your lifetime's effort" (LG, 130). The speaker echoes Dante's first words on beginning the ascent of Mount Purgatory, *"Dianzi, nell'alba che procede al giorno"* (9, 52), in his first line: "In the uncertain hour before the morning" (LG, 78). The first line is a veiled reference to Dante; so too is the last. A horn also sounds in Dante, at the entrance to the final circle of Hell: *"Ma io senti' sonare un alto corno."*[10] Bennett adds the following:

> But it is still rewarding to read the passage alongside that Canto on the Temple Classics edition that Eliot used and that perhaps prompted him to render *locotto aspetto* as "the baked features" (TC "baked aspect")—originally "those scorched brown features" (cf TC "the scorching of his visage" for *il viso abruciato*). It will then appear that he has compressed the opening dialogue into one question and transferred Brunetto's *"Qual maraviglia!"* (TC "what a wonder!") to his interlocutor who says: "The wonder that I feel is easy". In the *Inferno* it is the poet who has to bend down, being on a higher bank than Brunetto (cf XV.44: *il capo chino*); in "Little Gidding" the downturned face is the stranger's. The pair walk together in London, as in hell. Some trace of Brunetto's discourse is discernible in the later tercets, beginning "And he: 'I am not eager to rehearse/My thought and theory . . . ' " (cf *"E quegli"*, XV.31, *"Ed egli"*, 55). The unexpected figure of the cattle in the byre—"the full-fed beast shall kick the empty pail"—makes the same impact as Dante's gnomic "far from the goat shall be the grass" (72), which is followed by "Let the Fiesolan beast make fodder of themselves" (73), and "let the boor turn his mattock" (96).[11]

For a more detailed study of the importance of Dante in this scene, see the first section of chapter IV.

Eliot. All ghostly encounters, at the deepest level, are encounters with the self. Hamlet meets the voice within himself; Dante's ghosts are reflections of Dante; Wilfred Owen meets his own severed head in "The Show." Each ghost is ultimately a mirror of the soul. Eliot sees his "invisible twin," as he had Auden say, at the intersection time. The most critical influence upon *Four Quartets* is that of Eliot himself. *Burnt Norton* grew out of "lines and fragments that were discarded in the course of the production of Murder in the Cathedral."[12] "Autumn weather" (HG, 184) throws back to "La Figlia che Piange"; the whole conception of the scene complements the encounter with Stetson in *The Waste Land*. *Little Gidding* repeatedly returns to earlier quartets and earlier poetry in the attempt to bring about a summation and a renewal.

The Family Reunion is gathered together again in *Four Quartets*. Agatha tells Harry that he will "learn hereafter"[13] of his necessary purgation in the war. So, in the early draft, does the ghost: *"Those who have known purgatory here know it hereafter—so shall you learn"* (HG, 186). Before he goes off to become cannon-fodder, Harry says:

> I have been wounded in a war of phantoms,
> Not by human beings—they have no more power than I.
> The things I thought were real are shadows, and the real
> Are what I thought were private shadows.[14]

As in *Little Gidding*, the real is spectral; the shadow of war is a hideous reality. Agatha speaks of this terrifying crossover at the beginning of the play:

> When the loop in time comes—and it does not come for
>   everybody—
> The hidden is revealed, and the spectres show themselves.[15]

The loop in time comes again in *Little Gidding*, and then the spectres show themselves. The importance of *The Family Reunion* for *Little Gidding* is discussed within chapter IV.

MacNeice. MacNeice has been seen to share Eliot's touchstones, with "Hypocrite auditeur, mon semblable, mon frère," and "We are dying, Egypt, dying."[16] MacNeice often borrows directly from Eliot; occasionally the traffic of allusion passes in the opposite direction. The ghosts in Canto

XV of *Autumn Journal* are one and many, strange and familiar: "But something about their faces is familar; / Where have we seen them before?"[17] MacNeice's descent into the hell of the London Underground in Canto I parallels similar descents in Eliot's *Burnt Norton* and Williams' *All Hallows' Eve*. The replacement of unstressed syllables for rhyme words in *Little Gidding* follows MacNeice in *Autumn Journal*. MacNeice, like Auden and Williams, submitted his war work to Eliot in his capacity as the director of Faber & Faber. With his extraordinary powers of retention and his life-long concern for the maintaining of a literary tradition, Eliot may very well have fully realized the potential of his position.

Mallarmé. In *"Le Tombeau d'Edgar Poe,"* Mallarmé celebrates the black purity of Poe's words, his ability to give *"un sens plus pur aux mots de la tribu."* This line is lifted into the ghost's speech: "speech impelled us / To purify the dialect of the tribe" (LG, 126–27). Eliot had high praise for Mallarmé's line in his *"Note sur Mallarmé et Poe,"* an article translated into French by Ramon Fernandez for the *Nouvelle Revue Française* in 1926:

> *Dans* Ulalume *par exemple, et dans* Un Coup de Dés, *cette incantation, qui insiste sur la puissance primitive du Mot* (Fatum), *on est manifeste. En ce sens le vers de Mallarmé, qui s'applique si bien à lui-même, constitue une brillante critique de Poe*: donner un sens plus pur aux mots de la tribu.[18]

For Eliot, the principles of pure speech are manifest in *Un Coup de Dés* as much as "Ulalume," in Mallarmé as much as Poe; both prefigure the ghost's purification of the word. For a further discussion of Eliot's "Note on Mallarmé," see Christopher Ricks, "A Note on *Little Gidding*."

Owen. Perhaps the single most important outside poetic influence upon this passage is that of Wilfred Owen's "Strange Meeting." The poets of the Second World War continually struggled under the shadow of the poets of the First. Eliot, as always, avoids this struggle by subsuming the past tradition into his own work. "Strange Meeting," indisputably the greatest English poem of the First World War, directly informs *Little Gidding*, the greatest of the Second. Both are encounters at night during wartime. Both involve two figures, the one a speaker very much like the poet, the other a familiar ghost, "intimate and unidentifiable." The openings are very similar in tone, with long still vowels lengthening the descriptive lines: "In the uncertain hour before the morning" (LG, 78),

"Down some profound dull tunnel, long since scooped" (l. 2). Owen's title is concealed in Eliot's encounter:

> Too strange to each other for misunderstanding,
> In concord at this intersection time
> Of meeting nowhere. (LG, 104–106)*

Owen's German soldier is "the enemy you killed, my friend" (l. 40); Eliot's ghost is also a mirror of Eliot himself.

Shakespeare. The most obvious antecedent for Eliot's ghost is Hamlet's father. In his review of *Four Quartets*, Charles Williams notes 'a reference to the "refining fire" of that purgatory in which the ghost of the elder Hamlet dwelled."⁹ That fire, in Shakespeare, is expressly purgatorial

> And for the day confin'd to fast in fires,
> Till the foul crimes done in my days of nature
> Are burnt and purg'd away. (I. v. 11–13)

The ghost "faded on the blowing of the horn" (LG, 149), echoing the disappearance of Hamlet's father, who "faded on the crowing of the cock" (I. i. 157). The dancing at the close—"you must move in measure, like a dancer" (LG, 146)—also raises the ghost of Octavius: Mark Antony mocks him for wearing "His sword e'en like a dancer" (III. xi. 36).

Shelley. The image of "two worlds become much like each other" in *Little Gidding* (LG, 122), and in *The Family Reunion*, may be borrowed from Shelley as well as Arnold. In *Prometheus Unbound*, Zoroaster meets his *doppelgänger*:

> The Magus Zoroaster, my dead child,
> Met his own image walking in the garden.

*Owen's title is itself taken from Shelley's *Revolt of Islam*, wherein another written encounter is enacted:

> And one, whose spear had pierced me, leaned beside,
> With quivering lips and humid eyes; —and all
> Seemed like some brothers on a journey wide
> Gone forth, whom now strange meeting did befall [...].
> (*Revolt of Islam*, Canto V)

For more on Shelley's presence in *Little Gidding* II, see below.

That apparition, sole of men, he saw.
For know there are two worlds of life and death:
One that which thou beholdest; but the other
Is underneath the grave, where do inhabit
The shadows of all forms that think and live
Till death unite them and they part no more. (I. ll. 192–99)

Both Eliot and Williams draw upon these lines to express a spectral visitation. Pauline returns to them in *Descent into Hell*; Eliot quotes them in
full in *The Cocktail Party* (1949), as Dr. Reilly describes his premonition
of Celia Coplestone's death.[20] Shelley's "two worlds of life and death"
coalesce in Eliot's and Williams' idea of an intersection time. With Shelley,
Eliot presents the real and the nether worlds as mirror-images, allowing
intercourse between them.

Shelley also inspired the encounter in a much more general way. In
"What Dante Means to Me," Eliot cites Shelley's *Triumph of Life* for "some
of the greatest and most Dantesque lines in English."[21] He quotes a long
passage from that poem, and concludes "Well, this is better than I could
do."[22] Shelley demonstrated that the reimagination of Dante in English
style was possible; his presence in *Little Gidding* may be merely inspira-
tional but is nevertheless indelible.

Swift. The echo of Swift is not actually Eliot's: it was provided by John
Hayward. Swift's epitaph in St. Patrick's Cathedral, Dublin contains the
phrase: *"Ulterius cor lacerare nequit."* Hayward wrote these words against
the second draft, suggesting "laceration" for the "laughter at what ceases
to amuse" (LG, 136–37; cf. HG, 193). Eliot adopted the term, entering
Swift into the lists of writers compounded within the ghost.

Tennyson. As Litz has written, "Poem VII of *In Memoriam*, describing
Tennyson's Hamlet-like encounter with the ghost of Hallam during a dawn
patrol, casts its shadow over Part II of *Little Gidding*."[23] In 1942, Eliot
published in *The Listener* an uncharacteristically passionate article on Tennyson's *In Memoriam*, in which he quotes the seventh section:

He is not here; but far away
   The noise of life begins again,
   And ghastly thro' the drizzling rain
On the bald street breaks the blank day.[24]

This article is titled "The Voice of His Time"; Eliot, a century later, is becoming the voice of his. Eliot also adopts in this movement Tennyson's ruminative style, as earlier in the second movement, and in *East Coker*, he adapted Tennyson's "wainscot mouse," found in both *Maud*—"the shrieking rush of the wainscot mouse" (I. vi. 71)—and "Mariana": "the mouse / Behind the mouldering wainscot shriek'd" (ll. 63–64).

Williams. A third poet from whom Eliot borrowed while editor of Faber & Faber was Charles Williams. Like Auden's *The Double Man* and MacNeice's *Autumn Journal*, Williams' novel *Descent into Hell*, which Eliot read for Faber & Faber in 1937, leads directly into *Little Gidding*. The ghost of John Struther walks from *Descent into Hell* straight into Eliot's fourth quartet. Dead, Struther appears to Pauline in the street at dawn, who thinks as she sees him "a ghost in the fire was a ghost in the street."[25] Struther's purgatory compounds the philosophies of St. John and Dante, climbing a ladder of bone and passing through a refining fire. He appears with "the echo of the trumpet [...] or of a siren."[26] Eliot's ghost follows the same twisting path, and leaves with the sound of both trumpet and siren: "And faded on the blowing of the horn" (LG, 149). The extraordinary parallels between Williams and Eliot are discussed in the third section of chapter V.

Yeats. In the draft of the ghost's speech, the primary figure behind the dead master is unquestionably Yeats. The ghost *"spoke with an alien voice,"* of *"my alien people with an archaic tongue."* The ghost is buried *"on a distant shore,"* as Yeats was, having *"spent my life in that unending fight / To give the people speech"* (HG, 186–87). Eliot writes these references out, not wanting to limit the ghost's penumbra of reference: "The visionary figure has now become somewhat more definite and will no doubt be identified by some readers with Yeats though I do not mean anything so precise as that" (HG, 176). The presence of Yeats is retained, but in a more subtle way. The dancing image comes from "Byzantium" as well as from Blake:

> Dying into a dance
> An agony of trance,
> An agony of flame that cannot singe a sleeve. (ll. 30–32)

As Lipking has written, Yeats' image is itself inspired by Blake's drawing, to bring the wheel full circle.

Yeats' last play, *Purgatory*, was written in 1939. Eliot found the title inappropriate, saying that "I cannot accept a purgatory in which there is no hint, or at least no emphasis upon Purgation."[27] In Yeats' *Purgatory*, the ghosts of the Old Man's parents return to haunt him into a false expiation: his father is "A dead, living, murdered man!"[28] In the *New English Weekly* proof version of *Little Gidding*, now at Princeton, the speaker is "always dead, / And still alive" (HG, 179). This echo is written out as well.

Notes

Preface

1. Tom Harrisson, "War Books," *Horizon*, IV, #24 (December 1941), 417.

2. *Ibid.*, 432.

3. *Ibid.*, 436.

4. David Jones, *In Parenthesis* (New York: Chilmark Press, 1961), xii.

5. Elizabeth Bowen, *Ivy Gripped the Steps and Other Stories* (New York: Knopf, 1946), viii.

6. Jeffrey Smitten and Ann Daghistany, eds., *Spatial Form in Narrative* (Ithaca, N.Y.: Cornell University Press, 1981), 14.

7. Randall Stevenson, *The British Novel Since the Thirties* (London: Batsford, 1986), 68–69.

8. George Orwell, "London Letter to *Partisan Review*," 15 April 1941, in *The Collected Essays, Journalism and Letters of George Orwell*, II (Harmondsworth: Penguin with Secker & Warburg, 1970), 139.

9. Cyril Connolly, *et al.*, "Why Not War Writers? A Manifesto," *Horizon*, IV, #22 (October 1941), 236.

10. "To the Poets of 1940," *Times Literary Supplement*, 30 December 1939, 755.

11. A. A. Milne, "Song for a Soldier," in *Behind the Lines* (New York: Dutton, 1940), 31.

12. Catherine Reilly, *English Poetry of the Second World War* (London: Mansell, 1986), vii.

13. *Ibid.*, xiv.

14. Malcolm Muggeridge, *The Thirties* (London: Collins, 1967), 332.

15. Harold Nicolson, 1 September 1938, *Diaries and Letters, 1930–1939*, ed. Nigel Nicolson (London: Collins, 1966), 358.

16. Nicolson, 28 August 1939, *Ibid.*, 413.

17. Virginia Woolf, 28 August 1938, *The Diary of Virginia Woolf*, ed. Anne Olivier Bell, V (London: Harcourt Brace Jovanovich, 1984), 164.

18. Woolf, 20 September 1938, *Ibid.*, 173.

19. Stephen Spender, quoted in Samuel Hynes, *The Auden Generation* (New York: Viking, 1977), 381.

20. Keith Douglas, "Poets in This War " [May 1943], in *A Prose Miscellany*, comp. and ed. Desmond Graham (Manchester: Carcanet, 1985), 117–18.

21. *Ibid.*, 119–20.

22. Keith Douglas, *Collected Poems* (London: Faber & Faber, 1966), 129.

23. Roy Fuller, *Collected Poems, 1936–1961* (London: Deutsch, 1962), 55.

24. Alun Lewis, *Raiders' Dawn and Other Poems* (New York: Macmillan, 1942), 17.

25. C. Day Lewis, *Collected Poems* (London: Cape with the Hogarth Press, 1954), 228.

26. C. Day Lewis, *The Georgics of Virgil* (London: Cape, 1940), 9.

27. Quoted in Hynes, *The Auden Generation*, 381–82.

28. *Ibid.*, 382.

29. Quoted by William Rock, "Neville Chamberlain and the Pursuit of War," Western / North American Conference in British Studies, 16 October 1986.

30. Evelyn Waugh, *The Sword of Honour Trilogy* (Harmondsworth: Penguin, 1984), 271.

31. T. S. Eliot, "Poetry in Wartime," *Common Sense*, XI, #10 (October 1942), 351.

32. *Ibid.*

33. *Ibid.*

34. Patric Dickinson, *Soldiers' Verse* (London: Müller, 1945), v.

35. Eliot, "Poetry in Wartime," 351.

36. *Ibid.*

37. Douglas, "Poets in This War," 118.

38. *Ibid.*, 120.

39. "Why Not War Writers? A Manifesto," 236.

40. [Evelyn Waugh], "Letter - Why Not War Writers?," *Horizon*, IV, #24 (December 1941), 438.

41. Evelyn Waugh, *Put Out More Flags* (Harmondsworth: Penguin, 1943), 73.

42. Connolly, "Comment," *Horizon*, III, #13 (January 1941), 5.

43. Wilfred Owen, *The Collected Poems of Wilfred Owen* (New York: New Directions, 1965), 35.

CHAPTER I

While England Slept

1. H. G. Wells, *The Outline of History* (New York: Macmillan, 1930), 1080.

2. Aldous Huxley, *Eyeless in Gaza* (New York: American Reprint Co., 1975), 64.

3. George Orwell, "War-time Diary," 8 June 1940, in *The Collected Essays, Journalism and Letters of George Orwell*, II, 392.

4. *Ibid.*

5. Quoted in Sir Winston Churchill, *The Gathering Storm*, vol. 1 of *The Second World War* (Boston: Houghton Mifflin, 1948), 297.

6. Nicolson, 28 September 1938, *Diaries*, 370–71.

7. Churchill, *The Gathering Storm*, 326.

8. *Ibid.*, 205.

9. Nicolson, 20 September 1938, *Diaries*, 362.

10. Louis MacNeice, *Autumn Journal*, VIII, in *Collected Poems of Louis MacNeice*, ed. E. R. Dodds (London: Faber & Faber, 1966), 117.

11. Colin Seymour-Ure and John Schoff, *David Low* (London: Secker & Warburg, 1985), 94.

12. George Orwell, *Keep the Aspidistra Flying* (1936; rpt. Harmondsworth: Penguin with Secker & Warburg, 1981), 26.

13. George Orwell, *Homage to Catalonia* (New York: Harcourt Brace Jovanovich, 1952), 231–32.

14. George Orwell, *Coming Up for Air* (New York: Harcourt Brace Jovanovich, [1939]), 267.

15. Linda Shires, *British Poetry of the Second World War* (New York: St. Martin's Press, 1985), 21.

16. Evelyn Waugh, "Work Suspended," in *Work Suspended and Other Stories* (Harmondsworth: Penguin, 1982), 117.

17. Hynes, *The Auden Generation*, 341.

18. W. H. Auden and Christopher Isherwood, *Journey to a War* (New York: Random House, 1939), 11.

19. *Ibid.*, 20.

20. *Ibid.*, 274.

21. Stephen Spender, "Thoughts During an Air Raid," *New Republic*, 95, 18 May 1938, 42.

22. C. Day Lewis, *Overtures to Death* (London: Cape, 1938), 15.

23. *Ibid.*, 17.

24. MacNeice, *Autumn Journal*, V.

25. Orwell, *Coming Up for Air*, 127.

26. *Ibid.*, 198.

27. Hynes, *The Auden Generation*, 341.

28. *The Times*, 10 July 1939, 10, col. 5.

29. Christopher Fry, *The Boy with a Cart*, in *Selected Plays* (Oxford: Oxford University Press, 1985), 7.

30. Muggeridge, *The Thirties*, 107–108.

31. Woolf, 11 April 1939, *Diary*, V, 214.

32. Graham Greene, *The Ministry of Fear* (Harmondsworth: Penguin, 1974), 20.

33. Nicolson, 31 August 1939, *Diaries*, 416.

34. Evelyn Waugh, *The Letters of Evelyn Waugh*, ed. Mark Amory (Harmondsworth: Penguin, 1982), 198.

Purgatory: Waiting in the War

1. T. S. Eliot, *Four Quartets* (London: Harcourt Brace Jovanovich, 1971), EC, 123.

2. Michael Innes, *The Secret Vanguard* (New York: Berkley Medallion, 1965), 35.

3. Margery Allingham, *The Tiger in the Smoke* (Harmondsworth: Penguin with Chatto & Windus, 1957), 27.

4. *Ibid.*, 37.

5. Graham Greene, "While Waiting for a War," in *Granta*, 17 (Autumn 1985), 13–29.

6. Muggeridge, *The Thirties*, 222.

7. Woolf, 5 September 1938, *Diary*, V, 166.

8. Anthony Powell, *At Lady Molly's*, vol. 4 of *A Dance to the Music of Time* (New York: Popular Library, 1976), 171.

9. Muggeridge, *The Thirties*, 333.

10. Cyril Connolly, "Comment," *Horizon*, I, #1 (January 1940), 5.

11. Muggeridge, *The Thirties*, 334.

12. Waugh, *Put Out More Flags*, 7.

13. W. C. Brodie, Diary, Second World War Papers, Imperial War Museum, 13.

14. Mollie Panter-Downes, *London War Notes, 1939–1945* (New York: Farrar, Straus & Giroux, 1971), 43; 21.

15. Leonard Woolf, *The Journey not the Arrival Matters* (London: The Hogarth Press, 1969), 9–10.

16. W. H. Auden, *The Double Man* (New York: Random House, 1941), 46.

17. J. R. R. Tolkien, Letter to Peter Hastings, September 1954, *The Letters of J. R. R. Tolkien*, ed. Humphrey Carpenter (Boston: Houghton Mifflin, 1981), 195.

18. Lucy Redpath, *Dante and the Present War* (Westminster: Dacre Press, [1941]), 34.

19. *Ibid.*, 32.

20. T. S. Eliot, "What Dante Means to Me," rpr. as "Talk on Dante," *Adelphi*, 27, #2 (1951), 108.

21. Eliot, Letter to John Hayward, 27 August 1942, quoted in Dame Helen Gardner, *The Composition of* Four Quartets, rev. ed. (London: Faber & Faber, 1980), 65.

22. Stephen Spender, "Dante in English," rev. of *Purgatorio*, trans. Laurence Binyon, *New Statesman and Nation*, 17, 14 January 1939, 58.

23. Stephen Spender, *Letters to Christopher* (Santa Barbara: Black Sparrow Press, 1980), 132.

24. Christopher Isherwood, Letter to Edward Upward, 20 August 1955, quoted in Brian Finney, *Christopher Isherwood* (New York: Oxford University Press, 1979), 224.

25. T. S. Eliot, "Yeats," in *On Poetry and Poets* (New York: Farrar, Straus & Cudahy, 1957), 302.

26. Eliot, *Four Quartets*, LG, 150–53.

27. Virginia Woolf, *Between the Acts* (Harmondsworth: Penguin, 1953), 124.

28. Waugh, *Put Out More Flags*, 60.

29. C. S. Lewis, *The Great Divorce* (New York: Macmillan, 1946), 39.

30. Samuel Beckett *et al.*, *Our Exagmination Round His Factification for Incamination of* Work in Progress (London: Faber & Faber, 1972), 21–22.

31. Eliot, *Four Quartets*, LG, 155–56.

32. Ezra Pound, *Literary Essays of Ezra Pound* (London: Faber & Faber, 1954), 400.

33. Louis MacNeice, *Out of the Picture* (New York: Harcourt, Brace & Company, 1938), 105.

34. Dr. L. E. Elliott-Binns, *Dante and the World To-day* (Cambridge, W. Heffer & Sons, 1939).

35. Zoé Oldenbourg, *Massacre at Montségur*, trans. Peter Green (New York: Pantheon, 1961), 78ff.

36. David Jones, *In Parenthesis* (New York: Chilmark Press, 1961), xv.

37. E. R. Dodds, introd., Louis MacNeice, *The Strings are False* (London: Faber & Faber, 1965), 12.

38. T. S. Eliot, *The Family Reunion* (London: Faber & Faber, 1939), 121.

39. Eliot, *Four Quartets*, LG, 122.

40. Charles Williams, *Descent into Hell* (1949; rpt. Grand Rapids: Eerdmans, 1985), 132.

41. Eliot, *The Family Reunion*, 105.

42. *Ibid.*, 104–105.

43. Evelyn Waugh, 17 July 1940, *The Diaries of Evelyn Waugh, 1911–1965*, ed. Michael Davie (Harmondsworth: Penguin, 1979), 473; Woolf, 10 September 1938, *Diary*, V, 167.

44. Quoted in George Kearns, *Guide to Ezra Pound's* Selected Cantos (New Brunswick: Rutgers University Press, 1980), 8.

45. Beckett, *Our Exagmination*, 22.

Myth: The Tesseract of Literature and History

1. Hynes, *The Auden Generation*, 9.

2. W. H. Auden, introd., *Intimate Journals*, by Charles Baudelaire, trans. Christopher Isherwood (Boston: Beacon Press, 1947), xiii.

3. Bernard Bergonzi, *Reading the Thirties: Texts and Contexts* (Pittsburgh: University of Pittsburgh Press, 1978), 6.

4. *Ibid.*, 6–7.

5. Hynes, *The Auden Generation*, 382.

6. T. S. Eliot, " 'Ulysses', Order, and Myth," rev. of *Ulysses*, *Dial* (November 1923), 483.

7. Quoted in *The Modern Tradition*, eds. Ellmann & Feidelson (New York: Oxford University Press, 1965), 681.

8. Mircea Eliade, *The Myth of the Eternal Return*, Bollingen Ser. #46 (Princeton: Princeton University Press, 1974), 153.

9. Joseph Frank, *The Widening Gyre* (New Brunswick, N.J.: Rutgers University Press, 1963), 59.

10. *Ibid.*, 60.

11. Philip Rahv, *The Myth and the Powerhouse* (New York: Farrar, Straus & Giroux, 1965), 6.

12. *Ibid.*, 7.

13. *Ibid.*, 21.

14. W. B. Yeats, *Purgatory*, in *Collected Plays of W. B. Yeats* (London: Macmillan, 1952), 687.

15. Anthony Powell, *The Kindly Ones*, vol. 6 of *A Dance to the Music of Time* (New York: Popular Library, 1976), 87.

16. Douglas, *A Prose Miscellany*, 47–48.

17. C. Day Lewis, *Overtures to Death*, 60.

18. Orwell, *Coming Up for Air*, 221.

19. Muggeridge, *The Thirties*, 312.

20. Williams, *Descent into Hell*, 22.

21. *Ibid.*, 19.

22. H. G. Wells, *Babes in the Darkling Wood* (New York: Alliance, 1940), 177.

23. Orwell, *Coming Up for Air*, 235.

24. Henry Green, *Back* (New York: New Directions, 1981), 53.

25. Waugh, *The Sword of Honour Trilogy*, 83.

26. Innes, *The Secret Vanguard*, 128.

27. Nicholas Blake [C. Day Lewis], *Minute for Murder* (New York: Perennial, 1977), 106.

28. James M. Curtis, "Spatial Form in the Context of Modernist Aesthetics," in *Spatial Form in Narrative*, eds. Smitten and Daghistany, 176.

29. B. Nathorst, quoted in Walter Burkert, *Structure and History in Greek Mythology and Ritual* (Berkeley: University of California Press, [1979]), 11.

30. Auden, *The Double Man*, 189.

31. Eliot, *Four Quartets*, LG, 105.

32. Carl Jung, *Collected Works*, vol. 8 (Princeton: Princeton University Press, 1972), 440.

33. Northrop Frye, *The Anatomy of Criticism* (Princeton: Princeton University Press, 1971), 99.

34. Northrop Frye, *Fables of Identity* (New York: Harcourt, Brace & World, 1963), 58–59.

35. Frye, *The Anatomy of Criticism*, 117.

CHAPTER II

1. Alex Zwerdling, *Virginia Woolf and the Real World* (Berkeley: University of California Press, 1986), 302. Chapter II is revised from "*Between the Acts* and the Coming of War," *Novel*, 10, #3 (1977), 220–36.

2. Leonard Woolf, *The Journey not the Arrival Matters*, 56.

3. *Ibid.*

4. Virginia Woolf, "The Moment: Summer's Night," in *Collected Essays* (London: The Hogarth Press, 1966), II, 296.

5. For "Anon" and "The Reader," see Virginia Woolf, ' "Anon" and "The Reader": Virginia Woolf's Last Essays,' ed. Brenda Silver, *Twentieth Century Literature*, 25 (Fall/Winter 1979), 356–441.

6. *The Times*, 22 April 1938, 14, col. 4; *The Times*, 26 April 1938, 16, col. 4.

7. E. M. Forster, *A Passage to India* (Harmondsworth: Penguin, 1936), 30.

8. Renée Watkins, "Survival in Discontinuity," *Massachusetts Review*, X, #2 (Spring 1969), 356–57.

9. E. M. Forster, *The Abinger Pageant*, in *Abinger Harvest* (New York: Harcourt, Brace & World, 1964), 350.

10. *Ibid.*, 363.

11. Virginia Woolf, *Jacob's Room* (London: Harcourt Brace Jovanovich, 1950), 113.

12. Virginia Woolf, *Mrs. Dalloway* (London: The Hogarth Press, 1929), 123; 124.

13. Werner Deiman, "History, Pattern, and Continuity in Virginia Woolf," *Contemporary Literature*, XV, #1 (Winter 1974), 53.

14. Forster, *The Abinger Pageant*, 363.

15. *The Times*, 16 July 1934, 10, col. 5.

16. Virginia Woolf, Letter to R. C. Trevelyan, [25 July 1938], *Letters of Virginia Woolf*, ed. Nigel Nicolson and Joanne Trautmann, VI (New York: Harcourt Brace Jovanovich, 1980), 258.

17. E. M. Forster, *England's Pleasant Land* (London: The Hogarth Press, 1940), 22.

18. *Ibid.*, 78.

19. Michael Kennedy, *The Works of Ralph Vaughan Williams* (London: Oxford University Press, 1964), 560.

20. Woolf, *Jacob's Room*, 113.

21. Forster, *England's Pleasant Land*, 8.

22. *Ibid.*, 62.

23. See, as Leaska suggests, P. N. Furbank, *E. M. Forster, A Life*, II (London: Secker & Warburg, 1978), 141–43.

24. *The Times*, 20 May 1938, 13, col. 3.

25. J. Hillis Miller, *Fiction and Repetition* (Cambridge, Mass.: Harvard University Press, 1982), 204–205.

26. Churchill, *The Gathering Storm*, 292.

27. Zwerdling, *Virginia Woolf and the Real World*, 307.

28. E. M. Forster, "Post-Munich," in *Two Cheers for Democracy* (London: Edward Arnold & Company, 1951), 33–35.

29. Nicolson and Trautmann, eds., *Letters*, VI, xvii.

30. Zwerdling, *Virginia Woolf and the Real World*, 304.

CHAPTER III

1. MacNeice, *The Strings are False*, ed. and introd. E. R. Dodds, 169–70.

2. Quoted in Siegfried Kracauer, *From Caligari to Hitler: A Psychological History of the German Film* (Princeton: Princeton University Press, 1947), 248.

3. *Ibid.*

4. Hynes, *The Auden Generation*, 341.

5. Orwell, *Coming Up for Air*, 265.

6. MacNeice, *The Strings are False*, 35.

7. Dodds, introd., *Ibid.*, 12.

8. W. H. Auden, "Creatures," in *Another Time* (New York: Random House, 1940), 7.

9. Henry Green, *Pack My Bag* (London: The Hogarth Press, 1940), 194.

10. *Ibid.*, 32.

11. *Ibid.*, 211.

12. R. L. Cook, "Louis MacNeice: An Appreciation," *The Poetry Review*, 38 (May/June 1947), 163.

13. Orwell, *Coming Up for Air*, 198.

14. Louis MacNeice, *Poems 1925–1940* (New York: Random House, 1940), xiii.

15. *Ibid.*

16. Louis MacNeice, Letter to Eliot, 22 November 1938, quoted in Robyn Marsack, *The Cave of Making: The Poetry of Louis MacNeice* (Oxford: Clarendon Press, 1982), 43.

17. Louis MacNeice, *Modern Poetry* (London: Oxford University Press, 1938), 59–60.

18. MacNeice, *Out of the Picture*, 125–26.

19. *Ibid.*, 87–88.

20. *Ibid.*, 113.

21. James Joyce, *Ulysses* (New York: Random House, 1961), 186.

22. Orwell, *Homage to Catalonia*, 231–32.

23. MacNeice, *Modern Poetry*, 25.

24. Louis MacNeice, *The Poetry of W. B. Yeats* (New York: Oxford University Press, 1941), viii.

25. MacNeice, *Out of the Picture*, 16.

26. *Ibid.*, 72.

27. Marsack, *The Cave of Making*, 47.

28. MacNeice, *The Strings are False*, 171.

29. MacNeice, *Modern Poetry*, 59.

30. MacNeice, *Poems 1925–1940*, xiii.

31. W. H. Auden, "Archaeology," in *Collected Poems* (New York: Random House, 1966), 663.

32. Philip Larkin, obituary notice for Louis MacNeice, *New Statesman*, 6 September 1963, 294, quoted in Marsack, *The Cave of Making*, 155.

33. Stephen Spender, *The Still Centre* (London: Faber & Faber, 1939), 12.

34. Nicolson, 31 December 1938, *Diaries*, 384.

35. Stephen Spender, *The Thirties and After* (New York: Random House, 1978), 53.

36. George Orwell, *A Collection of Essays* (New York: Harcourt Brace Jovanovich, 1953), 238.

37. Christopher Isherwood, *Mr. Norris Changes Trains* (London: The Hogarth Press, 1937), 33.

38. MacNeice, *The Strings are False*, 174.

39. Louis MacNeice, "The Poet in England Today," *The New Republic*, 102, 25 March 1940, 412–13.

40. Churchill, *The Gathering Storm*, 123.

41. Anthony Powell, *Casanova's Chinese Restaurant*, vol. 5 of *A Dance to the Music of Time* (New York: Popular Library, 1976), 229.

42. Powell, *The Kindly Ones*, vol. 6 of *A Dance to the Music of Time*, 2.

43. David Gascoyne, *Collected Poems* (Oxford: Oxford University Press, 1965), 84.

44. Louis MacNeice, *Plant and Phantom* (London: Faber & Faber, 1941), 18. "Departure Platform" was not published in *Collected Poems*.

45. Gascoyne, *Collected Poems*, 81.

46. *Radio Portrait of Louis MacNeice*, narr. Goronwyn Rees, BBC, 7 September 1966.

47. MacNeice, *Out of the Picture*, 55.

48. MacNeice, *The Poetry of W. B. Yeats*, 1.

49. W. B. Yeats, "Song of the Happy Shepherd," in *The Collected Poems of W. B. Yeats* (New York: Macmillan, 1956), 7.

50. Spender, *The Still Centre*, 20.

51. Christopher Isherwood, *Down There on a Visit* (New York: Simon & Schuster, 1962), 143.

52. MacNeice, *Out of the Picture*, 46.

53. Mentioned in C. S. Lewis, Letter to Owen Barfield, 8 February 1939, *Letters of C. S. Lewis*, ed. W. H. Lewis (London: Geoffrey Bles, 1966), 163.

54. Auden, *Another Time*, 13.

55. Joyce, *Ulysses*, 143.

CHAPTER IV

The Way Up

1. T. S. Eliot, Interview with Donald Hall, *Paris Review*, 21 (Spring/Summer 1959), 60.

2. T. S. Eliot, Interview with John Lehmann, *New York Times Book Review*, 29 November 1953, 5.

3. Melville Chaning-Pearce, rev. of *Little Gidding*, *Nineteenth Century*, 133 (February 1943), 74.

4. *Ibid.*, 76.

5. Stephen Spender, "The Year's Poetry, 1940," *Horizon*, III, #14 (February 1941), 140.

6. F. O. Matthiessen, "Eliot's Quartets," rev. of *Four Quartets*, *Kenyon Review*, 5 (Spring 1943), 171–73.

7. T. S. Eliot, "Poetry in Wartime," *Common Sense*, XI, #10 (October 1942), 351.

8. Peter Ackroyd, *T. S. Eliot: A Life* (New York: Simon & Schuster, 1984), 264.

9. Paul Goodman, "T. S. Eliot: The Poet of Purgatory," rev. of *Little Gidding*, *The New Leader*, 14 August 1943, 7.

10. T. S. Eliot, " 'Ulysses', Order, and Myth," rev. of *Ulysses*, *Dial* (November 1923), 483.

11. Charles Williams, rev. of *Purgatorio*, trans. Laurence Binyon, *London Mercury*, 39 (November 1938), 84.

12. Delmore Schwartz, "Anywhere Out of the World," rev. of *Little Gidding*, *The Nation*, 157, 24 July 1943, 102–103.

13. T. S. Eliot, "Dante," in *Selected Essays, 1917–1932* (New York: Harcourt, Brace & Company, 1932), 217.

14. T. S. Eliot, "What Dante Means to Me," rpr. as "Talk on Dante," *Adelphi*, 27, #2 (1951), 106.

15. *Ibid.*, 108.

16. *Ibid.*, 109.

17. *Ibid.*

18. *Inferno* 15, 26; 15, 30.

19. Eliot, "What Dante Means to Me," 108–109.

20. Matthiessen, "Eliot's Quartets," 174.

21. Eliot, "Dante," 216–17.

22. J. A. W. Bennett, ' "Little Gidding": A Poem of Pentecost,' *Ampleforth Journal*, 79 (Spring 1974), 64.

23. Wilfred Owen, "Strange Meeting," l. 25.

24. Eliot, *The Family Reunion*, 69.

25. *Ibid.*, 97.

26. *Ibid.*, 105.

27. *Ibid.*, 121.

28. *Ibid.*, 136.

29. W. T. Levy and V. Scherle, *Affectionately, T. S. Eliot* (Philadelphia: Lippincott, 1968), 15.

30. Auden and Isherwood, *Journey to a War*, 274.

31. See my ' "*Only connect*...": Crashaw and Four Elegies in Bodleian MS. Tanner 465,' *Papers of the Bibliographical Society of America*, 81, #4 (Winter 1987).

32. A. Walton Litz, "From Burnt Norton to Little Gidding: The Making of T. S. Eliot's *Four Quartets*," rev. of HG, *Review*, 2 (1980), 17.

33. T. S. Eliot, Letter, *New English Weekly*, XXVI, #15, 25 January 1945, 112.

34. T. S. Eliot, *The Use of Poetry and the Use of Criticism* (London: Faber & Faber, 1933), 78–79.

35. T. S. Eliot, "Rhapsody on a Windy Night," ll. 23–25.

36. T. S. Eliot, "Yeats," in *On Poetry and Poets* (New York: Farrar, Straus & Cudahy, 1957), 299.

37. T. S. Eliot, "A Note on War Poetry," in *London Calling: A Salute to America*, ed. Storm Jameson (New York: Harper, 1942), 237.

38. Bowen, *Ivy Gripped the Steps and Other Stories*, xiv.

39. Eliot, "A Note on War Poetry," 238.

40. Goodman, "T. S. Eliot: The Poet of Purgatory," 7.

41. Chaning-Pearce, rev. of *Little Gidding*, 75.

The Way Down

1. Quoted in Eloise Hay, *T. S. Eliot's Negative Way* (Cambridge, Mass.: Harvard University Press, 1982), 154.

2. Charles Williams, *Poetry at Present* (Oxford: Clarendon Press, 1930), 173.

3. Charles Williams, *The Figure of Beatrice* (London: Faber & Faber, 1943), 8.

4. *Ibid.*, 9.

5. Redpath, *Dante and the Present War*, 29–30.

6. Charles Williams, *The Descent of the Dove* (New York: Pellegrini & Cudahy, 1939), 132.

7. T. S. Eliot, "A Lay Theologian," rev. of *The Descent of the Dove, New Statesman and Nation*, 18, 9 December 1939, 866.

8. Williams, *The Descent of the Dove*, 129.

9. J. A. W. Bennett, ' "Little Gidding": A Poem of Pentecost,' *Ampleforth Journal*, 79 (Spring 1974), 61.

10. T. S. Eliot, "Fragments of a Prologue," *The New Criterion*, IV, #4 (October 1926), 713.

11. Williams, *Poetry at Present*, 173.

12. T. S. Eliot, Letter to Paul Elmer More, 17 February 1932, Paul Elmer More Papers, 3, #3, Firestone Library, Princeton.

13. T. S. Eliot, "Paul Elmer More," *Princeton Alumni Weekly*, XXXVII, #17, 5 February 1937, 373.

14. Hay, *T. S. Eliot's Negative Way*, 11.

15. Eliot, Letter to More, 2 June 1930, More Papers.

16. Charles Williams, "A Dialogue on Mr. Eliot's Poem," rev. of *Four Quartets, The Dublin Review*, 212 (April 1943), 116.

17. *The Complete Works of Saint John of the Cross*, trans. E. Allison Peers (Westminster, Maryland: The Newman Press, 1953), I, 18.

18. Charles Williams, "The Poetry of Health," rev. of *East Coker, Time and Tide*, 5 October 1940, 990.

19. T. S. Eliot, *After Strange Gods* (London: Faber & Faber, 1934), 40–41.

20. T. S. Eliot, *The Waste Land and Other Poems* (New York: Harcourt Brace Jovanovich, 1962), 41; 52.

21. Hay, *T. S. Eliot's Negative Way*, 179–80.

22. Melville Chaning-Pearce, rev. of *Little Gidding, Nineteenth Century*, 133 (February 1943), 77.

23. G. Schmidt, 'An Echo of Buddhism in T. S. Eliot's "Little Gidding," ' *Notes and Queries* (September 1973), 330, referring to the translations of Henry Warren.

24. Walpola Rahula, *What the Buddha Taught*, rev. ed. (New York: Grove Press, 1974), 45.

25. *The Bhagavad Gita*, trans. Franklin Edgerton (New York: Harper, 1944), II, 38.

26. Christopher Isherwood, appx., *The Song of God: Bhagavad-Gita*, trans. Isherwood and Prabhavananda, introd. Aldous Huxley (New York: New American Library, 1944), 139.

27. T. S. Eliot, "Last Words," *Criterion*, 18 (January 1939), 274.

28. T. S. Eliot, "Waiting at the Church," *New English Weekly*, XVIII, 9, 19 December 1940, 99.

29. *Ibid.*

30. *The Complete Works of St. John of the Cross*, I, 441.

31. Eliot, Letter to More, Shrove Tuesday 1928, More Papers.

32. Eliot, Letter to More, 3 August 1929, *Ibid.*

33. Auden, *The Double Man*, 189.

34. Williams, *The Descent of the Dove*, 57.

CHAPTER V

"My 'purgatorial' story"

1. Lewis, Letter to Dom Bede Griffiths, O.S.B., 21 December 1941, *Letters*, 197.

2. Lee Rossi, *The Politics of Fantasy, C. S. Lewis and J. R. R. Tolkien* (Ann Arbor: UMI Research Press, [1984]), 112.

3. Humphrey Carpenter, *The Inklings* (London: Allen & Unwin, 1978), 132.

4. Quoted in *Ibid.*, 194.

5. J. R. R. Tolkien, Letter to Christopher Tolkien, 31 May 1944, *The Letters of J. R. R. Tolkien*, ed. Humphrey Carpenter (Boston: Houghton Mifflin, 1981), 83.

6. Tolkien, Letter to Jane Neave, 8–9 September 1962, *Ibid.*, 320.

7. Carpenter, *The Inklings*, 194.

8. *Ibid.*

9. Tolkien, Letter to Peter Hastings, September 1954, *Letters*, 195.

10. *Ibid.*, 196.

11. Tolkien, Letter to Neave, *Ibid.*, 321.

12. Humphrey Carpenter, *Tolkien* (Boston: Houghton Mifflin, 1977), 194–96.

13. Tolkien, Letter to Stanley Unwin, 19 December 1939, *Letters*, 44.

14. Tolkien, Letter to Neave, *Ibid.*, 321.

15. Quoted in Carpenter, *Tolkien*, 203.

16. Tolkien, Letter to Caroline Everett, 24 June 1957, *Letters*, 257.

17. Tolkien, Letter to Allen & Unwin, 23 February 1961, *Ibid.*, 306–307.

18. J. R. R. Tolkien, *The Fellowship of the Ring* (New York: Ballantine, 1965), foreword, 12.

19. Quoted in Carpenter, *Tolkien*, 190.

20. Tolkien, Letter to Joanna de Bortadano, [April 1956], *Letters*, 246.

21. Tolkien, *The Fellowship of the Ring*, 72.

22. *Ibid.*, foreword, 11.

23. Tolkien, Letter to Unwin, 13 October 1938, *Letters*, 41.

24. Leonard Woolf, *The Journey not the Arrival Matters*, 9–10.

25. Charles Williams, *All Hallows' Eve* (1948; rpt. Grand Rapids: Eerdmans, 1985), 83.

26. C. S. Lewis, *The Lion, the Witch, and the Wardrobe* (New York: Macmillan, 1950), 1.

27. C. S. Lewis, *The Last Battle* (New York: Collier, 1970), 183.

28. Tolkien, Letter to Priscilla Tolkien, 26 November 1963, *Letters*, 341.

C. S. Lewis and the Perversion of Purgatory

1. MacNeice, *Autumn Journal*, X, in *Collected Poems*, 121.
2. Quoted in Hynes, *The Auden Generation*, 378.
3. Auden, *The Double Man*, 187.
4. Lewis, Letter to Miss Jane Douglass, 27 October 1963, *Letters*, 308.
5. Lewis, Letter to Sister Penelope, C.S.M.V., 17 September 1963, *Ibid.*, 307.
6. Lewis, Letter to Dom Bede Griffiths, O.S.B., 8 May 1939, *Ibid.*, 165.
7. Lewis, Letter to Sister Penelope, 10 April 1941, *Ibid.*, 193.
8. Waugh, *Put Out More Flags*, 60.
9. Williams, *All Hallows' Eve*, 22.
10. J. R. R. Tolkien, "Leaf by Niggle," in *Poems and Stories* (London: Allen & Unwin, 1980), 210.
11. Quoted in Carpenter, *The Inklings*, 194n.
12. C. S. Lewis, *The Screwtape Letters and Screwtape Proposes a Toast* (New York: Macmillan, 1961), xi.
13. *Ibid.*, 31.
14. John D. Sinclair, trans., *Purgatorio*, vol. 2 of *The Divine Comedy of Dante Alighieri* (1939; rpt. New York: Oxford University Press, 1961), 390.
15. Quoted in Carpenter, *The Inklings*, 187.
16. C. S. Lewis, *A Preface to* Paradise Lost (New York: Oxford University Press, 1961), i–ii.
17. Lewis, Letter to W. H. Lewis, 11 February 1940, *Letters*, 177.
18. Lewis, *A Preface to* Paradise Lost, 102–103.

Further Co-inherence

1. David Evans, "T. S. Eliot, Charles Williams, and the Sense of the Occult," *Accent*, 14 (Spring 1954), 148.
2. T. S. Eliot, "The Significance of Charles Williams," rpr. as introd. to Williams, *All Hallows' Eve*, ix.
3. Alice Hadfield, *An Introduction to Charles Williams* (London: Robert Hale, 1959), 156.
4. Carpenter, *The Inklings*, 97.
5. Michael Holroyd, *Lytton Strachey* (London: Heinemann, 1968), II, 675.
6. Quoted in Carpenter, *The Inklings*, 193.
7. *Ibid.*, 179.
8. W. H. Auden, *Secondary Worlds* (London: Faber & Faber, 1968), 21–45.
9. Rossell Robbins, "A Possible Analogue for *The Cocktail Party*," *English Studies*, 34 (August 1953), 165–67; Lois G. Thrash, "A Source for the Redemption Theme in *The Cocktail Party*," *Texas Studies in Literature and Language*, IX, #4 (Winter 1968), 547–53.
10. Charles Williams, *The Greater Trumps* (1950; rpt. Grand Rapids: Eerdmans, 1976), 30; 102.
11. *Ibid.*, 95.
12. *Ibid.*, 228.

13. Lewis, *The Great Divorce*, 106.

14. Carpenter, *The Inklings*, 110.

15. Evans, "The Sense of the Occult," 148–55.

16. T. S. Eliot, Letter, *New English Weekly*, XV, #4, 11 May 1939, 66.

17. T. S. Eliot, "A Lay Theologian," rev. of *The Descent of the Dove*, *New Statesman and Nation*, 18, 9 December 1939, 864.

18. Eliot, "The Significance of Charles Williams," xiii.

19. Charles Williams, "A Dialogue on Mr. Eliot's Poem," rev. of *Four Quartets*, *The Dublin Review*, 212 (April 1943), 115.

20. *Ibid.*

21. *Ibid.*, 117.

22. *Ibid.*, 120.

23. Eliot, *The Family Reunion*, 113.

24. *Ibid.*, 18.

25. Quoted in F. O. Matthiessen, *American Renaissance* (London: Oxford University Press, 1957), 295n.

26. T. S. Eliot, *The Cocktail Party* (New York: Harcourt, Brace & Company, 1950), 183. Eliot's text is slightly different from Shelley's.

27. Robbins, "A Possible Analogue," 166.

28. Williams, "A Dialogue on Mr. Eliot's Poem," 120–21.

29. Williams, *Poetry at Present*, 173.

30. Charles Williams, "Reunion," rev. of *The Family Reunion*, *Time and Tide*, 8 April 1939, 450.

31. Eliot, "The Significance of Charles Williams," xiv.

32. Anne Ridler, ed. and introd., *The Image of the City*, by Charles Williams (London: Oxford University Press, 1958), xlii.

33. Dorothy Sayers, trans., *The Comedy of Dante Alighieri* (Harmondsworth: Penguin, 1949; 1955), dedication.

34. Quoted in Carpenter, *The Inklings*, 80.

35. Hadfield, *An Introduction*, 156.

36. Quoted in Charles Williams, "St. John of the Cross," *Time and Tide*, 23, 27 June 1942, 522.

37. *Ibid.*

38. Charles Williams, *War in Heaven* (New York: Pellegrini & Cudahy, 1949), 64; 271.

39. Williams, *The Descent of the Dove*, vii.

40. *Ibid.*, 181.

41. Tolkien, "Leaf by Niggle," in *Poems and Stories*, 220.

42. Eliot, "A Lay Theologian," 864.

CHAPTER VI

Four Works Suspended

1. Evelyn Waugh, *Vile Bodies* (Boston: Little, Brown & Company, 1930), 314.

2. *Ibid.*, 315.

3. Innes, *The Secret Vanguard*, 14.

4. George Orwell, "Decline of the English Murder," in *The Collected Essays, Journalism and Letters of George Orwell*, IV (New York: Harcourt, Brace & World, 1968), 98.

5. Margery Allingham, *Coroner's Pidgin* (London: Heinemann, 1945), 158.

6. *Ibid.*, 49.

7. Julian Symons, *Bloody Murder* (London: Faber & Faber, 1972), 148.

8. *Ibid.*, 19.

9. *Ibid.*, 148–49.

10. Waugh, *The Sword of Honour Trilogy*, 255.

11. *Ibid.*, 451.

12. Evelyn Waugh, "My Father's House," *Horizon*, IV, #24 (December 1941), 336.

13. Evelyn Waugh, *Work Suspended* (London: Chapman & Hall, 1942), front matter.

14. Waugh, Letter to Arthur Waugh, [5 December 1941], *Letters*, 158.

15. Waugh, *Work Suspended*, 1942 edition, 2; 1.

16. Robert Murray Davis, "Textual Problems in the Novels of Evelyn Waugh," *Papers of the Bibliographical Society of America*, 63 (1969), 45.

17. Waugh, *Work Suspended*, 1942 edition, 118.

Sitting in Limbo

1. Evelyn Waugh, *Put Out More Flags*, rev. ed. (London: Butler & Tanner, 1967), preface.

2. Woolf, 22 March 1938, 24 May 1938, *Diary*, V, 131; 142.

3. Woolf, 7 August 1938, *Ibid.*, V, 160.

4. Waugh, "Work Suspended" in *Work Suspended and Other Stories*, 113; Evelyn Waugh, *Brideshead Revisited* (Boston: Little, Brown & Company, 1945), 127.

5. Woolf, *Mrs. Dalloway*, 173; 170.

6. Christopher Sykes, *Evelyn Waugh: A Biography* (Boston: Little, Brown & Company, 1975), 207.

7. Waugh, *Put Out More Flags*, 1967 edition, preface.

8. Quoted in Quentin Bell, *Virginia Woolf, A Biography* (New York: Harcourt Brace Jovanovich, 1972), II, 213.

9. Waugh, *The Sword of Honour Trilogy*, 19.

10. Virginia Woolf, *The Waves* (London: The Hogarth Press, 1933), 22.

11. Evelyn Waugh, *Black Mischief* (New York: Farrar & Rinehart, 1932), 82–83.

12. Woolf, *Mrs. Dalloway*, 123.

13. Evelyn Waugh, "Fan-fare," *Life*, 20, 8 April 1946, 58.

The Operation of Divine Grace

1. Waugh, Letter to Nancy Mitford, 7 January 1945, *Letters*, 196.

2. Waugh, 21 May 1944, 21 March 1944, *Diaries*, 566; 560.

3. Waugh, *Vile Bodies*, 22.

4. Waugh, Letter to A. D. Peters, 30 September 1944, *Letters*, 189; Letter to Mitford, *Ibid.*, 196.

5. Evelyn Waugh, "Fan-fare," *Life*, 20, 8 April 1946, 56.

6. Waugh, *Brideshead Revisited* (London: Chapman & Hall, 1960), 9.

7. Waugh, "Work Suspended," in *Work Suspended and Other Stories*, 113.

8. Waugh, Letter to Ronald Knox, 14 May 1945, *Letters*, 206.

9. Waugh, Letter to Mitford, *Ibid.*, 196.

10. Ford Madox Ford, *The Good Soldier* (New York: Vintage, 1955), 46.

11. *Ibid.*, 255.

12. Waugh, *Brideshead Revisited*, 1960 edition, 8.

13. P. A. Doyle, "Brideshead Rewritten," *Catholic Book Reporter*, 2 (May 1962), 10.

14. Waugh, *Brideshead Revisited*, 1960 edition, 9.

15. *Ibid.*, 288.

16. Waugh, 9 May 1944, *Diaries*, 564–65.

17. "Yet Another Visit to Brideshead," *Times Literary Supplement*, 16 September 1960, 594.

18. Waugh, *The Sword of Honour Trilogy*, 61.

Soldiers Three

1. Waugh, 7 September 1940, *Diaries*, 479.

2. Waugh, 7 September 1940, *Ibid.*, 480.

3. Waugh, 18 January 1940, *Ibid.*, 461.

4. Anthony Powell, *To Keep the Ball Rolling* (Harmondsworth: Penguin, 1983), 92.

5. Waugh, 26 August 1939, *Diaries*, 437–38.

6. Waugh, 18–20 August 1940, *Ibid.*, 475.

7. Waugh, *Brideshead Revisited* (Boston: Little, Brown & Company, 1945), 5–6.

8. Waugh, *Vile Bodies*, 132.

9. Aldous Huxley, *Antic Hay* (London: Heinemann, 1940), 142.

10. Waugh, *Brideshead Revisited*, 48.

11. Ford Madox Ford, *Parade's End* (New York: Vintage, 1979), 731.

12. *Ibid.*, 299.

13. Stevenson, *The British Novel Since the Thirties*, 75.

14. Ford, *Parade's End*, 738.

15. Keith Douglas, *From Alamein to Zem Zem* (Oxford: Oxford University Press, 1979), 82.

16. John Russell, *Anthony Powell: A Quintet, Sextet, and War* (Bloomington: Indiana University Press, 1970), 185.

17. *Ibid.*, 190.

18. Powell, *To Keep the Ball Rolling*, 181.

19. Green, *Pack My Bag*, 210.

20. T. S. Eliot, "Poetry in Wartime," *Common Sense*, XI, #10 (October 1942), 351.

21. Keith Douglas, "Poets in This War," [May 1943], in *A Prose Miscellany*, 120.

CHAPTER VII

1. Eliot, *Four Quartets*, DS, 93–96.
2. T. S. Eliot, "Tradition and the Individual Talent," in *Selected Essays, 1917–1932*, 10.
3. Churchill, *The Gathering Storm*, 11.
4. Allingham, *The Tiger in the Smoke*, 37.
5. Elizabeth Bowen, *The Heat of the Day*, 82.
6. Elizabeth Bowen, *The Death of the Heart* (New York: Avon, 1979), 110; 144.
7. *Ibid.*, 176.
8. Bowen, *Ivy Gripped the Steps and Other Stories*, xii.
9. Quoted in Allan Austin, *Elizabeth Bowen* (New York: Twayne, 1971), 113–14.
10. Dorothy Sayers, trans., *Purgatorio*, 192.
11. Allingham, *The Tiger in the Smoke*, 205.
12. *Ibid.*, 193.
13. *Ibid.*, 197–98.
14. Margery Allingham, *The Oaken Heart* (New York: Doubleday, 1941), 166.
15. Allingham, *The Tiger in the Smoke*, 221.
16. *Ibid.*, 173.
17. Allingham, *The Oaken Heart*, 180–81.
18. *Ibid.*, 182.
19. Lord Angus Holden, *Purgatory Revisited: A Victorian Parody* (Essex: The Anchor Press, 1949), 11.
20. Quoted in Finney, *Christopher Isherwood*, 224.
21. John Le Carré, *A Perfect Spy* (New York: Bantam, 1986), 83–84.
22. Green, *Back*, 246.
23. Greene, *The Ministry of Fear*, 16.

APPENDIX

1. Woolf, 29 April 1938, *Diary*, V, 138.
2. Eliot, *The Family Reunion*, 121.
3. Auden, *The Double Man*, 189.
4. *Ibid.*, 187.
5. *Ibid.*, 12.
6. Charles Baudelaire, "Les Sept Vieillards," in *Les Fleurs du Mal* (Paris: Club des Libraires de France, 1959), 197.
7. Lawrence Lipking, *The Life of the Poet* (Chicago: University of Chicago Press, 1981), 13.
8. A. Walton Litz, "From Burnt Norton to Little Gidding: The Making of T. S. Eliot's *Four Quartets*," rev. of HG, *Review*, 2 (1980), 18.

9. *Inferno* 15, 30.

10. *Inferno* 31, 12.

11. J. A. W. Bennett, ' "Little Gidding": A Poem of Pentecost,' *Ampleforth Journal*, 79 (Spring 1974), 65–66.

12. T. S. Eliot, Interview with John Lehmann, *New York Times Book Review*, 29 November 1953, 5.

13. Eliot, *The Family Reunion*, 105.

14. *Ibid.*, 106–107.

15. *Ibid.*, 18.

16. MacNeice, *Out of the Picture*, 46; MacNeice, "The Sunlight on the Garden," in *Collected Poems*, 84.

17. MacNeice, *Autumn Journal*, XV, in *Collected Poems*, 130.

18. Quoted in Christopher Ricks, "A Note on *Little Gidding*," *Essays in Criticism*, 25, #1 (January 1975), 147–48. The article is unobtainable in the original English.

19. Charles Williams, "A Dialogue on Mr. Eliot's Poem," rev. of *Four Quartets*, *The Dublin Review*, 212 (April 1943), 121.

20. Williams, *Descent into Hell*, 19; Eliot, *The Cocktail Party*, 183.

21. T. S. Eliot, "What Dante Means to Me," rpr. as "Talk on Dante," *Adelphi*, 27, #2 (1951), 111.

22. *Ibid.*, 112.

23. Litz, "From Burnt Norton to Little Gidding," 8.

24. Quoted in T. S. Eliot, "The Voice of His Time," in *The Listener*, XXVII, 683, 12 February 1942, 212.

25. Williams, *Descent into Hell*, 161.

26. *Ibid.*, 167.

27. T. S. Eliot, "Yeats," in *On Poetry and Poets*, 302.

28. W. B. Yeats, *Purgatory*, in *Collected Plays*, 687.

Selected Bibliography

Ackroyd, Peter. *T. S. Eliot: A Life*. New York: Simon & Schuster, 1984.

Aistrop, Jack and Moore, Reginald. *Bugle Blast: An Anthology from the Services*. London: Allen & Unwin, 1943.

Allingham, Margery. *Coroner's Pidgin*. London: Heinemann, 1945.

———. *The Oaken Heart*. New York: Doubleday, 1941.

———. *The Tiger in the Smoke*. Harmondsworth: Penguin with Chatto & Windus, 1957.

———. *Traitor's Purse*. Harmondsworth: Penguin with Heinemann, 1950.

Astor, Sidney. *1939: The Making of the Second World War*. New York: Simon & Schuster, 1973.

Auden, W. H. *Another Time*. New York: Random House, 1940.

———. *Collected Poems*. New York: Random House, 1976.

———. *The Double Man*. New York: Random House, 1941.

———. "Hell." *Harper's Bazaar*, LXXIV, 1 January 1940, 118.

———. *Look, Stranger!* London: Faber & Faber, 1936.

———. *The Orators*. London: Faber & Faber, 1932.

———. "The Poet in Wartime." *New Republic*, 103, 18 July 1940, 59–60.

———. *Secondary Worlds*. London: Faber & Faber, 1968.

Auden, W. H., introd. *Intimate Journals*. By Charles Baudelaire. Trans. Christopher Isherwood. Boston: Beacon Press, 1947.

Auden, W. H. and Isherwood, Christopher. *Journey to a War*. New York: Random House, 1939.

———. *On the Frontier*. New York: Random House, 1938.

Beckett, Samuel. *Murphy*. New York: Grove Press, 1970.

Beckett, Samuel, *et al. Our Exagmination Round his Factification for Incamination of* Work in Progress. London: Faber & Faber, 1972.

Bell, Quentin. *Virginia Woolf, A Biography*. 2 vols. New York: Harcourt Brace Jovanovich, 1972.

Benham, David. "Lowry's Purgatory: Versions of 'Lunar Caustic.'" *Canadian Literature*, 44 (Spring 1970), 28–37.

Bennett, J. A. W. ' "Little Gidding": A Poem of Pentecost.' *Ampleforth Journal*, 79 (Spring 1974), 60–73.

Bergonzi, Bernard. *Reading the Thirties: Texts and Contexts*. Pittsburgh: University of Pittsburgh Press, 1978.

Binyon, Laurence. *The Burning of the Leaves*. London: Macmillan, 1944.

Binyon, Laurence, trans. *The Divine Comedy [The Portable Dante]*. New York: Viking, 1948.

Bishop, John. "The Hamlet of Louis MacNeice." Rev. of *Autumn Journal*. *The Nation*, 11 May 1940, 602–604.

[Bishop, John.] *Two One-Act Plays*. London: The Russia-Today Society, [1941].

Blake, Nicholas [C. Day Lewis]. *Malice in Wonderland*. New York: Harper, 1940.

———. *Minute for Murder*. New York: Perennial, 1977.

———. *The Smiler with the Knife*. London: Collins, 1939.

Bowen, Elizabeth. *The Death of the Heart*. New York: Avon, 1979.

———. *The Heat of the Day*. New York: Avon, 1976.

———. *Ivy Gripped the Steps and Other Stories*. New York: Knopf, 1946.

———. Rev. of *Between the Acts*. *New Statesman and Nation*, 22, 19 July 1941, 63–64.

Brand, Christianna. *London Particular*. [Published in America as *Fog of Doubt*.] New York: Carroll & Graf, 1984.

Brittain, Vera. *England's Hour*. New York: Macmillan, 1941.

———. *Humiliation with Honor*. New York: Fellowship Publications, 1943.

———. *Testament of Experience*. London: Gollancz, 1957.

Britton, George and Helena. Letters to Florence Britton Elkus, 1938 – 1945. 2 vols. Second World War Papers, Imperial War Museum.

Brodie, W. C. Diary. Second World War Papers, Imperial War Museum.

Browne, E. Martin. *The Making of T. S. Eliot's Plays*. Cambridge: Cambridge University Press, 1969.

Bush, Ronald. *T. S. Eliot, A Study in Character and Style*. New York: Oxford University Press, 1983.

Campbell, Roy. *Flowering Rifle*. London: Longmans, Green & Company, 1939.

Carpenter, Humphrey. *The Inklings*. London: Allen & Unwin, 1978.

———. *Tolkien*. Boston: Houghton Mifflin, 1977.

Caso, Adolph, ed. *Dante in the Twentieth Century.* Vol. 1 of *Dante Studies*. Boston: Dante University of America Press, 1982.

Chambers, R. L. *The Novels of Virginia Woolf.* London: Oliver & Boyd, 1947.

Chaning-Pearce, Melville. Rev. of *Little Gidding*. *Nineteenth Century*, 133 (February 1943), 74–78.

Chase, James Hadley [Rene Raymond]. *No Orchids for Miss Blandish*. London: Jarrolds, 1939.

Christie, Agatha. *The Moving Finger*. London: Collins, 1943.

———. *There is a Tide*. New York: Dodd, Mead & Company, 1948.

Churchill, Sir Winston. *The Gathering Storm*. Vol. 1 of *The Second World War*. Boston: Houghton Mifflin, 1948.

Commager, Henry. *The Story of the Second World War*. Boston: Little, Brown & Company, 1945.

Connolly, Cyril. "Comment." *Horizon*, I, #1 (January 1940), 5–6.

———. "Comment." *Horizon*, III, #13 (January 1941), 5–7.

———. *Enemies of Promise*. London: Routledge & Sons, 1938.

Connolly, Cyril, *et al.* "Why Not War Writers? A Manifesto." *Horizon*, IV, #22 (October 1941), 236–39.

Cook, R. L. "Louis MacNeice: An Appreciation." *The Poetry Review*, 38 (May/June 1947), 161–70.

Crick, Bernard. *George Orwell: A Life*. Harmondsworth: Penguin, 1980.

Crispin, Edmund [Bruce Montgomery]. *Holy Disorders*. London: Lippincott, 1946.
———. *The Moving Toyshop*. London: Lippincott, 1946.
———. *Swan Song*. 1947; rpt. New York: Avon, 1981.
Dahl, Roald. *Going Solo*. London: Cape, 1986.
———. *Over to You*. New York: Reynal & Hitchcock, 1946.
Dante Alighieri. *Inferno*. Vol. 1 of *The Divine Comedy*. Ed. Sinclair. 1939; rpt. New York: Oxford University Press, 1961.
———. *Purgatorio*. Vol. 2 of *The Divine Comedy*. Ed. Sinclair. 1939; rpt. New York: Oxford University Press, 1961.
Davis, Robert Murray. "The Serial Version of *Brideshead Revisited*." *Twentieth Century Literature*, 15 (1969), 35–43.
———. "Textual Problems in the Novels of Evelyn Waugh." *Papers of the Bibliographical Society of America*, 63 (1969), 41–46.
Day Lewis, C. *Collected Poems*. London: Cape with the Hogarth Press, 1954.
———. *The Georgics of Virgil*. London: Cape, 1940.
———. *Overtures to Death and Other Poems*. London: Cape, 1938.
Day Lewis, Sean. *Cecil Day-Lewis: An English Literary Life*. London: Weidenfeld & Nicolson, 1980.
Deiman, Werner. "History, Pattern, and Continuity in Virginia Woolf." *Contemporary Literature*, XV, #1 (Winter 1974), 49–66.
DiBattista, Maria. *Virginia Woolf's Major Novels: The Fables of Anon*. New Haven: Yale University Press, 1980.
Dickinson, Patric. *Soldiers' Verse*. London: Müller, 1945.
Douglas, Keith. *Collected Poems*. London: Faber & Faber, 1966.
———. *From Alamein to Zem Zem*. Oxford: Oxford University Press, 1979.
———. "Poets in This War." In *A Prose Miscellany*. Comp. and ed. Desmond Graham. Manchester: Carcanet, 1985, 117–20.
Douglas, Roy. *The Advent of War, 1939–1940*. London: Macmillan, 1978.
Dowie, William John. "Religious Fiction in a Profane Time: Charles Williams, C. S. Lewis and J. R. R. Tolkien." Diss. Brandeis 1970.
Doyle, P. A. "Brideshead Rewritten." *Catholic Book Reporter*, 2 (May 1962), 9–10.
Eliade, Mircea. *Myth and Reality*. Vol. 1 of World Perspectives. New York: Harper & Row, 1963.
———. *The Myth of the Eternal Return*. Bollingen Series, #46. Princeton: Princeton University Press, 1974.
Eliot, T. S. *After Strange Gods*. London: Faber & Faber, 1934.
———. *The Cocktail Party*. New York: Harcourt, Brace & Company, 1950.
———. "Dante." In *Selected Essays, 1917–1932*. New York: Harcourt, Brace & Company, 1932, 199–237.
———. "The Development of Leibniz's Monadism." *Monist*, XXVI, #4 (October 1916), 534–56.
———. *The Family Reunion*. London: Faber & Faber, 1939.
———. *Four Quartets*. London: Harcourt Brace Jovanovich, 1971.
———. "Fragments of a Prologue." *The New Criterion*, IV, #4 (October 1926), 713.
———. *The Idea of a Christian Society*. London: Faber & Faber, 1939.

———. Interview with Donald Hall. *Paris Review*, 21 (Spring/Summer 1959), 47–70.

———. Interview with John Lehmann. *New York Times Book Review*, 29 November 1953, 5, 44.

———. "Last Words." *Criterion*, 18 (January 1939), 269–75.

———. "A Lay Theologian." Rev. of *The Descent of the Dove*. *New Statesman and Nation*, 18, 9 December 1939, 864–66.

———. Letter. *New English Weekly*, XV, #4, 11 May 1939, 66.

———. Letter. *New English Weekly*, XXVI, #15, 25 January 1945, 112.

———. Letter to Gorton. 19 October 1941. Gen. Mss. [misc.], Eliot, #8. Firestone Library, Princeton.

———. Letters to Allen Tate. Allen Tate Papers, 19. Firestone Library, Princeton.

———. Letters to Paul Elmer More. Paul Elmer More Papers, 3, #3. Firestone Library, Princeton.

———. "A Note on War Poetry." In *London Calling: A Salute to America*. Ed. Storm Jameson. New York: Harper, 1942.

———. "Notes Towards a Definition of Culture." *New English Weekly*, 21 January 1943–11 February 1943, 117–46.

———. "Paul Elmer More." *Princeton Alumni Weekly*, XXXVII, #17, 5 February 1937, 373–74.

———. "Poetry in Wartime." *Common Sense*, XI, #10 (October 1942), 351.

———. *Quatre Quatuors*. Trans. Pierre Leyris. Notes supplied by John Hayward. Paris: Éditions du Seuil, [1950].

———. "The Significance of Charles Williams." *The Listener*, XXXVI, 936 (19 December 1946), 894–95. Rpr. as introd. to Charles Williams, *All Hallows' Eve*. 1948; rpt. Grand Rapids: Eerdmans, 1985, ix–xviii.

———. "The Three Voices of Poetry." In *On Poetry and Poets*. New York: Farrar, Straus & Cudahy, 1957, 96–112.

———. " 'Ulysses', Order, and Myth." Rev. of *Ulysses*. *Dial* (November 1923), 480–83.

———. *The Use of Poetry and the Use of Criticism*. London: Faber & Faber, 1933.

———. "The Voice of His Time." *The Listener*, XXVII, 683, 12 February 1942, 211–12.

———. "Waiting at the Church." *New English Weekly*, XVIII, 9, 19 December 1940, 99.

———. "What Dante Means to Me." Rpr. as "Talk on Dante." *Adelphi*, 27, #2 (1951), 106–14.

———. "Yeats." In *On Poetry and Poets*. New York: Farrar, Straus & Cudahy, 1957, 295–308.

[Eliot, T. S.] "Mr. Charles Williams." Obituary. *The Times*, 17 May 1945, 7. Unsigned.

Elliott-Binns, Dr. L. E. *Dante and the World To-day*. The Bishop Gore Memorial Lecture, Westminster Abbey, 18 November 1938. Cambridge: W. Heffer & Sons, 1939.

Empson, William. *The Gathering Storm*. London: Faber & Faber, 1940.

Evans, David. "T. S. Eliot, Charles Williams, and the Sense of the Occult." *Accent*, 14 (Spring 1954), 148–55.

Feder, Lillian. *Ancient Myth in Modern Poetry*. Princeton: Princeton University Press, 1971.

Feiling, Keith. *The Life of Neville Chamberlain*. London: Macmillan, 1947.

Finney, Brian. *Christopher Isherwood, A Critical Biography*. New York: Oxford University Press, 1979.

Ford, Ford Madox. *The Good Soldier*. New York: Vintage, 1955.

———. *Parade's End*. New York: Vintage, 1979.

Forster, E. M. *The Abinger Pageant*. In *Abinger Harvest*. New York: Harcourt, Brace & World, 1964, 349–63.

———. *England's Pleasant Land*. London: The Hogarth Press, 1940.

———. "Omega and Alpha." Rev. of Roger Fry. *New Statesman and Nation*, 10 August 1940, 140–41.

———. *Two Cheers for Democracy*. London: Edward Arnold & Company, 1951.

Frank, Joseph. *The Widening Gyre: Crisis and Mastery in Modern Literature*. New Brunswick, N.J.: Rutgers University Press, 1963.

Fry, Christopher. *The Boy with a Cart*. In *Selected Plays*. Oxford: Oxford University Press, 1985, 1–46.

Frye, Northrop. *The Anatomy of Criticism*. Princeton: Princeton University Press, 1971.

———. *Fables of Identity*. New York: Harcourt, Brace & World, 1963.

Fuller, Edmund, *et al. Myth, Allegory and Gospel; An Interpretation of J. R. R. Tolkien, C. S. Lewis, G. K. Chesterton [and] Charles Williams*. Minneapolis: Bethany, 1974.

Fuller, Roy. *Collected Poems, 1936–1961*. London: Deutsch, 1962.

Furbank, P. N. *E. M. Forster, A Life*. Vol. 2. London: Secker & Warburg, 1978.

Gardner, Dame Helen. *The Composition of* Four Quartets. Rev. ed. London: Faber & Faber, 1980.

Gascoyne, David. *Collected Poems*. Oxford: Oxford University Press, 1965.

Gillespie, Diane. "Virginia Woolf's Miss LaTrobe." *Women & Literature*, 5, #1 (Spring 1977), 38–46.

Goldman, Mark. "Virginia Woolf and E. M. Forster: A Critical Dialogue." *Texas Studies in Literature and Language*, VII, #4 (Winter 1966), 387–400.

Goodman, Paul. "T. S. Eliot: The Poet of Purgatory." Rev. of *Little Gidding*. *The New Leader*, 14 August 1943, 7.

Gordon, Lyndall. *Virginia Woolf: A Writer's Life*. Oxford: Oxford University Press, 1984.

Graham, Desmond. *Keith Douglas, 1920–1944*. London: Oxford University Press, 1974.

Graves, Robert. *No More Ghosts*. London: Faber & Faber, 1940.

———. "The Poets of World War II." In *The Common Asphodel*. London: Hamish Hamilton, 1949, 307–11.

———. "War Poetry in this War." *The Listener*, 26, 23 October 1941, 566.

Green, F. L. *Odd Man Out*. London: Michael Joseph, 1945.

———. *On the Night of the Fire*. London: Michael Joseph, 1939.

Green, Henry [Henry Yorke]. *Back*. New York: New Directions, 1981.

———. *Caught*. London: The Hogarth Press, 1943.

———. *Loving, Living, Party-Going*. Harmondsworth: Penguin, 1978.

———. "The Lull." *New Writing and Daylight* (Summer 1943), 11–21.

———. *Pack My Bag*. London: The Hogarth Press, 1940.

Greene, Graham. *Brighton Rock*. New York: Viking, 1951.

———. *The End of the Affair*. New York: Viking, 1961.

———. *The Ministry of Fear*. Harmondsworth: Penguin, 1974.

———. "While Waiting for a War." *Granta*, 17 (Autumn 1985), 13–29.

Hadfield, Alice. *Charles Williams: An Exploration of His Life and Work*. New York: Oxford University Press, 1983.

———. *An Introduction to Charles Williams*. London: Robert Hale, 1959.

Hamilton, Patrick. *Hangover Square: Or the Man with Two Minds*. New York: Random House, 1942.

———. *The Slaves of Solitude*. London: Constable, 1972.

Harries, Meirion and Susie. *The War Artists: British Official War Art of the Twentieth Century*. London: Michael Joseph, 1983.

Harrisson, Tom. "War Books." *Horizon*, IV, #24 (December 1941), 416–37.

Hay, Eloise. *T. S. Eliot's Negative Way*. Cambridge, Mass.: Harvard University Press, 1982.

Hewison, Robert. *Under Siege: Literary Life in London 1939–1945*. London: Weidenfeld & Nicolson, 1977.

Hillegas, Mark Robert, ed. *Shadows of Imagination: The Fantasies of C. S. Lewis, J. R. R. Tolkien, and Charles Williams*. Carbondale: Southern Illinois University Press, 1969.

Hirshfield, Claire. "The Strange Death of Mrs. Ryder." *Evelyn Waugh Newsletter*, 18, #2 (Autumn 1984), 1–3.

Holden, Lord Angus. *Purgatory Revisited: A Victorian Parody*. Essex: The Anchor Press, 1949.

Huxley, Aldous. *Antic Hay*. London: Heinemann, 1940.

———. *Eyeless in Gaza*. New York: American Reprint Co., 1975.

———. *Grey Eminence: A Study in Religion and Politics*. New York: Harper, 1941.

Hynes, Samuel. *The Auden Generation*. New York: Viking, 1977.

Innes, Michael [J. I. M. Stewart]. *The Case of the Journeying Boy*. New York: Perennial, 1983.

———. *The Secret Vanguard*. New York: Berkley Medallion, 1965.

Isherwood, Christopher. *Down There On a Visit*. New York: Simon & Schuster, 1962.

———. *Mr. Norris Changes Trains*. London: The Hogarth Press, 1937.

Isherwood, Christopher and Prabhavananda, Swami, trans. *The Song of God: Bhagavad-Gita*. Introd. Aldous Huxley. New York: New American Library, 1944.

James, Henry. "*Daniel Deronda*: A Conversation." *Atlantic Monthly*, XXXVIII (December 1876), 684–94.

———. "The Jolly Corner." In *The Complete Tales of Henry James*. Vol. 12. London: Rupert Hart-Davis, 1964, 193–232.

Jameson, Storm, ed. *London Calling: A Salute to America*. New York: Harper, 1942.

Jones, David. *In Parenthesis*. New York: Chilmark Press, 1961.

Juan de la Cruz. *The Complete Works of Saint John of the Cross*. Vol. 1. Trans. E. Allison Peers. Westminster, Maryland: The Newman Press, 1953.

———. *The Poems of Saint John of the Cross*. Trans. Barnstone. Bloomington: Indiana University Press, [1968].

Jung, C. G. *Memories, Dreams, Reflections*. Ed. Aneila Jaffé. New York: Pantheon, 1963.

Kearns, Cleo. *T. S. Eliot and Indic Traditions*. Cambridge: Cambridge University Press, 1987.

Kennedy, Michael. *The Works of Ralph Vaughan Williams*. London: Oxford University Press, 1964.

Keyes, Sidney. *The Collected Poems of Sidney Keyes*. New York: Henry Holt & Company, 1947.

Kojecky, Roger. *T. S. Eliot's Social Criticism*. London: Faber & Faber, 1971.

Kondo, Incho. "Virginia Woolf and E. M. Forster." *Eigo Seinen*, CXVI, #1 (February 1970), 64–66.

Kracauer, Siegfried. *From Caligari to Hitler: A Psychological History of the German Film*. Princeton: Princeton University Press, 1947.

Larkin, Philip. *A Girl in Winter*. New York: St. Martin's Press, 1962.

———. *Jill*. New York: The Overlook Press, 1976.

———. "The War Poet." Rev. of *The Collected Poems of Wilfred Owen*. In *Required Writing*. New York: Farrar, Straus & Giroux, 1984.

Le Carré, John. *A Perfect Spy*. New York: Bantam, 1986.

Le Goff, Jacques. *The Birth of Purgatory*. Trans. Arthur Goldhammer. Chicago: University of Chicago Press, 1985.

Lehmann, John. *I am My Brother*. New York: Reynal & Company, 1960.

———. *New Writing in England*. New York: Critics Group Press, 1939.

[Lehmann, John.] *New Writing and Daylight*, Summer 1943. London: The Hogarth Press, 1943.

Levy, William Turner and Scherle, Victor. *Affectionately, T. S. Eliot, The Story of a Friendship: 1947–1965*. Philadelphia: Lippincott, 1968.

Lewis, Alun. *Raiders' Dawn and Other Poems*. New York: Macmillan, 1942.

Lewis, C. S. *The Great Divorce*. New York: Macmillan, 1946.

———. *Letters of C. S. Lewis*. Ed. W. H. Lewis. London: Geoffrey Bles, 1966.

———. *The Lion, the Witch, and the Wardrobe*. New York: Macmillan, 1950.

———. *A Preface to* Paradise Lost. New York: Oxford University Press, 1961.

———. *The Screwtape Letters and Screwtape Proposes a Toast*. New York: Macmillan, 1961.

Lewis, John. *The Left Book Club: An Historical Record*. London: Gollancz, 1970.

Lightfoot, Marjorie J. "*Purgatory* and *The Family Reunion*: In Pursuit of Prosodic Description." *Modern Drama*, 7, #3 (December 1964), 256–66.

Litz, A. Walton. "From Burnt Norton to Little Gidding: The Making of T. S. Eliot's *Four Quartets*." Rev. of Helen Gardner, *The Composition of* Four Quartets. *Review*, 2 (1980), 1–18.

Lobdell, Jared, ed. *A Tolkien Compass*. La Salle, Ill.: Open Court, 1975. Esp. Kaufmann, U. Milo, "Aspects of the Paradisiacal in Tolkien's Work," and Plank, Robert, ' "The Scouring of the Shire": Tolkien's View of Fascism.'

Lowry, Malcolm. *Lunar Caustic.* Introd. Conrad Knickerbocker. London: Cape, 1968.

———. *Under the Volcano.* Harmondsworth: Penguin, 1962.

McDougal, Stuart, ed. *Dante Among the Moderns.* Chapel Hill: University of North Carolina Press, [1985].

McDougald, Roman. *Purgatory Street.* New York: Simon & Schuster, 1946.

McKinnon, William T. *Apollo's Blended Dream.* London: Oxford University Press, 1971.

MacNeice, Louis. *Autumn Journal.* London: Faber & Faber, 1939.

———. *The Collected Poems of Louis MacNeice.* Ed. E. R. Dodds. London: Faber & Faber, 1966.

———. *The Dark Tower and Other Radio Scripts.* London: Faber & Faber, 1947.

———. *The Earth Compels.* London: Faber & Faber, 1938.

———. *I Crossed the Minch.* London: Longmans, Green & Company, 1938.

———. *The Last Ditch.* Dublin: Cuala Press, 1940.

———. *Modern Poetry: A Personal Essay.* London: Oxford University Press, 1938.

———. *Out of the Picture.* New York: Harcourt, Brace & Company, 1938.

———. *Plant and Phantom.* London: Faber & Faber, 1941.

———. *Poems 1925–1940.* New York: Random House, 1940.

———. "The Poet in England Today." *The New Republic,* 102, 25 March 1940, 412–13.

———. *The Poetry of W. B. Yeats.* New York: Oxford University Press, 1941.

———. *The Strings are False.* Ed. and introd. E. R. Dodds. London: Faber & Faber, 1965.

MacNeice, Louis and Auden, W. H. *Letters from Iceland.* London: Faber & Faber, 1967.

Margolis, John D. *T. S. Eliot's Intellectual Development: 1922–1939.* Chicago: University of Chicago Press, 1972.

Marsack, Robyn. *The Cave of Making: The Poetry of Louis MacNeice.* Oxford: Clarendon Press, 1982.

Martz, Louis. "The Wheel and the Point: Aspects of Imagery and Theme in Eliot's Later Poetry." *Sewanee Review,* 55, #1 (Winter 1947), 126–47.

Matthiessen, F. O. "Eliot's Quartets." Rev. of *Four Quartets. Kenyon Review,* 5 (Spring 1943), 171–73.

Mendelson, Edward. *Early Auden.* New York: Viking, 1981.

Merton, Thomas. *The Secular Journal of Thomas Merton.* New York: Farrar, Straus & Cudahy, 1959.

———. *The Seven Storey Mountain.* New York: Harcourt, 1948.

Miller, J. Hillis. *Fiction and Repetition.* Cambridge, Mass.: Harvard University Press, 1982.

Milne, A. A. *Behind the Lines.* New York: Dutton, 1940.

———. *Peace with Honour.* London: Methuen, 1934.

Moore, D. B. *The Poetry of Louis MacNeice.* Leicester: Leicester University Press, 1972.

More, Paul Elmer. *The Catholic Faith.* Princeton: Princeton University Press, 1931.

Mosley, Leonard. *On Borrowed Time: How World War II Began.* London: Weidenfeld & Nicolson, 1969.

Muggeridge, Malcolm. *The Thirties*. London: Collins, 1967.

Muir, Edwin. *The Narrow Place*. London: Faber & Faber, 1943.

Musa, Mark, trans. *Dante's Purgatory*. Bloomington: Indiana University Press, 1981.

Nicolson, Harold. *Diaries and Letters, 1930–1939*. Ed. Nigel Nicolson. London: Collins, 1966.

———. *The War Years, 1939–1945*. Ed. Nigel Nicolson. New York: Athenaeum, 1967.

Okey, Thomas, *et al.*, trans. *La Divina Commedia*. London: Dent [Temple Classics], 1933.

Oldenbourg, Zoé. *Massacre at Montségur*. Trans. Peter Green. New York: Pantheon, 1961.

Orwell, George. *An Age Like This, 1920–1940*. Vol. 1 of *The Collected Essays, Journalism and Letters of George Orwell*. Eds. Sonia Orwell and Ian Angus. New York: Harcourt, Brace & World, 1968.

———. *My Country Right or Left, 1940–1943*. Vol. 2 of *The Collected Essays, Journalism and Letters of George Orwell*. Eds. Sonia Orwell and Ian Angus. Harmondsworth: Penguin with Secker & Warburg, 1970.

———. *As I Please, 1943–1945*. Vol. 3 of *The Collected Essays, Journalism and Letters of George Orwell*. Eds. Sonia Orwell and Ian Angus. New York: Harcourt, Brace & World, 1968.

———. *In Front of Your Nose, 1945–1950*. Vol. 4 of *Collected Essays* [v.s.].

———. *Coming Up for Air*. New York: Harcourt Brace Jovanovich, [1939].

———. *Homage to Catalonia*. New York: Harcourt Brace Jovanovich, 1952.

———. *Keep the Aspidistra Flying*. 1936; rpt. Harmondsworth: Penguin with Secker & Warburg, 1981.

Owen, Wilfred. *The Collected Poems of Wilfred Owen*. New York: New Directions, 1965.

Page, Leitch, and Knightley. *Philby: The Spy Who Betrayed a Generation*. London: Sphere, 1977.

Panovsky, Ernst. "Et in Arcadia Ego." In *Meaning and the Visual Arts*. New York: Doubleday, 1955, 295–320.

Panter-Downes, Mollie. *London War Notes, 1939–1945*. New York: Farrar, Straus & Giroux, 1971.

Powell, Anthony. *A Dance to the Music of Time*. 12 vols. New York: Popular Library, 1976. Esp. vols. 4–10: *At Lady Molly's, Casanova's Chinese Restaurant, The Kindly Ones, The Valley of Bones, The Soldier's Art, The Military Philosophers, Books Do Furnish A Room*.

———. *To Keep the Ball Rolling*. Harmondsworth: Penguin, 1983.

Press, John. *Louis MacNeice*. London: Longmans, Green & Company, 1965.

Quinones, Richard. *Mapping Literary Modernism*. Princeton: Princeton University Press, 1985.

Rahula, Walpola. *What the Buddha Taught*. Rev. ed. New York: Grove Press, 1974.

Rahv, Philip. *The Myth and the Powerhouse*. New York: Farrar, Straus & Giroux, 1965.

Raymond, Rene and Langdon, David. *Slipstream: A Royal Air Force Anthology*. London: Eyre and Spottiswoode, 1946.

Redpath, Lucy. *Dante and the Present War*. Westminster: Dacre Press, [1941].

Rees, Goronwyn, narr. *Radio Portrait of Louis MacNeice*. BBC, 7 September 1966.

Reibetanz, Julia Maniates. *A Reading of* Four Quartets. Ann Arbor, Michigan: UMI Research Press, 1983.

Reilly, Catherine. *English Poetry of the Second World War: A Biobibliography*. London: Mansell, 1986.

Richardson, Maurice. *London's Burning*. London: Robert Hale, 1941.

Ricks, Christopher. "A Note on *Little Gidding*." *Essays in Criticism*, 25, #1 (January 1975), 145–53.

Ridler, Anne, ed. and introd. *The Image of the City and Other Essays*. By Charles Williams. London: Oxford University Press, 1958.

Robbins, Rossell Hope. "A Possible Analogue for *The Cocktail Party*." *English Studies*, 34 (August 1953), 165–67.

———. *The T. S. Eliot Myth*. New York: Schuman, 1951.

Rock, William. "Neville Chamberlain and the Pursuit of War." Western / North American Conference on British Studies. 16 October 1986.

Rossi, Lee. *The Politics of Fantasy, C. S. Lewis and J. R. R. Tolkien*. Ann Arbor: UMI Research Press, [1984].

Roy, Emil. *Christopher Fry*. London: Feffer & Simons, 1968.

Roy, Sandra. *Josephine Tey*. Boston: Twayne, 1980.

Russell, John. *Anthony Powell: A Quintet, Sextet, and War*. Bloomington: Indiana University Press, 1970.

Ryf, Robert. *Henry Green*. New York: Columbia University Press, 1967.

Sansom, William. *Fireman Flower*. London: Chatto & Windus, 1944.

Sartre, Jean-Paul. *The War Diaries, November 1939—March 1940*. New York: Pantheon, 1984.

Sayers, Dorothy. *Begin Here: A War-time Essay*. London: Gollancz, 1940.

———. *The Wimsey Papers. The Spectator*, weekly, 1939–1940.

Sayers, Dorothy, trans. *The Comedy of Dante Alighieri*. Harmondsworth: Penguin, 1949; 1955; 1962.

Schmidt, G. 'An Echo of Buddhism in T. S. Eliot's "Little Gidding." ' *Notes and Queries* (September 1973), 330.

Schwartz, Delmore. "Anywhere Out of the World." Rev. of *Little Gidding. The Nation*, 157, 24 July 1943, 102–103.

Seymour-Ure, Colin and Schoff, John. *David Low*. London: Secker & Warburg, 1985.

Shires, Linda. *British Poetry of the Second World War*. New York: St. Martin's Press, 1985.

Sinclair, John D., trans. *Purgatorio*. 1939; rpt. New York: Oxford University Press, 1961.

Singleton, Charles. *Purgatorio*, vol. 2 [commentary]. Bollingen Series, #80. Princeton, Princeton University Press, 1973.

Sitwell, Osbert. *Open the Door!* New York: Smith & Durrell, 1941.

Sitwell, Sacheverell. *Poltergeists*. London: Faber & Faber, 1940.

Smitten, Jeffrey and Daghistany, Ann, eds. *Spatial Form in Narrative*. Ithaca: Cornell University Press, 1981.

Spears, Monroe. *The Poetry of W. H. Auden*. New York: Oxford University Press, 1963.

Spender, Stephen. "Books and the War." *Penguin New Writing*, January and November 1941.

———. *Collected Poems, 1928–1953*. London: Faber & Faber, 1955.

———. "Dante in English." Rev. of Dante's *Purgatorio*, trans. Laurence Binyon. *New Statesman and Nation*, 17, 14 January 1939, 56–58.

———. "The Greeks in the Black-Out." *New Statesman and Nation*, 18, 14 October 1939, 528.

———. "High-Brow Firemen." *New Statesman and Nation*, 23, 3 January 1942, 12–13.

———. *Letters to Christopher*. Santa Barbara: Black Sparrow Press, 1980.

———. *Poetry Since 1939*. London: Richard West, 1978.

———. *Ruins and Visions*. London: Faber & Faber, 1942.

———. "September Journal." In *Journals, 1939–1983*. London: Faber & Faber, 1985, 21–56.

———. *The Still Centre*. London: Faber & Faber, 1939.

———. *The Thirties and After*. New York: Random House, 1978.

———. "Thoughts During an Air Raid." *New Republic*, 95, 18 May 1938, 42.

———. "War Poetry in this War." *The Listener*, 26, 16 October 1941, 539.

———. *World Within World*. London: Hamish Hamilton, 1951.

———. "The Year's Poetry, 1940." *Horizon*, III, #14 (February 1941), 138–48.

Spender, Stephen, introd. *Air Raids*. London: Oxford University Press, 1943.

Stadtfeld, Frieder. "Virginia Woolfs Letzter Roman: More Quintessential Than the Others." *Anglia*, 91, #1 (1973), 56–76.

Stevenson, Randall. *The British Novel Since the Thirties*. London: Batsford, 1986.

Stokes, Edward. *The Novels of Henry Green*. London: The Hogarth Press, 1959.

Storrs, Sir Ronald and Graves, Philip. *A Record of the War, September 1939—September 1940*. 4 vols. London: Hutchinson, 1939–40.

Strachey, John. *Digging for Mrs Miller: Some Experiences of an Air-Raid Warden*. New York: Random House, 1941.

Swinfen, Ann. *In Defence of Fantasy*. 1971; rpt. Boston: Routledge & Kegan Paul, 1984.

Swingler, Randall. "The English Twilight." *Our Time*, 1, #3 (May 1941), 5–9.

Sykes, Christopher. *Evelyn Waugh: A Biography*. Boston: Little, Brown & Company, 1975.

Symons, Julian. *Bloody Murder*. London: Faber & Faber, 1972.

———. *Confusions about X*. London: The Fortune Press, [1942].

———. *The Thirties: A Dream Revolved*. London: Faber & Faber, 1975.

Taylor, A. J. P. *English History, 1914–1945*. Oxford: Oxford University Press, 1965.

Tey, Josephine [Elizabeth Mackintosh]. *Brat Farrar*. London: Davies, 1949.

Thomas, Dylan, *et al. The New Apocalypse*. London: The Fortune Press, [1939].

Thrash, Lois G. "A Source for the Redemption Theme in *The Cocktail Party*." *Texas Studies in Literature and Language*, IX, #4 (Winter 1968), 547–54.

Titmuss, Richard. *Problems of Social Policy*. London: Longmans, Green & Company, 1950.

Todd, Ruthven. *Garland for the Winter Solstice*. Boston: Little, Brown & Company, [1961].

Tolkien, J. R. R. "Leaf by Niggle." In *Poems and Stories*. London: Allen & Unwin, 1980.

———. *The Letters of J. R. R. Tolkien*. Ed. Humphrey Carpenter. Boston: Houghton Mifflin, 1981.

———. *The Lord of the Rings*. 3 vols. New York: Ballantine, 1965.

Tolley, A. T. *The Poetry of the Thirties*. London: Gollancz, 1975.

Trevelyan, George. *The History of England*. London: Longmans, Green & Company, 1937.

Turner, E. S. *The Phoney War on the Home Front*. London: Quality Book Club, 1961.

Unger, Leonard. *Eliot's Compound Ghost: Influence and Confluence*. University Park: The Pennsylvania State University Press, 1981.

Upward, Edward. *Journey to the Border*. London: The Hogarth Press, 1938.

Urang, Gunnar. *Shadows of Heaven: Religion and Fantasy in the Writing of C. S. Lewis, Charles Williams, and J. R. R. Tolkien*. Philadelphia: Pilgrim Press, 1971.

Warner, Rex. *The Aerodrome: A Love-Story*. London: John Lane, 1941.

———. *The Wild-Goose Chase*. New York: Knopf, 1938.

Watkins, Renée. "Survival in Discontinuity." *Massachusetts Review*, X, #2 (Spring 1969), 356–76.

Waugh, Auberon. "They Came to Number Three - Evelyn Waugh." *Evelyn Waugh Newsletter*, 20, #3 (Winter 1986), 1–3.

Waugh, Evelyn. *Basil Seal Rides Again*. London: Chapman & Hall, 1963.

———. *Brideshead Revisited*. Boston: Little, Brown & Company, 1945.

———. *Brideshead Revisited*. Rev. ed. London: Chapman & Hall, 1960.

———. *The Diaries of Evelyn Waugh, 1911–1965*. Ed. Michael Davie. Harmondsworth: Penguin, 1979.

———. "Fan-fare." *Life*, 20, 8 April 1946, 53–60.

———. *The Letters of Evelyn Waugh*. Ed. Mark Amory. Harmondsworth: Penguin, 1982.

———. "My Father's House." *Horizon*, IV, #24 (December 1941), 329–41.

———. *Put Out More Flags*. Harmondsworth: Penguin, 1943.

———. *Put Out More Flags*. Rev. ed. London: Butler & Tanner, 1967.

———. *The Sword of Honour Trilogy*. Harmondsworth: Penguin, 1984.

———. "Tactical Exercise." In *Tactical Exercise [and Other Stories]*. Boston: Little, Brown & Company, 1954.

———. *Vile Bodies*. Boston: Little, Brown & Company, 1930.

———. "Work Suspended." Rev. ed. In *Work Suspended and Other Stories*. Harmondsworth: Penguin, 1982.

———. *Work Suspended*. London: Chapman & Hall, 1942.

[Waugh, Evelyn.] "Letter - Why Not War Writers?" *Horizon*, IV, #24 (December 1941), 437–38. Unsigned.

Waugh, Evelyn, introd. *Fireside Fusilier*, by the Earl of Wicklow. Dublin: Clonmore & Reynolds, 1958.

Weatherhead, A. Kingsley. *Stephen Spender and the Thirties*. Lewisburg: Bucknell University Press, 1975.

Wells, H. G. *Babes in the Darkling Wood*. New York: Alliance, 1940.

———. *The Outline of History*. New York: Macmillan, 1930.

Weymouth, Anthony. *A Psychologist's War-Time Diary*. London: Longmans, Green & Company, 1940.

Williams, Charles. *All Hallows' Eve*. 1948; rpt. Grand Rapids, Mich.: Eerdmans, 1985.

———. *Descent into Hell*. 1949; rpt. Grand Rapids, Mich.: Eerdmans, 1985.

———. *The Descent of the Dove*. New York: Pellegrini & Cudahy, 1939.

———. "A Dialogue on Mr. Eliot's Poem." Rev. of *Four Quartets*. *The Dublin Review*, 212 (April 1943), 114–22.

———. *The Figure of Beatrice*. London: Faber & Faber, 1943.

———. *The Greater Trumps*. 1950; rpt. Grand Rapids, Mich.: Eerdmans, 1976.

———. *Poetry at Present*. Oxford: Clarendon Press, 1930.

———. "The Poetry of Health." Rev. of *East Coker*. *Time and Tide*, 21, 5 October 1940, 990.

———. *Reason and Beauty in the Poetic Mind*. Oxford: Clarendon Press, 1933.

———. *Religion and Love in Dante*. Westminster: Dacre Press, [1941].

———. "Reunion." Rev. of *The Family Reunion*. *Time and Tide*, 8 April 1939, 450–51.

———. Rev. of *Purgatorio*, trans. Laurence Binyon. *London Mercury*, 39 (November 1938), 84.

———. *Rochester*. London: A. Barker, [1935].

———. "St. John of the Cross." *Time and Tide*, 23, 27 June 1942, 522.

———. *Seed of Adam and Other Plays*. London: Oxford University Press, 1948.

———. *War in Heaven*. New York: Pellegrini & Cudahy, 1949.

Wilson, Edmund. *The Thirties*. New York: Farrar, Straus & Giroux, 1980.

Woolf, Leonard. *Barbarians at the Gate*. London: Gollancz, 1939.

———. *Downhill All the Way*. London: The Hogarth Press, 1967.

———. *The Journey not the Arrival Matters*. London: The Hogarth Press, 1969.

Woolf, Virginia. ' "Anon" and "The Reader": Virginia Woolf's Last Essays.' Ed. Brenda Silver. *Twentieth Century Literature*, 25 (Fall/Winter 1979), 356–441.

———. *Between the Acts*. Harmondsworth: Penguin, 1953.

———. *The Diary of Virginia Woolf*. Ed. Anne Olivier Bell. 5 vols. Esp. vols. 3–5: 1925–1930, 1931–1935, 1936–1941. London: Harcourt Brace Jovanovich, 1980; 1982; 1984.

———. *Jacob's Room*. London: Harcourt Brace Jovanovich, 1950.

———. *The Letters of Virginia Woolf*. Eds. Nigel Nicolson and Joanne Trautmann. VI, 1936–1941. New York: Harcourt Brace Jovanovich, 1980.

———. "The Moment: Summer's Night." In *Collected Essays*, vol. 2. London: The Hogarth Press, 1966, 293–97.

———. *Mrs. Dalloway*. London: The Hogarth Press, 1929.

———. *Pointz Hall: The Earlier and Later Typescripts of* Between the Acts. Ed. Mitchell Leaska. New York: University Publications, 1983.

———. *Roger Fry, A Biography*. London: The Hogarth Press, 1940.

———. "A Sketch of the Past." In *Moments of Being*. New York: Harcourt Brace Jovanovich, 1976, 61–138.

———. "Thoughts on Peace in an Air Raid." In *Collected Essays*, vol. 4. London: The Hogarth Press, 1967, 173–77.

———. *Three Guineas*. London: Harcourt Brace Jovanovich, 1966.

Woon, Basil. *Hell Came to London; A Reportage of the Blitz During 14 Days.* London: Davies, 1941.

Wright, Gordon. *The Ordeal of Total War, 1939–1945.* New York: Harper & Row, 1968.

Wright, Marjorie Evelyn. "The Cosmic Kingdom of Myth; A Study in the Myth-Philosophy of Charles Williams, C. S. Lewis and J. R. R. Tolkien." Diss. Illinois 1960.

Wright, S. Fowler. *Prelude in Prague: A Story of the War of 1938.* London: George Newnes, 1935.

Yeats, W. B. *Purgatory.* In *The Collected Plays of W. B. Yeats.* London:Macmillan, 1952, 679–90.

Zorn, Marilyn. "The Pageant in Between the Acts." *Modern Fiction Studies,* II, #1 (February 1956), 31–35.

Zwerdling, Alex. "*Between the Acts* and the Coming of War." *Novel,* 10, #3 (Spring 1977), 220–36.

———. *Virginia Woolf and the Real World.* Berkeley: University of California Press, 1986.

[Unsigned.] "To the Poets of 1940." *Times Literary Supplement,* 30 December 1939, 755.

[Unsigned.] "Yet Another Visit to Brideshead." *Times Literary Supplement,* 6 December 1960, 594.

Index

The author gratefully acknowledges permission to quote from the following works.

MARGERY ALLINGHAM
Excerpts from *The Tiger in the Smoke*. Reprinted by permission of the Estate of Margery Allingham and The Hogarth Press.

W. H. AUDEN
Excerpts from *W. H. Auden, Collected Poems*, edited by Edward Mendelson. Copyright © 1976 by Edward Mendelson, William Meredith and Monroe K. Spears, Executors of the Estate of W. H. Auden. Reprinted by permission of Random House, Inc. and Faber & Faber Ltd.

T. S. ELIOT
Excerpts from *The Family Reunion*. Copyright © 1939 by T. S. Elliot, © renewed 1967 by Esme Valerie Eliot. Reprinted by permission of Harcourt Brace Jovanovich, Inc. and Faber & Faber Ltd.

Excerpts from "Burnt Norton," "East Coker," "The Dry Salvages," and "Little Gidding," in *Four Quartets*. Copyright © 1943 by T. S. Eliot, © renewed 1971 by Esme Valerie Eliot. Reprinted by permission of Harcourt Brace Jovanovich, Inc. and Faber & Faber Ltd.

C. S. LEWIS
Excerpts from *The Great Divorce*. Reprinted by permission of William Collins Sons & Co Ltd.

LOUIS MACNEICE
Excerpts from *The Collected Poems of Louis MacNeice*, edited by E. R. Dodds. Copyright © 1966 by Faber & Faber Ltd. Reprinted by permission of Faber & Faber Ltd.

Excerpts from *The Strings are False*, edited by E. R. Dodds. Published by Faber & Faber, Ltd., 1965. Reprinted by permission of David Higham Associates and Victor Gollancz Ltd.

GEORGE ORWELL
Excerpts from *Coming Up for Air*. Reprinted by permission of Harcourt Brace Jovanovich, Inc., the estate of Sonia Brownell Orwell, and Secker & Warburg.

Excerpts from *Homage to Catalonia*. Copyright © 1952, © renewed 1980 by Sonia Brownell Orwell. Reprinted by permission of Harcourt Brace Jovanovich, Inc., the estate of Sonia Brownell Orwell, and Secker & Warburg.